LLEWELLYN'S

2022

Magical Almanac

Featuring

H. Byron Ballard, Elizabeth Barrette, Stephanie Rose Bird,
Mireille Blacke, Danielle Blackwood, Blake Octavian Blair,
Chic and S. Tabatha Cicero, Monica Crosson, Kate Freuler,
Michael Furie, Sasha Graham, Raechel Henderson,
JD Hortwort, James Kambos, Kelden, Lupa,
Daniel Moler, Mickie Mueller, Diana Rajchel,
Suzanne Ress, Astrea Taylor, Melissa Tipton,
Charlynn Walls, Charlie Rainbow Wolf,
Stephanie Woodfield, and Natalie Zaman

Llewellyn's 2022 Magical Almanac

ISBN 978-0-7387-6045-2. Copyright © 2021 by Llewellyn Publications. All rights reserved. Printed in the United States. Llewellyn Publications is a registered trademark of Llewellyn Worldwide Ltd.

Editing and design by Lauryn Heineman
Cover illustration © Rebecca Solow
Calendar pages design by Llewellyn Art Department
Calendar pages illustrations © Fiona King

Interior illustrations: Meraylah Allwood: pages 40, 43, 70, 76, 188, 193, 245, and 248; © Kathleen Edwards: pages 5, 8, 62, 85, 89, 176, 218, 223, and 273; © Kate Freuler: page 269; © Wen Hsu: pages 1, 17, 23, 37, 47, 67, 101, 167, 169, 172, 213, 217, 234, 239, 257, 260, 265, and 277; © Jessica Krcmarik: pages 27, 30, 80, 181, 185, 197, 200, and 252; © Amber Zoellner: pages 12, 50, 55, 92, 98, 209, 226, and 230

All other art by Dover Publications and Llewellyn Art Department

Special thanks to Amber Wolfe for the use of daily color and incense correspondences. For more detailed information, please see *Personal Alchemy* by Amber Wolfe.

You can order Llewellyn annuals and books from *New Worlds*, Llewellyn's catalog. To request a free copy of the catalog, call 1-877-NEW-WRLD toll-free or visit www.llewellyn.com.

Astrological data compiled and programmed by Rique Pottenger. Based on the earlier work of Neil F. Michelsen.

Llewellyn Worldwide Ltd.
2143 Wooddale Drive
Woodbury, MN 55125

Table of Contents

Earth Magic

Air Magic

2022 Almanac

Fire Magic

Water Magic

Coloring Magic

Earth Magic

The Magick of Hair

Kate Freuler

One of the most popular and often misunderstood ingredients in spells and magick is human hair. We've all heard variations of the same story: an evil witch plucks a curl from an unsuspecting person's head, and later the victim falls ill, dies, or experiences some other horrible fate. Using hair in Witchcraft is often portrayed in this evil, nefarious light. Even when removed from the context of witchery, collecting a person's hair is generally considered alarming, stalker-like behavior nowadays. However, it hasn't always been that way. In Victorian times, it was considered romantic to exchange locks with a loved one, and jewelry was constructed from the tresses of the deceased to be worn with pride and reverence. Many groups of people around the world past and present have associated the hair on their heads with spirituality and power in various ways. It's often believed to house spirit, life energy, or a connection to the Divine. Some people never, ever cut their hair throughout their entire lives for religious reasons, whereas others, such as monastic Buddhists, shave it off as part of their sacred practice.

During the witch hunts, sometimes the accused person would have their head and body shorn during questioning. This was to reveal any witch's marks they may be hiding and, more importantly, to strip them of their power. It was believed that witches hid spells and magick in their hair and that loosening a witch's braid or bun would unleash evil and sinful sexual energy.

Clearly, hair is loaded with mystical meaning. It invokes strong feelings no matter what the time

A Little Bit of Magic

SOME PEOPLE ONLY TRIM THEIR HAIR ON THE NEW MOON BECAUSE THEY BELIEVE IT ENCOURAGES GROWTH AND KEEPS HAIR HEALTHIER.

period, and it's worth wondering why. It could be that people of all persuasions feel instinctively that their hair is intensely personal and therefore powerful, containing a bit of their soul or at least an intimate piece of themselves.

In modern Witchcraft, hair can be used in many spells, from healing to love to protection and, yes, even cursing. This is because a lock of hair is a perfect ingredient for what is called sympathetic, or imitative, magick.

Hair in Sympathetic Magick

Sympathetic magick is the term used to describe the act of energetically connecting an object to a person and working magick upon them through the object. Sympathetic magick can be used for almost any magickal goal, both positive and negative.

A good example of sympathetic magick is the use of a doll or poppet. A doll is made from clay or cloth bearing the features and physical characteristics of an individual. Symbolic acts are performed upon the doll, which will cause similar experiences to befall the person. To create a strong energetic tie between the doll and the target of the spell, something belonging to the person needs to be added to the doll's stuffing or surface. Hair is the perfect ingredient for this, for a few reasons: It contains their DNA, which is completely unique to them alone. It's a part of their physical body and has absorbed their thoughts, feelings, and experiences. It also contains their energy, soul, or aura (depending which terminology you prefer). While it's certainly possible to perform sympathetic magick through energy work and focus alone, having a personal belonging, especially something as intimate as hair, helps strengthen the connection between the person and the object.

Using Hair in Spells

When using hair in spells, some magickal practitioners advise that you always ask permission of the person involved beforehand. Since you can use hair in spells for healing, prosperity, and other positive things, like-minded people might be perfectly willing to give you some of their hair. Of course, bear in mind, if they're *not* like-minded, they might find the request strange to say the least! Here are some basic spells making use of human hair in various ways.

Healing Spell Bottle

This is a spell to help someone who is ill or suffering in some manner. In this case, the hair will be surrounded by objects bearing healing energy, thus causing the owner of the hair to be enveloped by healing influences as well.

You will need:

Piece of hair from the person in need of healing
Bottle or jar with a tight lid
3 cotton balls
Tea tree oil
Quartz crystal
Dried lavender, chamomile, and jasmine to fill the entire bottle or jar

Find a quiet spot to cast your spell. Hold the piece of hair in your hand and visualize the person it belongs to. Imagine them fully cured, happy, and healthy. Place the hair into the bottle.

The next step uses the tea tree oil and the cotton balls. Tea tree oil is known for its purifying properties and, in this case, signifies the cleansing of illness or unwanted forces. The cotton balls represent a soft and gentle energy that will surround the person while they heal. Put a drop of tea tree oil on each cotton ball, and put them in the jar. Imagine the person in question surrounded by softness, comfort, and nurturance while recovering.

Take the dried jasmine and inhale its scent. Imagine it glowing with a restful light blue aura. Place it in the jar. Repeat this with the other herbs, filling the jar or bottle. Place the quartz crystal on the top of the herbs to amplify the power of the other ingredients, and then put the lid on tightly.

Now the hair is surrounded by softness, cleansing energy, and herbs with healing vibrations. Because this is sympathetic or imitative magick, the person you are doing the spell for is also surrounded by these benevolent forces.

Keep the healing bottle in a warm, sunny spot. Each day, hold the bottle and spend some time visualizing the person in perfect health. Continue to do this until they improve.

Remember to combine this spell with appropriate medical care.

Protective Armor Spell

In this spell, you'll surround a piece of hair with a protective seal, thus guarding the person it came from with an energetic shield. You can do this spell for yourself or someone else.

You will need:

Piece of cardboard to protect your work surface from melting wax
Square of black paper
Piece of hair belonging to the person you'd like to protect
Olive oil
Black candle
Lighter

Put the cardboard on your work surface to prevent it getting ruined by melting wax. Lay the piece of black paper down, and then place the hair in the center of the paper. Visualize the person it belongs to as clearly as possible. Carefully fold the paper around the hair, bending all the corners in so the hair cannot fall out. Make it into the smallest possible compact shape. Set it on the cardboard.

Put a dab of olive oil on your fingers. Anoint the candle by rubbing the oil into it, starting at the bottom and massaging the oil up to the middle of the candle. Repeat this motion from the top of the candle, down to the middle. While you do this, visualize the person represented in the spell surrounded by a protective sphere of energy.

Light the black candle. Hold it at an angle, and let the wax drip onto the folded paper. While you do this, repeat the chant, "A layer of armor protects (name) from all harm." Continue to drip the wax onto all sides of the folded paper, rotating it as necessary, until it is completely covered in a shell of black hardened wax. Blow out the candle.

Anytime you feel that there's a need for a boost of protective energy, light the candle and drip more wax onto the amulet, thickening the "armor" surrounding the person.

Keep the amulet in a safe place. Once the protection spell is no longer necessary, dispose of the amulet or bury it. If the black candle isn't all gone, you can keep it for future protective spells.

Spell to Break a Bond

This spell is to be done when you wish to remove yourself from another person's sphere of influence or cut energetic ties with them for any reason. This is best performed during the dark moon.

You will need:

Piece of hair belonging to the person in question
Piece of your own hair
Scissors
Bowl
Fireproof dish

Charcoal disk
Lighter
Dried bay leaves

Hold the two hairs together. Visualize the bond between yourself and the other person, which may be toxic and unhealthy. Allow yourself to feel the emotions this invokes, as you gaze at the entwined hair. You might feel sadness, anger, regret, or other unpleasant things while doing this. Now imagine your feelings are forming a mass of energy in front of your heart/chest area. This may look like a scribbled chaotic mess, a sad murky blob, or something else, depending on your relationship with the person and the nature of its discord. Visualize this mass of energy moving into the hairs.

Place the bowl in front of you. Using the scissors, cut the hairs into as many tiny pieces as you can, being sure to catch all the fragments in the bowl. If the hairs are too short for this, you can snip the scissors in the air around the hairs to symbolically cut what binds you.

Light the charcoal disk and put it in a fireproof dish. Carefully transfer the hair pieces from the bowl onto the disk. As they hiss and burn, imagine the unhealthy ties that bind you together transforming into smoke and floating away.

Place a bay leaf on the charcoal disk. As it burns, allow the smoke to cleanse the area. Waft the smoke with your hand onto your face and body, feeling the purifying energy. You can burn as many bay leaves as you wish until you feel the spell is done.

You have now begun to free yourself from the unhealthy attachment. After a spell of this kind, there may be changes in your life, such as a breakup, a shift of circumstances, or some other upheaval. Keep in mind that in a truly toxic situation, this type of change is for the best.

Animal Hair

When it comes to hair magick, we can't forget about our animal friends. If you have a beloved pet or animal companion, you can incorporate their fur into magick too.

Animal companions are often a source of comfort to us and therefore represent a sense of home, belonging, love, and reassurance. There are lots of creative ways to include your pet's hair in your magick. For example, if you make your own candles, place a single strand of their hair in the wax to add some extra good vibes. If your animal, such as a dog, is the guardian of your home, you can add some of their fur to protection amulets of all kinds.

An animal's hair will bring the energy of its species into any spell. Cat hair could be used in workings for independence and hunter energy, dog hair for loyalty and friendship, and rabbit hair for prosperity. You can add a tiny bit of the fur to herb mixes, incense, sachets, and other magickal crafts.

Black Cat Witch's Amulet

Black cats are universally associated with Witchcraft and the occult. A black cat is often portrayed as the ultimate Witch's familiar and is believed by some to house a spirit or otherworldly being. Sometimes they're considered good luck, other times bad luck. Over time, the image of the black cat has become a repository of witchy attributes and associations.

Even if you don't consider yourself a cat person, you can make and wear this amulet to call upon the archetypal traits of the famous black cat: luck, connection to spirits, mysticism, and, of course, Witchcraft power. This amulet is meant to increase magickal abilities, aid in occult studies, and generally bring out your inner Witch.

You will need:
Small tiger's eye crystal that will fit in the bottle
Small glass bottle with a cork, available at craft shops
Pinch of dried catnip
3 strands of hair from a black cat
Glue
Piece of cord or string long enough to go around your neck

On the night of the Full Moon, find a quiet place to make your amulet. It's preferable that you're able to see the Moon, but if you can't, visualize it in your mind instead.

Hold the tiger's eye up toward the Moon. Think about how a cat's eye glows in the dark just like the Moon does, and say,

Cat's eye, cat's eye,
Moon shining bright.
Guide my way in darkness
Like a black cat in the night.

Add it to the bottle. The stone represents your inner vision, helping you see mystical undercurrents and increasing your psychic senses.

Put the catnip in the bottle. Catnip attracts most cats and is a favorite tempting treat for them. Say,

Fetch and summon, come to be.
Black cat spirit, come to me.

Place the cat hairs in the bottle. Say,

Black cat power is here with me,
With secrets, luck, and wile.
A Witch's companion spirit
Now lives within this vial.

Put the cork in the bottle and glue it in place. When it's dry, string it on the cord and wear it as an amulet during rituals and spells or in situations when you need extra power from the black cat spirit.

Other Hair Magick

Hair magick can be performed without removing a single piece from your head. There are lots of ways to add some enchantment to your hair care routine, to attract the energies you desire, and to repel those you don't.

Essential Oils: You can add a few drops of essential oil to your shampoo or conditioner. Remember to only add a small amount so it doesn't compromise the product. Try mint for prosperity, rosemary for protection, or chamomile for peace.

Braids: If you have long hair, you can use knot magick to attract your desires. While braiding your hair, visualize what you would like to bring into your life. When you tie the elastic in place, state, "It is done." Repeat this every time you braid your hair until the thing you seek comes to you.

Cleansing: Every New Moon, pull the hair out of your hairbrush and safely burn it while letting go of everything you no longer need. This will clear out all the stagnant energy from the last Moon cycle, clearing the way for growth and new beginnings.

Crystals: Quartz crystal amplifies your personal power and boosts spiritual awareness. Place a quartz crystal in your bottle of shampoo or other hair product. The energy from the quartz crystal will linger every time you wash your hair. You can do this with other crystals as well according to what you want to attract. Just make sure the crystals you choose won't be ruined by being immersed in liquid.

How to Create a Magical Threshold

James Kambos

In the literal sense, a threshold is the strip of wood, metal, or brick that forms a protective barrier at the bottom of an exterior door, especially the front door. Years ago when many people lived on farms and the front door was near the barnyard, the threshold served to keep out grain debris (thresh), dust, dirt, and cold air, hence the term *threshold*. Gradually in cultures around the world, a threshold took on a special, magical significance. Being the point of entry to most homes, the threshold became a magical area that served to keep out negative forces and evil spirits. At the same time, it was believed to be the place where good fortune could be drawn into the home. The ancient Greeks, for instance, would select a favorite goddess or god to protect specific exterior doors. As a sign of thanks, they'd leave small gifts at each entrance for their chosen deity.

Over time, the entire entry area of a home began to be associated with magic. The front door, porch, windows, and front steps were all thought to attract magical energies—good and bad. Different cultures soon began to develop their own folk magic traditions about how to keep negative energies out while drawing positive energies inside the home.

Here are some ideas for you to try so you can create your own magically charged threshold. By using some traditional folk magic, you'll be able to turn your home's entrance into a welcoming magical haven.

Let's begin by looking at how to use the color blue as an aid to blocking negative energy from entering the home.

Out of the Blue

Ever since the ancient Persians thought the sky was blue because they believed Earth rested on a large sapphire, blue has been associated with protection magic. If there's one color that's favored for its use at, or near, an entrance to bring good fortune into a home, blue is the hands-down favorite.

From the American South to Mexico to Moroccan villages, I've seen porch ceilings, front doors, and window trim painted various shades of blue, being used to guard homes from misfortune just as it's been done for centuries. But why is blue the number-one choice for protecting thresholds? Since blue is associated with the heavens, it's possible that blue is thought to possess healing and protective powers. Also, blue has long been thought to protect against the evil eye.

Even today in the American South, sometimes you'll see front porch ceilings painted a beautiful pale blue. This blue is known as "haint blue." *Haint*, a word of uncertain origin, is an evil spirit. The belief is that haints will be drawn to the blue ceiling and think it's the sky, then continue upward away from the home, instead of going inside.

In Mexico and the American Southwest, many homes have front doors and window trim painted a vivid turquoise blue. Again, it's thought to repel mischievous spirits. Once while traveling in the Atlas Mountains of Morocco, I came to a village where most front doors were painted royal blue. I was told it was done to "send back" the glare of the evil eye.

For many of us, it's not practical to paint our front door and other areas blue. But there are other ways you can use this magical color near your threshold to protect your home. For example, adding a blue garden gazing ball near your door or in a flower bed isn't just attractive—it's protective too. It reflects negativity. Adding a blue ribbon to a wreath on your front door will do the same. Don't forget, you can also paint some outdoor flowerpots blue.

Now let's take a look at some plants that are also useful in protecting your home's threshold.

Plant a Protective Barrier

Plants aren't just for beauty or landscaping. Plants, herbs, and flowers can also serve as a buffer between your threshold and the negative energy of the outside world. All plants are living entities that emit energy. As such, they're a valuable aid in protecting and creating a magical threshold. Here are some plants with highly protective vibrations perfect for this purpose.

Since many of you may have limited space around your threshold, I'll start with a few plants that can be grown in pots. They can easily be placed by your front door or on a small terrace. It just takes a few to give you magical results.

A potted fern is one of the easiest and most magical plants you can grow by your threshold. They've graced doorsteps since the Victorian era, and it's easy to see why. Their lush greenery brings a sense of calm and their foliage has strong protective vibrations. They guard against all evil. Including a few stems in a vase arrangement will bring their magical powers inside too.

Cheery geraniums are another protective plant that can be enjoyed potted near the threshold. Red geraniums are very protective. When cut and placed in a vase inside, they can protect the interior of a home also. Outside they repel most negativity. Pink geraniums draw friendship, and white geraniums are soothing. Don't forget, scented geraniums can also be grown in pots near the threshold. Depending on the scent you select, scented geraniums can calm you or repel evil. For some quick magic, try rubbing the leaf of a rose-scented geranium on an exterior doorknob to protect the home from emotional upsets in general.

One other plant that offers exceptional magical qualities when potted and placed near the threshold is the pansy. Known for drawing love and friendship, pansies also do well during cool weather and thrive in spring and autumn when other plants might not do well. I've even had pansies bloom outside my front door in Ohio on New Year's Day.

Now let's take a look at some plants that can protect your threshold and be planted in a bed, border, or garden near your entrance.

Cherished for generations, the peony is one of the most carefree and powerful magical plants that can be planted near your threshold. Known in Grandma's day by the

A LITTLE BIT OF MAGIC

The custom of a groom carrying his bride across the threshold dates back to the Middle Ages. It was believed this would prevent the bride from bringing any bad luck into the newlywed's first home.

folk name *piney*, they've been used in medicine and magic since ancient times. Planted near the threshold, the peony protects against evil spirits. It was even used in exorcisms long ago. Cut for a vase arrangement, peonies will also protect the inside of the home. Blooming begins in May, but the entire plant has protective powers. It blooms in white, cream, red, and various shades of pink. I know you'll find one you'll love.

If you want to keep the evil eye, negative spirits, and unwanted visitors away from your threshold, plant a few lily bulbs. These tall beauties grow three to four feet high. Not only will they bring protection to your doorstep, but they'll also add charm. As a bonus, their trumpet-shaped flowers are a magnet for hummingbirds.

When thinking about planting a protective barrier or plants and flowers near your threshold, let's not forget to mention roses. The flower of peace, love, and friendship, the rose is also highly protective when planted near the entrance of a home. It helps prevent negativity from entering any dwelling. Just scattering a few rose petals near the threshold will ease domestic tensions. This will also neutralize any dark energy left behind by an unpleasant visitor who has just left. Today there are many easy-care roses available, so you needn't worry about fussing over them. To keep their magical qualities active, don't spray them with toxic sprays. However, today's easy-to-grow roses shouldn't need spraying. Simply plant them and enjoy their protective qualities.

There are many other plants you may use to protect your threshold, but these are some of the most powerful I've encountered. They are also easy to find.

Last, for generations, spells and charms have been used to protect many thresholds. I'd like to end by sharing one with you.

A Threshold Spell

For this spell, you'll need some salt, a few drops of lemon juice or vinegar, and one clove of crushed garlic. Begin by sprinkling some salt along your threshold. In a small dish, mix together a few grains of salt, the lemon juice or vinegar, and the crushed garlic. Now, bury the garlic near your front door. Next, with a broom, sweep the salt you've sprinkled along your threshold away from your door. Continue sweeping the salt away from your home and off your porch or steps if you have them. As you sweep, say this charm:

Spirits dark and spirits that I dread,
Leave this threshold where I tread.

Repeat this spell once a year, or more if you feel it's necessary.

However you choose to do it, treating your threshold as a magical space will protect your home and family.

Pentacles: What Are They?

Chic and S. Tabatha Cicero

The pentagram is the single most recognizable symbol of magic. When you mention the word *pentagram*, most Wiccans, magicians, and Neopagans know exactly what you mean: the traditional five-pointed star used in several of our spiritual traditions and ritual work. But there is a host of similar words that tend to confuse even the most knowledgeable practitioner of magic: *pentacle, pantacle, pentangle,* and *pentalpha.* Are these the same thing as a pentagram, or are they different?

Etymology

For many, the word *pentacle* specifically means an encircled pentagram. It can be inscribed on a disk made of wood, parchment, wax, or metal or a pendant. Pentacles were usually circular in shape and painted or engraved with emblems appropriate to the magical work at hand. Medieval grimoires are filled with pentacles ornamented with various forms of symbolism.

Some insist that the word *pentacle* always refers to the symbol of the encircled pentagram because of its emphasis on the root *penta*, derived from the Greek *pente* meaning "five." But as we shall see, the symbolism on a pentacle can take many forms, far beyond the five-pointed star.

The familiar pentagram is sometimes called the "Blazing Star," "wizard's foot," the "Star of the Magi," and the "Star of the Microcosm." It is sometimes called the *pentalpha* because it can be constructed out of five Greek letter *alphas*(A) arranged in a star formation. So the figure of the *pentalpha* is synonymous with the *pentagram.*

Readers will occasionally come across the word *pentangle*, which comes from the Latin word *angulus,* or "angle." It refers to a shape with five angles. For many, this is also identical with the pentagram. However, in Golden Dawn terminology, any geometric poly*angle* (meaning "many angles") has two forms: a poly*gon* and a poly*gram.* The suffix *-gon* (derived from the Greek *gonia,* meaning "angle") signifies dispersion, distribution, and radiation of a force, whereas *gram* (stemming from the Greek *grammē* meaning "line" as well as "something written") indicates concentration and sealing. A pentangle can be either a pentagon (meaning "five angles," a nonintersecting five-sided shape) or a pentagram (meaning "five lines," a self-intersecting star-shaped figure).

The word *pentacle* comes from the medieval Latin *pentaculum,* combining *penta* (five) with the suffix *-culum,* which was often used to form nouns that represented tools or instruments. According to some, it may also mean a "small painting," indicating the symbols drawn on a talisman. Occasionally the variant *pentacula* is used in the same way. From roots of these words, it seems only natural that readers would assume that pentacles and pentagrams are one and the same. But historically a pentacle could have any magical symbol inscribed upon it, not just a pentagram.

The *Oxford English Dictionary* tells us that a pentacle was "a certain figure (or a material object, e.g. something folded or interlaced, of that shape) used as a symbol, esp. in magic; app. properly the same as pentagram; but also used for various other magical symbols, esp. the hexagram or six-pointed star formed by two interlaced triangles." The text also describes a pentacle as something worn around the neck as an amulet, and some would connect it with the French *pentacol* or *pendacol,* from *pend* ("hang"), *à* ("to"), and *col, cou* ("neck"), indicating a jewel or ornament hung around the neck. It seems likely that *pentacol* is the source for what magicians know as a pentacle.

An alternative spelling is *pantacle,* which was coined by nineteenth-century French occult revivalist Éliphas Lévi. This version replaces the Greek root *penta* with *panta,* or "all," marking a pantacle as a synthetic tool that contains *all* the magical doctrine or symbolism needed to carry out the pantacle's specific purpose. And the purposes for creating pantacles (or pentacles, as we shall refer to them here) can be as varied as the purposes for creating talismans—the possibilities are endless.

An Elemental Tool

One of the earliest magical texts that describe pentacles is the *Heptameron,* dating at least to 1581. The pentacles it describes consist of sacred sigils and names of good spirits along with holy letters, geometric figures, scriptural verses, and names of God, often mixed or compounded together in a harmonious fashion. The main pentacle illustrated in the grimoire is the "Grand Pentacle of Solomon," shown inscribed with a hexagram.

Numerous pentacles illustrate the well-known grimoire *The Key of Solomon the King,* sometimes called *The Greater Key of Solomon,* dating to the fifteenth or sixteenth century. These pentacles are attributed to the seven planets: seven different pentacles for Saturn, seven for Jupiter, seven for Mars, seven for Sol, five for Venus, five for Mercury, and six for Luna. They were to be constructed on the day and hour of their assigned planet from suitable metals, engraved with symbols or inscribed on "virgin paper" with the appropriately colored inks, and sewn into the front of the magician's linen robe over the chest. When invoking, the magician would lay his hand upon the pentacle over his heart to form a powerful connection with the energies it contained.

Whether hung from the neck or not, pentacles are usually shaped as disks or flat circles. Author Donald Michael Kraig recommended making a protective pentacle out of a flat wooden disk carved in such a way as to be concave. Constructed in this manner, any unwanted energy hitting the pentacle would bounce back to its source of origin.

The pentacle can be said to represent a container for the magical forces inscribed on it. It is used to encircle these forces and bring them into physical or earthly manifestation.

The tarot suit of pentacles is ascribed to the element of earth. The old medieval tarot suit of coins was renamed pentacles by Éliphas Lévi. In 1909 the Rider-Waite-Smith Tarot, created by author and Golden Dawn Initiate Arthur Edward Waite, became the first published tarot deck to incorporate the suit of pentacles, symbolized by a golden disk inscribed with a pentagram. Waite's creation became the design upon which Wiccan style pentacles were based.

Some Wiccan pentacles take the form of simple pentagrams engraved on a circular disk of wax or copper. Others are more elaborate, containing a series of pentagrams, triangles, and astrological symbols. It is considered a symbol of the Earth Mother and is often the centerpiece of the Wiccan altar. Objects are placed on the pentacle to be consecrated or blessed.

In the Golden Dawn system of magic, the pentacle is the ritual implement of the element of earth. It normally takes the form of a flat wooden disk approximately five to six inches in diameter, and it is used in the Adept grades to invoke and to banish the spirits and energies of earth. Along with the Fire Wand, Water Cup, and Air Dagger, the Earth Pentacle is considered one of the four

Elemental Weapons or Elemental Tools assigned to the elements and the four letters of the Great Hebrew Godname *YHVH* (*Yod Heh Vav Heh*), also known as the Tetragrammaton. All the elements are thought to have a sympathetic bond between them; each element is thought to exist within the others, but to a lesser degree. So even if only one of the Elemental Weapons is to be used in a ritual, the others should also be present for the sake of balance and completeness. Therefore, they are usually placed on top of the magician's altar thus: Air Dagger in the east, Fire Wand in the south, Water Cup in the west, and Earth Pentacle in the north.

Like the Grand Pentacle of Solomon, the Golden Dawn's Earth Pentacle is inscribed with a hexagram but in white. The outer rim of the pentacle is also painted white, with the names and sigils of Hebrew godnames, archangels, angels, and spirits inscribed in black. The white circular border emphasizes the surrounding element of spirit, which binds and harmonizes the other four elements. Behind the hexagram are the four colors of Malkuth, the tenth Sephirah on the Qabalistic Tree of Life and the only one that is attributed to the element of earth. Malkuth represents far more than earth, however. As the Sephirah of final manifestation, Malkuth represents all energies on the physical plane: all elements, all planets, all zodiacal signs, all organisms, and so on.

All four of the Elemental Tools can be fully considered talismans in their own right, and of these four, the design of the Earth Pentacle certainly looks the most talisman-like. But unlike regular talismans, each of the Elemental Tools is meant to be wielded like the proverbial magic wand in ritual: invoking or banishing elemental energies into the temple, or charging other talismans with that same energy.

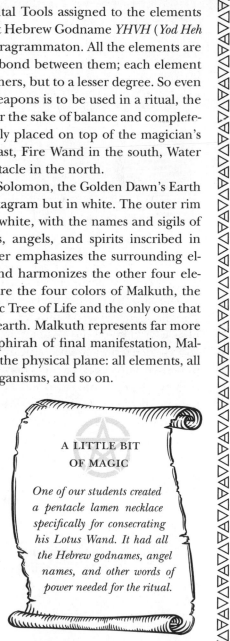

A LITTLE BIT OF MAGIC

One of our students created a pentacle lamen necklace specifically for consecrating his Lotus Wand. It had all the Hebrew godnames, angel names, and other words of power needed for the ritual.

Elemental Tools are normally kept within one's working temple space, while talismans are usually wrapped and carried around on the magician's person or placed where their energies are needed most.

The Earth Pentacle is the only one of the Elemental Tools that could conceivably be worn over the chest, like the pentacles described in the grimoires. In one of the higher-grade rituals of the Golden Dawn, the design of the Earth Pentacle (minus the Hebrew and sigils) is worn as a lamen by an officer who invokes elemental earth. The word *lamen* comes from the Latin word for "plate" and indicates a symbolic breastplate that signifies the magician's rank, authority, or power. A lamen is a magical pendant (pentacle!) worn by the magician in ritual. It is usually two to four inches in diameter and is suspended from a cord, ribbon, chain, or collar so that it hangs over the heart, the location of the Sephirah Tiphareth within the human aura.

Magicians often create lamens that mirror the design of whatever forces, angels, or spirits they are working with in a particular ritual, including their sigils, figures, and Hebrew names on the front of the lamen and a protective symbol such as a pentagram, hexagram, or Rose Cross on the back, next to the magician's chest.

Crafting Your Own Pentacle

A pentacle can be a container or reservoir for all manner of magical energies. It can be created to be the centerpiece of your magical altar like the Wiccan pentacle, or it can be crafted to be wielded as an active ritual tool like the Golden Dawn's Earth Pentacle. It can be made and charged as a simple talisman or constructed to be worn as a lamen on the chest. The design possibilities are endless, but the following list of suggestions can be used as a starting point:

Construction
- Construct it out of sturdy material such as wood or a good-quality poster board or mat board.
- Use paints that are easy to work with, such as acrylic.
- Use a good clear finish such as a spray-on nonyellowing lacquer or a clear brush-on finish such as acrylic gloss gel medium.

- Make the diameter five to six inches for an altar pentacle, two to four inches for a talisman, and two to three inches for a lamen.

Symbolism
- Paint the outer circle white for spirit.
- Include your own magical motto or mystical name.
- Use colors attributed to the forces you want to invoke.
- Include names in Hebrew or English (or both) of the divine forces, deities, or angels you want to invoke.
- Include symbols, geometric figures, or sigils of the forces you want to invoke. (Consult our book *Golden Dawn Magic* for divine, angelic, and color correspondences.)

A Pentacle of Universal Forces

This pentacle can be used to invoke or banish elemental, planetary, sephirotic, or zodiacal energies. The front of the pentacle is inscribed with a dodecagram surrounding a pentagram. The five points of the pentagram can be employed for their respective elemental powers, while the twelve points of the dodecagram can be utilized for their

zodiacal forces. The sigil of any angel can be astrally traced in the central circle.

On the reverse side of the pentacle, the points of the hexagram can be used to invoke or banish planetary energies as well as their Sephirotic counterparts. The three Supernal Sephiroth (Kether, Chokmah, and Binah) can all be invoked using the Saturn point, while both Yesod and Malkuth correspond to the Lunar point. The powers of the Sun and the Sephirah of Tiphareth lie within the center of the hexagram.

The two sides of the pentacle can be painted in the neutral, achromatic colors of white, black, and gray, or the star points and sigils of the energies can be fully embellished in the colors attributed to them.

Simple Consecration Ritual for Your Pentacle

You don't need a full temple space. A corner of your bedroom will do. A convenient tabletop, desktop, dresser top, or mantle top can be covered with a white or black cloth and used as a temporary altar. It's best if the altar top faces east but not absolutely necessary. Candles and incense will help set a solemn mood and focus your intention. Have a white linen or silk bag nearby for wrapping your pentacle. Place your pentacle on the center of your altar top.

Begin with slow rhythmic breathing to relax the mind and body. When ready, perform the Qabalistic Cross by touching (1) the top of your head, (2) center of your chest, (3) right shoulder, and (4) left shoulder while intoning "Atah" (head), "Malkuth" (chest), "Ve-Geburah" (right shoulder), "Ve-Gedulah" (left shoulder). Clasp your hands together and intone "Le-Olahm, amen." The meaning of this is "Thou art the kingdom, the power, and the glory, forever, unto the ages." Imagine a vibrant cross of brilliant divine light in the center of your body, connected by the points you have activated.

Place your hands directly over your pentacle, thumb touching thumb and index finger touching index finger so that your hands form a triangle over the pentacle. Then say,

The heaven is above and the earth is beneath. And between the light and the darkness, the energies vibrate. I call upon the Sacred Source of All that

exists, by the majesty of the divine names and words of power YOD HEH VAV HEH, ADONAI, EHEIEH, and AGLA, to bestow this present day and hour, and confirm their mystic and potent influence upon the energies linked to the sigils on this Pentacle of the Universal Forces, which I hereby dedicate to purity and occult work, and may its grasp strengthen me in the work of the magic of light!

Imagine a halo of light surrounding your pentacle, charging it with divine power and light. Take as much time as you need before thanking the Sacred Source of All and any other personal deities or angels who may have aided your ritual. Finally, wrap your consecrated pentacle in the white linen or bag. Take some time to contemplate the ritual you have completed before extinguishing any candles and ending the rite.

Your pentacle can now be used whenever you wish to work with any of the energies whose symbols are inscribed on it. When calling upon a specific energy, grasp the pentacle so that your thumb, the digit assigned to the element of spirit, touches the symbol of the force you wish to work with.

You can also use the pentacle as a magical basis for charging other talismans, placing objects on it for consecration or blessing.

The pentacle is a very adaptable tool that can be embellished with any symbolism desired and used for an endless variety of magical goals. Designing and crafting your own personal pentacle will not only give you practical experience in pentacle making, it is also a creative magical act of consecration in and of itself. This simple implement might just surprise you with its versatility and effectiveness.

Resources

Oxford English Dictionary. S.v. "pentacle." 2nd ed. Oxford, UK: Oxford University Press, 1989. https://www.oed.com/oed2/00174753.

Peter de Abano. *Heptameron, or Magical Elements*. Electronic transcription by Joseph H. Peterson. Twilit Grotto Esoteric Archives. Last modified November 10, 2020. http://www.esotericarchives.com/solomon /heptamer.htm.

Knowing the Land Itself
Lupa

P agans are, by and large, a people of the land. For some of us, our spirituality stems from connections to the land of our ancestors, and so we may explore and practice rites and ways that were formed through many years of living in particular places, even if they are far away. For others, the land is a source of materials for magic, including stones, herbs, and incenses, among other curiosities. And still others root themselves deeply in whatever physical land they may find themselves treading, whether for a day or a lifetime, learning its contours and meeting the various beings who share space there. Many combine all three of these relationships to the land, and perhaps even more.

Look at how many of us orient ourselves to the ground beneath our feet. We open our rituals by greeting or otherwise bringing attention to the directions; north, south, east, and west may even be joined by up and down in some traditions, pointing an arrow straight into the center of the earth herself. Some of us may call on notable nearby landforms and their spirits, whether mountains or waterways, broad plains or valleys. Even the most abstract spiritual and divine forms often have direct links to earthly places and phenomena.

My path has always relied heavily on the soil and the wild things that spring from it, the plants and fungi that weave the mycorrhizal tangle together, and the animals whose lives are inextricably woven in with them. These are the easiest manifestations of the land's fertility for us to access, for we ourselves arc animals, the mammal *Homo sapiens*. We are minerals and carbon and water and other vital molecules all wrapped up in a living package and all sourced from the food that we eat and water we drink.

But how often do we look beneath this biological surface to the geology, hydrology, and related studies? It's one thing to know

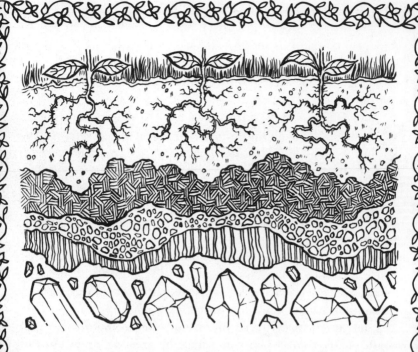

that rose quartz can be used for healing, particularly when emotions are involved. It's another thing to know that it formed from magma, is one of the hardest stones (7 on the Mohs scale), and is generally pulled from the ground through open pit mining. But those are just the minutiae of one particular sort of crystal. What about the ecosystem that it comes from?

Look at the granite that quartz is most often cradled within. What sorts of plants like that type of silica-rich stone as a base for their soil? How have the elements weathered and water shaped the solid stone over time? How long ago did the magma that became this stone erupt out of the ground, and what beings might have witnessed this awesome sight?

Deep Time

It can be incredibly difficult to truly conceptualize the immense amount of time that has passed since Earth first formed from material of the circumstellar disk that orbited around our newborn

Sun, over four and a half *billion* years ago. To someone for whom a century may be a lifetime, it's challenging to think of a timespan of 45 million centuries, never mind how much has happened on our one planet in that time.

And yet if we want to really dig deep into the story of the land, we must also dig deep into time. *Deep time*, in fact, is a term that was first used by author John McPhee in his book *Basin and Range*, though the concept of geologic time in Western geology stems from James Hutton, an eighteenth-century Scottish geologist. Deep time is not just noting remarkable dates and numbers in the history of Earth but really considering how long ago it was and how far apart certain phenomena were in time. One of the best-known examples of this is how the dinosaur *Tyrannosaurus rex*, which appeared about 81 million years ago and went extinct with the K-T event 65 million years ago, is closer to us in time than to *Stegosaurus* species, which all died out about 150 million years ago.

Carl Sagan's Cosmic Calendar is a popular way to visualize the history of the universe, and Earth's history can also be mapped out on a twenty-four hour clock. If the Earth formed at midnight in a shiny new cycle, it wouldn't be until 4:00 am that life appeared, preceded by three hours of the planet being a ball of molten rock constantly bombarded by various meteorites, and then taking another hour or so to cool down enough to form liquid water and a somewhat firm surface. The very oldest fossils of microscopic beings we have are from around 5:36 am. Single-celled algae, some of the very first photosynthesizers, didn't show up until a little after 2:00 that afternoon. The first jellyfish appeared in the oceans at 8:48 pm, followed by trilobites at 9:04 pm. Plants didn't even make it onto land until eight minutes to 10:00, and the dinosaurs sauntered onto the planet fashionably late at 10:56 pm. You'd have to wait until 11:39 pm to see your very first mammal, and we ourselves didn't arrive to the party until 11:58:43, just a second and a half ago.

We may think of trilobites as ancient, primitive animals because they did live so very long ago, but there was so much time that occurred before them! It took over half of the Earth's life-span for anything to be able to photosynthesize, and yet we take plants for granted. And depending on where you live, there may be rocks beneath you that could tell stories of the time before anything lived on the land, when it was dry and open and endless and broken only by the life-giving oceans. Really blows your mind if you think about it long enough!

Deep Time Walk

One of my favorite tools for experiencing deep time, even if only in a teacup, is Deep Time Walk. Created by a vibrant team of scientists, actors, programmers, and other professionals, it is a tool meant to help people grasp the age of the Earth through visual and kinesthetic means. The free Deep Time Walk app for any smartphone serves as a guided meditation as you walk 4.6 kilometers (scaled to Earth's 4.6 billion years); the same script (or summaries thereof) is also available to purchase as an audiobook, bookmark-size timeline, printed book, and set of cards.

If you are capable of safely walking 4.6 kilometers (2.86 miles), whether in one shot or in sections, this is a marvelous way to help you really picture the magnificence of deep time. Use the smartphone app, audiobook, or the script and/or cards if you're able to pay attention to them while you walk. Plot out your route beforehand; I have used a free account at Runkeeper.com as a way to plan walks or runs by distance (just act as though you are about to record a walk or run you've already done as a way to access the plot map). If you can't make the walk, you can also simply sit or lie down wherever you are most comfortable; just make sure you put the app into mobility-assist mode. You don't need any sort of wi-fi or other signal, either, to make it work.

Before you begin your walk (or meditation), look around your starting point. Think for a moment about how even though we think of the land around us as being enduring, its present form is recent and temporary and will continue to change due to erosion, sedimentation, and other natural forces, as well as through human activities as long as we're around. You might greet the directions to help center yourself, ground yourself in the land beneath you, or utilize whatever practices you normally do to open a ritual. Then say or think the following:

I open myself to the ancient Earth,
And prepare to journey to her birth.
May Time be so kind as to share
What wonders may be found from here to there.

Then start your walk. Allow yourself to be as immersed in it as you safely can be, and pause whenever you need a break or take time to process the immensity of what you are exploring. There is no time limit; audiobooks can be paused, scripts and cards picked up again, and the app follows your motion. What is important is that you are able to focus to the best of your ability and digest your explorations at your own pace.

You might also mark important points in your walk as you go along. You could put a knot in a long cord every time something truly strikes you, creating a record as you go along. If you're using the cards, you might separate out the ones that represent the most meaningful events and save them for later meditation. If you have the time, you can try journaling throughout your journey.

When you reach the end and have had some time to process, you can close your ritual with the following words:

I thank the Earth for what I've learned today
And those who have helped me on my way.
May context and understanding guide me
And wonder and awe always find me.

You can go through the Deep Time Walk as many times as you like. In addition to this rite, I've also used the app as a way to contact spirits of beings that lived (or otherwise existed) at various times of Earth's history, pausing at the right point after "traveling" back to their time. Plus it's just a fun thing to do to spice up an otherwise ordinary walk on a nice day!

Deep into the Earth

Once you have some appreciation for the immensity of deep time, it's time to apply it to the land you live on! Start by finding out as much as you can about the geologic history of where you live. A fabulous free resource is the smartphone app Rockd, which not only tells you what sorts of formations, stones, and soils you live on, but also can tell you something of the geologic history of that place. Don't have a smartphone? Macrostrat.org has links to a wealth of geologic maps that let you explore your area from any computer with internet access. Or you can go old school and check out books on your local and regional geology; ask your friendly neighborhood librarian for suggestions, or contact local rockhound groups.

Make sure you also understand how water and air have shaped the land. How has the wind carved away stone with the sand that it carries and the storms that ride its currents? What sorts of rivers, lakes, and other bodies of water currently exist where you are? Can you find information on how the boundaries and beds of these waterways have shifted over time? Are there any that once existed there in the past but are gone today? Consider how erosion from rain has changed how the land is shaped, slowly wearing away mountaintops and flooding the streams and rivers. Even ice may shatter stone, and many places are scarred by the tracks of great glaciers from many thousands of years ago.

Once you have this basic understanding of the geological history of where you live, you can use the following guided meditation to connect with it more deeply.

Guided Meditation

If you are able, go outside to someplace where you can see the contours of the land. It might be on a hill or where you can see a road cutaway showing the layers of stone. It might be in the middle of a wide field or plain stretching as far as the eye can see. Even if you are staying in your own home, try to find a good picture that represents your land and perhaps a handful of the soil found nearby.

Make yourself as comfortable as you can, in physical contact with the ground if possible. Slow your breathing and close your eyes. Then imagine that your awareness is sinking into the ground like a taproot, down through your skin and into soil. Explore that soil for a moment, countless tiny particles in a thin layer across the land, shot through with plant roots and fungal hyphae and the tunnels of tiny creatures and so many bacteria and other microscopic beings that the soil is alive! Consider how in millions of years this very soil that you touch may someday become shale or sandstone or some other sedimentary rock.

Now explore deeper, below the soil. Remember what you learned about what's beneath your home; allow yourself time to "dig" down through the layers of geological history, millions of years measured in inches and feet. Think about how the stone first came to be, whether as magma, ash, or cinders from a volcano; sediment washed up by watery currents; or older stone pressed into new forms by heat and tectonic forces. Think about what beings may have first walked upon the stone when it was young and open to the sky, and how their memories may still be recorded there in spirit, if not in form.

Remember the water that has sluiced across the layers of land here time and time again. Think of the rain falling down on ancient mud flats and sandy beaches, sizzling on fresh magma, cutting channels through beds of volcanic ash. Imagine how ponds and lakes have formed in depressions, deepened, then filled in again to become meadows and forests that press the old silt beds down into the earth.

And when you are ready, come back to yourself, but bring back a thin core of these layers with you. Embed them into yourself so that whenever you call upon the elements, you know their presence in the history of the land. When you go outside, know that you are poised on the newest page of a book of ancient history, contributing your tiny part to the grandest story the land has ever told.

Resources

"History of Earth in 24-Hour Clock." Flowing Data. October 9, 2012. https://flowingdata.com/2012/10/09/history-of-earth-in-24-hour-clock/.

McPhee, John. *Basin and Range*. New York: Farrar, Straus and Giroux, 1980.

Oswald, Peter and Stephan Harding. *Deep Time Walk*. Deep Time Walk CIC, 2019. Android 4.0 or later. Audio by Jeremy Mortimer and Jo Langton.

Ashé of Your Deepest Ancestry

Stephanie Rose Bird

I am many things: Green Witch, Hoodoo practitioner, shaman, visionary, and, though I seldom mention it, genealogist. This article will bring together eclectic Paganism and a specific area of magick that I've found myself delving into repeatedly over the years, something I call ancestry magick.

Let's begin by building on a few Yoruban language concepts, such as the meaning of the word *àṣẹ,* or *ashé.* The Yoruba are a powerful and influential group of people, whom some refer to as a tribe, from Nigeria and its environs. After, I will speak to my enthusiasm, as an eclectic Pagan, for digging for and finding my roots through DNA tests. Last, I will leave you with a project to enrich your personal spiritual practice.

Ashé

Before going further, it is necessary that the reader is grounded in the meaning of the central concepts being discussed. *Ashé* is a Yoruban word sometimes also written as *àṣẹ.* As an author, ashé is very intriguing to me because it concerns itself specifically with words. Ashé words are powerfully thought, spoken, or written words.

By their very act of being, they are full of meaning, one of the most important being potential.

Ashé has become a greeting African Americans use. It is a blessing, wish, and hope for one another. When spoken, we are hoping the receiver will be able to approach their potential. We wish it with reverence and respect. It speaks to the potentiality we all hold inside.

I am bringing ashé into the conversation of ancestry magick as a way of acknowledging the potential we derive simply from our DNA link to our ancestors. Let's be real: this link is not all peaches and cream. There is a scale of darkness and light to some of the deeds of our ancestors. At this time, when we look for and discuss the ashé of our ancestors, we are discussing the positive side. We seek to celebrate the potentiality that our association with these predecessors offers.

Roots and Seeds: Deep Ancestry

Spirituality, healing, and magick complement your ancestry. I have always been excited about culture, background, and heritage. Interestingly enough, I have found that those people I thought of as an "other" culture actually live deep inside of me right next to those I consider my dominant cultures or, in short, those whom I claim as being in my lineage.

You have no idea how very excited I was when DNA ancestry kits appeared on the market about a decade or so ago. Once these kits became available, I was on them, almost immediately. I have been purchasing them, one by one, for nearly ten years and have done about ten distinctive tests, some with the same company several times for more comprehensive results.

Many years before it became as popular as it is today, I embarked on a deep ancestry journey in search of my DNA ancestry kin. "Deep" means going well beneath the surface of getting to know about your parents, grandparents, and great grandparents. After all, for some, that information is simply not available anyway. My parents were married and raised us together, but my father's father was not in his life or ours. Apart from learning more about this rather important line of people, I worked hard building my family tree from what was known and discovered. I relied heavily on my membership to Ancestry.com, where I scanned documents such as marriage, birth, and death records; baptism reports; and the all-important census reports. In addition, I gave the Dawes Rolls a good going over to track any Native American background.

Slowly but surely, I came to understand the relationship between my relatives and my ancestry test results through genealogy work with an expert in the field. I would have been lost without her at that point in time; unless you are a scientist, the results could leave you in a world of confusion. The DNA consultant was wonderful and helped me sort through the studies various companies produced. She went further to help me think of looking for my paternal grand-father's line so it could have some presence on my tree as well.

Likely, you can imagine the sense of empowerment this gave me. Being of African descent and of my generation, I had often heard that we, as African Americans, were stripped of our language, customs, beliefs, and tribal affiliations. Sadly, this is true, yet I've always strongly believed there are still ways of getting back to our roots. Eclectic Paganism, specifically Wicca, Hoodoo, and Witchcraft, along with engagement with the gods and goddesses through spells and conjuration, incantations, chants, prayers, and altar work alongside herb magick, helps open the way. All these beautiful Pagan practices enhance the nuggets that become available through DNA ancestry results.

Ancestry Magick

When you tie Gaia-based spiritual engagement together with your deep ancestry knowledge, you are on the path to unlocking the mysteries of your innermost self, a path called ancestry magick. My book *Sticks, Stones, Roots & Bones* shares a cross-cultural examination of magickal traditions transformed into usable incantations, rituals, spells, and tricks for the eclectic Pagan reader. It is focused around my multicultural heritage with an African foundation—I find magick in heritage and in culture. Ancestry magick taps into these vibrant spirits in my bones and in yours.

Ancestry magick is a unique spiritual practice that invites us to embrace the ashé (potentiality) of our full ancestry. In the world we are living in, it may sound hard to believe, but we are not white, black, brown, yellow, or red. We are a rainbow of magickal possibilities, as demonstrated through deep ancestry examination of our DNA. While at first researching your ancestry seems mysterious and daunting, as you work the different types of ancestry magick of deep heritage, you'll find that inevitably it touches your heart and expands your soul.

As you dig more and more into your ancestry, you will find surprises and mysteries. There may even be a disappointment or two for a plethora of reasons. Once you have taken a DNA test, have gone through your DNA test results, and have a good understanding of them, the first thing I suggest you do is make a spiritual family tree. This will require obtaining a tree and magickal natural objects. It also requires deep reflection.

Spiritual Family Tree

You might celebrate Yule with a tree. I do. I'm inviting you to embrace tree energy in your home as a way to get comfortable and in touch with your family tree from a magickal point of view. You'll begin with a meditation, stop by a garden center to purchase the tree, and then perform a tree dressing for a plant you'll keep in your home, decorating it as you might a Yule tree around the holidays. There are many fine and varied choices for your tree:

- Norfolk island pine
- Yucca
- Palm species
- Money tree
- Ficus
- Meyer lemon or other fruit you can grow indoors

You will need:
Purple cloth
Matches or lighter
White column-shaped candle, vanilla or unscented
Fireproof candle plate
Cauldron, dutch oven, or stock pot (optional)
Salt water (optional)
Smudge stick (optional)
Van Van Oil (optional)
Spring water or other type of water (optional)
5 to 7 meaningful small objects that speak to a handful or so of
    your heritages or places (cities, town, villages) you or your an-
    cestors come from
Permanent marker
Brown paper or parchment
Twine, fishing line, or thread

If at all possible, go to a natural body of water to reflect. After all, long before we had mirrors, we went to see ourselves in moving bodies of natural water. Think of Narcissus.

Near the natural water place a purple cloth to sit on. Purple is a highly spiritual color on many paths.

Use pranayama to breathe more and more slowly, more and more fully, until you feel completely relaxed. Pranayama is a meditative technique that focuses on the connection between breath and clarity. You may begin with eight breaths inhaled through your nose, letting your jaw relax. Keep the mouth soft but closed. Breathe out, dispelling all the air from your chest in an eight count. You may continue until you feel clear and light or after doing three counts of eight.

Next, light a white columnar candle near you on a firesafe plate. A tempered glass or earthenware plate would be perfect.

If you can't go to a local river, pond, or lake, you can use a cauldron. Cleanse your cauldron thoroughly with salt water. Dry it and smudge it out with a smudge stick, using twelve counterclockwise circular sweeps. Drop in seven to nine drops of Van Van Oil. In Hoodoo, this oil is known to open the way. Then fill the cauldron with spring water.

In your heightened state, select a tree to represent your family tree. This may be a miniature Norfolk pine tree, a ficus, or another plant that you find available or that calls out to you. Snuff out the candle, quickly, using wet fingers, after the meditation is completed.

Go to a plant nursery or home and garden center to purchase a potted tree to keep indoors.

Return home and look over your DNA results again. Now, gather the objects to put on your tree. Hold each object in your hand for at least five minutes and reflect on its connection to your ancestry. What ashé does it hold? Write a single word on the back of it with a permanent marker if possible, or hang a torn piece of brown paper bag or parchment next to it with the word written on it with a pencil or marker.

Use twine, fishing line, or other threadlike material (I like synthetic waxed sinew from a craft store) to creatively string these objects on your tree. You will continue to fill it as you see fit over time.

The tree is not static but alive, changing, growing. The ritual is ongoing, as are your discoveries and intuitive developments; this is not a Christmas tree that has been cut down, decorated, and discarded.

Be mindful about how you feed your tree. Listen for its messages. Does it prefer clean spring water, rainwater, lightning water? Be careful about its light conditions and other necessities too. Does it require a grow light? Misting? Research the plant's needs, but also listen well. Let the spirits in your bones guide you. Nurture your evolving DNA family tree. Enjoy your journey into DNA ancestry magick!

Mugwort, My Love

H. Byron Ballard

Mugwort is a common and invasive weed wherever it grows, but the magical qualities of this homely plant cannot be overstated. Its botanical name is *Artemisia vulgaris*, a coupling of words that reminds us of the plant's sacred connection to the Divine as well as the everyday practical value it imparts. It's sexier cousin—*Artemisia absinthium*—gives us the "green fairy" drink, absinthe, and is used as a fumigant to rid a household of fleas and other tiny, terrible vermin. As with most plants, mugwort is part of a vast and successful family that shares certain characteristics of leaf, stem, and growth pattern. The artemisias are in the family Asteraceae and have fragrant and beautiful leaves that are green on top and silvery gray-green underneath. With the Sun above and the Moon below, mugwort is a plant that bridges the gap between night and day and rules the gloaming and the twilight. This is especially apt when we look at its history and its usefulness.

If an herb's English name ends in *-wort*, it means the plant is used as a medicine or food. *Wort* comes from the Old English word *wyrt*, which means plant or herb, so that a practice called *wort-cunning* is done by dint of knowing the properties and uses of local plants. Mugwort appears in the tenth-century "Nine Herbs Charm" as *mucgwyrt* and in the wonderful old *Leechbook of Bald*. This pedigree belies its humble place in Appalachian folkways, but it is good to remember that our old buddy mugwort has a long-standing place in herbal healing.

It is used traditionally to regulate irregular menstrual cycles, for stomach issues like colic, and for both constipation and diarrhea. Mugwort is a mild abortifacient, and that may be a reason for a cautious approach. In traditional Asian medicine, it is called *moxa* and is burned to heat acupuncture needles as well as burned in a healing process called moxibustion.

Our particular artemisia is called mugwort because it was used in making beer in Europe, before the introduction of hops as a bittering agent. It is still used in warming, light-alcohol ales that are easy to brew and delicious to drink. One recipe is sweetened with sorghum molasses and delivers a gently bubbly drink. We can assume that the earlier use of mugwort as bitters in a vat of good ale was quite satisfactory.

Gathering Mugwort

As with any unfamiliar plant, wear gloves when harvesting mugwort. It rarely causes an allergic reaction but certainly can, and it is better to be careful until you know how the plant's juices will affect you. Most herbs should be harvested in the early morning before the sun has had a chance to dry the plant out. The parts of the plant that are used are the leaves and stems, and they may be used either fresh or dried, depending on the application.

Mugwort is easy to identify when foraging and grows well in a soil that retains some moisture but drains well. It flourishes in sun and partial shade, though it can sometimes be found in shady spots too. It is a weed. It isn't fussy. The leaves look like the leaves of its cousin chrysanthemum, and most people have an idea of what that looks like because of their use in autumn seasonal decorations—pumpkins, gourds, and golden mums inhabit the porch steps of many a suburban home and are readily available for purchase at the grocery and hardware store.

All the artemisias are easy to grow, if that is your preference. They are perennials and tend to be invasive, so growing a specimen plant in a large container may be your best bet. If you find yourself harvesting and using it for all the things it's good for, you might end up keeping a patch that happily regrows.

As a culture, we are growing more intentional about the plants we use for sacred smoke in ritual and other uses. Cultural appropriation is a legitimate concern, and finding plant materials other than white sage (which is also overharvested in the wild) is a pleasant study. It gives us a lovely excuse to explore the plants that are native to us. Many dried plants can be used as sacred smoke, but, as always, check with a plant guide or herbalist to make sure the plant is safe to burn.

A bundle of dried mugwort—perhaps with the addition of lavender, rosemary, or mint—makes a natural and culturally appropriate smudge stick. Tie it up with some cotton, wool, or hemp string, not too thick.

Mugwort Infused Oil

Mugwort oil is useful for dressing objects like ritual tools and candles and for anointing hands and foreheads for workings and ceremonies. Take a small glass jar with a reclosable, screw-on lid—about six ounces is a good place to start. Loosely fill it three-quarters full with fresh mugwort, then add in a vegetable oil to near the top. Screw the lid on and give it a good shake. Leave it in a cool, dark place for a Moon cycle, shaking it every few days until the month is over. Remove the gooey green material by pouring the oil through a sieve or strainer. (The goo can go into your compost pile.) You may want to filter it again through cheesecloth to remove the last bits of leaf and stem, but it isn't necessary. You can wipe out the original jar and pour the filtered oil back in for storage, but most people prefer to pour it into a decorative bottle before shelving it. It is important that oils be kept in a cool, dark place, and an amber or dark green bottle

is useful in keeping light from degrading the oil. It is also important to label the bottle with the kind of oil it contains as well as the
date it was bottled. You think you will remember but chances are
you won't. Best to label everything.

Dreams and Sleep

Mugwort is one of three sovereign plants in my personal practice. The other two are rue (*Ruta graveolens*) and vervain (*Verbena
hastata* is the one I use). They rank so highly because we continue
to experiment with them and find new uses.

Mugwort has been long prized as a dream tonic. Whether in-
gested as a warm evening tea, burned as an incense, or used fresh,
this herb is often recommended to people who are suffering
from either a dearth of dreams or oppressive or frightening ones.
If you're having trouble remembering your dreams and desire to
do so, mugwort can bring your dreams up so they stick in your
memory upon waking. When used with an end-of-day routine

that includes a set bedtime, a dark and quiet resting place, and an early retirement of electronic devices, mugwort is an aid to relaxation, deep sleep, and vivid dreams.

On the other hand (and especially given the challenging times we are living in now), some people are plagued with far too vivid dreams, with nightmares and night terrors. Disturbed and erratic sleep patterns contribute not only to fatigue during daylight hours but, if prolonged, can impact our general good health and well-being. Children can be particularly susceptible to scary or confusing images that return in their deep sleep. A simple sun catcher in the shape of a beloved character or animal and placed in the child's window can shield the sleeper from the scarier elements, and creating a regular tucking-in ritual will also help. Listen to the child's concerns and especially note the story of the dreams and the characters. Dreams may hold clues to things your child is facing but is unable to articulate. And the same is true for you.

In both of these scenarios, our friend mugwort can also come to the rescue. Create a strong tisane by brewing up a cup of fresh or dried mugwort. Another suggestion is to cut branches of fresh mugwort and place them under the pillow but inside the pillowcase. The pungent scent is released all night long as you move about in your sleep. Replace the branches every night until your dreams have regulated themselves and are restful and informative.

As you might imagine, this plant is also useful for lucid dreaming and for trance work. Used as a sacred smoke or incense or drunk as a tisane, it is a light aid in trance. As with any plant material, follow all precautions about allergies, use during pregnancy or lactation, and drug interactions before using mugwort.

Mugwort Tisane
If using the fresh herb, cut the leaves and stems early in the day and rinse in tepid water to remove any soil or insects. Allow the herb to dry on a kitchen towel until you are ready to use it. Stuff the plant material into a glass jar or a teapot, but don't pack it too tightly. Pour boiling water into the pot and leave it to steep for

at least an hour, allowing it to cool in the process. It can be used to lightly mist the pillow and top edge of the quilt. There isn't a strong scent when brewed this way, so you may choose to add a drop of lavender oil to your tisane.

Parting the Veil

This glorious plant—with the Sun above it and the Moon below— has another secret to share with us, and its efficacy with dream-work gave herbalists and magic practitioners the hint to wander down another of artemisia's pathways. Many of us consider that there is an energetic veil or wall between the worlds of matter and spirit. Mugwort may be useful to easing open a gateway and is being used by some death midwives and doulas to ease the passage into death and the worlds beyond for those waiting at that liminal edge. For those caregivers who are sitting by the bedside of a beloved elder, the same mugwort water that helps a child to a peaceful sleep can be used as a cooling compress on the forehead of the dying. A cotton ball can apply this gentle soother to wrists, inner elbows, or ankles. Our companion mugwort finds a place in this powerful rite of passage. As with dreamwork, fresh branches may be placed inside the pillowcase or tucked into a green bouquet on the bedside table.

••• ☽ •••

Artemisia—sacred to Artemis in the West—has been used folklorically in many places and cultures throughout history. It is no surprise that it fits so neatly into the healing pharmacopoeia of Appalachia. For sleep and dreams or disturbed digestive tracts, this humble, sturdy, and magical plant should have a prominent place on your herb shelf, in your garden, and in your practice.

Air Magic

Air Magic Hacks

Astrea Taylor

L ike fish immersed in water, we live in a world saturated with the element of air. Wherever we go and whatever we do, air is one of the most accessible elements to us. It's readily available whenever we need it—it's a mere breath away. Air helps us elevate, communicate, concentrate, expand, change, and bring about different mindsets. There are many ways to utilize the magical element of air in our everyday lives. Over the years, I've discovered a few hacks that help me bring this amazing element more into my life.

Conscious Breath, Magical Breath

There's a huge difference between breathing automatically and breathing with awareness. Conscious breathing is one of the simplest ways to experience the element of air, and it's also a great warmup for any air magic.

To breathe consciously, take a deep breath. Feel the life-giving air enter your nose, slide down your throat, and enter your lungs. Hold the breath for a moment. On your exhalation, feel your lungs contract and your breath slide over your throat and out. Pause at the end of the exhalation, and then continue breathing with the same awareness.

Once you can breathe consciously, you can step it up to inhale the magical energy in the element of air. Begin to breathe with more power. With every deep, strong inhale, draw into yourself the positive aspects of the element of air. Breathe in change, communication, and mental ability. Exhale resistance to change, blocks to communication, and mental stagnation. Inhale the energies of expansion, elevation, and focus. Exhale closed-mindedness, rigidity, and ambivalence. With each inhalation, imagine you're taking in all the good that's present in the air around you. Allow this uplifting energy to bring your mind and spirit into more blissful realms.

Cultivate a Frequency

As our breaths rise and fall, we create a rhythm or a frequency of energy. The wavelengths of our breathing patterns are with us all the time, and they contribute greatly to our mental and spiritual states. We hold the power to change our vibe with our breath. In other words, we can match the rhythm of our breaths to the energy we desire most. To cultivate a specific frequency, consider the mindset that would benefit you most at the moment, and breathe at a pace that supports it. You could envision the process of finding your frequency as if you're turning a knob on an old-fashioned stereo, trying to find a radio station. Once you find your desired frequency, do your best to maintain it. The trick is to keep from backsliding into your previous frequency or a resting state.

For some people, cultivating a breath frequency will be an easy hack. If you're not sure, figure out if you need to go higher or lower. Do you want a high-energy, focused mind, or an ecstatic spiritual state? If so, try breathing more rapidly. Do you need more relaxation, peace, and contentment? Breathe more slowly. Adjust your breathing rate until you find a pace that suits your needs.

The great thing about creating a breath frequency is that it can be used nearly everywhere you go. For instance, you can breathe strong, purposeful breaths in the morning to give you energy to start your day. When you go to work, evaluate what energy is most suitable for the day, and dial into that frequency. Upon returning home, shift to a supportive breathing pattern for that environment. When it's time for your magical work, this could mean breathing slower to cultivate a relaxed state of mind or breathing faster to find bliss.

Send a Message through the Realm of Air

The element of air is always flowing, churning, and blowing new energy into our lives. Even when there's no physical breeze in our world, the magical realm of air still rolls through our world like a dense, never-ending fog made of spirits and energy. When we send our intentions into the world, we tap into this highly transmissive realm. The magical realm of air facilitates nonphysical communication.

Psychically sensitive people can send and receive messages by being in tune with it.

Before beginning, there are a few things you'll need to do. The first is to get permission from a friend to send and receive psychic messages with you. The second is to tune in to the ever-changing energy of the magical realm of air. Establish a general baseline of the sound and the energy, and then practice filtering the baseline out of your awareness while remaining connected with the magical realm of air.

Whenever you want to send a message, call to mind the background energy of the magical realm of air. It's sort of like picking up a landline telephone and hearing a dial tone. Envision your friend's face floating in the air before you, and speak a message in your mind. You may be tempted to shout your message to make sure it's heard, but a tone that sounds more like your natural speaking voice will probably be received more easily. As long as your voice stands out from the background energy of the magical realm of air, it should be fine. Your message will ride along the invisible, magical airwaves, and not unlike wi-fi, it will cross time and space and reach your friend an instant later. Imagine your friend receiving it and acknowledging it.

To receive a psychic message, pay attention to when you suddenly hear the background noise of the magical realm of air. Filter out the static and try to hear your friend's voice. There are many ways to receive messages—some people receive audibly, and others feel messages. Learn which method you're best at and use it to your advantage.

Discernment is sometimes necessary when receiving these kinds of messages. If the message is harmless, like a request to pick up chocolate, you can probably trust the message enough without wondering whether it was sent from your friend or not. However, if the message is questionable, be skeptical. Check with your friend to verify the message before believing it.

Think like a scientist: repeat the process until you find methods that work best for you. Successful transmissions often depend on how sensitive you and your friend are and how open the receiver is at the time. Troubleshoot issues with actual communication and repetition.

Airy Walks

Whenever I feel troubled or I want to change my mindset, I go outside and take a walk. I've found it's a great way to get in touch with the magical element of air. Physically, walks increase our breathing rates and circulation, creating aerobic respiration on a whole-body, cellular level. Walks also have numerous magical applications as well. Here are my favorite hacks to do on my "airy walks."

- While you're walking, look up at the vast sky above you. Connect with how big it is in all directions. You may start to feel your energy expand and decompress as you take in its enormous beauty.
- Pagans and Witches talk about the practice of grounding a lot, but hardly anyone talks about the magical practice of elevating. It's just as important, and it can raise your energy and give you fresh perspectives. To elevate, align your mind or your upper

chakras with the sky high above you. Imagine that your arms are branches, and feel them grow upward into the sky. Envision them being caressed by a gentle breeze. Allow these sensations to lift you up. Another way to elevate is to connect with a flying bird or a cloud passing overhead.

- Trees, bushes, and other plants are so in tune with the element of air that even when there's no breeze that we can feel, they may be dancing in an unseen wind. While walking, look for leaves or branches that are waving at you. Wave back at them or acknowledge them mentally. If you feel moved to do so, ask them for a message. They may just share some arcane wisdom with you.
- As you walk, gather a ball of air energy around yourself. This is an uplifting experience that's easy for anyone who has ever played with a ball of energy in their hands. To gather a ball of energy while you walk, swing your arms naturally. Cup your hands slightly so that when your arm is moving backward and toward you, your hand brings energy toward the center of your body. Continue walking this way until you've gathered a ball of energy around you that doesn't seem to be growing any bigger. With a deep breath, breathe it in.

Charge the Air with Intention

One of the most practical and magical applications that I've enjoyed lately is to infuse the air with my intentions. This is a great way to promote a certain emotion or feeling at a location. It creates a purposeful atmosphere that's best suited for your needs.

Before beginning, you may wish to cleanse the space by bell, besom, or incense. A good cleansing will neutralize any negative energy in the space, but the end result is neutral energy, not positive energy. It's sort of like washing a dish—you remove the food particles and germs from it, but at the end of your cleansing, it's just an empty dish. It's certainly not filled with pie or stroganoff or some other delectable food.

There's nothing wrong with neutral energy, but in an environment, it can create an energy gradient that could bring some high-energy people down. It also could make energy raising more labor-intensive and tiring, which is not ideal in a magical setting.

Charging the air with intentions ensures that you won't be starting from scratch. It magnifies your magical and mundane workings by lifting them up before you've even begun. It can also change any lingering energy patterns in that area. Depending on how successful your magic is, it might even reduce your need to cleanse the space as often.

The first step to charging the air with your intentions is to choose a location. Once you're there, evaluate what happens there and what you wish would happen there. With that in mind, create an intention that states what you want the space to do: "This living room is a place of relaxation, love, and happiness." "My home office helps me focus so I can create my best work." "This park is a clean and safe space. Anyone who comes here will respect the land or feel the urge to leave immediately." "My ritual space is a protected and sacred area that facilitates powerful magic."

Be specific, and use language that is positive and present tense. Write your intention down so you can refer to it during this practice and whenever you wish to use it again in the future.

When you're ready to charge the air with your intention, stand in the center of the space with your feet about hip-width apart. Feel the energy of the air. Start to breathe more consciously, and then connect with the magical element of air.

Once you feel the magical element of air within you, draw a deep breath and speak your intention out loud. If that's not possible, speak it in your mind. Your words will be imbued with the magical element of air. Envision your magical words traveling through the place as a specific color and vibration or feeling. See your intention touching and coloring the items in your immediate area. Hold this image in your mind for about ten seconds before releasing it. Breathe regularly for a few rounds.

A Little Bit of Magic

TO GET IN TOUCH WITH AIR, IMAGINE THE SKY IS A VAST, INVISIBLE OCEAN WHERE OUR COMMUNICATIONS TRAVEL AND SPIRITS FLY.

When you're ready to do this again, breathe strongly again to take in the magical element of air within you. Allow it to build for a few breaths. When you feel up for it, take an even deeper breath than the last time. Let the magical element of air fill your lungs. Recite your intention a second time, louder than before. Envision your intention as an even more vibrant color and vibration that connects with all the molecules in the air around you. See this energy interact with the first intention—see it build upon the energy there and strengthen it. For about twenty seconds, imagine that your intention fills the area. Release the image and breathe naturally for a moment.

When you're ready for the last push, inhale the magical element of air again. Let it grow within you, then take your deepest breath yet, inhaling as much of the magical element of air into your lungs as possible. Recite your intention with your loudest voice. Envision the energy of your words saturating the place entirely, building upon the other layers of intention in the room with the most intense color and vibration. Hold this in your mind for about thirty seconds, and then release it.

To tether the intention to the room, imagine there's a thread in the energy that you could pluck that connects to the center of the energy, sort of like a cloud on a string. Grasp the invisible thread and tie it to something that won't be cleansed soon, such as a light fixture or a tree branch. Do this again a few times around the space. These threads will help anchor the energy there. Close your eyes and envision the threads holding the intention for a minute. When you're satisfied with your magic, thank the element of air for its assistance.

Your charged intention can last for anytime from a couple of hours to several months. It depends on the strength of your intention, the strength of your energy, and how much traffic it sees. Recharge the intention every once in a while, especially if it dissipates quickly.

If anyone else uses the space, be aware of whether they would consent to you altering the energy or not. It's likely that your coven wouldn't mind if you created a spiritual intention in your group ritual room. When consent gets blurry, though, be aware of your ethics and repercussions from your actions.

Transformative Bubbles

Just the thought of blowing bubbles transports me back to happy childhood summers, when I needed nothing more than a bottle of bubbles, a wand, and sunshine. The swirling, rainbow opalescence of bubbles is so dazzling, and I always feel so peaceful watching them float in the air. By themselves, bubbles are great for lifting spirits. It's nearly impossible to feel negative around them. But of course, we're Witches, so we're going to make bubbles that magically transform our energy to match our desires.

Buy a translucent bottle of bubbles in a color that corresponds to the energy you wish to cultivate. For example, a blue bottle could bring serenity, and a purple bottle would be perfect for spirituality. A bottle in a sunny color can bring cheer, and a red bottle would call forth love. It doesn't hurt to spend a few extra dollars on this purchase—it could mean the difference between bubbles that last for a couple of seconds and ones that last for much longer.

Remove the label and cleanse the outside of the bottle with soap and water. Allow it to air dry. Next, place the bottle in moonlight or sunlight, whichever corresponds best with your intention. Full moonlight will call forth a gentle, emotional energy, and sunlight will instill the bubbles with a more powerful, logical energy. As the bottle bathes in the light, ask for a blessing from the Sun or the Moon for your purposes: for example, "I call upon the energy of the moon to bless these bubbles with emotional wisdom and magic."

When you're ready to enchant your bubbles, drop a crystal that's not water-soluble into the charged liquid. Some of the best crystals for this are clear quartz, rose quartz, citrine, and amethyst. Say what you wish it to do: for example, "With this piece of amethyst, I call upon the energy of serenity."

Place your hands around the bottle and repeat your intention one more time: "I call upon the energy of serenity to bless these bubbles." Create the energy of serenity in your mind and body, and then send the serenity through your hands and into the bottle. When the energy transfer feels complete, cap the bubbles and write the purpose on the bottle with a permanent marker. Keep it on your air shrine to charge them up for later use.

The next time you're feeling the opposite emotion of the magical transformative bubbles, take your bubbles outside and open them up. Dip the wand in the solution, hold it before you, draw a deep breath, and say something like, "I release the emotion of anger and encase it in serenity" or "I release any blocks I have to feeling serenity."

Blow into the wand. You'll have to blow out at just the right speed—too fast and the bubbles will pop. Too slow and nothing will come out. Find the just-right breath to create bubbles.

When you blow the bubbles, see them as the energy that you wished to release trapped in a shell of your desired energy. In our examples, that would be anger encased in serenity. Watch the bubbles float away from you, and feel the emotion leave you. Repeat as many times as you need to release the emotion.

Magick in the Air: Homemade Incense

Monica Crosson

The sweetly scented smoke from incense made by the grinding of tree resins and herbs, spices, and bits of bark weaves its tendrils throughout my ritual space, purifying the area and dispelling the negative energy that so easily slips between the fibers of our lives. Creating incense that I use in magick is as important to me, as a practitioner whose magick takes her to the edge of the otherworld, as the ritual itself. I remain fully present as I go into the wild (or even my backyard garden) to gather materials for my ritual smoke, stopping to commune with trees or say hello to animals who pass my way. As I grind and mix my ingredients, I keep focused on my magickal intent, seeing my results clearly in my mind as I chant words of power over the mixture. During ritual, the scent of my incense rises warm and familiar, helping me deepen my connection to the spirits who occupy the land surrounding me. I feel at peace and at one with the elements I work with.

If you are using smoke to honor the spirits of the land that surround you, doesn't it make sense to make incense from ingredients found or grown in your own region? Gathering resins or plant material from your local wild areas, or from your own backyard garden, allows you to make a deeper connection with *your* region and relieves some pressure from popular resinous trees and plant material whose demand is leading to overharvesting.

Resins from conifers such as pine, fir, cedar, spruce, and hemlock are just as wonderful as the more exotic resins that we are familiar with. And though they carry subtle differences in scent and energy, they are no less powerful. For example, resins from trees in the pine family are a great substitute for resins of non-native trees such as *Protium copal* (copal tree) of Central America and the *Boswellia sacra* (frankincense tree) whose sustainability is under threat because of its popularity. Common garden herbs such as sage, rosemary, and lavender, which can be grown in your backyard or in pots, along with the bark, berries, and leafy material from many of your local deciduous trees and shrubs make a magickally potent addition to your incense blends.

Coniferous Trees that Best Produce Resin	
Cedar	Use in incense blends for calm, spirituality, healing, and denoting sacred space.
Fir	Use in magick for ancestral work, healing, blessings, and past-life regression.
Hemlock	Coniferous hemlock can be used in magick for transformation and illumination. It blends well with lavender and is for meditative blends.
Juniper	The resin, berries, bark, and wood have a calming and relaxing effect and have been used to sharpen mental clarity, for protection, and to raise spiritual energy.
Larch	Use in mixes for connecting with the otherworld, for confidence, and for protection.
Pine	Can be used as a substitute for copal or frankincense in blends and is used for healing, cleansing, strength, and grounding.
Redwood	Use to connect with the otherworld, abundance, healing, and protection.
Spruce	Use in magick for constancy, versatility, and determination.

What Is Resin?

Resin is a main component in most incense blends. I know you are familiar with resins such as frankincense, sandalwood, and dragon's blood that are purchased dried and arrive neatly packaged. But do you know what a resin actually is? Resin is produced in special resin cells in plants to protect them from insects or pathogens and is made in response to an injury to the plant. Resins can be produced through the bark of a tree, the flowers of an herb, or the buds of a shrub and can occur as part of other compounds, such as latex.

Some folks use the terms *sap* and *resin* interchangeably, and though both are secreted by plants, sap is a thin, sweet liquid that carries nutrients to the living parts of the tree. Resin, on the other hand, is a sticky secretion that is located in the outer cells of the tree and is produced as a seal that prevents infection when a tree is injured. Gathering your own resin is actually easier than you might realize, and you are benefited with the knowledge that your material was gathered ethically and with love.

Harvesting Resin

You will need:
Designated dull knife or small metal paint scraper
Jars, baggies, or wax paper to hold the resin
Gloves (optional)

You know that thick, sticky substance you see dripping down the trunk of a tree typically where damage has been done? That is resin. You can easily harvest it by using a dull knife to gently remove the resin from the bark. But remember to keep away from the injured part of the tree and harvest only the drips or what has collected on the ground. The resin acts as a bandage to help keep infection at bay, and you don't want to further injure the tree by opening the wound. If you keep resin in a plastic bag, it will remain sticky. To dry it, place on a cookie sheet in the sun or a warm dry place and wait . . . but be patient: it can take months for resin to dry completely.

Another option (what I do) is to harvest already dried resin from the tree. The pieces can be removed very easily from the trunk and around the base of the tree with little mess.

Remember, resin is very sticky and does not clean up easily. Alcohol works for cleaning your tools, and olive oil, shortening, and hand cleaners such as Goop work on your skin.

After your collected resin has dried, the easiest way to utilize it is to simply burn small chunks of it on a charcoal block in whatever amount you may require. Remember to test a small amount first to see how much smoke you get. You might be surprised at how little you will need.

Other Plant Material

Once you have collected and dried your resin, you may want to add dried plant material or essential oil to create a unique incense blend that is suited to your magickal needs.

Correspondences for Common Woody and Fragrant Material	
Alder	Use in mixes for journeying, for self-love, and to ease fear.
Angelica	Use in mixes for protection and clearing negativity.
Ash	Burn the bark of ash in blends for prosperity, protection, and good health.
Aspen	Use for protection, antitheft, and eloquence.
Basil	Use in blends for improving memory, to cleanse and purify, and to induce calm.
Bay	Use to promote healing, sharpen psychic abilities, for protection, and for purification.
Birch	Use in magick for new beginnings, protection, resilience, and inspiration.
Chamomile	Use for peace, healing, divination, and dreamwork.
Dill	Sporting beautiful fragrant fronds, dill is used in blends for love, money, and protection.
Elecampane	Use to work with elves, for purification, and for divination.
Elderberry	The perfect addition to working magick with the fae, for protection, or to break curses.
Eucalyptus	You can't beat this tree's cleansing abilities. Great for protection and to zap negative influences from your surroundings.
Fennel	Use fennel in blends for courage, strength, and transformation.
Fern	Use in faery magick, for luck, for health, and for protection.
Ginseng	Use for love, lust, prosperity, and protection.
Hawthorn	Use in magick for protection, faery magick, and happiness.

Correspondences for Common Woody and Fragrant Material	
Lavender	The smoke of lavender creates a calming, peaceful atmosphere and can be used in mixes for loving vibes, to induce sleep, for meditation, for purification, and for healing.
Lemon Peel	Use dried peel in mixes for summertime rituals, cleansing, happiness, and friendship. Great added to a ritual bath.
Maple	Use in magick for prosperity and love.
Mint	Can be used in mixes to aid in meditation, sleep, and psychic awareness. Use for love, for peaceful vibes, and to stimulate mental clarity.
Mullein	Use for protection, strength, and astral travel.
Mugwort	Use to cleanse a space of negative energies, for dreamwork, and in divination.
Orange Peel	Dried citrus can add an uplifting scent to your incense blends and can be used in blends for mental clarity, for luck, for joy, or to raise energy.
Poplar	Use the sticky, sweet resinous buds in magick for success, money, endurance, hope, and rebirth.
Rose	The lovely dried petals of the rose can be used in incense blends for love and healing and to promote a peaceful vibe.
Rosemary	Can be used in mixes for peace of mind, for luck, to stimulate mental clarity, for protection, for healing, and to designate spiritual space.
Sage	Use in mixes for cleansing, promoting spirituality, increased memory, and healing.
St. John's Wort	Use for happiness, positivity, and protection.
Thyme	Lends well to blends for health, healing, strength, and purification.
Yarrow	Use in mixes for psychic awareness before divination and for clarity.

Making Magick

The fragrant scent of smoke created by incense has a long history that goes back thousands of years. Throughout its history, it has been used to mask the sometimes-odorous scent of human habitation, to purify sacred or religious sanctuaries, to carry prayers, to chase away malevolent spirits, to elevate meditative states, or for healing purposes.

Every autumn, a few of my magically inclined friends gather with me in my gazebo under a canopy of golden leaves to grind our favorite herbs, resins, and barks that we have gathered from the forest or grew in our own gardens and share our recipes. We make incense to purify and to ease the weary soul. We create blends to attract prosperity and draw love. We have mixes to coax sleep and to comfort the anxious mind. Those who have them bring a mortar and pestle, and everyone contributes with favorite resins, herbs, berries, spices, and bits of dried bark to share with the group. The autumn air stirs, lending its magick to our own smoke that rises from tiny cauldrons that smolder with aromatic herbs as we tell stories and share knowledge. Gathering with coven-mates or friends to create incense blends is a wonderful way to get the creative energy flowing and share techniques and recipes.

Here are a few recipes, how-tos and correspondence lists to get you started.

Noncombustible Incense

Noncombustible incense is made up of loosely ground aromatic plant material, resins, and essential oils and releases its smoke when

sprinkled onto a hot ember (typically an incense charcoal tablet) in a censer or a heat-proof container. What's great about noncombustible incense is that it's easy to make, you're in control of the ingredients, and you can specialize blends to fit your intentions.

You will need:
Mortar and pestle
Coffee grinder (optional; works great for hawthorn or juniper
    berries but destroys some of the essential oils for most material)
Essential oils (optional)
Self-lighting charcoal tabs
Censer or firesafe container

Creating your own incense blends helps you infuse your personal power into the incense. And by using resin that you collected, along with either homegrown or locally sourced dry plant material, you will find that there is not only a pleasant difference in the scent of the smoke but a stronger energy that raises gooseflesh.

Grind your material. Then add optional essential oils. Store in a jar in a warm, dry place and your incense will keep for years. Noncombustible incense can be burned on a charcoal tab in a censer or other firesafe container.

Incense Balls

These are a favorite of mine to make and are a fun way to get the kids involved when creating incense.

You will need:
Dry fragrant materials such as dried herbs (lavender, rosemary,
    mugwort, thyme, sage, etc.) and/or dried resin
Mortar and pestle
Sticky resin that is cleaned (as best you can) of bark, twigs, and
    needles
Essential oils (optional)
Cookie sheet

Coarsely grind fragrant materials and optional essential oil with a mortar and pestle, then take a pea-sized glob of resin and knead it together with dry fragrant incense materials. You can use the back of a spoon or some other tool for kneading to keep your hands clean. When you are finished, your resin balls should have enough dry ingredients added to no longer feel sticky.

Spread them out evenly on the cookie sheet and set it in a warm place with good circulation.

To use them, simply burn them on a charcoal block in a heat-proof container.

Incense Blends

Time to Unwind (Calm or Meditation)
2 parts pine resin
1 part lavender buds
½ part cedar bark

Raise the Roof (To Raise Energy)
2 parts juniper resin
1 part orange peel
½ part rosemary

Get Off Your Butt (Motivation)
2 parts spruce resin
½ part thyme
½ part St. John's wort

Meditation Blend
2 parts coniferous hemlock resin
1 part lavender
½ part garden sage

Divination Blend
2 parts pine resin
1 part yarrow
½ part mugwort
¼ part chamomile
¼ part elecampane

How to Summon a Grief Eater

Sasha Graham

Practical magic is powerful. Having helpful spirit companions is like money in the bank (or like toads in a Witch's brew). The more you have, the better off you are.

One of the most useful techniques I've ever come across was inspired by my travel and research in the Tibetan Himalayas. I was delighted to discover that Tibetan monks, nuns, and Tantric yoginis work with their spiritual iconography the same way I work with archetypal tarot energy. This is how I learned of a grief eater.

We Witches despise not getting what we want. We are used to having our way with the world (even though we know our sacred universal dance is a two-step; we never work magic alone). We know we are always given just the very thing we need at any moment. Yet it stings when our desires are not met. Acceptance of disappointment, darkness, and sadness is part of being whole and healthy.

A grief eater will aid you when you are moving through sadness, picking up fractured pieces, and tending to your soul. A grief eater soothes emotional and mental issues as well as challenging daily situations. Call upon a grief eater to make life bearable through the grieving process. Access it when your heart has been shattered. Use it to vanquish a repetitive or painful thought cycle.

The Magician's Secret

Working with a grief eater is a three-step process. First, integrate the Magician's secret of reality. Second, select and invoke the grief eater you want to work with. Third, ask for permission and begin working with the grief eater.

The Magician's secret of reality resides inside the tarot deck. Observe the Magician card in any historical tarot from the Italian Visconti deck to the French Marseilles to Pamela Colman Smith's Magician card. Each Magician is depicted the same way. He stands

behind a table with the four suit symbols of tarot upon it: wand, cup, sword, and pentacle. It is a reminder that the tools you need are always in front of you. The secret of reality also hides among his tools.

Wands align with elemental fire. We feel tarot's wands in our body when we experience passion, desire, and energy. We observe energy in others and feel it when our cheeks flush red with excitement. But we can't hold passion in our hands. It is intangible. Cups align with elemental water, and we experience tarot's cups via emotions, imagination, and love. We make things using our creativity, yet fantasies aren't something we can place in a box. We know empathy when we feel it. But love and dreams are not something we can touch with our fingers. Swords align with elemental air. Tarot's swords move through our body as thoughts, ideas, and the stories we tell ourselves and others. We can write or articulate a thought when we speak. But a thought isn't something we can actually touch or taste. Ideas and calculations are intangible. Pentacles align with elemental earth. We can feel tarot's pentacles with our blood, bones, and body. Elemental earth is *everything* we can see, feel, touch, taste, and smell. Have you figured out the Magician's secret? It contains the secret of who you are.

We are not our passions. We feel excitement, identify with the exhilaration, but it isn't us. We are not our emotions. We experience waves of feeling driving us to act. But it isn't us. We are not our feelings. Wild ideas and narratives fill our ever-calculating minds. But we are not our thoughts. A thought is simply something we have. Earth is the only element we can see, touch, taste, hear, and smell.

The Magician's secret: three-quarters of the world is invisible. The universe doesn't exist "out there." It exists inside *us!*

Who are we? We are the intelligence gazing through our eyes. We are the active observer. We are the Magician. This secret gives us the space to choose how we respond to any emotion, idea, or impulse. We can choose to respond to anything with our deepest authenticity. The Magician does not cast magic on the outside world. He casts the magic on himself.

It is easy to be a magical witchy creature when life is humming along beautifully. But what about when we brush up against the hard stuff? What can we do when life gets in the way? The grief eater is a relationship you can cultivate to help you through life's toughest times. A grief eater is energy you will befriend and whom you will feed your negative thought patterns and dark emotions to.

Choosing Your Grief Eater

Choose your grief eater through a familiar and comfortable association. It can be a god energy, archetypal energy, or plant energy. The god or goddess should align within your spiritual system. Hecate, Brigid, and Kali make excellent choices. The Death card from tarot makes a perfect grief eater because Death will devour your

grief and reprocess it into something new. Trust your instincts for this work. You can choose an herb or tree (but not an animal). Motherwort herb is highly recommended due to its soothing qualities, but you can select any herb or tree energy you like and have access to.

Sit before your chosen image or in front of the herb or tree you have chosen to work with at twilight. As the setting Sun casts long shadows and the sky turns pink and purple, light a candle and gaze at your chosen goddess, tarot card, or plant. Focus intently. Observe everything. What does it look like? What does it smell like? What are the colors? How does it make you feel?

Close your eyes and continue to explore the goddess, archetype, or plant. Move close to the energy and officially welcome it into your life. Explain your situation to the energy and ask for permission to transfer your negative, repetitive, dark, or heartbreaking thought patterns to it. Allow the energy to speak for itself. If the energy gives you permission to work with it, you may ask if there are any additional messages it would like to share with you.

Keep the grief eater's image close by in the coming days. Every time you feel yourself overcome with challenging emotions or destructive, sad, or heartbreaking thoughts, bring the image of your grief eater to mind. Take a deep breath, close your eyes. In your mind's eye, allow the grief eater to absorb the negative or repetitive thoughts and emotions. This will give you space to heal and the ability to change the thought pattern, and it creates room to grow.

Thank your grief eater by making charitable donations in its name or by planting herbs, trees, or flowers. Working with energies and spirits is a two-way relationship. It mirrors the "regular" relationships in our life. Always treat a sacred pact with good manners and respect to keep your bond healthy and strong.

Namaste and so mote it be.

Mapping the Magic

Natalie Zaman

In 1791 when the location of the nation's permanent capital was being debated, one thing was certain: the new city would be named *Washington* after the nation's first president and Revolutionary War hero. George Washington was a legend in his own lifetime—but he was also practical and played an active role in planning America's capital. The city, a ten-mile square, is a grid intersected by diagonal streets. At the intersections, circles were placed, one for each of the original thirteen colonies. The plan included a survey of the land as well as the sky to determine the placement of buildings and the alignment of streets and structures so that they'd mirror the stars and planets. If you look closely at a map of the area, distinct forms take shape in those precisely laid-out lines:

A compass, a tool used for surveying that features heavily in Masonic symbolism, is formed by Pennsylvania Avenue Northwest and Maryland Avenue Southwest. This compass seems to be intersected by a builder's square formed by Louisiana Avenue Northwest and Washington Avenue Southwest. But that's not all.

Starting at the White House, follow Connecticut Avenue Northwest until you reach DuPont Circle, then trace down, this time on Massachusetts Avenue. Eventually, you'll reach Mount Vernon Square where it joins up with K Street. Follow K Street westward until you hit Washington Circle Northwest. Look at your map. Can you see a star with points terminating at the White House, DuPont Circle, Mount Vernon Square, Logan Circle, and Washington Circle Park—if only Rhode Island Avenue would continue on for another few blocks?

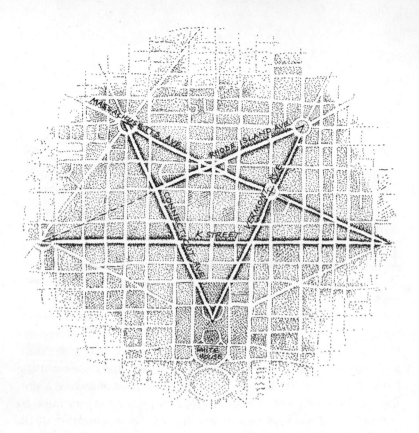

The star or pentacle has a great deal of significance: it can symbolize the elements, points of astrology and astronomy, and humanity and its place in the world. But does it appear in Washington's street plan by chance or by design? Exactness can be found throughout the city. For example, the Washington Monument was intended to sit in the exact center of Washington, DC. The placement had to be changed, as the chosen spot turned out to be on ground that was too unstable to bear the monument's weight. A 400-foot adjustment had to be made, slightly skewing the sacred geometry of the site. (The intended site is marked with a smaller, stubbier obelisk known as the Jefferson Pier.)

There is also the alignment of the streets. One of Thomas Jefferson's fondest wishes was to make America independent in all things, which included establishing the country's own meridian—

that invisible line of light that determines the measure of time in any given place. That meridian aligns with the Sun at high noon and drives a path through DC right down 16th Street Northwest, often called the "Corridor of Light." It cuts through the heart of the pentacle formed by the streets above the White House and passes over the intended site of the Washington Monument. The four obelisks that frame the eastern entrance to Meridian Hill Park, 16th Street's northern terminus, catch the Sun as it makes its way over the city each day. If you happen to be in DC at either equinox, the moving Sun aligns perfectly between these obelisks at the exact moment of the Wheel's turning. These things are not new ideas.

Centuries before the American Revolution, construction began on St. Peter's Basilica in Rome. Astrologers were consulted about when to start building and what direction the main doors should face. This, coupled with the fact that the church would sit over the purported tomb of Peter himself, contributed to making the basilica a nexus that continues to draw energy as well as countless pilgrims to Rome. If you go to St. Peter's, climb to the top of the dome and look out over the city. It is only too clear that avenues, buildings, and statues "line up." Rome is full of hints of its underlying planning, from squares like the Piazza Navona, whose fountains offer unique views when you gaze down their center lines, to keyholes that, when peeped through, offer a distant vision of St. Peter's in miniature, framed in ancient metal and wood.

Planning and mapping is creative placemaking, time making, energy channeling, and life changing—and need not be limited to massive projects like city and cathedral building. You can put the power of maps and planning to work for you to bring positive change to your life and habits—read on!

A Map for Safe Travel

It's probable that, in the wake of the COVID-19 pandemic, more and more people will take to the roads rather than the rails and skies for work and for play. Increased traffic means increased chances for mishaps. Perform this map ritual for safe travel, whether you're going on a far-flung trip or making your daily commute.

You will need:

Peppermint essential oil for protection (also good for keeping alert!)

1 black or light blue candle (blue and black for their protective qualities). Alternatively, you can make a road candle with a sheet of black beeswax and a light blue taper or pillar candle. Cut the beeswax into long strips of equal widths and wind them around the taper or pillar to form a "road" that spirals around the candle. Be sure to press the beeswax strips gently but firmly onto the pillar so that they stick. (You can also use a hair dryer to heat up the wax a bit so that it adheres better.) Once the candle is made, dress it with the oil.

Black and light blue markers

12–14-inch lengths of black and light blue ribbons

If you did not make the road candle described above, dress the blue or black candle with the peppermint oil. Light it and use its flame to focus. When you're ready, log in to Google Maps or your favorite on-line service to create a map of your route. Take your time and include all the stops you plan to make, then print the map.

Using the black marker, trace your route, visualizing yourself arriving at each destination safely. Write a mantra out along your route (feel free to change and adapt!):

There and back,
Keep me on track,
Safe and sound
'Til the journey's end.

Now take the light blue marker and with broad, outward strokes, color the route that will give your path a protective aura in case of detours or changes of plans.

Roll the map up, repeating the mantra, then tie with the ribbons. Why roll rather than fold the map? After all, most maps (of my era, anyway) were folded (and infuriatingly difficult to refold!). The rolling motion makes for smooth, swift travel. Creases made by folding symbolically cut lines through maps, which may incorporate stops or blocks into your travel plans.

Keep the map with you when you travel. Safe journeys!

A Map Spell for Health

Bilbo Baggins liked maps. He kept one in his hall "of the Country Round with all his favorite walks marked in red ink." Tolkien himself was an avid walker and was known for taking long strolls that lasted for hours, even into old age—but I wonder if he knew the power of the color red and the energy and vitality with which it is associated. (My guess is that he did!)

Movement is so important for health. I don't know about you, but some of my best ideas, solutions to problems, and aha moments come to me when I'm on my daily walk. Movement clears my head and frees my mind. One of the reasons I've been able to stick to my walking regimen is the plan I made for it. I have a few favorite walking routes, and while I love walking in new places and the discoveries that I make while on them, a familiar trek that I've mapped out, first on paper and then repeated until the steps are second nature, is grand for walking meditation. On these walks I can move on autopilot (being aware of my surroundings, of course) and let my mind wander where it will. This mental and physical exercise has been of great comfort and benefit to me—and it's easy to do.

You will need:

Map of the area where you walk, bike, or hike. What if you can't get out or if you have mobility challenges? Indoor spaces are very mappable, whether it's an indoor shopping mall or your own home. The exercise of mapping out space where you live can also be very handy for clearing paths, removing tripping hazards, and becoming aware of sharp corners on furniture.

Blue (for inner peace) and/or purple (for enlightenment) markers. I prefer highlighters so that I can see and read the map details even when I've colored over them. You can also substitute other colors depending on what you want to do: red for vitality and high energy, yellow for inner joy, orange for creativity, green for healing, etc.

Mantra that supports your goals (See more on goals in the next exercise.)

Log in to Google Maps or your favorite online service to create a map of your route. Trace your finger along the route; take note of cross streets, changes in terrain, and landmarks.

Trace the route with the blue or purple marker, visualizing yourself moving along it safely and at a comfortable pace. Write your mantra out along your route. Keep it simple—one line or less so that you can remember it without having to refer to it. When you're physically moving along the route, it will help you focus and clear your mind.

Just as with the Map for Safe Travel, roll it up. Store it in the shoes you'll use when you visit your route. You can keep the map with you, of course, but storing it in the shoes you'll be wearing is like charging a battery.

This mapping exercise can also be used for trips to the grocery store. Perhaps the store is where you find you can be most mobile. Many supermarkets have their aisles mapped out online or provide paper copies that show where everything is. Try mapping the aisles where you will just be walking in green and those where you will stop and shop in red.

A Treasure Map for Life Goals

There are other kinds of maps besides the ones that mark out physical geography, whether in the sky or on the earth. I've taken to making "life road maps" to make plans. For years I'd lived by to-do lists (and still do to an extent), but as I grow older, I find myself becoming more *process* than goal oriented. Making goals and not achieving them has made me feel like I've failed in some way. Everyone's heard the old sayings "It's the journey, not the destination" and "Getting there is half the fun!" Focusing on the journey is different from goal setting. Nine times out of ten you probably spend more time on your journey than at the destination. And when you think about it, is the destination ever really the "end"?

When it comes to my life road maps, I try not to look further out than a year. Oh, I have visions of a distant future, but they're just that: nebulous dreams of which I can't quite make out all the details. I include things I'd like to see happen over the course of the next twelve months—*like to see* being the operative words here. I am learning—and have to be reminded at times—not to have many, if any, expectations, as things can change in seconds and upset any "plans" I've made.

Life mapping is an easy, though contemplative, ritual.

You will need:
Pencils (with erasers!)
Paper
Pens or markers
Journal

Set aside an hour or so when you won't be disturbed (easier said than done, sometimes!) and create sacred space as you normally would.

Begin with shape: using the pencil, draw the landmass of your year. What shape will it take? Try not to think about it too much and just let your hand wander. You can ink it in later, but to start, I always use pencil to give myself the leeway of changing my mind in the planning stages. Later on, when things are "permanent," it makes for interesting reading at the end of the year when you're looking back on the map in hindsight.

Once you have the shape, make a list of the things you would like to see happen—and what "topography" you associate with them. Is a certain task a "mountain"? Does an activity you enjoy flow like a river? What is boggy to you? What bustles like a city? Or a farm? Take the time to free associate.

Once you have a solid list of all the things you'd like to see happen in the year, start penciling them in on the map. Draw

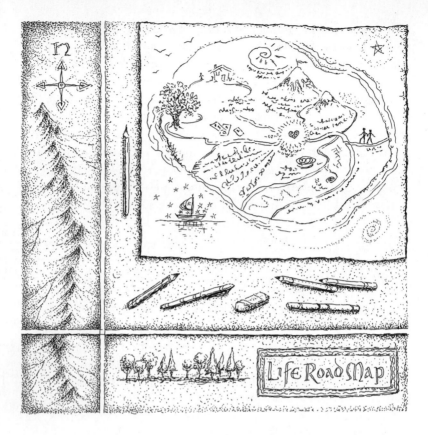

the topography associated with it. Think spatially: How far away would they be from each other? For example, let's say two things you'd like to see happen are that you want to be more physically active (rather than aiming to lose ten pounds) and that you want to change your environment (rather than something specific like moving to another state). How far away from each other are these items? Is one dependent on the other? Take the time to explore these questions as you place these items on the map—or just let your subconscious place them where they "feel" right. There is no wrong way to do this.

You may find your year getting rather crowded. You may want to move or delete some of your planning—or perhaps set it aside. In the last year or so, my maps have included a harbor with ships full of wishes waiting to "disembark" or "unload."

Once you are happy with your map, you can ink in over the pencil. You can make this as artistic as you like, or it can be simple. Put the map in a place where you can see it, and as you move forward, mark your steps out. Use different colors, keeping in mind the energies associated with them (see the previous two rituals for suggestions). You may find that moving toward one destination lines you up to move on to another. You may find that you start many journeys, stop them, and then pick them up again. Make notes on your map as you progress through your year.

When is a good time to begin? I like to do life maps on or near my birthday, but there is always January 1, Samhain, any of the sabbats, or any day that has meaning for you—any day at all. It is always a good time to plan for a new beginning!

Resources

Black, Annetta. "The Aventine Keyhole." Atlas Obscura. Accessed August 30, 2020. https://www.atlasobscura.com/places/the-aventine-keyhole -rome-rome-italy.

Harris, Molly. "The Horoscope of St. Peter's." National Endowment for the Humanities. December 12, 2013. https://www.neh.gov/divisions /research/featured-project/the-horoscope-st-peter%E2%80%99s.

Tolkien, J. R. R. *The Hobbit.* New York: Houghton Mifflin, 2001. Page 24.

The Creation and Use of Spirit Houses

Kelden

The practice of Witchcraft is a spiritual one, meaning it involves direct contact and allyship with various types of spirits. Witches have a long history of working side by side with a variety of otherworldly beings, whether they be deities, ancestors, familiars, fetches, land wights, or the Fair Folk. Having a strong rapport with the spirit world is of utmost importance when it comes to practicing the art of Witchcraft. For one, spirits are incredible sources of magical wisdom, and they are, at times, willing to impart this knowledge upon a curious and sincere seeker. Additionally, it is by establishing bonds with spirits that Witches often enter a symbiotic relationship in which offerings are exchanged for guidance, protection, or other blessings.

There are many ways to connect with spirits, and there are just as many by which we can help foster the growth of a budding relationship. One of my favorite methods for working with and honoring a specific spirit is to create them their very own home. The building of these homes, which are generally called spirit houses, can be found in many different cultures around the world. Perhaps one of the best-known examples of spirit houses comes from Thailand. Here, people construct ornate little dwellings known as the *san phra phrum* that are often placed on or near one's property. Another example comes from Iceland, where you will find quaint miniature homes known as *álfhól*, which are built for the purpose of housing the *Huldufólk*, or elven folk. Universally, spirit houses are created in order to provide ethereal creatures with shelter in hopes that they might in turn bestow protection, luck, abundance, or other blessings. Depending upon the temperament of the spirit, these houses are also believed to help keep unruly beings busy, and thus preventing them from causing chaos elsewhere.

Growing up, I spent many a day out in the woods building tiny homes out of sticks, leaves, rocks, and other natural materials. These structures were meant to become a place of lodging for the Fair Folk, who were some of the first spirits I ever worked with as a young Witch. By lovingly creating habitats for these spirits, I was able to connect with them and honor the magic that they had brought to the world around me. Additionally, these wee abodes became an excellent place for leaving gifts of gratitude, such as small bowls of milk and honey (both traditional offerings said to be enjoyed by the Fair Folk). I was never worried about coming back later and finding that the house I had worked so hard on had collapsed or was otherwise in disarray, as I always took this to mean that the Fair Folk had enjoyed a rowdy party before moving on.

Today, whenever I want to create a more permanent structure, I will often utilize the small, plain birdhouses which you can find at most craft stores. These pinewood birdhouses come in a variety of shapes and sizes and are typically pretty inexpensive. Because of their bare-bones design, the birdhouses can be decorated in an endless variety of ways, even better if done in accordance to the spirit's preferences. I recommend using natural items such as moss, twigs, rocks, bark, shells, and bones to adorn the structure. Additionally, the house can be filled with attractive baubles such as small bells, colorful knotted cords or ribbons, mirror disks, vibrant glass beads, and shiny coins. These items are meant to entertain the spirit and provide them with a beautiful environment, which they are sure to enjoy.

When completed, a spirit house can be placed in a sacred or special spot indoors or outdoors. If placing the house inside, you might want to rest it upon an altar and set candles and bowls for offerings nearby. Make sure, though, to keep the area around the house neat and tidy, including dusting away dirt and keeping away any clutter. If placing the house outside, you could very well build it into your garden or put it on an outdoor altar. However, depending upon the location and the materials used to build the house, be prepared for it to slowly break down over time as it's exposed to the elements.

Creating a Spirit House

If there is a particular otherworldly being that you work with who you believe would enjoy having a space of their own, you can try your hand at building a spirit house. In order to do so, you will first need to gather the following items.

You will need:

Plain wooden birdhouse. You can find unfinished pine birdhouses in various shapes and sizes at most craft stores.

Paint or wood stain in any colors you so desire

Brushes or rags to apply paint or stain

Wood burner (optional)

Natural decorations (moss, twigs, rocks, bark, shells, bones, etc.)
Hot glue gun or other sturdy fixative
Attractive baubles (small bells, colorful knotted cords or ribbons,
mirror disks, vibrant glass beads, shiny coins, etc.)

Begin by applying an even layer of paint or stain to your house, allowing ample time for it to dry before applying a second coat if need be. Once the house has been painted or stained, you may wish to add different symbols, such as any sigil associated with the spirit who will reside within the house, using additional paint or with a wood burner. Next, use the hot glue gun or other fixative to add natural elements to the house. For example, you might wish to glue a layer of moss on the roof or create siding using twigs or rocks. Finally, fill the house with attractive baubles by passing them through the entrance hole. Don't worry if these items fall inside haphazardly, as this will only add to the spirit's joy and entertainment.

Ritual to Enchant Your Spirit House

When your spirit house is ready to be inhabited, you can perform the following ritual to bless and enchant the home, effectively inviting the spirit to take up residence.

You will need:
Your spirit house
White votive candle
Offering (a bit of bread, honey, whiskey, or whatever else your
spirit may have a preference for)

Begin by placing your spirit house in its designated spot, such as upon your altar, by your front door, or some other auspicious location. Next, place the votive candle to one side of the house (be careful, making sure not to put it too close!) and the offering on the other. Now, light the candle, which will act as a magical beacon to draw the intended spirit to its new house. As the candle burns, recite the following incantation thrice:

I built this house, both fine and best,
For a kindly spirit to dwell and rest.
That it may be their rightful home,
A living space to call their own.

Close your eyes and reach out to your spirit ally, informing them of the new space that you have created just for them. Invite the spirit to inhabit the house and to make it their own. Then, once you feel ready, open your eyes. You will want to give the spirit some space in order for them to enter the house and explore a bit. Although, you will want to be nearby so that you can keep an eye on the burning candle! The candle should burn for an hour (or less if it naturally burns out), at which time you may extinguish it. If, for whatever reason, your spirit has not found its way to their new house, perform the ritual again the following night.

Chocolate: The User-Friendly Entheogen

Elizabeth Barrette

C hocolate is famous as a sweet treat, but not many people know its magical side. It's also an entheogen, connecting the mortal with the Divine. Yes, chocolate is literally the food of the gods in some traditions! It has physical benefits, emotional benefits, and magical uses too. Come explore the magical world of chocolate.

Cultivation and Processing

Cacao trees only grow in limited habitat, around the Tropic of Cancer and Tropic of Capricorn. Vulnerable to wind and sun, they naturally inhabit the shady understory of mature forests. This poses a challenge to cacao farmers. In some places, they cut down forests to create monoculture plantations, using artificial barriers to block wind and make shade. More sustainable practices, sometimes called "shade grown" and used for coffee as well, require interplanting cacao with other species, such as banana trees. This practice provides a more natural environment less prone to pests and diseases, while preserving more habitat and gaining multiple crops from the same land. It also instills more energy in the cacao beans.

It takes five to ten years for a tree to mature enough to produce fruit. Cacao blossoms form right on the trunk. Only a fraction of them mature into pods. When the pods ripen, they turn brown. The seeds are removed and fermented for five to six days. This lowers the bitterness while raising the complexity of other flavors. Then the beans are dried for one to two weeks. At that point they are cleaned and graded, then packed and shipped away.

Cacao beans are usually roasted and hulled to extract the kernels, then crushed into nibs, but raw nibs are also available. The nibs can be roasted again and then ground to paste using high- or low-heat methods. The result is called chocolate liquor, the base for making bars and many other products.

A chocolatier may blend chocolates from many different places or source materials only from one region or even one plantation. Some buy their chocolate from a manufacturer in order to make confections, while others have a "bean to bar" production line. These variations in cultivation and processing create the wide range of flavors available.

All this time and effort required to produce chocolate is part of what gives it so much magical power. If you buy gourmet chocolate, that adds the expense of fine ingredients as well. Some types, like single-origin or ruby chocolate, are also rare and bring that energy. You can see why it adds a lot to a spell or ritual.

Types of Chocolate

The cacao bean can be turned into many different products, from the variations of candy commonly called "chocolate" to individual ingredients. Each has its own characteristics. Ideally, look for pure ones without artificial additives. Diluting real chocolate with synthetic stuff lowers both its nutritional value and its mystical energy.

Various certifications assist shoppers in finding the best chocolate. Organic chocolate avoids harsh chemicals. Fair trade chocolate aims to protect the people who grow and process it. Sustainable chocolate is grown in ways that support the environment instead of threatening it. Raw cacao products retain more nutrients and vital energy, things that heat and other commercial processes can destroy. I use "clinical-grade chocolate" to describe the range that has

the best medicinal properties, so dark milk to dark chocolate that is organic and preferably sustainable. This is the stuff you want in your emotional first aid kit or on the altar as an entheogen.

White Chocolate

White chocolate has an ivory color. It contains cocoa butter but no cocoa solids. Yes, it is real chocolate, because cocoa butter comes from the cocoa bean. Sometimes it has vanilla added, which should also be genuine. "White baking chips" or similar products made with partially hydrogenated oil and other artificial ingredients are not chocolate and do not work the same.

Milk Chocolate

Milk chocolate is medium brown. It ranges from about 10 to 45 percent cocoa solids. The high end of that range is sometimes called dark milk chocolate, a good choice if dark chocolate is too bitter for you. Milk chocolate is light and sweet, very popular in candy and desserts.

Dark Chocolate

Dark chocolate ranges from deep brown to almost black. It contains about 50 to 99 percent cocoa solids. This gives it more active components if you're looking for the medicinal or mystical benefits. The flavor tends to be bitter and sour, but some of the better examples just taste dark and complicated.

Ruby Chocolate

Ruby chocolate is new, made from cacao beans with pronounced fruity notes and then processed to enhance those qualities. Despite the name, it is bright rose pink rather than red. It contains around 30 to 50 percent cocoa solids, similar to milk chocolate, but tastes totally different. Ruby chocolate has a vivid berry flavor with a sharp tangy edge, even though there's no fruit in it. However, it's often combined with fruit in candy confections. It goes exceptionally well with floral flavors too. The tangy profile matches well with ascorbic acid (vitamin C) if you like "sour sugar" as a dust coat on candy.

Unsweetened Chocolate

Unsweetened chocolate is almost black. It is 100 percent pure cocoa solids, without the milk or sugar used to make chocolate candy. It has a rough, dusty, bitter taste with lots of chocolate character. Unsweetened chocolate is meant as a cooking ingredient, so it works in savory as well as sweet recipes.

Cacao Powder

Cacao powder, or cocoa powder, is almost pure cocoa solids. It can be sweetened or unsweetened, cooked or raw. The natural form is darker and acidic, while Dutch process cocoa powder has been alkalinized for a mellower flavor and redder color. Only the natural form will react with baking soda to form bubbles, so Dutch process cocoa needs a different leavener, such as baking powder. Cacao powder works as a superfood boost in smoothies, even if you don't have a high-speed blender.

Chocolate Mix

Chocolate mix is a blend of cocoa powder, milk powder, sugar, and often other ingredients for flavoring and texture. Usually it matches milk chocolate, but there are dark and white versions also. It is used to make beverages such as hot chocolate or chocolate milk. However, it can also be used to flavor cookies, make puddings, coat truffles, and other creative applications. This is one of the few cases where those extra ingredients offer new abilities instead of just diluting the flavor. Turning a bar into a beverage is rather more complicated.

Cacao Nib

Cacao nibs are tiny bits of cacao beans that have been fermented, dried, and crushed. They may or may not be roasted. They have a dark brown to almost black color, with a tender crunchy texture. The nibs are intensely bitter, complex, and chocolaty. If you feel that most chocolate is too sweet, try these instead. They can be used like miniature chocolate chips in cookies or as a topping. More often, they are ground up to intensify the flavor of milk or dark chocolate in a recipe. They're also ideal for savory chocolate recipes such as molé sauce. If you have a high-speed blender, drop cacao nibs in smoothies as a superfood boost.

Cocoa Butter

Cocoa butter is the fat from the cacao bean. It is semisolid to solid at room temperature, with ivory to pale brown color. This is what makes chocolate melt so well, giving it a rich, creamy texture. The flavor is mild and slightly sweet. In addition to culinary uses, this part of chocolate has many applications for skin, hair, and other body care.

Benefits of Chocolate

The cacao plant offers many benefits. It is important to distinguish the source, however, because cocoa solids and cocoa butter do some different things. Most of the mood-boosting effects are in the solids and most of the body-care effects are in the butter, although there is some overlap. This is why the usual recommendation is to use dark chocolate for clinical or mystical purposes, but sometimes what you want is actually the butter part. Let's take a look at some of the benefits cacao can offer.

Dark chocolate has a high nutrient content. An average bar has most of a day's supply of copper and manganese, two-thirds of necessary iron, and over half of magnesium. It also includes potassium, selenium, and zinc. This is another reason to choose organic, shade-grown chocolate: the better soil practices promote higher nutrients in the final food compared to beans grown on depleted soil.

Theobromine may relieve coughing. Some recipes for home-made cough syrup therefore mix cacao powder with other traditional ingredients like cayenne, black pepper, horehound, or honey. It also makes an excellent cover for medicinal flavors.

Flavonoids in dark chocolate improve cardiac and circulatory health. This lowers the risk of heart attack or stroke and keeps blood flowing properly. Flavonoids also help balance the metabolism, including the sugar cycle.

Flavonols can improve memory in older people. However, processing reduces them, and the addition of eggs, milk, sugar, and so on dilutes them even more. Consider using raw, pure cacao powder or nibs in rituals to support mental acuity. Flavonols also boost resistance to sunburn, improve vision, and lower blood pressure.

Flavonols and other compounds in chocolate promote the formation and release of endorphins. This improves mood by generating feelings of pleasure and satisfaction.

Cocoa polyphenols lift mood, giving credence to the use of chocolate to cheer up. Although eating junk food while upset is not a good idea, eating mood-boosting foods like dark chocolate, salmon, or fresh fruit can help. Keep some dark chocolate in your emotional first aid kit.

Chocolate can reduce food cravings, especially for salty or sweet foods. Its richness quickly satisfies such needs. Dark chocolate is often sold in small squares that work well as a supplement or a craving-crusher.

Chocolate also raises energy and lowers fatigue. It can help with chronic low energy, and it works well in recovery drinks or snacks after exertion.

As a food, cocoa butter provides the fat-soluble vitamins K and E. It also makes a delicious carrier if you want to add more fat-soluble vitamins from other ingredients—for instance, vitamin A from dairy and bright yellow or orange produce and vitamin D from dairy and oranges.

Cocoa butter also moisturizes skin and hair. Therefore, it reduces dandruff. It deep-conditions hair, relieving frizz. It soothes sensitive skin, lowers the risk of stretch marks, and improves scar appearance. Its antioxidants remove free radicals, thus minimizing the tendency for wrinkles and age spots. Cocoa butter appears in many body products, such as lip balm, lotion bars, and conditioners.

Chocolate as an Entheogen

Entheogens are substances used to connect with higher powers. Many do this by making dramatic changes in state of consciousness, while others are more subtle or work simply by attracting divine attention. Almost all entheogens have serious protections designed to discourage casual use, which makes them risky. But chocolate is the most user-friendly entheogen. It doesn't have booby traps, and its effects are gentle enough that they don't cause risks either. It just lifts the mood a bit, opening the user to feelings of pleasure and satisfaction.

Chocolate is associated with various deities. Ixcacao is the Mayan goddess of chocolate. The Mayans also worship Ek Chuah as the chocolate god, and chocolate is the favored food of their rain god Kon. The Aztec goddess Xochiquetzal is associated with chocolate and also oversees flowers, fruit, and fertility. The Aztecs also associated chocolate with Quetzalcoatl, the feathered serpent. Modern Pagans sometimes speak of the chocolate spirit as a goddess, Chocolata.

You can see how the collateral associations echo chocolate's generally mellow vibe. Rain, flowers, fruit, fertility, creation—those are all positive things with nurturing and sensual characteristics. Chocolate isn't about cracking open the cosmic egg to reveal the secrets of the universe. It's about being here now, enjoying life and your body. So it's designed to be used easily and often.

White, milk, and ruby chocolate are often offered to goddesses. Dark milk chocolate and dark chocolate are often offered to gods. Additional flavors—ginger, cinnamon, chile, vanilla, jasmine, rose, orange, raspberry—offer another way to connect with a deity if you know the correspondences for their favorite herbs, spices, fruits, flowers, or other edibles. As with any magical activity, stacking multiple correspondences strengthens the connection. You could actually put out four bars of chocolate to evoke four different deities, and based on the extra ingredients, everyone would know which was whose.

Spells and Rituals

As a magical substance, chocolate appears in a variety of spells and rituals. Sometimes it is the whole focus. Both the Aztecs and the Maya did rituals honoring chocolate. Modern Pagans have a more whimsical version in "The Chocolate Ritual," which has been published in numerous venues.

It is possible to buy divine figures molded from chocolate. In my coven, we have used these in several rituals, first blessing them and then breaking them for the cakes and ale portion. They serve a similar purpose to baking a bread god, a way to embody the divine that we can take into our own bodies.

You can also mold chocolate into symbolic shapes, much like shaped candles are used to define the focus of a spell or ritual. Candy molds come in infinite variety. Consider birds (air magic, communication), coins (money, success), dragons (fire magic, protection), eggs (Ostara, fertility), eyes (vision, psychic powers), flowers (earth magic, garden blessing), hands (healing, benediction), hearts (love, friendship), horseshoes (luck, animal magic), seashells (water magic, cycles), and stars (astrology, wishes). Bite-size pieces also work great for cakes and ale. One year we even got a hollow chocolate Yule log packed with individual chocolates.

Chocolate naturally comes in white, brown, almost black, and pink. If you need other colors, you can tint white chocolate with candy coloring to make any color. There are even edible metallic powders to make it silvery, golden, or pearly. That makes chocolate ideal for work that relies on color magic.

Conclusion

Chocolate is subtle but powerful. This energy can be enhanced with careful growing and processing. The raw beans may be turned into many delicious products. The benefits of chocolate are physical, emotional, and spiritual. Now that you know more about it, you can use it to better effect in your spells and rituals. Enjoy!

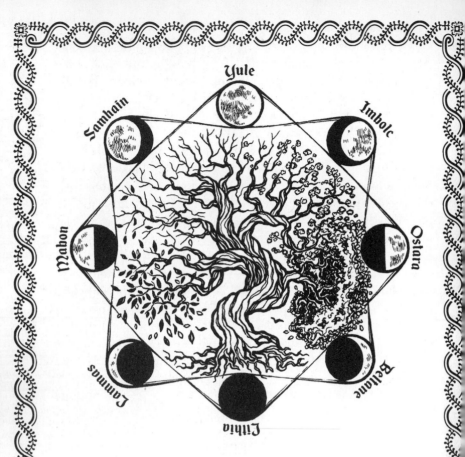

Seasonal Magic

Suzanne Ress

Most practitioners of magic are aware of the importance of the Moon's phases in spells and other magic work. We know about the Wheel of the Year, divided into eight equal parts, each part with its own name, the name of an ancient festival, also known as the four greater and the four lesser sabbats in Wicca and Witchcraft. But how tuned in are we to nature and its eternal cycle of birth, life, and death? It's easy enough to celebrate Samhain, Imbolc, Beltane, or Yule with holiday decorations, special foods and traditions, but what is really at the bottom of each of these seasonal celebrations and how do we get in touch with that for magical use?

Nature's cycle is all around us, all the time, and we are a part of it. At certain times nature's incredible power is quite clear—a hurricane, the open ocean, a violent rainstorm, strong winds—but even when we aren't paying it any attention, the power is still there, and it is the greatest source of magical energy, an energy that can be focused and used to make magic work more effectively.

For each of the four seasons, there is an element. These were recognized and used by alchemists in medieval times: fire, air, water, and earth. When we conduct magic rituals and spells, it is common to draw down or give thanks to each of these four elements. Each element rules a geographical direction: fire rules south, air rules north, water rules west, and earth rules east. The masculine elements are air and fire; the feminine are water and earth. It follows, then, that south and north are masculine directions, and the seasons associated with them, summer and winter, are masculine seasons. Likewise, earth, spring, water, and autumn are feminine. Along with the elements, each season has a corresponding planet, color, jewel, and fluid.

Knowing the symbols of each season will help you choose appropriate materials, locations, and types of spells and magic, but being in touch with nature will give you the power to make your magic work.

Spring Magic

Spring is associated with growth, new life, motherhood, and new beginnings. Even if you are a city dweller, it's hard not to notice tiny new green leaves on the trees, birds' songs as they build their nests and prepare to lay eggs, milder weather, and longer days starting at the equinox and reaching their peak at the solstice. Our earth turns on its axis, closer to the Sun during this period, and the increased sunlight signals plants to grow and mammals to shed winter coats and mate.

For many people, spring is the happiest season of the year because it signifies new hope, resurrection of new life that has faded and come to a standstill over the winter. This is the first part of the light half of the year.

When life is bursting out all around us, this is the most opportune time for magic of increase, whether that means an increase in wealth, health, happiness, luck, love, or anything else.

In everyday magic, spring is a great time to honor all living things, including trees. Perhaps you could plant a tree or meditate beside or against one, concentrating on the life flowing through the tree's roots underground, from the Sun's rays through the tree's leaves above you, and all through the tree's sturdy, slow-growing trunk. Spring is an excellent time to appreciate how the important people in our lives enrich and help us grow and to thank them with some small gesture or natural gift, such as a flower, plant, or seeds.

Spring is auspicious for working spells having to do with love, money, and success, in particular. When you choose materials for a spell worked in spring, pay careful attention to colors (yellow, green), scents (flowery), all sensual aspects, and your position, which should be with your feet firmly planted on the earth and facing east.

A Spring Spell for Growth and Increase
Scented green candle
Scented yellow candle
Matches or a lighter
4 paperwhite bulbs
Small pot filled with potting soil
1 tablespoon of yellow flower petals (dandelions are perfect)

Set these items on your altar so that you can reach them while facing eastward.

This spell can be cast at any time between dawn and midday in early spring. You will primarily be calling upon power from the Sun, but do the spell on the day of a full or waxing Moon.

Light the green candle and say,

I call upon the powers of Mother Nature to help increase _____ (love, money, success, whatever) in my (or someone else's) life.

Light the yellow candle and say,

I call upon the powers of the Sun to aid in this increase.

Take the bulbs between your cupped hands and picture each one of them representing one step in the increase you seek. Picture this in as great a detail as possible. When you are ready, say,

I plant my desire for increase deep in the nourishing earth, and as the days lengthen and the green parts unfurl and rise up out of the soil, so shall my desire grow and seek the light.

Plant the bulbs in the pot, flat side down. Sprinkle the yellow petals over the soil and place the pot in a sunny windowsill. As the flowers grow and bloom, so will that which you desire.

Summer Magic

Summer is masculine, ruled by Mars. Its jewel is the red ruby, its fluid blood, its direction south, and its element fire. Its color is red, and the salamander is its magical being.

Summer, which officially begins at Midsummer, or the summer solstice, is when the length of days seems to stand still for a great long time. Although the days are really getting shorter after June 21, this happens very slowly, especially at first, so it seems as if there are weeks and weeks of gloriously long, bright summer days.

Summer is also, coincidentally, when most people spend a great deal more time outdoors, enjoying the warmth and the full-blown green leafy trees and thunderstorms and heavily scented flowers. Spending more time outdoors makes people more outward-thinking and feeling, which is likely due in part to sunlight's effect on our bodies. High doses of vitamin D are relaxing, may ease anxiety and depression, and promote healthy bones, teeth and muscles. Additionally, the deep greenery of trees, grass, hedges, shrubs, and other plants surrounding us is believed to be relieve stress and heal.

Summer is the best time for magic having to do with strength, energy, new opportunities, change, health, and bounty. In daily life you will likely meet more people, both new and old, than in any other season, and this gives you a chance to spread good energy and strength with every human interaction you have no matter how minor or major. Feel nature's strength flowing through your body and spirit, and share it with everyone you meet in some way.

Spellwork in summer can be extremely powerful because nature is at her fullest and will really pack a punch to your efforts.

A Summer Spell for Psychic Strength

Pinch of sand from a beach
Pinch of graveyard dirt
Pinch of dirt from a five-way intersection (not asphalted!)
Pinch of dirt from a mountain
Iron nail or a red stone
Small red bag

Collect all the items into the red bag and close it tightly (you may first put them in a small plastic bag that goes into the red bag, to be more secure).

On an evening outdoors around a friendly bonfire gathering when the Moon is waxing or full, hold the mojo bag secretly in your left hand, and, closing your eyes, concentrate on the warmth of the fire and of the people around you. Imagine the flames entering into your body, flowing all through you and filling you with strength and warm, positive feelings. Now imagine the strength all flowing into your left arm, into your left hand, and into the mojo bag. Keep your eyes closed until all this warmth and strength is transferred to the bag. Then silently say the words,

Ignite this mojo bag with strength and warmth that I can call on at any time for psychic ability.

Slip the bag into your left pocket. When you go to bed, secret the bag away to a hidden place to the left of your head as you sleep. Each night as you go to sleep, meditate on the powerful mojo bag near your head, and your psychic strength will increase every day for the rest of the summer.

Autumn Magic

Around the autumn equinox, also called Mabon, on September 21 or so in the Northern Hemisphere, feminine energy again takes the reins. Autumn is the time to prepare for the settling in, the dark time. As days grow shorter and nights ever longer and cooler, our thoughts begin to turn inward.

Autumn's element is water, as in the womb or the Moon-ruled ocean. Autumn's color is calming blue, its jewel lapis, its planet the thoughtful Saturn, and its direction west. Now cooling rains come, and the last fruits of summer's labor are harvested.

Autumn is the time for banishing magic, getting rid of unnecessary habits or relationships. It is a time for magic that changes the interior of things and people, magic for the home and hearth.

The feeling now is sunset or twilight, burning wood, wind and rain, comfort inside oneself and one's home. Concentrate on these feelings as you move through the season. Daily magic now might include small home improvements and getting rid of clutter, a change in interior decor, cooking, baking, handicrafts, and indoor hobby projects that bring you personal satisfaction. Cozy evenings by firelight and walks in the woods to collect nuts, mushrooms, or colored leaves, are activities that will bring you in touch with autumn's natural energy.

Spellwork in autumn is best done by moonlight, and the waning Moon is the most suitable time.

An Autumn Banishing Spell

Blue candle
Black candle
Lighter or matches
Knife
1 apple, preferably one that was grown near you.
1 fresh mint leaf
1 black ribbon or cord
Wooden skewer or toothpicks

On the evening of a waning Moon, face west with both of the candles in front of you. As you light the blue candle, say these words:

I light the blue for the presence of helpful feminine energy.

Picture cleansing water flowing underground, away from you, through brooks and streams and rivers and into oceans and seas. As the water flows it carries away debris and waste.

Light the black candle and say,

I call upon the waning powers of the Moon, who rules these cleansing flowing waters, to banish the thing I shall not name.

As you say these words, visualize the thing you wish to banish as a dark blob with a feeling attached to it, but nameless and unformed.

Cut the apple in half horizontally so that its inner pentagram is revealed. Rub the lower half inside with the mint leaf while visualizing the dark blob. Put the two halves of the apple back together with the mint leaf between them and fasten them together securely with the wooden skewer, then wrap it up with the black cord or ribbon. Blow out the black candle and cry out,

So mote it be!

Gently extinguish the blue candle and give it thanks.

Bury the apple immediately, not on your property or anywhere you normally pass by. As the apple rots away underground, so shall your problem diminish and disappear.

Winter Magic

Winter's element is air; its direction north; its liquid milk; its jewelry silver, crystal, and diamond; its color white; and its planet Jupiter. It is masculine.

Winter is the time for drawing ourselves inward. The nights are long and we have much time for contemplation, and time to gather knowledge through books, websites, tarot card readings, films, and cozy conversations. With all the knowledge your brain is absorbing in winter, dreams become especially important, as they reflect and stabilize your new knowledge. Winter is a good time to keep a dream diary and use it to help yourself work through and find hidden insights from your psyche and daily life.

A Winter Dream Bath
Taken before you retire, a dream bath will relax you, bring you meaningful dreams, and help you to remember them. Prepare a mixture of the following:

1 handful dried hibiscus flowers
1 handful dried rose petals
1 teaspoon dried mugwort
7 dried bay leaves

Toss the mixture into your steaming bathwater, and add 1 teaspoon orange flower water. Light candles all around the bath and turn off the electric lights. Submerge yourself in the scented water. Watch the flickering candle flames and breathe deeply of the scented steam. Picture your exhaled breath mingling with the steam and the warm air above the candles. After a while, close your eyes and relax completely. Stay as long as you like.

When you are ready, emerge from the water, wrapping yourself in clean white terrycloth towels or a bathrobe. Blow out the candles with your magical breath and go to bed. Sweet dreams!

2022 Almanac

The Date

The date is used in numerological calculations that govern magical rites. Below is a calendar for 2022.

JANUARY

```
JANUARY                FEBRUARY                MARCH                   APRIL
               1           1  2  3  4  5           1  2  3  4  5                    1  2
 2  3  4  5  6  7  8     6  7  8  9 10 11 12     6  7  8  9 10 11 12     3  4  5  6  7  8  9
 9 10 11 12 13 14 15    13 14 15 16 17 18 19    13 14 15 16 17 18 19    10 11 12 13 14 15 16
16 17 18 19 20 21 22    20 21 22 23 24 25 26    20 21 22 23 24 25 26    17 18 19 20 21 22 23
23 24 25 26 27 28 29    27 28                   27 28 29 30 31          24 25 26 27 28 29 30
30 31

MAY                     JUNE                    JULY                    AUGUST
 1  2  3  4  5  6  7           1  2  3  4                       1  2     1  2  3  4  5  6
 8  9 10 11 12 13 14     5  6  7  8  9 10 11     3  4  5  6  7  8  9     7  8  9 10 11 12 13
15 16 17 18 19 20 21    12 13 14 15 16 17 18    10 11 12 13 14 15 16    14 15 16 17 18 19 20
22 23 24 25 26 27 28    19 20 21 22 23 24 25    17 18 19 20 21 22 23    21 22 23 24 25 26 27
29 30 31                26 27 28 29 30          24 25 26 27 28 29 30    28 29 30 31
                                                31

SEPTEMBER               OCTOBER                 NOVEMBER                DECEMBER
          1  2  3                          1           1  2  3  4  5              1  2  3
 4  5  6  7  8  9 10     2  3  4  5  6  7  8     6  7  8  9 10 11 12     4  5  6  7  8  9 10
11 12 13 14 15 16 17     9 10 11 12 13 14 15    13 14 15 16 17 18 19    11 12 13 14 15 16 17
18 19 20 21 22 23 24    16 17 18 19 20 21 22    20 21 22 23 24 25 26    18 19 20 21 22 23 24
25 26 27 28 29 30       23 24 25 26 27 28 29    27 28 29 30             25 26 27 28 29 30 31
                        30 31
```

The Day

Each day is ruled by a planet that possesses specific magical influences:

MONDAY (MOON): Peace, sleep, healing, compassion, friends, psychic awareness, purification, and fertility.

TUESDAY (MARS): Passion, sex, courage, aggression, and protection.

WEDNESDAY (MERCURY): The conscious mind, study, travel, divination, and wisdom.

THURSDAY (JUPITER): Expansion, money, prosperity, and generosity.

FRIDAY (VENUS): Love, friendship, reconciliation, and beauty.

SATURDAY (SATURN): Longevity, exorcism, endings, homes, and houses.

SUNDAY (SUN): Healing, spirituality, success, strength, and protection.

The Lunar Phase

The lunar phase is important in determining the best times for magic.

THE WAXING MOON (from the New Moon to the Full) is the ideal time for magic to draw things toward you.

THE FULL MOON is the time of greatest power.

THE WANING MOON (from the Full Moon to the New) is a time for study, meditation, and little magical work (except magic designed to banish harmful energies).

The Moon's Sign

The Moon continuously "moves" through the zodiac, from Aries to Pisces. Each sign possesses its own significance.

ARIES: Good for starting things, but lacks staying power. Things occur rapidly, but quickly pass. People tend to be argumentative and assertive.

TAURUS: Things begun now last the longest, tend to increase in value, and become hard to alter. Brings out appreciation for beauty and sensory experience.

GEMINI: Things begun now are easily changed by outside influence. Time for shortcuts, communication, games, and fun.

CANCER: Stimulates emotional rapport between people. Pinpoints need, supports growth and nurturance. Tends to domestic concerns.

LEO: Draws emphasis to the self, central ideas, or institutions, away from connections with others and other emotional needs. People tend to be melodramatic.

VIRGO: Favors accomplishment of details and commands from higher up. Focuses on health, hygiene, and daily schedules.

LIBRA: Favors cooperation, social activities, beautification of surroundings, balance, and partnership.

SCORPIO: Increases awareness of psychic power. Precipitates psychic crises and ends connections thoroughly. People tend to brood and become secretive.

SAGITTARIUS: Encourages flights of imagination and confidence. This is an adventurous, philosophical, and athletic Moon sign. Favors expansion and growth.

CAPRICORN: Develops strong structure. Focus on traditions, responsibilities, and obligations. A good time to set boundaries and rules.

AQUARIUS: Rebellious energy. Time to break habits and make abrupt changes. Personal freedom and individuality is the focus.

PISCES: The focus is on dreaming, nostalgia, intuition, and psychic impressions. A good time for spiritual or philanthropic activities.

Color and Incense of the Day

The color and incense for the day are based on information from *Personal Alchemy* by Amber Wolfe, and relate to the planet that rules each day. This information can be taken into consideration along with other factors when planning works of magic or when blending magic into mundane life. Please note that the incense selections listed are not hard and fast. See page 266 for a list of color correspondences. If you cannot find or do not like the incense listed for the day, choose a similar scent that appeals to you.

Holidays and Festivals

Holidays and festivals and many cultures and nations are listed throughout the year. The exact dates of many ancient festivals are difficult to determine; prevailing data has been used.

Time Zones

The times and dates of all astrological phenomena in this almanac are based on **Eastern Standard Time (EST)**. If you live outside of the Eastern time zone, you will need to make the following adjustments:

PACIFIC STANDARD TIME: Subtract three hours.

MOUNTAIN STANDARD TIME: Subtract two hours.

CENTRAL STANDARD TIME: Subtract one hour.

ALASKA: Subtract four hours.

HAWAII: Subtract five hours.

DAYLIGHT SAVING TIME (ALL ZONES): Add one hour.

*Daylight Saving Time begins at 2 am on March 13, 2022,
and ends at 2 am on November 6, 2022.*

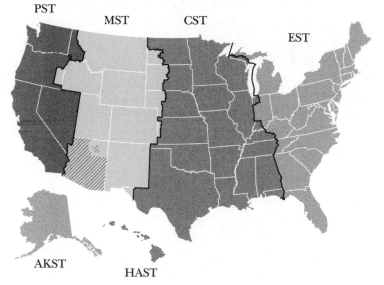

Please refer to a world time zone resource for time adjustments for locations outside the United States.

2022 Sabbats
and Full Moons

January 17	Cancer Full Moon 6:48 pm
February 2	Imbolc
February 16	Leo Full Moon 11:56 am
March 18	Virgo Full Moon 3:18 am
March 20	Ostara (Spring Equinox)
April 16	Libra Full Moon 2:55 pm
May 1	Beltane
May 16	Scorpio Full Moon 12:14 am
June 14	Sagittarius Full Moon 7:52 am
June 21	Midsummer (Summer Solstice)
July 13	Capricorn Full Moon 2:38 pm
August 1	Lammas
August 11	Aquarius Full Moon 9:36 pm
September 10	Pisces Full Moon 5:59 am
September 22	Mabon (Fall Equinox)
October 9	Aries Full Moon 4:55 pm
October 31	Samhain
November 8	Taurus Full Moon 6:02 am
December 7	Gemini Full Moon 11:08 pm
December 21	Yule (Winter Solstice)

All times are Eastern Standard Time (EST)
or Eastern Daylight Time (EDT)

2022 Sabbats in the Southern Hemisphere

Because Earth's Northern and Southern Hemispheres experience opposite seasons at any given time, the season-based sabbats listed on the previous page and in this almanac section are not correct for those residing south of the equator. Listed here are the Southern Hemisphere sabbat dates for 2022:

February 2	Lammas
March 20	Mabon (Fall Equinox)
May 1	Samhain
June 21	Yule (Winter Solstice)
August 1	Imbolc
September 22	Ostara (Spring Equinox)
November 1	Beltane
December 21	Midsummer (Summer Solstice)

Birthstone Poetry

Birthstone poetry in the monthly calendar
reprinted from
The Occult and Curative Powers of Precious Stones
by William T. Fernie, M.D.
Harper & Row (1981)

Originally printed in 1907 as
*Precious Stones: For Curative Wear; and Other Remedial Uses;
Likewise the Nobler Metals*

January

1 Saturday
New Year's Day • Kwanzaa ends
Waning Moon
Moon phase: Fourth Quarter
Color: Brown

Moon Sign: Sagittarius
Moon enters Capricorn 6:02 pm
Incense: Magnolia

2 Sunday
First Writing Day (Japanese)
Waning Moon
New Moon 1:33 pm
Color: Orange

Moon Sign: Capricorn
Incense: Juniper

3 Monday
St. Genevieve's Day
Waxing Moon
Moon phase: First Quarter
Color: Silver

Moon Sign: Capricorn
Moon enters Aquarius 5:44 pm
Incense: Clary sage

4 Tuesday
Kamakura Workers' Festival (Japanese)
Waxing Moon
Moon phase: First Quarter
Color: Gray

Moon Sign: Aquarius
Incense: Cedar

5 Wednesday
Bird Day
Waxing Moon
Moon phase: First Quarter
Color: White

Moon Sign: Aquarius
Moon enters Pisces 7:17 pm
Incense: Lavender

6 Thursday
Epiphany
Waxing Moon
Moon phase: First Quarter
Color: Purple

Moon Sign: Pisces
Incense: Carnation

7 Friday
Tricolor Day (Italian)
Waxing Moon
Moon phase: First Quarter
Color: Rose

Moon Sign: Pisces
Incense: Cypress

January

8 Saturday

Midwives' Day (Bulgarian)
Waxing Moon
Moon phase: First Quarter
Color: Blue

Moon Sign: Pisces
Moon enters Aries 12:26 am
Incense: Rue

Sunday

Feast of the Black Nazarene (Filipino)
Waxing Moon
Second Quarter 1:11 pm
Color: Yellow

Moon Sign: Aries
Incense: Almond

10 Monday

Feast of St. Leonie Aviat
Waxing Moon
Moon phase: Second Quarter
Color: White

Moon Sign: Aries
Moon enters Taurus 9:47 am
Incense: Narcissus

11 Tuesday

Carmentalia (Roman)
Waxing Moon
Moon phase: Second Quarter
Color: Maroon

Moon Sign: Taurus
Incense: Basil

12 Wednesday

Revolution Day (Tanzanian)
Waxing Moon
Moon phase: Second Quarter
Color: Topaz

Moon Sign: Taurus
Moon enters Gemini 10:08 pm
Incense: Bay laurel

13 Thursday

Twentieth Day (Norwegian)
Waxing Moon
Moon phase: Second Quarter
Color: Green

Moon Sign: Gemini
Incense: Balsam

14 Friday

Feast of the Ass (French)
Waxing Moon
Moon phase: Second Quarter
Color: Coral

Moon Sign: Gemini
Incense: Orchid

January

15 Saturday
Korean Alphabet Day
Waxing Moon
Moon phase: Second Quarter
Color: Gray

Moon Sign: Gemini
Moon enters Cancer 11:11 am
Incense: Sage

16 Sunday
Teachers' Day (Thai)
Waxing Moon
Moon phase: Second Quarter
Color: Amber

Moon Sign: Cancer
Incense: Marigold

☺ Monday
Martin Luther King Jr. Day
Waxing Moon
Full Moon 6:48 pm
Color: Ivory

Moon Sign: Cancer
Moon enters Leo 11:03 pm
Incense: Hyssop

18 Tuesday
Feast of St. Athanasius
Waning Moon
Moon phase: Third Quarter
Color: Gray

Moon Sign: Leo
Incense: Ylang-ylang

19 Wednesday
Edgar Allan Poe's birthday
Waning Moon
Moon phase: Third Quarter
Color: Brown

Moon Sign: Leo
Sun enters Aquarius 9:39 pm
Incense: Honeysuckle

20 Thursday
Feast of St. Euthymius the Great
Waning Moon
Moon phase: Third Quarter
Color: Turquoise

Moon Sign: Leo
Moon enters Virgo 9:02 am
Incense: Jasmine

21 Friday
Husband's Day (Icelandic)
Waning Moon
Moon phase: Third Quarter
Color: Purple

Moon Sign: Virgo
Incense: Mint

January

22 Saturday

St. Vincent's Day (French)
Waning Moon
Moon phase: Third Quarter
Color: Indigo

Moon Sign: Virgo
Moon enters Libra 5:03 pm
Incense: Patchouli

23 Sunday

Feast of St. Ildefonsus
Waning Moon
Moon phase: Third Quarter
Color: Gold

Moon Sign: Libra
Incense: Hyacinth

24 Monday

Alasitas Fair (Bolivian)
Waning Moon
Moon phase: Third Quarter
Color: Lavender

Moon Sign: Libra
Moon enters Scorpio 10:57 pm
Incense: Neroli

☽ Tuesday

Burns Night (Scottish)
Waning Moon
Fourth Quarter 8:41 am
Color: Red

Moon Sign: Scorpio
Incense: Ginger

26 Wednesday

Australia Day
Waning Moon
Moon phase: Fourth Quarter
Color: Yellow

Moon Sign: Scorpio
Incense: Lilac

27 Thursday

Holocaust Remembrance Day
Waning Moon
Moon phase: Fourth Quarter
Color: White

Moon Sign: Scorpio
Moon enters Sagittarius 2:34 am
Incense: Clove

28 Friday

St. Charlemagne's Day
Waning Moon
Moon phase: Fourth Quarter
Color: Pink

Moon Sign: Sagittarius
Incense: Thyme

29 Saturday
Feast of St. Gildas
Waning Moon
Moon phase: Fourth Quarter
Color: Black

Moon Sign: Sagittarius
Moon enters Capricorn 4:09 am
Incense: Ivy

---

30 Sunday
Gasparilla Pirate Festival (Floridian)
Waning Moon
Moon phase: Fourth Quarter
Color: Amber

Moon Sign: Capricorn
Incense: Frankincense

---

31 Monday
Independence Day (Nauru)
Waning Moon
Moon phase: Fourth Quarter
Color: Gray

Moon Sign: Capricorn
Moon enters Aquarius 4:43 am
Incense: Lily

January Birthstones

By her in January born
No gem save Garnets should be worn;
They will ensure her constancy,
True friendship, and fidelity.

Modern: Garnet   Zodiac (Capricorn): Ruby

February Birthstones

The February-born shall find
Sincerity, and peace of mind,
Freedom from passion and from care,
If they the Amethyst will wear.

Modern: Amethyst   Zodiac (Aquarius): Garnet

☽ **Tuesday**
Lunar New Year (Tiger)
Waning Moon
New Moon 12:46 am
Color: Bayberry

Moon Sign: Aquarius
Incense: Rosemary

2 Wednesday
Imbolc • Groundhog Day
Waxing Moon
Moon phase: First Quarter
Color: Marjoram

Moon Sign: Aquarius
Moon enters Pisces 6:00 am
Incense: Ginger

3 Thursday
St. Blaise's Day
Waxing Moon
Moon phase: First Quarter
Color: Apricot

Moon Sign: Pisces
Incense: Bay laurel

4 Friday
Independence Day (Sri Lankan)
Waxing Moon
Moon phase: First Quarter
Color: Vanilla

Moon Sign: Pisces
Moon enters Aries 9:57 am
Incense: Balsam

5 Saturday
Constitution Day (Mexican)
Waxing Moon
Moon phase: First Quarter
Color: Pine

Moon Sign: Aries
Incense: Thyme

6 Sunday
Bob Marley's birthday (Jamaican)
Waxing Moon
Moon phase: First Quarter
Color: Heliotrope

Moon Sign: Aries
Moon enters Taurus 5:52 pm
Incense: Sandalwood

7 Monday
Feast of St. Richard the Pilgrim
Waxing Moon
Moon phase: First Quarter
Color: Hyssop

Moon Sign: Taurus
Incense: Juniper

February

◐ Tuesday
Prešeren Day (Slovenian)
Waxing Moon
Second Quarter 8:50 am
Color: Black

Moon Sign: Taurus
Incense: Geranium

9 Wednesday
St. Maron's Day (Lebanese)
Waxing Moon
Moon phase: Second Quarter
Color: Brown

Moon Sign: Taurus
Moon enters Gemini 5:27 am
Incense: Lavender

10 Thursday
Feast of St. Scholastica
Waxing Moon
Moon phase: Second Quarter
Color: Purple

Moon Sign: Gemini
Incense: Mulberry

11 Friday
National Foundation Day (Japanese)
Waxing Moon
Moon phase: Second Quarter
Color: Pink

Moon Sign: Gemini
Moon enters Cancer 6:27 pm
Incense: Alder

12 Saturday
Revolution Day (Tanzanian)
Waxing Moon
Moon phase: Second Quarter
Color: Blue

Moon Sign: Cancer
Incense: Sandalwood

13 Sunday
Parentalia
Waxing Moon
Moon phase: Second Quarter
Color: Yellow

Moon Sign: Cancer
Incense: Eucalyptus

14 Monday
Valentine's Day
Waxing Moon
Moon phase: Second Quarter
Color: Silver

Moon Sign: Cancer
Moon enters Leo 6:17 am
Incense: Narcissus

February

15 Tuesday
Lantern Festival (Chinese)
Waxing Moon
Moon phase: Second Quarter
Color: Maroon

Moon Sign: Leo
Incense: Cedar

Wednesday
Nichiren's birthday
Waxing Moon
Full Moon 11:56 am
Color: Yellow

Moon Sign: Leo
Moon enters Virgo 3:42 pm
Incense: Honeysuckle

17 Thursday
Quirinalia (Roman)
Waning Moon
Moon phase: Third Quarter
Color: Turquoise

Moon Sign: Virgo
Incense: Myrrh

18 Friday
St. Bernadette's Third Vision
Waning Moon
Moon phase: Third Quarter
Color: White

Moon Sign: Virgo
Sun enters Pisces 11:43 am
Moon enters Libra 10:51 pm
Incense: Yarrow

19 Saturday
Flag Day (Turkmenian)
Waning Moon
Moon phase: Third Quarter
Color: Black

Moon Sign: Libra
Incense: Patchouli

20 Sunday
World Day of Social Justice
Waning Moon
Moon phase: Third Quarter
Color: Amber

Moon Sign: Libra
Incense: Marigold

21 Monday
Presidents' Day
Waxing Moon
Moon phase: Third Quarter
Color: Lavender

Moon Sign: Libra
Moon enters Scorpio 4:19 am
Incense: Neroli

February

22 Tuesday
Caristia (Roman)
Waning Moon
Moon phase: Third Quarter
Color: White

Moon Sign: Scorpio
Incense: Basil

◑ Wednesday
Mashramani Festival (Guyanan)
Waning Moon
Fourth Quarter 5:32 pm
Color: Topaz

Moon Sign: Scorpio
Moon enters Sagittarius 8:29 am
Incense: Bay laurel

---

24 Thursday
Regifugium (Roman)
Waning Moon
Moon phase: Fourth Quarter
Color: Green

Moon Sign: Sagittarius
Incense: Nutmeg

---

25 Friday
St. Walburga's Day (German)
Waning Moon
Moon phase: Fourth Quarter
Color: Pink

Moon Sign: Sagittarius
Moon enters Capricorn 11:27 am
Incense: Rose

---

26 Saturday
Zamboanga Day (Filipino)
Waning Moon
Moon phase: Fourth Quarter
Color: Gray

Moon Sign: Capricorn
Incense: Rue

---

27 Sunday
Independence Day (Dominican)
Waning Moon
Moon phase: Fourth Quarter
Color: Orange

Moon Sign: Capricorn
Moon enters Aquarius 1:36 pm
Incense: Orange

---

28 Monday
Kalevala Day (Finnish)
Waning Moon
Moon phase: Fourth Quarter
Color: Ivory

Moon Sign: Aquarius
Incense: Rosemary

March

1 Tuesday

Mardi Gras (Fat Tuesday)
Waning Moon
Moon phase: Fourth Quarter
Color: Red

Moon Sign: Aquarius
Moon enters Pisces 3:53 pm
Incense: Lily

Wednesday

Ash Wednesday
Waning Moon
New Moon 12:35 pm
Color: White

Moon Sign: Pisces
Incense: Cinnamon

---

3 Thursday

Doll Festival (Japanese)
Waxing Moon
Moon phase: First Quarter
Color: Purple

Moon Sign: Pisces
Moon enters Aries 5:43 pm
Incense: Marjoram

---

4 Friday

Blue Dragon Festival (Chinese)
Waxing Moon
Moon phase: First Quarter
Color: Coral

Moon Sign: Aries
Incense: Jasmine

---

5 Saturday

Navigium Isidis Festival (Roman)
Waxing Moon
Moon phase: First Quarter
Color: Blue

Moon Sign: Aries
Incense: Yarrow

---

6 Sunday

Alamo Day (Texan)
Waxing Moon
Moon phase: First Quarter
Color: Yellow

Moon Sign: Aries
Moon enters Taurus 3:00 am
Incense: Magnolia

---

7 Monday

Vejovis Festival (Roman)
Waxing Moon
Moon phase: First Quarter
Color: Silver

Moon Sign: Taurus
Incense: Almond

8   **Tuesday**

International Women's Day
Waxing Moon
Moon phase: First Quarter
Color: White

Moon Sign: Taurus
Moon enters Gemini 1:40 pm
Incense: Ylang-ylang

---

9   **Wednesday**

Teachers' Day (Lebanese)
Waxing Moon
Moon phase: First Quarter
Color: Brown

Moon Sign: Gemini
Incense: Lilac

☾   **Thursday**

Tibet Uprising Day
Waxing Moon
Second Quarter 5:45 am
Color: Green

Moon Sign: Gemini
Incense: Mulberry

---

11   **Friday**

National Foundation Day (Japanese)
Waxing Moon
Moon phase: Second Quarter
Color: Purple

Moon Sign: Gemini
Moon enters Cancer 2:24 am
Incense: Alder

---

12   **Saturday**

Girl Scouts' birthday
Waxing Moon
Moon phase: Second Quarter
Color: Indigo

Moon Sign: Cancer
Incense: Magnolia

---

13   **Sunday**

Feast of St. Leander of Seville
Waxing Moon
Moon phase: Second Quarter
Color: Amber

Moon Sign: Cancer
Moon enters Leo 3:32 pm
Incense: Frankincense
Daylight Saving Time begins at 2 am

---

14   **Monday**

Pi Day
Waxing Moon
Moon phase: Second Quarter
Color: Ivory

Moon Sign: Leo
Incense: Hyssop

March

15 Tuesday
Fertility Festival (Japanese)
Waxing Moon
Moon phase: Second Quarter
Color: Scarlet

Moon Sign: Leo
Incense: Geranium

16 Wednesday
Purim begins at sundown
Waxing Moon
Moon phase: Second Quarter
Color: Topaz

Moon Sign: Leo
Moon enters Virgo 12:59 am
Incense: Honeysuckle

17 Thursday
St. Patrick's Day
Waxing Moon
Moon phase: Second Quarter
Color: Crimson

Moon Sign: Virgo
Incense: Balsam

☺ Friday
Sheila's Day (Irish)
Waxing Moon
Full Moon 3:18 am
Color: Rose

Moon Sign: Virgo
Moon enters Libra 7:26 am
Incense: Orchid

19 Saturday
Minna Canth's birthday (Finnish)
Waning Moon
Moon phase: Third Quarter
Color: Brown

Moon Sign: Libra
Incense: Sandalwood

20 Sunday
Ostara • Spring Equinox
Waning Moon
Moon phase: Third Quarter
Color: Orange

Moon Sign: Libra
Sun enters Aries 11:33 am
Moon enters Scorpio 11:45 am
Incense: Juniper

21 Monday
Juarez Day (Mexican)
Waning Moon
Moon phase: Third Quarter
Color: Gray

Moon Sign: Scorpio
Incense: Clary sage

March

22 Tuesday
World Water Day
Waning Moon
Moon phase: Third Quarter
Color: Maroon

Moon Sign: Scorpio
Moon enters Sagittarius 2:59 pm
Incense: Ginger

23 Wednesday
Pakistan Day
Waning Moon
Moon phase: Third Quarter
Color: Yellow

Moon Sign: Sagittarius
Incense: Lavender

24 Thursday
Day of Blood (Roman)
Waning Moon
Moon phase: Third Quarter
Color: Purple

Moon Sign: Sagittarius
Moon enters Capricorn 5:54 pm
Incense: Apricot

☽ Friday
Tolkien Reading Day
Waning Moon
Fourth Quarter 1:37 am
Color: Pink

Moon Sign: Capricorn
Incense: Yarrow

26 Saturday
Prince Kuhio Day (Hawaiian)
Waning Moon
Moon phase: Fourth Quarter
Color: Blue

Moon Sign: Capricorn
Moon enters Aquarius 8:55 pm
Incense: Patchouli

27 Sunday
Passover begins at sundown
Waning Moon
Moon phase: Fourth Quarter
Color: Gold

Moon Sign: Aquarius
Incense: Hyacinth

28 Monday
Weed Appreciation Day
Waning Moon
Moon phase: Fourth Quarter
Color: White

Moon Sign: Aquarius
Incense: Neroli

March

29 Tuesday
Feast of St. Eustace of Luxeuil
Waning Moon
Moon phase: Fourth Quarter
Color: Red

Moon Sign: Aquarius
Moon enters Pisces 12:32 am
Incense: Cedar

30 Wednesday
Seward's Day (Alaskan)
Waning Moon
Moon phase: Fourth Quarter
Color: Brown

Moon Sign: Pisces
Incense: Bay laurel

31 Thursday
César Chávez Day
Waning Moon
Moon phase: Fourth Quarter
Color: Turquoise

Moon Sign: Pisces
Moon enters Aries 5:30 am
Incense: Carnation

March Birthstones

Who in this world of ours, her eyes
In March first opens, shall be wise.
In days of peril, firm and brave,
And wear a Bloodstone to her grave.

Modern: Aquamarine
Zodiac (Pisces): Amethyst

April

☽ Friday
All Fools' Day • April Fools' Day
Waning Moon
New Moon 2:24 am
Color: Coral

Moon Sign: Aries
Incense: Mint

---

2 Saturday
Ramadan begins at sundown
Waxing Moon
Moon phase: First Quarter
Color: Gray

Moon Sign: Aries
Moon enters Taurus 12:50 pm
Incense: Sage

---

3 Sunday
Feast of St. Mary of Egypt
Waxing Moon
Moon phase: First Quarter
Color: Amber

Moon Sign: Taurus
Incense: Eucalyptus

---

4 Monday
Megalesia (Roman)
Waxing Moon
Moon phase: First Quarter
Color: Lavender

Moon Sign: Taurus
Moon enters Gemini 11:04 am
Incense: Lily

---

5 Tuesday
Tomb-Sweeping Day (Chinese)
Waxing Moon
Moon phase: First Quarter
Color: Black

Moon Sign: Gemini
Incense: Cinnamon

---

6 Wednesday
Tartan Day
Waxing Moon
Moon phase: First Quarter
Color: Topaz

Moon Sign: Gemini
Incense: Marjoram

---

7 Thursday
Motherhood and Beauty Day (Armenian)
Waxing Moon
Moon phase: First Quarter
Color: Green

Moon Sign: Gemini
Moon enters Cancer 11:30 am
Incense: Nutmeg

April

8 Friday
Buddha's birthday
Waxing Moon
Moon phase: First Quarter
Color: White

Moon Sign: Cancer
Incense: Rose

☽ Saturday
Valor Day (Filipino)
Waxing Moon
Second Quarter 2:48 am
Color: Blue

Moon Sign: Cancer
Incense: Pine

---

10 Sunday
Palm Sunday
Waxing Moon
Moon phase: Second Quarter
Color: Gold

Moon Sign: Leo
Moon enters Leo 12:00 am
Incense: Almond

---

11 Monday
Juan Santamaría Day (Costa Rican)
Waxing Moon
Moon phase: Second Quarter
Color: Silver

Moon Sign: Leo
Incense: Narcissus

---

12 Tuesday
Children's Day (Bolivian and Haitian)
Waxing Moon
Moon phase: Second Quarter
Color: Gray

Moon Sign: Leo
Moon enters Virgo 10:07 am
Incense: Basil

---

13 Wednesday
Thai New Year (ends April 15)
Waxing Moon
Moon phase: Second Quarter
Color: Yellow

Moon Sign: Virgo
Incense: Lavender

---

14 Thursday
Black Day (South Korean)
Waxing Moon
Moon phase: Second Quarter
Color: Turquoise

Moon Sign: Virgo
Moon enters Libra 4:46 pm
Incense: Clove

April

15 Friday
Good Friday • Passover begins at sundown
Waxing Moon
Moon phase: Second Quarter
Color: Rose

Moon Sign: Libra
Incense: Thyme

Saturday
World Voice Day
Waxing Moon
Full Moon 2:55 pm
Color: Indigo

Moon Sign: Libra
Moon enters Scorpio 8:23 pm
Incense: Rue

17 Sunday
Easter
Waning Moon
Moon phase: Third Quarter
Color: Orange

Moon Sign: Scorpio
Incense: Juniper

18 Monday
Sechseläuten (Swiss)
Waning Moon
Moon phase: Third Quarter
Color: White

Moon Sign: Scorpio
Moon enters Sagittarius 10:16 pm
Incense: Rosemary

19 Tuesday
Primrose Day (British)
Waning Moon
Moon phase: Third Quarter
Color: Red

Moon Sign: Sagittarius
Sun enters Taurus 10:24 pm
Incense: Ylang-ylang

20 Wednesday
Drum Festival (Japanese)
Waning Moon
Moon phase: Third Quarter
Color: Brown

Moon Sign: Sagittarius
Moon enters Capricorn 11:52 pm
Incense: Bay laurel

21 Thursday
Tiradentes Day (Brazilian)
Waning Moon
Moon phase: Third Quarter
Color: Crimson

Moon Sign: Capricorn
Incense: Myrrh

April

22 Friday
Earth Day • Orthodox Good Friday
Waning Moon
Moon phase: Third Quarter
Color: Purple

Moon Sign: Capricorn
Incense: Violet

Saturday
Passover ends
Waning Moon
Fourth Quarter 7:56 am
Color: Brown

Moon Sign: Capricorn
Moon enters Aquarius 2:17 pm
Incense: Sandalwood

24 Sunday
Orthodox Easter
Waning Moon
Moon phase: Fourth Quarter
Color: Yellow

Moon Sign: Aquarius
Incense: Hyacinth

25 Monday
Robigalia (Roman)
Waning Moon
Moon phase: Fourth Quarter
Color: Gray

Moon Sign: Aquarius
Moon enters Pisces 6:15 am
Incense: Clary sage

26 Tuesday
Chernobyl Remembrance Day (Belarusian)
Waning Moon
Moon phase: Fourth Quarter
Color: Scarlet

Moon Sign: Pisces
Incense: Ginger

27 Wednesday
Freedom Day (South African)
Waning Moon
Moon phase: Fourth Quarter
Color: White

Moon Sign: Pisces
Moon enters Aries 12:10 pm
Incense: Honeysuckle

28 Thursday
Floralia (Roman)
Waning Moon
Moon phase: Fourth Quarter
Color: Purple

Moon Sign: Aries
Incense: Jasmine

April

29 Friday
Showa Day (Japanese) • *Arbor Day*
Waning Moon
Moon phase: Fourth Quarter
Color: Coral

Moon Sign: Aries
Moon enters Taurus 8:19 pm
Incense: Vanilla

 Saturday
Walpurgis Night
Waning Moon
New Moon 4:28 pm
Color: Blue

Moon Sign: Taurus
Incense: Ivy

April Birthstones

She who from April dates her years,
Diamonds shall wear, lest bitter tears
For vain repentance flow; this stone
Emblem for innocence is known.

Modern: Diamond
Zodiac (Aries): Bloodstone

May

1 **Sunday**
Beltane • Ramadan ends
Waxing Moon
Moon phase: First Quarter
Color: Amber

Moon Sign: Taurus
Incense: Heliotrope

---

2 **Monday**
National Education Day (Indonesian)
Waxing Moon
Moon phase: First Quarter
Color: Lavender

Moon Sign: Taurus
Moon enters Gemini 6:47 am
Incense: Rosemary

---

3 **Tuesday**
Roodmas • Teacher Appreciation Day
Waxing Moon
Moon phase: First Quarter
Color: White

Moon Sign: Gemini
Incense: Cinnamon

---

4 **Wednesday**
Star Wars Day
Waxing Moon
Moon phase: First Quarter
Color: Yellow

Moon Sign: Gemini
Moon enters Cancer 7:05 pm
Incense: Marjoram

---

5 **Thursday**
Cinco de Mayo (Mexican)
Waxing Moon
Moon phase: First Quarter
Color: Turquoise

Moon Sign: Cancer
Incense: Nutmeg

---

6 **Friday**
Martyrs' Day (Lebanese and Syrian)
Waxing Moon
Moon phase: First Quarter
Color: Pink

Moon Sign: Cancer
Incense: Alder

---

7 **Saturday**
Pilgrimage of St. Nicholas (Italian)
Waxing Moon
Moon phase: First Quarter
Color: Black

Moon Sign: Cancer
Moon enters Leo 7:50 am
Incense: Sage

May

☽ Sunday
Mother's Day
Waxing Moon
Second Quarter 8:21 pm
Color: Gold

Moon Sign: Leo
Incense: Almond

---

9 Monday
Lemuria (Roman)
Waxing Moon
Moon phase: Second Quarter
Color: White

Moon Sign: Leo
Moon enters Virgo 6:53 pm
Incense: Neroli

---

10 Tuesday
Independence Day (Romanian)
Waxing Moon
Moon phase: Second Quarter
Color: Gray

Moon Sign: Virgo
Incense: Bayberry

---

11 Wednesday
Ukai season opens (Japanese)
Waxing Moon
Moon phase: Second Quarter
Color: Topaz

Moon Sign: Virgo
Incense: Bay laurel

---

12 Thursday
Florence Nightingale's birthday
Waxing Moon
Moon phase: Second Quarter
Color: Green

Moon Sign: Virgo
Moon enters Libra 2:34 am
Incense: Carnation

---

13 Friday
Pilgrimage to Fátima (Portuguese)
Waxing Moon
Moon phase: Second Quarter
Color: Rose

Moon Sign: Libra
Incense: Yarrow

---

14 Saturday
Carabao Festival (Spanish)
Waxing Moon
Moon phase: Second Quarter
Color: Indigo

Moon Sign: Libra
Moon enters Scorpio 6:34 am
Incense: Magnolia

15 Sunday
Festival of St. Dymphna
Waxing Moon
Moon phase: Second Quarter
Color: Yellow

Moon Sign: Scorpio
Incense: Eucalyptus

16 Monday
St. Honoratus's Day
Waxing Moon
Full Moon 12:14 am
Color: Ivory

Moon Sign: Scorpio
Moon enters Sagittarius 7:50 am
Incense: Narcissus

17 Tuesday
Norwegian Constitution Day
Waning Moon
Moon phase: Third Quarter
Color: Black

Moon Sign: Sagittarius
Incense: Geranium

18 Wednesday
Battle of Las Piedras Day (Uruguayan)
Waning Moon
Moon phase: Third Quarter
Color: White

Moon Sign: Sagittarius
Moon enters Capricorn 8:02 am
Incense: Lilac

19 Thursday
Mother's Day (Kyrgyzstani)
Waning Moon
Moon phase: Third Quarter
Color: Purple

Moon Sign: Capricorn
Incense: Jasmine

20 Friday
Feast of St. Aurea of Ostia
Waning Moon
Moon phase: Third Quarter
Color: Pink

Moon Sign: Capricorn
Sun enters Gemini 9:23 pm
Moon enters Aquarius 8:53 am
Incense: Rose

21 Saturday
Navy Day (Chilean)
Waning Moon
Moon phase: Third Quarter
Color: Blue

Moon Sign: Aquarius
Incense: Pine

May

○ **Sunday**
Harvey Milk Day (Californian)
Waning Moon
Fourth Quarter 2:43 pm
Color: Amber

Moon Sign: Aquarius
Moon enters Pisces 11:49 am
Incense: Hyacinth

---

23 Monday
Victoria Day (Canadian)
Waning Moon
Moon phase: Fourth Quarter
Color: Gray

Moon Sign: Pisces
Incense: Clary sage

---

24 Tuesday
Education and Culture Day (Bulgaria)
Waning Moon
Moon phase: Fourth Quarter
Color: Maroon

Moon Sign: Pisces
Moon enters Aries 5:39 pm
Incense: Cedar

---

25 Wednesday
Missing Children's Day
Waning Moon
Moon phase: Fourth Quarter
Color: Brown

Moon Sign: Aries
Incense: Lavender

---

26 Thursday
Pepys's Commemoration (English)
Waning Moon
Moon phase: Fourth Quarter
Color: White

Moon Sign: Aries
Incense: Myrrh

---

27 Friday
Feast of St. Bede the Venerable
Waning Moon
Moon phase: Fourth Quarter
Color: Purple

Moon Sign: Aries
Moon enters Taurus 2:22 am
Incense: Violet

---

28 Saturday
St. Germain's Day
Waning Moon
Moon phase: Fourth Quarter
Color: Gray

Moon Sign: Taurus
Incense: Ivy

May

29 Sunday
Oak Apple Day (English)
Waning Moon
Moon phase: Fourth Quarter
Color: Orange

Moon Sign: Taurus
Moon enters Gemini 1:23 am
Incense: Juniper

Monday
Memorial Day
Waning Moon
New Moon 7:30 am
Color: Silver

Moon Sign: Gemini
Incense: Hyssop

31 Tuesday
Visitation of Mary
Waxing Moon
Moon phase: First Quarter
Color: Red

Moon Sign: Gemini
Incense: Basil

May Birthstones

Who first beholds the light of day,
In spring's sweet flowery month of May,
And wears an Emerald all her life,
Shall be a loved, and happy wife.

Modern: Emerald
Zodiac (Taurus): Sapphire

June

1   Wednesday
Dayak Harvest Festival (Malaysian)
Waxing Moon
Moon phase: First Quarter
Color: Yellow

Moon Sign: Gemini
Moon enters Cancer 1:49 am
Incense: Honeysuckle

---

2   Thursday
Republic Day (Italian)
Waxing Moon
Moon phase: First Quarter
Color: Crimson

Moon Sign: Cancer
Incense: Apricot

---

3   Friday
Feast of St. Clotilde
Waxing Moon
Moon phase: First Quarter
Color: Coral

Moon Sign: Cancer
Moon enters Leo 2:38 pm
Incense: Cypress

---

4   Saturday
Shavuot begins at sundown
Waxing Moon
Moon phase: First Quarter
Color: Brown

Moon Sign: Leo
Incense: Rue

---

5   Sunday
Constitution Day (Danish)
Waxing Moon
Moon phase: First Quarter
Color: Yellow

Moon Sign: Leo
Incense: Frankincense

---

6   Monday
National Day of Sweden
Waxing Moon
Moon phase: First Quarter
Color: White

Moon Sign: Leo
Moon enters Virgo 2:22 am
Incense: Neroli

◖   Tuesday
Vestalia begins (Roman)
Waxing Moon
Second Quarter 10:48 pm
Color: Gray

Moon Sign: Virgo
Incense: Ylang-ylang

June

8 Wednesday
World Oceans Day
Waxing Moon
Moon phase: Second Quarter
Color: Topaz

Moon Sign: Virgo
Moon enters Libra 11:23 pm
Incense: Lilac

9 Thursday
Heroes' Day (Ugandan)
Waxing Moon
Moon phase: Second Quarter
Color: Purple

Moon Sign: Libra
Incense: Balsam

10 Friday
Portugal Day
Waxing Moon
Moon phase: Second Quarter
Color: Pink

Moon Sign: Libra
Moon enters Scorpio 4:41 pm
Incense: Orchid

11 Saturday
Kamehameha Day (Hawaiian)
Waxing Moon
Moon phase: Second Quarter
Color: Blue

Moon Sign: Scorpio
Incense: Pine

12 Sunday
Independence Day (Filipino)
Waxing Moon
Moon phase: Second Quarter
Color: Gold

Moon Sign: Scorpio
Moon enters Sagittarius 6:31 pm
Incense: Almond

13 Monday
St. Anthony of Padua's Day
Waxing Moon
Moon phase: Second Quarter
Color: Silver

Moon Sign: Sagittarius
Incense: Narcissus

Tuesday
Flag Day
Waxing Moon
Full Moon 7:52 am
Color: Scarlet

Moon Sign: Sagittarius
Moon enters Capricorn 6:14 pm
Incense: Cinnamon

June

15 Wednesday
Vestalia ends (Roman)
Waning Moon
Moon phase: Third Quarter
Color: Brown

Moon Sign: Capricorn
Incense: Bay laurel

16 Thursday
Bloomsday (Irish)
Waning Moon
Moon phase: Third Quarter
Color: Turquoise

Moon Sign: Capricorn
Moon enters Aquarius 5:44 pm
Incense: Myrrh

17 Friday
Bunker Hill Day (Massachusetts)
Waning Moon
Moon phase: Third Quarter
Color: White

Moon Sign: Aquarius
Incense: Mint

18 Saturday
Waterloo Day (British)
Waning Moon
Moon phase: Third Quarter
Color: Black

Moon Sign: Aquarius
Moon enters Pisces 7:01 pm
Incense: Sage

19 Sunday
Juneteenth • Father's Day
Waning Moon
Moon phase: Third Quarter
Color: Orange

Moon Sign: Pisces
Incense: Heliotrope

◖ Monday
Flag Day (Argentinian)
Waning Moon
Fourth Quarter 11:11 pm
Color: Lavender

Moon Sign: Pisces
Moon enters Aries 11:37 pm
Incense: Clary sage

21 Tuesday
Litha • Summer Solstice
Waning Moon
Moon phase: Fourth Quarter
Color: Red

Moon Sign: Aries
Sun enters Cancer 5:14 am
Incense: Geranium

June

22 Wednesday
Teachers' Day (El Salvadoran)
Waning Moon
Moon phase: Fourth Quarter
Color: White

Moon Sign: Aries
Incense: Marjoram

23 Thursday
St. John's Eve
Waning Moon
Moon phase: Fourth Quarter
Color: Purple

Moon Sign: Aries
Moon enters Taurus 7:58 am
Incense: Clove

24 Friday
St. John's Day
Waning Moon
Moon phase: Fourth Quarter
Color: Rose

Moon Sign: Taurus
Incense: Thyme

25 Saturday
Fiesta de Santa Orosia (Spanish)
Waning Moon
Moon phase: Fourth Quarter
Color: Gray

Moon Sign: Taurus
Moon enters Gemini 7:13 pm
Incense: Sandalwood

26 Sunday
Pied Piper Day (German)
Waning Moon
Moon phase: Fourth Quarter
Color: Amber

Moon Sign: Gemini
Incense: Marigold

27 Monday
Seven Sleepers' Day (German)
Waning Moon
Moon phase: Fourth Quarter
Color: Ivory

Moon Sign: Gemini
Incense: Hyssop

Tuesday
Paul Bunyan Day
Waning Moon
New Moon 10:52 pm
Color: Black

Moon Sign: Gemini
Moon enters Cancer 7:53 am
Incense: Ginger

June

29 Wednesday

Haro Wine Battle (Spanish)
Waxing Moon
Moon phase: First Quarter
Color: Yellow

Moon Sign: Cancer
Incense: Lavender

30 Thursday

The Burning of the Three Firs (French)
Waxing Moon
Moon phase: First Quarter
Color: White

Moon Sign: Cancer
Moon enters Leo 8:40 pm
Incense: Mulberry

June Birthstones

Who comes with summer to this earth,
And owes to June her hour of birth,
With ring of Agate on her hand,
Can health, wealth, and long life command.

Modern: Moonstone or Pearl
Zodiac (Gemini): Agate

July

1 Friday
Canada Day • Tartan Day (Australian)
Waxing Moon
Moon phase: First Quarter
Color: Pink

Moon Sign: Leo
Incense: Orchid

2 Saturday
World UFO Day
Waxing Moon
Moon phase: First Quarter
Color: Indigo

Moon Sign: Leo
Incense: Patchouli

3 Sunday
Dog Days of Summer begin
Waxing Moon
Moon phase: First Quarter
Color: Orange

Moon Sign: Leo
Moon enters Virgo 8:31 am
Incense: Hyacinth

4 Monday
Independence Day
Waxing Moon
Moon phase: First Quarter
Color: Silver

Moon Sign: Virgo
Incense: Lily

5 Tuesday
Tynwald Day (Manx)
Waxing Moon
Moon phase: First Quarter
Color: Silver

Moon Sign: Virgo
Moon enters Libra 6:25 pm
Incense: Bayberry

◐ Wednesday
San Fermín begins (Spanish)
Waxing Moon
Second Quarter 10:14 pm
Color: Brown

Moon Sign: Libra
Incense: Marjoram

7 Thursday
Star Festival (Japanese)
Waxing Moon
Moon phase: Second Quarter
Color: Crimson

Moon Sign: Libra
Incense: Apricot

July

8 Friday

Feast of St. Sunniva
Waxing Moon
Moon phase: Second Quarter
Color: Rose

Moon Sign: Libra
Moon enters Scorpio 11:15 am
Incense: Alder

9 Saturday

Battle of Sempach Day (Swiss)
Waxing Moon
Moon phase: Second Quarter
Color: Blue

Moon Sign: Scorpio
Incense: Magnolia

10 Sunday

Nicola Tesla Day
Waxing Moon
Moon phase: Second Quarter
Color: Yellow

Moon Sign: Scorpio
Moon enters Sagittarius 4:34 am
Incense: Frankincense

11 Monday

Mongolian Naadam Festival (ends July 13)
Waxing Moon
Moon phase: Second Quarter
Color: Ivory

Moon Sign: Sagittarius
Incense: Narcissus

12 Tuesday

Malala Day
Waxing Moon
Moon phase: Second Quarter
Color: Maroon

Moon Sign: Sagittarius
Moon enters Capricorn 5:01 am
Incense: Basil

☺ Wednesday

Feast of St. Mildrith
Waxing Moon
Full Moon 2:38 pm
Color: Topaz

Moon Sign: Capricorn
Incense: Lilac

14 Thursday

Bastille Day (French)
Waning Moon
Moon phase: Third Quarter
Color: Green

Moon Sign: Capricorn
Moon enters Aquarius 4:13 am
Incense: Nutmeg

July

15 Friday
St. Swithin's Day
Waning Moon
Moon phase: Third Quarter
Color: Purple

Moon Sign: Aquarius
Incense: Cypress

16 Saturday
Fiesta de la Tirana (Chilean)
Waning Moon
Moon phase: Third Quarter
Color: Indigo

Moon Sign: Aquarius
Moon enters Pisces 4:18 am
Incense: Ivy

17 Sunday
Gion Festival first Yamaboko parade (Japanese)
Waning Moon
Moon phase: Third Quarter
Color: Gold

Moon Sign: Pisces
Incense: Heliotrope

18 Monday
Nelson Mandela International Day
Waning Moon
Moon phase: Third Quarter
Color: White

Moon Sign: Pisces
Moon enters Aries 7:17 am
Incense: Neroli

19 Tuesday
Flitch Day (English)
Waning Moon
Moon phase: Third Quarter
Color: Black

Moon Sign: Aries
Incense: Ginger

☽ Wednesday
Binding of Wreaths (Lithuanian)
Waning Moon
Fourth Quarter 10:19 am
Color: Yellow

Moon Sign: Aries
Moon enters Taurus 2:23 pm
Incense: Honeysuckle

21 Thursday
National Day (Belgian)
Waning Moon
Moon phase: Fourth Quarter
Color: Turquoise

Moon Sign: Taurus
Incense: Myrrh

22 Friday

St. Mary Magdalene's Day
Waning Moon
Moon phase: Fourth Quarter
Color: White

Moon Sign: Taurus
Sun enters Leo 4:07 pm
Incense: Vanilla

---

23 Saturday

Mysteries of St. Cristina (Italian)
Waning Moon
Moon phase: Fourth Quarter
Color: Brown

Moon Sign: Taurus
Moon enters Gemini 1:11 am
Incense: Rue

---

24 Sunday

Gion Festival second Yamaboko parade (Japanese)
Waning Moon
Moon phase: Fourth Quarter
Color: Amber

Moon Sign: Gemini
Incense: Marigold

---

25 Monday

Illapa Festival (Incan)
Waning Moon
Moon phase: Fourth Quarter
Color: Lavender

Moon Sign: Gemini
Moon enters Cancer 1:54 pm
Incense: Rosemary

---

26 Tuesday

St. Anne's Day
Waning Moon
Moon phase: Fourth Quarter
Color: Red

Moon Sign: Cancer
Incense: Cedar

---

27 Wednesday

Sleepyhead Day (Finnish)
Waning Moon
Moon phase: Fourth Quarter
Color: Brown

Moon Sign: Cancer
Incense: Bay laurel

Thursday

Independence Day (Peruvian)
Waning Moon
New Moon 1:55 pm
Color: White

Moon Sign: Cancer
Moon enters Leo 2:36 am
Incense: Balsam

July

29 Friday
Islamic New Year begins at sundown
Waxing Moon
Moon phase: First Quarter
Color: Coral

Moon Sign: Leo
Incense: Violet

---

30 Saturday
Micman Festival of St. Ann
Waxing Moon
Moon phase: First Quarter
Color: Gray

Moon Sign: Leo
Moon enters Virgo 2:11 pm
Incense: Sage

---

31 Sunday
Feast of St. Ignatius
Waxing Moon
Moon phase: First Quarter
Color: Gold

Moon Sign: Virgo
Incense: Eucalyptus

July Birthstones

The glowing Ruby shall adorn
Those who in warm July are born;
Then will they be exempt and free
From love's doubt, and anxiety.

Modern: Ruby
Zodiac (Cancer): Emerald

August

1 **Monday**
Lammas
Waxing Moon
Moon phase: First Quarter
Color: Gray

Moon Sign: Virgo
Incense: Lily

---

2 **Tuesday**
Porcingula (Pecos)
Waxing Moon
Moon phase: First Quarter
Color: White

Moon Sign: Virgo
Moon enters Libra 12:06 am
Incense: Basil

---

3 **Wednesday**
Flag Day (Venezuelan)
Waxing Moon
Moon phase: First Quarter
Color: Yellow

Moon Sign: Libra
Incense: Lavender

---

4 **Thursday**
Qixi Festival (Chinese)
Waxing Moon
Moon phase: First Quarter
Color: Purple

Moon Sign: Libra
Moon enters Scorpio 7:47 am
Incense: Carnation

◑ **Friday**
Carnival of Bogotá
Waxing Moon
Second Quarter 7:07 am
Color: Rose

Moon Sign: Scorpio
Incense: Thyme

---

6 **Saturday**
Hiroshima Peace Memorial Ceremony
Waxing Moon
Moon phase: Second Quarter
Color: Blue

Moon Sign: Scorpio
Moon enters Sagittarius 12:39 pm
Incense: Patchouli

---

7 **Sunday**
Republic Day (Ivorian)
Waxing Moon
Moon phase: Second Quarter
Color: Yellow

Moon Sign: Sagittarius
Incense: Juniper

August

8 Monday
Farmers' Day (Tanzanian)
Waxing Moon
Moon phase: Second Quarter
Color: Ivory

Moon Sign: Sagittarius
Moon enters Capricorn 2:39 pm
Incense: Hyssop

9 Tuesday
Nagasaki Peace Memorial Ceremony
Waxing Moon
Moon phase: Second Quarter
Color: Maroon

Moon Sign: Capricorn
Incense: Cedar

10 Wednesday
Puck Fair (ends Aug. 12; Irish)
Waxing Moon
Moon phase: Second Quarter
Color: White

Moon Sign: Capricorn
Moon enters Aquarius 2:45 pm
Incense: Marjoram

Thursday
Mountain Day (Japanese)
Waxing Moon
Full Moon 9:36 pm
Color: Turquoise

Moon Sign: Aquarius
Incense: Clove

12 Friday
Ghost Festival (Chinese)
Waning Moon
Moon phase: Third Quarter
Color: Purple

Moon Sign: Aquarius
Moon enters Pisces 2:44 pm
Incense: Rose

13 Saturday
Women's Day (Tunisian)
Waning Moon
Moon phase: Third Quarter
Color: Black

Moon Sign: Pisces
Incense: Ivy

14 Sunday
Independence Day (Pakistani)
Waning Moon
Moon phase: Third Quarter
Color: Orange

Moon Sign: Pisces
Moon enters Aries 4:43 pm
Incense: Marigold

August

15 Monday
Bon Festival (Japanese)
Waning Moon
Moon phase: Third Quarter
Color: Lavender

Moon Sign: Aries
Incense: Clary sage

16 Tuesday
Xicolatada (French)
Waning Moon
Moon phase: Third Quarter
Color: Black

Moon Sign: Aries
Moon enters Taurus 10:22 pm
Incense: Geranium

17 Wednesday
Black Cat Appreciation Day
Waning Moon
Moon phase: Third Quarter
Color: Brown

Moon Sign: Taurus
Incense: Honeysuckle

18 Thursday
St. Helen's Day
Waning Moon
Moon phase: Third Quarter
Color: Green

Moon Sign: Taurus
Incense: Jasmine

◑ Friday
Vinalia Rustica (Roman)
Waning Moon
Fourth Quarter 12:36 am
Color: White

Moon Sign: Taurus
Moon enters Gemini 8:06 am
Incense: Mint

20 Saturday
St. Stephen's Day (Hungarian)
Waning Moon
Moon phase: Fourth Quarter
Color: Indigo

Moon Sign: Gemini
Incense: Pine

21 Sunday
Consualia (Roman)
Waning Moon
Moon phase: Fourth Quarter
Color: Gold

Moon Sign: Gemini
Moon enters Cancer 8:29 pm
Incense: Heliotrope

August

22 Monday

Feast of the Queenship of Mary (English)
Waning Moon
Moon phase: Fourth Quarter
Color: Silver

Moon Sign: Cancer
Sun enters Virgo 11:16 pm
Incense: Neroli

23 Tuesday

National Day (Romanian)
Waning Moon
Moon phase: Fourth Quarter
Color: Scarlet

Moon Sign: Cancer
Incense: Bayberry

24 Wednesday

St. Bartholomew's Day
Waning Moon
Moon phase: Fourth Quarter
Color: Topaz

Moon Sign: Cancer
Moon enters Leo 9:09 am
Incense: Lilac

25 Thursday

Liberation of Paris
Waning Moon
Moon phase: Fourth Quarter
Color: Crimson

Moon Sign: Leo
Incense: Apricot

26 Friday

Heroes' Day (Namibian)
Waning Moon
Moon phase: Fourth Quarter
Color: Pink

Moon Sign: Leo
Moon enters Virgo 8:25 pm
Incense: Yarrow

Saturday

Independence Day (Moldovan)
Waning Moon
New Moon 4:17 am
Color: Brown

Moon Sign: Virgo
Incense: Sandalwood

28 Sunday

St. Augustine's Day
Waxing Moon
Moon phase: First Quarter
Color: Amber

Moon Sign: Virgo
Incense: Amber

29 Monday
St. John's Beheading
Waxing Moon
Moon phase: First Quarter
Color: Gray

Moon Sign: Virgo
Moon enters Libra 5:45 am
Incense: Rosemary

30 Tuesday
St. Rose of Lima Day (Peruvian)
Waxing Moon
Moon phase: First Quarter
Color: Red

Moon Sign: Libra
Incense: Cinnamon

31 Wednesday
La Tomatina (Valencian)
Waxing Moon
Moon phase: First Quarter
Color: White

Moon Sign: Libra
Moon enters Scorpio 1:11 pm
Incense: Bay laurel

August Birthstones

Wear Sardonyx, or for thee
No conjugal felicity;
The August-born without this stone,
'Tis said, must live unloved, and lone.

Modern: Peridot
Zodiac (Leo): Onyx

September

1 Thursday
Wattle Day (Australian)
Waxing Moon
Moon phase: First Quarter
Color: Green

Moon Sign: Scorpio
Incense: Balsam

---

2 Friday
St. Mammes's Day
Waxing Moon
Moon phase: First Quarter
Color: Rose

Moon Sign: Scorpio
Moon enters Sagittarius 6:39 pm
Incense: Violet

◑ Saturday
National Feast of San Marino
Waxing Moon
Second Quarter 2:08 pm
Color: Blue

Moon Sign: Sagittarius
Incense: Magnolia

---

4 Sunday
Feast of St. Rosalia
Waxing Moon
Moon phase: Second Quarter
Color: Yellow

Moon Sign: Sagittarius
Moon enters Capricorn 10:03 pm
Incense: Eucalyptus

---

5 Monday
Labor Day • Labour Day (Canadian)
Waxing Moon
Moon phase: Second Quarter
Color: White

Moon Sign: Capricorn
Incense: Clary sage

---

6 Tuesday
Hiroshima Peace Memorial Ceremony
Waxing Moon
Moon phase: Second Quarter
Color: Maroon

Moon Sign: Capricorn
Moon enters Aquarius 11:41 pm
Incense: Ginger

---

7 Wednesday
Independence Day (Brazilian)
Waxing Moon
Moon phase: Second Quarter
Color: Topaz

Moon Sign: Aquarius
Incense: Honeysuckle

8 Thursday
International Literacy Day
Waxing Moon
Moon phase: Second Quarter
Color: Purple

Moon Sign: Aquarius
Incense: Myrrh

9 Friday
Remembrance for Herman the Cheruscan (Asatru)
Waxing Moon
Moon phase: Second Quarter
Color: Pink

Moon Sign: Aquarius
Moon enters Pisces 12:42 am
Incense: Orchid

☻ Saturday
Mid-Autumn Festival (Chinese)
Waxing Moon
Full Moon 5:59 am
Color: Black

Moon Sign: Pisces
Incense: Rue

11 Sunday
Grandparents' Day
Waning Moon
Moon phase: Third Quarter
Color: Gold

Moon Sign: Pisces
Moon enters Aries 2:47 am
Incense: Frankincense

12 Monday
Mindfulness Day
Waning Moon
Moon phase: Third Quarter
Color: Silver

Moon Sign: Aries
Incense: Hyssop

13 Tuesday
The Gods' Banquet
Waning Moon
Moon phase: Third Quarter
Color: White

Moon Sign: Aries
Moon enters Taurus 7:39 am
Incense: Ylang-ylang

14 Wednesday
Holy Cross Day
Waning Moon
Moon phase: Third Quarter
Color: Brown

Moon Sign: Taurus
Incense: Lavender

September

15 Thursday
International Day of Democracy
Waning Moon
Moon phase: Third Quarter
Color: Crimson

Moon Sign: Taurus
Moon enters Gemini 4:16 pm
Incense: Clove

16 Friday
Independence Day (Mexican)
Waning Moon
Moon phase: Third Quarter
Color: Purple

Moon Sign: Gemini
Incense: Vanilla

Saturday
Teachers' Day (Honduran)
Waning Moon
Fourth Quarter 5:52 pm
Color: Gray

Moon Sign: Gemini
Incense: Pine

18 Sunday
World Water Monitoring Day
Waning Moon
Moon phase: Fourth Quarter
Color: Orange

Moon Sign: Gemini
Moon enters Cancer 3:59 am
Incense: Hyacinth

19 Monday
Feast of San Gennaro
Waning Moon
Moon phase: Fourth Quarter
Color: Lavender

Moon Sign: Cancer
Incense: Lily

20 Tuesday
St. Eustace's Day
Waning Moon
Moon phase: Fourth Quarter
Color: Red

Moon Sign: Cancer
Moon enters Leo 4:38 pm
Incense: Basil

21 Wednesday
UN International Day of Peace
Waning Moon
Moon phase: Fourth Quarter
Color: Yellow

Moon Sign: Leo
Incense: Lilac

September
♎

22 Thursday

Mabon • Fall Equinox
Waning Moon
Moon phase: Fourth Quarter
Color: Turquoise

Moon Sign: Leo
Sun enters Libra 9:04 pm
Incense: Mulberry

23 Friday

Feast of St. Padre Pio
Waning Moon
Moon phase: Fourth Quarter
Color: White

Moon Sign: Leo
Moon enters Virgo 3:53 am
Incense: Yarrow

24 Saturday

Schwenkenfelder Thanksgiving (German-American)
Waning Moon
Moon phase: Fourth Quarter
Color: Indigo

Moon Sign: Virgo
Incense: Ivy

☽ Sunday

Rosh Hashanah begins at sundown
Waning Moon
New Moon 5:55 pm
Color: Amber

Moon Sign: Virgo
Moon enters Libra 12:43 pm
Incense: Juniper

26 Monday

Feast of Santa Justina (Mexican)
Waxing Moon
Moon phase: First Quarter
Color: Ivory

Moon Sign: Libra
Incense: Rosemary

27 Tuesday

Meskel (Ethiopian and Eritrean)
Waxing Moon
Moon phase: First Quarter
Color: Gray

Moon Sign: Libra
Moon enters Scorpio 7:15 pm
Incense: Geranium

28 Wednesday

Confucius's birthday
Waxing Moon
Moon phase: First Quarter
Color: White

Moon Sign: Scorpio
Incense: Bay laurel

September

29 Thursday
Michaelmas
Waxing Moon
Moon phase: First Quarter
Color: Purple

Moon Sign: Scorpio
Incense: Carnation

---

30 Friday
St. Jerome's Day
Waxing Moon
Moon phase: First Quarter
Color: Coral

Moon Sign: Scorpio
Moon enters Sagittarius 12:03 am
Incense: Cypress

◈

September Birthstones

A maiden born when autumn leaves
Are rustling in September's breeze,
A Sapphire on her brow should bind;
'Twill cure diseases of the mind.

Modern: Sapphire
Zodiac (Virgo): Carnelian

October

1 Saturday
Armed Forces Day (South Korean)
Waxing Moon
Moon phase: First Quarter
Color: Brown

Moon Sign: Sagittarius
Incense: Magnolia

☾ Sunday
Gandhi's birthday
Waxing Moon
Second Quarter 8:14 pm
Color: Gold

Moon Sign: Sagittarius
Moon enters Capricorn 3:38 am
Incense: Marigold

---

3 Monday
German Unity Day
Waxing Moon
Moon phase: Second Quarter
Color: Gray

Moon Sign: Capricorn
Incense: Neroli

---

4 Tuesday
Yom Kippur begins at sundown
Waxing Moon
Moon phase: Second Quarter
Color: Black

Moon Sign: Capricorn
Moon enters Aquarius 6:20 am
Incense: Ginger

---

5 Wednesday
Republic Day (Portuguese)
Waxing Moon
Moon phase: Second Quarter
Color: White

Moon Sign: Aquarius
Incense: Marjoram

---

6 Thursday
German-American Day
Waxing Moon
Moon phase: Second Quarter
Color: Crimson

Moon Sign: Aquarius
Moon enters Pisces 8:47 am
Incense: Nutmeg

---

7 Friday
Nagasaki Kunchi Festival (ends Oct. 9)
Waxing Moon
Moon phase: Second Quarter
Color: Rose

Moon Sign: Pisces
Incense: Mint

October

8 Saturday
Arbor Day (Namibian)
Waxing Moon
Moon phase: Second Quarter
Color: Indigo

Moon Sign: Pisces
Moon enters Aries 11:57 am
Incense: Patchouli

Sunday
Sukkot begins at sundown
Waxing Moon
Full Moon 4:55 pm
Color: Orange

Moon Sign: Aries
Incense: Eucalyptus

10 Monday
Thanksgiving Day (Canadian)
Waning Moon
Moon phase: Third Quarter
Color: White

Moon Sign: Aries
Moon enters Taurus 5:04 pm
Incense: Narcissus

11 Tuesday
Meditrinalia (Roman)
Waning Moon
Moon phase: Third Quarter
Color: Maroon

Moon Sign: Taurus
Incense: Cedar

12 Wednesday
National Festival of Spain
Waning Moon
Moon phase: Third Quarter
Color: Brown

Moon Sign: Taurus
Incense: Honeysuckle

13 Thursday
Fontinalia (Roman)
Waning Moon
Moon phase: Third Quarter
Color: Green

Moon Sign: Taurus
Moon enters Gemini 1:08 am
Incense: Carnation

14 Friday
National Education Day (Polish)
Waning Moon
Moon phase: Third Quarter
Color: Coral

Moon Sign: Gemini
Incense: Alder

October

15 Saturday
The October Horse (Roman)
Waning Moon
Moon phase: Third Quarter
Color: Blue

Moon Sign: Gemini
Moon enters Cancer 12:11 pm
Incense: Sandalwood

16 Sunday
Sukkot ends
Waning Moon
Moon phase: Third Quarter
Color: Yellow

Moon Sign: Cancer
Incense: Heliotrope

☾ Monday
Dessalines Day (Haitian)
Waning Moon
Fourth Quarter 1:15 pm
Color: Ivory

Moon Sign: Cancer
Incense: Hyssop

18 Tuesday
Feast of St. Luke
Waning Moon
Moon phase: Fourth Quarter
Color: White

Moon Sign: Cancer
Moon enters Leo 12:45 am
Incense: Bayberry

19 Wednesday
Mother Teresa Day (Albanian)
Waning Moon
Moon phase: Fourth Quarter
Color: Topaz

Moon Sign: Leo
Incense: Bay laurel

20 Thursday
Feast of St. Acca
Waning Moon
Moon phase: Fourth Quarter
Color: Purple

Moon Sign: Leo
Moon enters Virgo 12:25 pm
Incense: Apricot

21 Friday
Apple Day (United Kingdom)
Waning Moon
Moon phase: Fourth Quarter
Color: Pink

Moon Sign: Virgo
Incense: Rose

October

22 Saturday
Jidai Festival (Japanese)
Waning Moon
Moon phase: Fourth Quarter
Color: Black

Moon Sign: Virgo
Moon enters Libra 9:24 pm
Incense: Sage

---

23 Sunday
Revolution Day (Hungarian)
Waning Moon
Moon phase: Fourth Quarter
Color: Amber

Moon Sign: Libra
Sun enters Scorpio 6:36 am
Incense: Hyacinth

---

24 Monday
Diwali
Waning Moon
Moon phase: Fourth Quarter
Color: Silver

Moon Sign: Libra
Incense: Rosemary

Tuesday
St. Crispin's Day
Waning Moon
New Moon 6:49 am
Color: Scarlet

Moon Sign: Libra
Moon enters Scorpio 3:18 am
Incense: Basil

---

26 Wednesday
Death of Alfred the Great
Waxing Moon
Moon phase: First Quarter
Color: Yellow

Moon Sign: Scorpio
Incense: Lilac

---

27 Thursday
Feast of St. Abbán
Waxing Moon
Moon phase: First Quarter
Color: White

Moon Sign: Scorpio
Moon enters Sagittarius 6:55 am
Incense: Balsam

---

28 Friday
Ohi Day (Greek)
Waxing Moon
Moon phase: First Quarter
Color: Rose

Moon Sign: Sagittarius
Incense: Yarrow

October

29 Saturday

National Cat Day
Waxing Moon
Moon phase: First Quarter
Color: Gray

Moon Sign: Sagittarius
Moon enters Capricorn 9:21 am
Incense: Pine

30 Sunday

John Adams's birthday
Waxing Moon
Moon phase: First Quarter
Color: Orange

Moon Sign: Capricorn
Incense: Almond

31 Monday

Halloween • Samhain
Waxing Moon
Moon phase: First Quarter
Color: Ivory

Moon Sign: Capricorn
Moon enters Aquarius 11:43 pm
Incense: Clary sage

October Birthstones

October's child is born for woe,
And life's vicissitudes must know;
But lay an Opal on her breast,
And hope will lull those foes to rest.

Modern: Opal or Tourmaline
Zodiac (Libra): Peridot

November

☽ Tuesday
All Saints' Day • Día de los Muertos
Waxing Moon
Second Quarter 2:37 am
Color: Gray

Moon Sign: Aquarius
Incense: Ylang-ylang

2 Wednesday
All Souls' Day
Waxing Moon
Moon phase: Second Quarter
Color: Brown

Moon Sign: Aquarius
Moon enters Pisces 2:46 pm
Incense: Lavender

3 Thursday
Culture Day (Japanese)
Waxing Moon
Moon phase: Second Quarter
Color: Turquoise

Moon Sign: Pisces
Incense: Mulberry

4 Friday
Mischief Night (British)
Waxing Moon
Moon phase: Second Quarter
Color: Purple

Moon Sign: Pisces
Moon enters Aries 7:07 pm
Incense: Vanilla

5 Saturday
Guy Fawkes Night (British)
Waxing Moon
Moon phase: Second Quarter
Color: Blue

Moon Sign: Aries
Incense: Patchouli

6 Sunday
St. Leonard's Ride (German)
Waxing Moon
Moon phase: Second Quarter
Color: Yellow

Moon Sign: Aries
Incense: Juniper

Daylight Saving Time ends at 2 am

7 Monday
Feast of St. Willibrord
Waxing Moon
Moon phase: Second Quarter
Color: Lavender

Moon Sign: Aries
Moon enters Taurus 12:15 am
Incense: Lily

November ♏

	Tuesday	
	Election Day (general)	Moon Sign: Taurus
	Waxing Moon	Incense: Cinnamon
	Full Moon 6:02 am	
	Color: Red	

9 Wednesday
Fateful Day (German) Moon Sign: Taurus
Waning Moon Moon enters Gemini 10:03 pm
Moon phase: Third Quarter Incense: Honeysuckle
Color: White

10 Thursday
Martin Luther's Birthday Moon Sign: Gemini
Waning Moon Incense: Jasmine
Moon phase: Third Quarter
Color: Purple

11 Friday
Veterans Day • Remembrance Day (Canadian) Moon Sign: Gemini
Waning Moon Moon enters Cancer 7:22 pm
Moon phase: Third Quarter Incense: Thyme
Color: Pink

12 Saturday
Feast Day of San Diego (Tesuque Puebloan) Moon Sign: Cancer
Waning Moon Incense: Rue
Moon phase: Third Quarter
Color: Indigo

13 Sunday
Festival of Jupiter Moon Sign: Cancer
Waning Moon Incense: Marigold
Moon phase: Third Quarter
Color: Orange

14 Monday
Feast of St. Lawrence O'Toole Moon Sign: Cancer
Waning Moon Moon enters Leo 7:48 am
Moon phase: Third Quarter Incense: Hyssop
Color: Silver

November

15 Tuesday
Seven-Five-Three Festival (Japanese)
Waning Moon
Moon phase: Third Quarter
Color: Scarlet

Moon Sign: Leo
Incense: Cedar

Wednesday
St. Margaret of Scotland's Day
Waning Moon
Fourth Quarter 8:27 am
Color: Yellow

Moon Sign: Leo
Moon enters Virgo 8:04 pm
Incense: Marjoram

---

17 Thursday
Queen Elizabeth's Ascension Day
Waning Moon
Moon phase: Fourth Quarter
Color: Crimson

Moon Sign: Virgo
Incense: Myrrh

---

18 Friday
Native American Heritage Day
Waning Moon
Moon phase: Fourth Quarter
Color: White

Moon Sign: Virgo
Incense: Mint

---

19 Saturday
National Adoption Day
Waning Moon
Moon phase: Fourth Quarter
Color: Gray

Moon Sign: Virgo
Moon enters Libra 5:58 am
Incense: Magnolia

---

20 Sunday
Revolution Day (Mexican)
Waning Moon
Moon phase: Fourth Quarter
Color: Amber

Moon Sign: Libra
Incense: Frankincense

---

21 Monday
Feast of the Presentation of Mary
Waning Moon
Moon phase: Fourth Quarter
Color: Ivory

Moon Sign: Libra
Moon enters Scorpio 12:16 pm
Incense: Clary sage

November

22 Tuesday
St. Cecilia's Day
Waning Moon
Moon phase: Fourth Quarter
Color: Maroon

Moon Sign: Scorpio
Sun enters Sagittarius 3:20 am
Incense: Geranium

Wednesday
St. Clement's Day
Waning Moon
New Moon 5:57 pm
Color: Topaz

Moon Sign: Scorpio
Moon enters Sagittarius 3:16 pm
Incense: Bay laurel

---

24 Thursday
Thanksgiving Day (US)
Waxing Moon
Moon phase: First Quarter
Color: White

Moon Sign: Sagittarius
Incense: Clove

---

25 Friday
Feast of St. Catherine of Alexandria
Waxing Moon
Moon phase: First Quarter
Color: Rose

Moon Sign: Sagittarius
Moon enters Capricorn 4:18 pm
Incense: Orchid

---

26 Saturday
Constitution Day (Indian)
Waxing Moon
Moon phase: First Quarter
Color: Black

Moon Sign: Capricorn
Incense: Pine

---

27 Sunday
Feast of St. Virgilius
Waxing Moon
Moon phase: First Quarter
Color: Gold

Moon Sign: Capricorn
Moon enters Aquarius 5:07 pm
Incense: Heliotrope

---

28 Monday
Republic Day (Chadian)
Waxing Moon
Moon phase: First Quarter
Color: White

Moon Sign: Aquarius
Incense: Neroli

November

29 Tuesday
William Tubman's birthday (Liberian)
Waxing Moon
Moon phase: First Quarter
Color: Red

Moon Sign: Aquarius
Moon enters Pisces 7:15 pm
Incense: Ginger

Wednesday
St. Andrew's Day (Scottish)
Waxing Moon
Second Quarter 9:37 am
Color: Yellow

Moon Sign: Pisces
Incense: Lilac

November Birthstones

Who first come to this world below,
With drear November's fog, and snow,
Should prize the Topaz's amber hue,
Emblem of friends, and lovers true.

Modern: Topaz or Citrine
Zodiac (Scorpio): Beryl

December

1 Thursday
Feast for Death of Aleister Crowley (Thelemic)
Waxing Moon
Moon phase: Second Quarter
Color: Turquoise

Moon Sign: Pisces
Moon enters Aries 11:41 pm
Incense: Balsam

---

2 Friday
Republic Day (Laotian)
Waxing Moon
Moon phase: Second Quarter
Color: Pink

Moon Sign: Aries
Incense: Cypress

---

3 Saturday
St. Francis Xavier's Day
Waxing Moon
Moon phase: Second Quarter
Color: Indigo

Moon Sign: Aries
Incense: Ivy

---

4 Sunday
Feasts of Shango and St. Barbara
Waxing Moon
Moon phase: Second Quarter
Color: Orange

Moon Sign: Aries
Moon enters Taurus 6:38 am
Incense: Juniper

---

5 Monday
Krampus Night (European)
Waxing Moon
Moon phase: Second Quarter
Color: Lavender

Moon Sign: Taurus
Incense: Narcissus

---

6 Tuesday
St. Nicholas's Day
Waxing Moon
Moon phase: Second Quarter
Color: White

Moon Sign: Taurus
Moon enters Gemini 3:49 pm
Incense: Bayberry

☺ Wednesday
Burning the Devil (Guatemalan)
Waxing Moon
Full Moon 11:08 pm
Color: Brown

Moon Sign: Gemini
Incense: Marjoram

December

8 **Thursday**
Bodhi Day (Japanese)
Waning Moon
Moon phase: Third Quarter
Color: Green

Moon Sign: Gemini
Incense: Mulberry

---

9 **Friday**
Anna's Day (Swedish)
Waning Moon
Moon phase: Third Quarter
Color: Coral

Moon Sign: Gemini
Moon enters Cancer 2:49 am
Incense: Violet

---

10 **Saturday**
Alfred Nobel Day
Waning Moon
Moon phase: Third Quarter
Color: Brown

Moon Sign: Cancer
Incense: Pine

---

11 **Sunday**
Pilgrimage at Tortugas
Waning Moon
Moon phase: Third Quarter
Color: Amber

Moon Sign: Cancer
Moon enters Leo 3:09 pm
Incense: Almond

---

12 **Monday**
Fiesta of Our Lady of Guadalupe (Mexican)
Waning Moon
Moon phase: Third Quarter
Color: White

Moon Sign: Leo
Incense: Rosemary

---

13 **Tuesday**
St. Lucy's Day (Scandinavian and Italian)
Waning Moon
Moon phase: Third Quarter
Color: Gray

Moon Sign: Leo
Incense: Cinnamon

---

14 **Wednesday**
Forty-Seven Ronin Memorial (Japanese)
Waning Moon
Moon phase: Third Quarter
Color: Topaz

Moon Sign: Leo
Moon enters Virgo 3:45 am
Incense: Lavender

December

15 Thursday
Consualia (Roman)
Waning Moon
Moon phase: Third Quarter
Color: Purple

Moon Sign: Virgo
Incense: Clove

☽ Friday
Las Posadas begin (end Dec. 24)
Waning Moon
Fourth Quarter 3:56 am
Color: Rose

Moon Sign: Virgo
Moon enters Libra 2:49 pm
Incense: Vanilla

17 Saturday
Saturnalia (Roman)
Waning Moon
Moon phase: Fourth Quarter
Color: Blue

Moon Sign: Libra
Incense: Sandalwood

18 Sunday
Hanukkah begins at sundown
Waning Moon
Moon phase: Fourth Quarter
Color: Gold

Moon Sign: Libra
Moon enters Scorpio 10:31 pm
Incense: Eucalyptus

19 Monday
Opalia (Roman)
Waning Moon
Moon phase: Fourth Quarter
Color: Silver

Moon Sign: Scorpio
Incense: Clary sage

20 Tuesday
Feast of St. Dominic of Silos
Waning Moon
Moon phase: Fourth Quarter
Color: Red

Moon Sign: Scorpio
Incense: Ginger

21 Wednesday
Yule • Winter Solstice
Waning Moon
Moon phase: Fourth Quarter
Color: White

Moon Sign: Scorpio
Sun enters Capricorn 4:48 pm
Moon enters Sagittarius 2:12 am
Incense: Bay laurel

December

22 Thursday
Feasts of SS. Chaeremon and Ischyrion
Waning Moon
Moon phase: Fourth Quarter
Color: Crimson

Moon Sign: Sagittarius
Incense: Apricot

Friday
Larentalia (Roman)
Waning Moon
New Moon 5:17 am
Color: Pink

Moon Sign: Sagittarius
Moon enters Capricorn 2:49 am
Incense: Mint

24 Saturday
Christmas Eve
Waxing Moon
Moon phase: First Quarter
Color: Indigo

Moon Sign: Capricorn
Incense: Rue

25 Sunday
Christmas Day
Waxing Moon
Moon phase: First Quarter
Color: Yellow

Moon Sign: Capricorn
Moon enters Aquarius 2:14 am
Incense: Marigold

26 Monday
Kwanzaa begins • Boxing Day • Hanukkah ends
Waxing Moon
Moon phase: First Quarter
Color: Gray

Moon Sign: Aquarius
Incense: Neroli

27 Tuesday
St. Stephen's Day
Waxing Moon
Moon phase: First Quarter
Color: Scarlet

Moon Sign: Aquarius
Moon enters Pisces 2:34 am
Incense: Basil

28 Wednesday
Feast of the Holy Innocents
Waxing Moon
Moon phase: First Quarter
Color: Yellow

Moon Sign: Pisces
Incense: Honeysuckle

December

Thursday
Feast of St. Thomas à Becket
Waxing Moon
Second Quarter 8:21 pm
Color: Green

Moon Sign: Pisces
Moon enters Aries 5:36 am
Incense: Jasmine

---

30 Friday
Republic Day (Madagascan)
Waxing Moon
Moon phase: Second Quarter
Color: Purple

Moon Sign: Aries
Incense: Alder

---

31 Saturday
New Year's Eve
Waxing Moon
Moon phase: Second Quarter
Color: Black

Moon Sign: Aries
Moon enters Taurus 12:08 pm
Incense: Magnolia

December Birthstones

If cold December gives you birth,
The month of snow, and ice, and mirth,
Place in your hand a Turquoise blue;
Success will bless whate'er you do.

Modern: Turquoise or Blue Topaz
Zodiac (Sagittarius): Topaz

Fire Magic

Working Magick for Protests, Organizations, and Activism

Raechel Henderson

At the end of May 2020, I felt I had reached a boiling point. I had been watching the protests that erupted all around the country after the murder of George Floyd. The violent police response to the peaceful protestors filled me with despair. I posted my support of Black Lives Matter to social media. I donated to bail funds. But it didn't feel like I was doing enough. I wanted to join the protests but couldn't. In that moment, caught between dread and frustration, I wrote to Hestia, praying to her:

Great Goddess Hestia, the first and the last, protect the protestors, protect the rebels, protect the people rising up against oppression.

Great Goddess Hestia, the most honored of the gods, encircle those who are fighting for a better world in your fiery protection. Keep them safe from bullets, keep them safe from tear gas, keep them safe from harm and malice.

Great Goddess Hestia, to whom the first and richest portion is given, aid those who have been denied so long their own due. Lift up their voices, lift up their actions, lift up their demand, and help them overcome.

Amen.

To those not familiar with her, it might seem strange to invoke Hestia in the context of Black Lives Matters protests. She is the Greek goddess of the state, and the state is supposed to gain its power from the people. Since the state was attacking citizens exercising their First Amendment rights, I knew she would side with the people over those in power.

It was comforting to be able to call on Hestia. In doing so, I remembered that there were even more ways I could assist those causes and issues I support. I could work magick to protect protestors and to amplify their message. Much of that spellwork didn't have to involve being at a protest to work, either. The mundane ways I was already engaging in movements and issues could be enhanced by the type of magick I was already employing in my personal life.

Letter Writing, Petitions, and Donations

Letter writing is understandably still one of the most effective means of communication with elected officials. If someone is taking the time to write out a letter, stuff it in an envelope, seal it, stamp it, and drop it in a mailbox, that tells a representative that the sender is willing to put in the effort to vote against them if they don't do what the sender wants. In the day and age of electronic mail that can be filtered and automatically responded to, letter writing is a valuable tool in the Social Justice Witch's arsenal. You can use magickal means to give your letter a greater chance at being better received.

Mix the juice of half a lemon with a few drops of water, then use a toothpick dipped in the "ink" to draw sigils on your letter-writing

paper. When the juice is dry, the sigil is invisible unless held up to a light. This is better done before you write or print your letter, as trying to write the sigil over the printing could make it run. You can also write the sigils in the margins of the letter after you have written if you prefer.

Burn lemon balm, clover, or ginger and bathe your letter in the smoke to give it more success of being persuasive. Or add a dab of honey to the envelope seal to "sweeten" your message.

Add sigils or emojis to the signature line of your emails to politicians for the same effect as the lemon juice sigils above.

Additionally, most online petitions provide a space to add your own thoughts to your signature. Use that space to magickally amplify your message by adding a sigil (drawn in ASCII) or emojis or even a magick phrase to support and bring about change.

Fundraising Money Spell

Make a money jar to support the fundraising efforts of any organizations you are supporting. In a jar with a lid, place a flyer or print out of their fundraiser information. If they don't have one, you can make one up or just write the name of the organization and what they need (money, donated items, etc.) on a piece of paper. Place the jar on your altar or in a place where you will interact with it every day. Each morning drop something into the jar that represents money and abundance. This can be coins, monopoly money, semi-precious stones, rings, mint leaves, and even cutouts from magazines that represent what the organization needs. After you drop in the daily contribution, close the jar up and give it a shake. Visualize donations raining down on the organization, fulfilling their goals and meeting their needs. Keep filling the jar until the fundraiser is over.

When donating money through electronic means (PayPal, Venmo, etc.), you can add emojis to a note to give the donation a magickal boost. Add three money bag emojis to attach energies of growth and abundance to your donation so that even more donations will flow into the organization's coffers.

Spellwork for Protesting

Joining a protest and making your voice heard can be empowering. You don't feel alone because you are surrounded by like-minded individuals. It can feel like you are engaging in meaningful action that makes an impact. You should be putting as much thought into the magick part of your protest as your signage.

Blessing and Protective Spells

Before you and others head out to a protest, you need to take certain precautions: you wear protective goggles and comfortable shoes, and you should also be protecting yourself magickally. Anoint yourself and others with an oil for protection and blessing. Call on your deities, spirit helpers, and ancestors to bless you before you head out. Before you return home after a protest, make sure you are cleansing yourself so you aren't bringing any negative energies or magicks home with you. You can do so either with a smoke bundle made from herbs like rosemary, mugwort, or juniper or with sound cleansing such as ringing bells around your body or dancing to a fast-moving song that lifts your spirits.

Protective Amulets for Protestors

Protective amulets are best if they are as innocuous as possible in case of arrest. Pouches full of herbs, stones, or other materia magica could lead to protestors getting held for drug possession or other trumped-up charges. Instead, opt for things like pieces of paper with sigils (which can look like doodles to the uninformed). If you want to leverage the protective properties of herbs, make an amulet out of bay leaves by marking them with a protective symbol like an eye, which protestors can carrying in their wallets or pockets.

Black Salt for Invisibility

Black salt is a mixture of herbs and salt that is used for protection, often sprinkled around a property. As there have been many instances of protestors being identified and later arrested or harassed by police, you can make use of black salt's protective properties in a slightly

different way. Burn chicory, fern, mistletoe, or poppy on a charcoal disc until everything has been consumed and the disc is completely burned out. Mix the ashes with salt to create your black salt. At a protest, sprinkle the salt behind you. The herbs all have properties of granting invisibility, and so the salt will help interfere with any attempts to identify you or other protestors for later reprisal.

Spells to Protect Protestors

Marching in a protest isn't for everyone, however. Many times protests aren't accessible, leaving people with disabilities on the sidelines. The possibility of injury or arrest can be other reasons people steer clear of protests. That doesn't mean they can't participate magickally from afar. Work the protection spell below before a protest to maintain the safety of those who are marching.

This spell works best when you are protecting specific people you know. You can generalize it by writing the name of organizations on the bay leaves, but the generalized nature of that will mean the protection is not as strong.

Cut a piece of blue fabric into a rectangle that measures nine by eleven inches. Gather a number of bay leaves equal to the people you are protecting. Write their names on the bay leaves, one name per leaf. Lay the bay leaves, stacked on each other, at the top of the fabric. Start folding the fabric toward you with the bay leaves in it. Say,

They are protected from violence, they are protected from retaliation, they are protected from opposition.

Ask your deity or any spirits you work with to lend their power to your spell. Keep the leaves wrapped until the protest is over, then unwrap and bury them. Cleanse the fabric and keep it for use when the next protest happens.

Hexing and Binding

Not every Witch is comfortable with hexing and binding, but both are valid and powerful magickal tools. CEOs of corporations that are polluting local waterways and environments; police officers who shoot, kill, or brutalize people; and politicians who take bribes and ignore calls for justice are all valid targets for offensive magick.

Even if you aren't comfortable with hexing and cursing, you can work a freezer spell. All you need is a picture of the target (a printout from a news article is fine), a container (a plastic baggie will do fine), and water. Place the picture in the baggie and fill it with water. You don't need much, just enough to cover the picture. Seal the baggie and place in the freezer. As you do so, say,

You are frozen. You can do no harm. You cannot move forward. You cannot progress.

The spell will aid in keeping the target from making any progress in their career or life. They'll basically be in stasis. Should they be brought to justice, you can remove the frozen picture from the freezer. The picture and ice can be buried and the container either cleansed or recycled.

You can add a piece of monopoly money, coins, or actual money to the freezer bag if you also want to freeze the target's finances. As the United States has a capitalist society, a foe's wallet is a legitimate target for binding.

Bring Your Deities into the Battle

There are a number of deities from numerous paths and religions one can work with in the context of supporting a chosen cause. There are even saints who can be called upon if you work within a Christian framework. I'm not suggesting the Social Justice Witch pick out a deity like they're picking out an ice cream flavor. That's a recipe for cultural appropriation and has the potential of getting on the wrong side of a god. Instead, look to the deities and spirits you work with first. Even your ancestors, if you communicate with them, might be willing to join in the magickal fight. (Be careful, though, if you bring your ancestors in the mix, and be sure that they would want to be involved. My grandfather, for example, fought in WWII and liberated a Nazi concentration camp, was a lifelong Democrat, and also used many racial slurs. While he would probably support freedom from tyranny, I'm not certain his presence would be particularly welcome in BLM matters.)

More than likely they already share a connection to what you are passionate about. If you are looking to support LGBTQ+ issues and work with Artemis (for example), you have an established connection all ready to go. If you aren't sure if the deity or spirit helpers you work with are interested in your causes, you can use meditation, divination, or prayer to ask them.

As Witches, we are not limited to only mundane methods of changing the world. Nor should we focus solely on magickal means. There's a balance to be struck between the two where real-world, effective revolution can be attained. If we ignore certain tools in our toolbox in favor of others, we'll only hamper our efforts. Marrying the magickal with the practical can only speed up the change we want to see in the world.

The Spell Undone:
A Look at Magical Reversals

Michael Furie

Have you ever cast a successful spell, only to then regret the outcome, but you were unsure of how to turn it around? Or conversely, have you cast a successful spell and been quite happy with the result, only to have it seemingly unravel at some point and everything return to the way it was before the spell was cast? Both of these things have happened to me, and my experiences in discovering why a spell unravels on its own have actually helped me understand the overall process of magical reversal. Magical reversal has the potential to be quite helpful in instances when we might consciously choose to undo our own magic, breaking the power of a spell in a formal way so that the previous flow of events can resume. To begin, a short overview of the essential aspects of spellcasting is needed. Though techniques and procedures vary greatly from one magical practice to another, some key elements and similarities are usually present in formal spellwork.

The Structure of Spellwork

In many types of spellwork, there is an essential ritual structure that may either be adhered to quite rigidly or may be only a bare guideline. In any event, keeping these points in mind is a good starting place to understanding not only how to create and cast successful spells but also how to reverse them if necessary. Such steps include purification of the self; setting up an altar or focal point; purification and preparation of the ritual area; setting the proper atmosphere; calling in guides, guardians, helpers, or deities; performing the specific spell; thanking and acknowledging any spiritual allies who were called; concluding the ritual; releasing the space; grounding; and "acting in accord." Each of these facets of ritual are still secondary to the creation of the actual magical message itself, and in my own work, this is achieved through the interplay of three important aspects of the mind: thinking, feeling, and willpower. The mental image of the end result is clearly thought out, and this is deeply infused with strong emotion. A key here is that the emotion used is how you want to feel when the goal is reached, and no other feeling is added. This powerful combination of thought and emotion is then released through the sheer force of will to a focal point

such as a candle or sent directly at the target of the working. These steps each play important roles in the honing of the message being transmitted in the actual spell. If all the components are properly executed, a clear and intense message can be sent. On the other hand, if vital areas are overlooked, there can be mixed messages, blockages, or unintended reversals.

Sudden Reversals

When it comes to successful spells suddenly reversing, I have had a couple of very specific events in the past that were disheartening to say the least. For example, many years ago I performed a banishing to remove a harmful person from not only my life but also the lives of several loved ones. Now, the spell worked at first: the harmful person suddenly got a new job and left the area. They had a new life, we had our lives back in order, and everything was good for a while. In my personal practice, I abide by an ethical guideline that includes work such as banishing and bindings, though the overall focus is intended to ensure those ends are achieved without harm and that they are only done when other options are not available or have proven insufficient. That being said, at the time I was incredibly relieved that the banishing I had performed had been effective, but little did I know that it was about to unravel. A few months later the person was suddenly back—not only back in town, but back at their old job and back around us all almost every day. Admittedly, I was crushed! Not just because of the huge blow to the magical ego that the complete reversal of a spell brings, but more importantly, the person was back and up to their old tricks again. It was as though they'd never left.

I tried to be philosophical about this turn of events and wondered what "greater good" or spiritual "lesson" I was supposed to glean from these experiences, but ultimately I felt defeated and, honestly, I also felt abandoned by Spirit since this particular working was so important to the quality of our lives at the time. Thankfully, I was eventually able to talk myself into stepping out of my ego and taking a broader look at the nature of my practice and what was missing in my work. Some of the questions that I had to ask myself included uncovering my own motivations and objectives for the working and whether or not I had actually made a genuine effort to thoroughly and properly perform each of the steps in the process so as to create and release a precise magical intention. Upon close examination, I determined that I'd properly conducted the working and did have the correct mindset, motivations, and a clear result in mind. Though this was comforting, I also discovered that I had overlooked two critical factors that help to direct and control the power of a spell. These factors are spellbinding and sealing.

Spellbinding and Sealing

Though the term *binding* often refers to the magical practice of casting a spell on a person in an attempt to get them to obey a direction of the spellcaster, usually known as a binding spell, this is not what is meant by the term *spellbinding*. To bind a spell to a person (as opposed to binding the person themselves) is to use a magical link to the subject of the spell so that the caster has a more complete magical connection to the target of the working. Such magical links often include locks of hair, nail clippings, or articles of clothing from the person, though more modern options include photographs, discarded tissues, or handwritten notes from the person. Each of these items carries varying degrees of energy from a person and can serve as a magical link, connecting the energy of a spell directly to its target. Using a magical link vastly improves the strength and effectiveness of any magic directed toward a specific person or animal and is a great benefit in cases such as healing or banishing, when direct contact with the target is frequently either not advised or possible.

Spell *sealing*, on the other hand, usually refers to making a formal action, gesture, or declaration at the end of a magical working in order to send the spell on its way and sever the connection between spell and caster. If we fail to break this connection, then our link to the magic will continually bleed away energy and confuse its message. The same is also true if we continue to dwell on it after it has been cast. Think of it like baking a cake: if we keep opening the oven door to check on it every few minutes, we dissipate the heat of the oven, and the cake either won't bake properly or will take much longer to do so. It is best to cast the spell, seal it to break our connection, and then let it go. That is one of the benefits of magical journaling. If we write down the dates and details of our spellwork, we can put them out of our minds with the comfort of knowing that we have all the important information written down for reference and later confirmation. In my experience, this makes it much easier to let it go and give the energy time to do its work. Some easy and effective techniques to seal a spell include drawing a pentagram in the air with a tool such as an athame or wand, clapping the hands to stop the outflow of energy, striking the altar with a wand, or ringing a bell.

Another method of sealing is to use a specific symbol that corresponds to your magical goal. Symbols of this type are often called sigils or magical seals, and these are perfect for the twofold purpose of binding the energy of the spell to its purpose and sealing it to keep its power intact. As with a pentagram, a sigil or seal can be drawn energetically in the air with an athame or wand as a means of accomplishing the work. One can also be drawn, painted, or inscribed on something physical, such as a charm, in order to keep its power intact. With a little bit of research, an appropriate symbol, sigil, or seal that corresponds to your magical goal can usually be found, and it is always possible to design your own, either with the guidance of books or as a spontaneous creation.

Intentionally Reversing a Spell

Using the techniques of spellbinding and sealing has immensely improved my magical success rate and eliminated my unintended reversal problem. Trying to reverse magic on purpose is, however, a useful skill to learn. Ideally, all magic should be well-thought-out, preplanned, and ethical so that it need not be reversed in the first place, but since mistakes or unforeseen shifts are possible, it is good to know reversal techniques just in case they may be needed. Now, when it comes to reversing a spell intentionally, it is important to remember that the more skillfully it was cast, the more complicated it will be to undo. The first thing to do is to gather as many of the original spell components as possible, especially the link that was the spellbinding; those pieces that are no longer available must be replaced.

A helpful technique to use is a mirroring altar setup in which each of the components are placed at the opposite point of where they were for the original spell. In other words, the candle that was on the left is now placed on the right and vice versa. Whatever the altar layout was for casting the spell, simply reverse it for this undoing. In some cases, magic that includes a reversal instruction will say to redo the entire spell backward, including the words, and that can be done if desired. Other steps are much more individualized depending on the specific working, but I provide some potentially helpful examples below.

An important key in any reversal will be to purify the magical link to the target of the spell. Strip it of its power and intent. If the link was in a charm bag or bottle, this should be opened and all of its bits and pieces cleansed. Photographs, locks of hair, and other links can be immersed in salt or saltwater to break down their magical charge. While this is going on, the candles can be lit and the original words of the spell can be said in reverse if desired, but I have found that a clearly stated need coupled with an earnest desire for the spell to be reversed and a strong feeling of the comfort this will bring have an excellent effect in undoing the work. A good general idea for words to use in a reversal spell could be something along the lines of this:

Spell once cast with intention true, the tide has turned and must now undo. Break the spell, reverse its course—I stop this magic at its source. The power undone and bonds are free, as I now will, so mote it be!

Of course, words can be specifically tailored to the exact situation and, if done so, would be most effective. Remember to fill yourself with not only the mental intention but also the strong emotion of how you want to feel when your goal is reached; this is true of all magic, whether it be to begin something or to reverse it. Keeping in mind the importance of thinking, feeling, willing, spellbinding, and sealing is a sure way to strongly increase your magical success.

Creating and Tending a Magical Hearth

Stephanie Woodfield

As a child, I was excited when we moved into a house that had a fireplace. Not that we needed one—today we have other means to heat our homes and cook our food. But there was something magical about it. Later when I moved out into my first apartment, I lamented the loss of that magical space. In my earliest years as a Witch, it was the place where I burned my Yule log, a place to light a small fire to burn papers etched with magical sigils for spellwork, and a place to burn offerings. I felt I had lost a vital tool in my magical practice. It wasn't like a cauldron or a wand that I could just bring with me to a new place. Or was it? Most modern homes do not have a hearth, and if they do, they are usually more for decorative purposes than practical. Luckily, you don't have to have an actual fireplace to practice hearth magic.

What Is a Hearth?

So what is a hearth anyway? In simple terms, it is a place to light a fire, usually within a home or public building. It's hard for us in modern times to wrap our heads around how revolutionary the idea of a fireplace was. In practical mundane terms, this was a center for domestic activity. It is where the cooking would have been done and a place where a family would gather to talk and tell stories by the warmth of the fire. Its warmth was the difference between surviving the bitter cold of winter and freezing. It offered safety, security, sustenance, and connection. These were fires that would have been banked at night but never fully put out, regardless of the time of the year. When they were extinguished, it was usually to be ritually relit from a sacred fire so its blessing and power could be brought into the home. It is perhaps not hard to see how something so vital to everyday life would come to be seen as magical.

While the hearth was the center of the home, in Greece this idea was expanded on within the community with the *prytaneion* and *bouleuterion*. These where the symbolic centers of the community where civic functions were held. These public hearths were sacred to Hestia, whose name literally means "hearth."

In Russia it was believed that every home had house spirits called *domovoi*, who lived in the ashes of the hearth. When a family moved, they took the ashes from their hearth and brought them to the new home so their house spirits would come with them. Similarly, in Ireland it was believed that the coals from the hearth of the old home should be used to light the fire in the new home so the household's luck was not left behind. This connection between the hearth and luck brought from the friendly spirits that inhabited it can also be seen in the items traditionally hung on the hearth. Placing horseshoes above a hearth is a folk custom observed in several cultures. Folk practices in London in the 1900s included placing various items and children's toys on the mantle for luck. If you have ever hung stockings above the fireplace hoping to get gifts in them on a wintery morning, you have also participated in such a folk practice.

While the hearth was a place to encourage the luck and protection of the household, it was also seen as a weak point. Many folktales feature malevolent beings, faeries, demons, and ghosts entering a home by way of the fireplace. Even today we continue the tradition of viewing spirits, like Santa Claus, though not an evil one, as entering the home through the chimney. In Britain protective charms called "witch marks" were carved near the hearth to prevent evil spirits from being able to enter the home or enter through the chimney. These "witch marks" were usually in the form of circles or Sun rosettes. During renovation, a vast cache of shoes was found buried beneath a fireplace in Cwm Gelli-Lago, Wales. It is thought they were put there as a charm to protect the house and prevent evil spirits from entering through the fireplace.

Where does all that leave us as modern practitioners? We clearly have a rich tradition of hearth magic. What most of us lack is an actual hearth. While I lived in a place that lacked a fireplace, I didn't feel like that meant I had to give up a meaningful practice. It was also a time in my life when I did not have a lot of money to spend on tools. Consequently, I found ways of working without tools or modifying things that I already had on hand. I thought, if I could do that with my other magical tools, why not with my hearth magic? The thing is you don't necessarily need a literal fireplace to practice hearth magic. The basic qualifiers of a hearth are that it is the symbolic or literal center of a home or public space and that there is some kind of sacred fire in that space. That's it. When we frame it from this perspective, the hearth of a home can be centered in many places and can be honored in many ways.

Finding Your Home's Spiritual Center

To begin our modern hearth magic, we first must identify the center of the home. This will be different in every household. This could be the literal center of the house or a symbolic one. A modern fireplace, while a powerful symbol, has in many ways moved away from being the center of the home. What room do you use the most? Where do people gather and feel comfortable in your home? Some folks could probably consider the family living room with a television a modern hearth since we gather around it, and many of us spend a good chunk of time there. The TV even has the ancient hearth's element of people gathering around it to tell stories. Similarly, from a modern point of view, if you enjoy cooking, your kitchen could be considered the spiritual center of the house and serve as your hearth. Or maybe it's a room you use for arts and crafts, igniting the creative fires of the mind.

Connecting to the Hearth Spirits

Being creative about what I considered a hearth also forced me to become more aware of the spirit of the place I lived. Houses new and old and even apartments have a spirit of place. Building a relationship to this spirit can be valuable to your hearth magic and to the stability and protection of your living space. When I lived in a place that already had a fireplace I made offerings to this spirit of place, but I hadn't built the deep connections to that spirit that I had in the places that I lived in after that. Mostly because the hearth was already there. When I had to build a symbolic hearth, I found I worked harder at building that relationship because I was essentially starting from scratch. I had to have the magical tool, the actual hearth, taken away before I really dug deep into what that magical tool really represented and meant to me. In the end, it made my practices more meaningful and powerful. Even if you do have a fireplace, spending the time connecting to your household spirit is essential to making your hearth practice flourish.

Your hearth could also be a place you make sacred to a particular hearth deity. If you find it difficult to connect to your local house spirit, hearth deities can also act as a go-between and help you build those connections. Where I currently live, there is an altar to Brigid next to our fireplace, and both the house spirits and Brigid are honored as part of my hearth practices.

Symbols and Items for Your Hearth

Once you have identified your home's "center," the next step is to create an altar. This can be something simple, like an electric candle or a real candle in a firesafe container. Next to your literal or symbolic flame, there should be a small bowl to make offerings or to burn items in. From there you can add whatever items you like. If you plan to honor your helpful house spirits, you might have items that represent or are appealing to those beings.

Protective symbols should also be placed here to symbolize the house and those living within it being protected from harm.

These could be actual objects or a symbol that you draw. They may be something linked to hearth customs in folklore, such as a horseshoe, or can be something that has personal meaning to you. Sun rosettes and equal-armed crosses work nicely. You could also use a stone, such as black tourmaline, that has the quality of neutralizing negative energy. Try a pair of nails tied with red string to create an equal-armed cross.

My own hearth altars over the years have been places to make regular offerings and ones to pay particular attention to on holidays connected to fire. During these times, I clean my hearth altar and add items to it to set certain intentions for that particular cycle of the year. When I moved into my first apartment, my hearth was an electric candle on a shelf next to the TV. Next to the candle I kept a drawing of a Sun rosette imbued with magic to protect the household, as well as a folded dollar bill with a sigil drawn on it to draw luck to the home, placed under the candle. It was simple and probably looked decorative to anyone who visited, yet it was a strong piece of personal magic, one that served me well. The more I centered my thoughts on this altar being the spiritual center of my home, the more powerful the magical work I did there became. Later, I moved into a home with an actual fireplace, but how I worked my hearth magic didn't really change. Your hearth can be literal or symbolic. The important thing to remember is to be creative and to make it your own.

A Modern Hearth Blessing

You will need:
Candle
Your favorite incense
Offering
Small bowl

This blessing is just a starting point and can be used as is or modified to suit the kind of hearth you will be working with.

Place your items on your hearth and light the candle. Light the incense, waft the smoke over the area, and visualize any unwanted energy dispersing. Take a moment to open your awareness and see your entire house from a bird's-eye view. In your mind, track its borders and see all the rooms in the home. Every home has a kind of spirit of its own, a spirit of that place. Try to connect with this spirit of place, sending out your intentions to protect the borders of this place and those who live within. You could also choose to see wealth and love flowing into the space.

I light my hearth's flame.
I stand at the sacred center of my home and heart.
May this flame be a flame of protection,
A flame of love and warmth,
A flame of (whatever you wish to draw into your space).
I leave this offering to (hearth deity, home spirits, etc.), who watch
over this space.
Bring your blessing and gentle protection.

Leave your offering in the bowl. Let the candle burn for a little while before extinguishing it. Make sure to visit your hearth regularly, renewing your intentions and making offerings.

Resources

Aveela, Ronesa. *A Study of Household Spirits of Eastern Europe.* N.p.: Bendideia Publishing, 2019.

Chainey, Dee Dee. *A Treasury of British Folklore: Maypoles, Mandrakes and Mistletoe.* London: National Trust, 2018.

The Despacho: An Offering of Sacred Reciprocity

Daniel Moler

I watch the circle of sisters and brothers gathered around, flashes of orange and yellow flickering off their faces in the deep night. We are caked in sweat from the baking heat of the fire. Some are dancing, most are singing; drums and rattles wail to call upon the spirits of the wild, inviting the mysteries of the unknown to come and witness the offering made in honor of Creation.

The youngest of us, a child, walks out of the tribal assembly toward the raging bonfire. She is carrying a bundle wrapped in paper and tied off with red ribbon, like a present. It is bulky and full of sweet-smelling oblations. As she approaches, the wild celebration ceases. With a shovel, I maneuver the scorching logs, sparks flitting into the air above us in a fireworks display swirling up to the stars. I arrange a space within the smoldering coals appropriately for the gift.

The child moves around the circle clockwise, touching each participant with the package. First the brow, then the heart, and finally the belly. After assisting her in blessing the entire circle, I point her to the spot I have prepared among the coals, an opening within the logs that should provide an easy space of access and safety for the disbursement. With me at her side for protection, she drops it in, and we step back.

The depth of silence among the crowd is deafening. Everyone's focus is pristine, centered on the offering as it catches the heat and begins to smolder. Curls of smoke begin to dance languidly around the paper, and we smell the copal and frankincense within. Flames lick the contents and the spirits consume the gift we have given in gratitude. Every person in the circle has a different view, but each is equally engrained in the process, deciphering what the burning despacho means to them. Some laugh, some cry, and all surrender to the relationship of reciprocity with the natural world.

What Is a Despacho?

A *despacho* is an offering made to *Pachamama* (Mother Earth) and the spirit guardians of the natural world. A shamanic practice originating from the indigenous Quechua people of Peru, it is a ritual artform that takes many shapes and styles within the tradition. There are despachos for healing, despachos for acquiring love or wealth, and even some designed to assist the transition of a soul into death. The ceremony for creating a despacho is often a community event but can also be done individually. Though there are numerous despacho kits one can find in the markets of Peru's Sacred Valley, anyone can build a despacho with the items they have at home or directly from nature.

Though it is a simple practice, it is an art in which one can become extremely advanced, like the *pampamesayoqs* (shaman healer-priests) of the Quechua, whose medicine of the despacho is so potent they can heal sickness in the community and repair sacred trust with the spirits of nature. In fact, that is the ultimate goal of the despacho: to build a rapport of sacred reciprocity between human and nature. This connection has rapidly dwindled over the centuries. The shamans of Peru (and indeed the world) agree that it is this severance with nature which causes our sickness and malaise as a species.

Ayni (EYE-NEE), the Quechua word for sacred reciprocity, is a system of currency between the earth and her children. It is a form of language that allows communication and connection with the world of spirit and soul. Ultimately, despite a despacho ceremony's specific purpose, its overall aim should be one of gratitude. It is the shamanic worldview that we are not just spiritually but literally the children of the earth . . . expressing thanks to Pachamama is where a true shamanic healer's power resides. Instead of the usual human paradigm of taking resources from our Mother, we should establish a routine of giving in return. How wonderful it is to have the gift of life, to be able to breathe and eat, to be able to experience all the ups and downs of existence! We have Pachamama to thank for that. As we give to her, she listens and will indeed talk back if you are willing to listen.

Ingredients of a Despacho

Ultimately, the despacho is an artform, and you are free to grow and evolve your own method of practice. However, here is a list of traditional items that I recommend you begin with in order to establish a solid foundation for your ritual craft:

Piece of White Paper: Make sure it is large enough to do your work of laying out your offerings. The reason it is white is because symbolically the color white represents the *Apus*, the sacred mountain spirits who are the emissaries of Spirit in the Quechua worldview. It can also mean the connection to the higher worlds important to you, whether that be angels, star relatives, the gods, etc.

Red Ribbon, String, or Yarn: This will be for tying up the despacho when it is complete. Red symbolically represents the blood of Pachamama, the source of all planetary life. It is the red (earth) and white (spirit or air) that are married together to represent the union of the above and below.

Flowers: A bountiful gift to the earth. Traditionally, red and white carnations or roses are used, but you can use all manner of floral arrangements that align with you. Who wouldn't give flowers to their mother?

Sugar, Candies, Sprinkles, and Cookies: All these things represent the sweetness of life, the sweetness of Pachamama.

Seeds of All Kinds: To represent renewal and new growth.

Incense: Meant to assist in carrying the prayers of your intention. Any manner of incense is suitable according to how it aligns to your intentions, though copal is most often used.

Other: Any number of other items can be used, depending upon what calls to you—spices, raisins, beads, glitter, cotton, coca or bay leaves, rice, cornmeal, tobacco, perfumes, and other herbs. The sky is the limit!

Building a Despacho

First, make sure you establish a clear intention for your ceremony. It is sometimes helpful to write down a statement of intent. You could ask for healing for yourself, to assist another in need, or even just to express gratitude. Whatever it is, be clear and focused. Lay out the paper flat in your ritual space. If you build a despacho outside, be sure to anchor the paper from the wind. Arrange your items around the paper in a careful fashion, ensuring each offering is in view for others (if you are in a group), and that the ritual intention of each offering is clear.

Pace yourself throughout the duration of the ceremony. In Peru sometimes a despacho ceremony can take hours, maybe even a full day. The shamans operate the ceremony with utmost reverence, as priestesses and priests of the earth. Move slowly and carefully as the priestess/priest that you are.

Now, according to your intention, you will spend some considerable time laying out the ritual ingredients on the paper. Use the petals from the flowers, the sugars, and other loose ingredients, all with the objective of creating a design on the paper that matches your end intention for the ceremony. When you create, align with the balance of universe, of the elements of the natural world: earth, air, fire, and water. Build a mandala with your offerings, a geometric configuration representing the holism of the cosmos, the microcosm and macrocosm joining in harmony through your hands and onto the two-dimensional paper before you. Imagine the Buddhist monks creating their sand mandalas, magnificent diagrams of perfection that will inevitably be swept away into the mysteries of the unknown. You are such a monk, a disciple of the Great Mystery, carefully and respectfully taking your time to build an astonishing design that is meditative, trance-like, and a gift to yourself and the invisible spirits who support you. Make the building of the despacho itself a meditation. Every action is a prayer. The key is to make beauty!

You do not have to use all the items gathered. Some practitioners have a stockpile of ritual items they use from ceremony to ceremony. You will end when it feels right to you, when the medicine feels right to be offered.

Offering a Despacho

When complete, take a moment to reflection upon the magnificence of your creation and how it relates to your own life. Now, gently fold the paper of the despacho—with the offerings inside—into a bundle. Start with the top third of the paper and fold down. Next, fold the bottom third up, then the left third, and finally the right third, inserting the right side into the left like a sleeve. Tie the bundle with the string or yarn.

There are numerous ways to offer a despacho to the earth. It is perfectly acceptable to bury a despacho in the soil or to release it in flowing water, but one of the more common ways of offering is through fire. Fire is an element for purging and releasing old things

and allowing new things to have room for growth. Also, it can be a source for focus and creation. It was the discovery of fire that changed the trajectory of human destiny, allowing us the ability to bring light into the darkness. Fire is indeed essential to the human experience, for it is through fire that we witness the unification of the spirit realm above and the earth below. The smoke of the offering will carry the prayers into the upper realms and throughout the land, a propitiation to the spirit guardians around us. The ashes will return to Pachamama to become new soil for growth and renewal.

When you have started your sacred fire, call forth the spirits through sacred sound makers such as drums or rattles. Praise their support for life through ecstatic dance and singing. Build up your own spiritual energy as the fire blazes. When you feel the timing is right, carefully use a tool to safely make a space within the coals for easy distribution of the despacho bundle. A common formation is situating the logs so that you are placing the despacho within the space of a U shape.

Before releasing the despacho in the fire, give everyone and yourself a final blessing by touching your brow (your third eye), your heart (the center of all being), and your stomach (for ritual feeding) as a way to receive a transition of medicine from your own creation. Traditionally, it is the youngest of the group who brings the despacho to the fire, provided they are old enough to be safe and assisted by an adult if necessary. When the bundle is offered, settle yourself into another state of meditation. All focus should be on the burning. The burning of a despacho is itself a practice of divination. Do you see things in the smoke, in the flames? Do you hear anything? What is the despacho saying to you? Do you see any shapes or faces in the embers that provide answers for the despacho's purpose? The key is to have your mind open to all possibilities, to be like a child. Bring yourself back to your own childhood and what it was like watching a fire. Allow your imagination to run wild. Do not concern yourself with anything around you other than what the fire has to say to you.

The building and burning of a despacho is an ancient ritual that has evolved over time. Do not concern yourself with doubtful notions, such as "Am I doing this right?" Bottom line: it is a craft that represents a sacred communion between you and Pachamama. Nobody else can tell you how to develop that relationship. Create your own practice. Experiment. Utilize the fire as a purging of old ways and an inspiration to create something new. Though fire in the modern world is often used as a tool of destruction, in ancient times it was utilized as a tool of creation. Be the creator you were meant to be. Through a regular practice of the despacho, you can establish a renewed trust and reciprocity with the natural world.

Making a Magickal Staff

JD Hortwort

Early on in my self-dedication as a solitary Pagan, I, like many novices, looked to acquire what might be called the tools of the trade. Some were easy to come by, like a cauldron or various herbs and candles. Others, according to the authorities I read, needed to be made by the Witch personally. Among those tools was a good staff.

Depending on the tradition, staffs are considered a means of directing the energy of air, similar to a wand only longer. Others say the staff is used to direct the fire element. I've even seen a few sources declare the staff controls earth elements. I believe the staff, which is usually in contact with the earth while always directed through air, can't be one or the other. It bridges the two. The link between air and earth is fire, and that is the elemental controlled by the staff.

However you use it, a staff is a fine magickal tool to have. But for the first humans, it probably didn't start out as such.

In the Beginning

One doesn't need a lot of imagination to see how staffs came into use. For early humans, a sturdy limb was an aid in walking, especially walking long distances. It would have come in handy to scare predators and other dangers away.

At some point it occurred to our early ancestors to strap an arrow-shaped stone on the end and fling the resulting weapon at any animal that was getting away too fast. At that point, the staff becomes a spear, usable not only to score a meal for the tribe but also to best a foe in battle.

A more peaceful use of a staff was as a herding tool. Some clever someone thought to bend the top of his or her staff into a hook to better control sheep or goats. The shepherd's crook was born.

According to a 1995 article in *Smithsonian Magazine* by Edwards Park, eventually everyone had a staff, each unique to a particular trade or position. Obviously, those with more money could afford finer woods or even metal. Anyone with a bit of talent and a carving tool could make their staff ornate. Those who had the funds but not the talent could afford to pay someone to do the carving for them.

In time, the staff became a symbol of authority and status. Religious leaders carried them during ceremonies. Rulers would have had fine staffs, gilded with precious metal and gems. Park also noted that Pharaoh Tutankhamun was buried with 130 staffs.

From the fifteenth through the eighteenth centuries in Europe and England, the quarterstaff was considered an essential weapon for combat and defense. A quarterstaff was a little different from a plain staff in that the length was specifically set at about six to nine feet, and sometimes it had a spike on the business end. How do we know this? At least two authors from these time periods, Richard Peeke in 1625 and Zachary Wylde in 1711, published books on how to fight with quarterstaffs.

The advent of gunpowder, pistols, and rifles took something of the utility of staffs out of combat. Slowly, the staff was shortened to about half a person's height.

The staff didn't go away entirely. We still see Christian icons, living and dead, represented with a staff as a symbol of authority. Gopalkrishna Gandhi, writing for *Telegraph India* in 2018, indicates the staff is virtually part of the dress code for religious members of Buddhist, Jain, and Hindu traditions.

Through popular fiction, we've come to expect magickal figures to carry a staff. Where would Gandalf be without his magickal tool cleverly disguised as a walking staff? You can create your own staff as well with a sturdy piece of wood, a little talent, and some time to properly dedicate your tool.

Making Your Staff

I made my first staff twenty years ago from an oak branch that was gifted to me by a stately oak in my front yard. I was taking a class on how to make your own magickal tools and trying to figure out where I was going to get the necessary wood for a staff. I came home from work a few days prior to the class to find an excellent piece of aged oak lying in the path leading to my front door.

I thanked the universe, made some modest adornments to my gift in the form of a quartz crystal at the top, some leather strapping for a grip, and some Pagan symbols burned onto the body of the staff. It still serves mc well during rituals today, in which I use it to draw a fiery sphere of protection around myself and any others who might be in the ritual circle.

We traditionally think of staffs as made from wood. There are exceptions. In the *Greek Magical Papyri*, Anubis is described as wielding an iron staff. Recent discoveries in northern Europe have uncovered the graves of women, thought to have been *völvas*, or seers, who were buried with iron staffs that are believed to indicate significant power or rank.

The average Pagan today probably isn't going to have access to either the materials or the equipment to forge an iron staff. Fortunately, wood is plentiful for most of us.

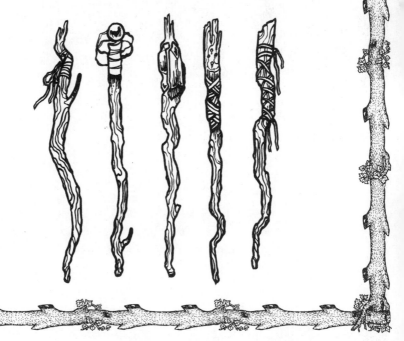

Magick workers are almost expected to have a staff. It is a symbol of authority and power. Made in the right way and used properly, it can be a valuable tool for Pagans of all traditions.

Most of the woodworkers I know advocate sourcing the wood for your staff from material that has been naturally cast off by the tree. You can also take advantage of downed trees—those that have been cut by utility companies, by a neighbor, or even by yourself, if you've had to take down a tree for safety purposes.

When looking for material for a staff, I don't take note of the date or time. Frankly, I often come across the right piece of wood on a casual walk through the woods. I don't want to leave it in the woods where there is a chance that I won't be able to find it again. If you plan to cut your own material and can do it, take the material in a waxing Moon on an appropriate day for the plant material. For example, if you check *Cunningham's Encyclopedia of Magical Herbs*, you'll see that oak is governed by the Sun. You would want to cut it on a Sunday during a waxing Moon.

If you want to make your staff specific to gender, the same resource will help you pick the right material. You'll find that most nut trees have masculine energy. Fruit trees fall under Venus and will have feminine energy. Conifers vary in gender energy; some are masculine, and others are feminine.

The size of the material will vary with the user. Staffs range in height from shoulder height to just above the head. Much more than that becomes unwieldy. The user should be able to comfortably grip the staff. Obviously, a small person's staff would have a smaller diameter than a larger person's staff. I find that a diameter of one and a half to three inches is a good range.

Material that has dried naturally will likely already be debarked. If you cut the material fresh, peel or scrape the bark off before you put it back to dry. In my experience, bark comes off much easier while fresh.

Try to find a place to dry or "cure" your staff where the wood will lie straight. If you have to prop it up in the corner of a room, check it periodically to ensure the wood isn't bowing. How long this will take will depend on the wood, how fresh it was when you collected it, and the conditions where you live. Allow at least two to three months for fresh wood. Even wood that has been naturally cast off will need a few weeks to dry out.

When you are ready to work on the material, you should take note of the timing. I prefer to work on staffs in a waxing Moon. If I plan to dedicate it to a specific deity, I work the material on that deity's special day if possible.

Regardless of the timing of your work, always have your purpose in mind as you work the material. I don't work on magickal tools while I'm upset or angry. There is purpose in my effort as I use an old sturdy pocket knife to remove any rough bark, inner bark, and the dried cambium layer underneath.

Once you are down to the wood, it's time to sand the material smooth. The sanding can be done by hand or by electric sander. Sanding paper is divided into grades or grit. The lower the number, the coarser the grit. An aged oak or hickory staff might require an 80 grit to start with in order to remove any leftover cambium layer of material. But you might be able to start with 100 to 120 grit for a softer wood, such as poplar. The goal is to get the staff to a smooth finish, almost like satin. You can tell from the feel when you've reached that point.

When the sanding is done, it's time for embellishment, if you want that. Some staffs have a fine look to them without more work—the grain of the wood is enough. But you can use a wood-burning tool to etch Pagan symbols or runes in the wood. I have found many people seem to like having stones representing the chakras embedded into the wood. It is a simple matter to drill the right size hole and sink the stone in with a bit of glue.

After the work is done, the staff can be treated with any of several oils to preserve it. I have used linseed, tung, and teak oils on various projects to great effect. Plan on applying at least three coats,

always sanding in between coats. Occasionally, I use varnish. Again, you should apply two to three coats with sanding in between.

I don't paint walking staffs, although you could do that. I assume you will be using your staff with some regularity. In my experience, paint rubs off at the grip and at the end that contacts the ground. That means you will need to frequently retouch the paint, which can be a hassle. On the other hand, you only need to reapply a wood oil once every year or so, depending on how much you use your staff.

Dedication

With the work done, a dedication of the tool is a good idea. This should be done during a waxing Moon on the day special to your patron deity. If you don't plan to dedicate the tool to a particular deity, pick either Sunday (for masculine woods) or Monday (for feminine woods).

Set your sacred space up according to your tradition. Use a red candle. If you are dedicating the staff to a particular deity, use an incense that is pleasing to that entity. Otherwise, frankincense or sandalwood incense is appropriate.

Raise your wards and call your protection. After lighting the incense and candle, take some time to bring yourself into a meditative state. Feel your connection to the universe. When you are ready, pick up your staff. Communicate in words or thought your need to the staff. You want it to help you navigate the ritual space. You want it to stabilize and protect you in the mundane world. You want it to help you direct the energy of fire in magickal workings.

Touch the staff from top to bottom. Pass it through the incense and over the candle fire. If you are calling a deity, ask that deity to lend his or her energy to your working.

When you feel the energy in the staff, your work is done. Ground yourself and open your ritual space. Treat your staff with respect. It's not a chew toy for the dog; it's not a rack to hang your cloak on. From time to time, use a clean cloth of natural fibers to rub it down and re-energize it.

This is a tool that can be with you for your entire magickal life. Cherish it and walk through that life in confidence.

Resources

Cunningham, Scott. *Cunningham's Encyclopedia of Magical Herbs*. St. Paul, MN: Llewellyn Publications, 1985. Page 185.

Dieter Betz, Hans, ed. *The Greek Magical Papyri in Translation*. Chicago: University of Chicago Press, 1986. Page 327.

Gandhi, Gopalkrishna. "The Curious History of the Walking Stick," *Telegraph India*, September 22, 2018. https://www.telegraphindia.com/opinion/a-proud-staff/cid/1669845.

Gardeła, Leszek. "Into Viking Minds: Reinterpreting the Staffs of Sorcery and Unravelling 'Seiðr.'" *Viking and Medieval Scandinavia* 4 (2008): 45–84. www.jstor.org/stable/45093195.

Park, Edwards. "The Object at Hand." *Smithsonian Magazine*, October 1995. https://www.smithsonianmag.com/articles/the-object-at-hand-1-102561973/.

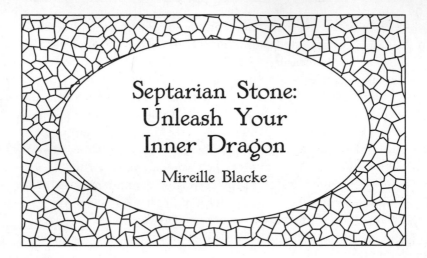

Septarian Stone: Unleash Your Inner Dragon

Mireille Blacke

Three words: *Game of Thrones*. I started watching the show after my coworkers endlessly gushed about it, and I became addicted. Admittedly, Jason Momoa's presence may have had something to do with it. Aside from Momoa's formidable Khal Drogo, season one featured a trio of dragon eggs. Massively significant throughout the series, they were a wedding gift to Khal Drogo's bride, Daenerys Stormborn of House Targaryen, the Khaleesi, and would eventually signify transformation, loyalty, power, and renewal. (Spoilers ahead! To avoid them, jump to "Mother of Bengals" on the next page and then skip the conclusion of the article, "Dracarys!")

As the series continued, themes of regeneration and resurrection emerged. Khal Drogo's funeral pyre at the end of season one birthed three baby dragons as the grief-stricken, childless Daenerys immolated herself (along with the sacred dragon eggs) in the pyre's flames but survived, transformed, in the ashes: the Khaleesi, now the Unburnt, Mother of Dragons.

In 2019, *GoT* ended its run after eight seasons. My job followed suit a year later, due to the novel coronavirus (COVID-19). By late 2020, my coworker connections fizzled; the pandemic pulverized us, like the Night King and his White Walkers during *GoT's* final season. Struggling to adapt and survive in the post-COVID world, the night really seemed dark and full of terrors.

Coincidentally, *GoT* soared again when the pandemic made TV binge-watching a national pastime. I smiled, since I knew that dragon eggs really did exist.

Enter septarian stone.

Mother of Bengals

Also known as dragon's stone, septarian stone's ovoid shape and stunning striated pattern resemble a dragon's egg. In myth and legend, dragons majestically symbolize cycles of destruction (fire) and regeneration, untamed beasts that draw their limitless power from the deepest recesses of Mother Earth, where they also might be protecting a mountain of gold. Both dragons and septaria convey timelessness, embodying the earth's ancient wisdom and protective energy.

When I stumbled upon my first septarian stone many years ago, it looked like a hatched dragon's egg from a fairy tale. Its striking coloring and "cracked" pattern also closely mirrored the wild, leopard-like markings of my much-adored Bengal cats. The "cracks" glittered with small, clear crystals; removing the egg's top revealed a sparkling interior, a sugar-crystalline druzy geode. I purchased the egg and started researching its origins.

I'll never forget how powerful that first septarian stone felt in my hands; holding a septarian stone leaves a strong impression that's hard to describe. No two stones look or feel the same, not all are egg-shaped with druzy features, and luckily, most of mine are so heavy, the Bengals can't knock them over!

Formation Process

Septaria are geological concretions, hard mineral masses of varying shapes, sizes, and compositions. Septaria typically consist of combinations of calcite, aragonite, limestone or chalcedony, pyrite, siderite, and barite. *Septarian* stems from the Latin word *septum*, meaning "partition," "wall," or "enclosure," referencing the prominent cracks, cavities, and fractures within the septarian stone.

The predominant formation theory begins fifty to seventy million years ago, during the Cretaceous Period. Following intermittent volcanic eruptions, mud balls (or nodules) were created by sediment accumulating around minerals from decaying ocean life. With the eventual ebb of the sea levels, the mud balls dried, shrunk, and cracked, producing the stunning septarian patterns we see today.

Higher sea levels during this time period deposited the precursors to septarian stones in parts of the United States (Arizona, Southern Utah) and Madagascar. Larger septarian formations have been identified along the coast of South Island, New Zealand, and the cliffs of England's Wessex Coast.

A notable septarian variation (lightning, black) was identified in the Lake Michigan area of the United States. The darker coloring of this particular stone comes from siderite, an iron-based mineral. Calcite-filled cavities create extraordinary lightning bolt patterns against the stone's brown/black backgrounds. Stunning pendants and jewelry are made from this septarian variety.

Geological experts may continue to argue about septarian stone's exact formation process for years to come. However, there is no debate that the dragon's stone is one of the most stunning creations the natural world has given us.

Metaphysical Properties of Septaria

Septarian stones hold the following energies: balance, calming, clarity, clear communication, emotional flexibility, focus, concentration, grounding, healing, honoring ancestors, joy, nurturing, patience, peace, positivity, protection, public speaking, renewal, self-acceptance, self-confidence, connecting with spirit guides, stability, strength, teamwork, tolerance, transformation, and wisdom (ancestral, earth). Concretion stones like septaria are said to be protective and nurturing; the earth element within septaria both grounds and shields "its person" physically, emotionally, and spiritually. In contrast, the fire element (i.e., dragon energy) is action-based and empowering, assisting with decision-making.

In society today, self-confidence or self-esteem may be negatively impacted by the perspective of others, to the degree that true self-acceptance is profoundly, positively life-altering. For many people, trauma history, negative body image, and low self-worth are often lifelong struggles. Communication is directional; choose to focus inward with positive self-talk, including daily kind, clear, firm affirmations of self-worth and value: "I honor the flaws that make me unique and badass. There's no one else like me, and my past experiences make me who I am today." At home or in the office, the timeless septaria and their physical cracks reminded me of that.

Though I'm logical and evidence-based, discovering that one septarian egg had a profound effect on my life.

Septarian Stone Shapes

A septarian stone's shape assists with its function. The following list briefly summarizes septarian shapes and associated properties and purposes:

Shape	Properties
Cube	Calling spirit guides, spiritual expansion, meditation, enlightenment
Egg	Universal wisdom, earth energy, grounding, shamanic journeying, tolerance, patience
Heart	Peaceful and graceful change, healing spiritual wounds, honoring the "cracks" within yourself, stability, self-acceptance
Obelisk	Protection, honor, designation of sacred space
Palm Stone	Meditation, spiritual transformation, guidance
Pillar	Earth wisdom, transformation, protection, meditation
Pillow	Transformation, embracing change, deep meditation
Sphere	Acceptance, wisdom, healing, peace, calling spirit guides/ancestors, deep earth wisdom, life-changing transformation

The term *druzy* can apply to any shape and has "cracked open," sugar crystalline, geode-like aspects. Additional septarian shapes include tumbled stones, freeform stones, standalone pieces, intact geodes, and carved creations (e.g., carved animal shapes, bookends, jewelry, and smudging bowls).

Septarian Stone and Sacred Space

Each septarian stone is unique, with its own shape, size, and origin story. The mineral composition also varies between stones. Each mineral component within the stone contributes its individual properties to the whole, and separate properties work synergistically. The following table briefly summarizes properties of minerals commonly found within septarian stones.

Stone	Properties
Aragonite	Grounding, truth, stability, understanding, perception
Barite	Spirit guide communication, meditation, calming, energy balance
Calcite	Calming, healing, wisdom, memory, spirituality, removes negativity
Chalcedony	Vitality, stamina, endurance, absorbs negativity, nurturing, kindness, generosity
Clear Quartz	Clarity, clearing negativity, amplification, self-awareness, manifesting, decision-making
Limestone	Healing, purification, grounding, balance, nurturing, positive thoughts
Pyrite	Protection, logic, creativity, mental stability, optimism, practicality, learning and perception, discerning deception, memory
Siderite	Career re-engagement, employment stability, positive thoughts and ideas
Smoky Quartz	Serenity, calmness, positive thoughts, stability, grounding, concentration, communication

Individual and collective properties of septaria are conducive to creating sacred space by fostering an atmosphere of healing, protection, clarity, and stability.

Magical Uses of Septarian Stone
Clearing: Smudging Bowl
Round or heart-shaped bowls are carved from larger pieces of septaria and work well for smudging or other ritual purposes. Choose a smudge stick for clearing purposes, such as cedar.

In addition to smudging sacred space, septarian bowls can be placed on your altar or close to your bed. Septarian dishes of different sizes and shapes appear throughout my house, storing smaller mineral stones; as table centerpieces, candy dishes, and jewelry holders; and decorating coffee tables. I recommend keeping routinely used septaria separate from ritual pieces.

Meditation: Cube and Sphere Stones

When carved into cubes or spheres, septaria become some of the most practical and versatile altar pieces or meditation tools. Septarian cubes and spheres both honor the four directions and four elements (earth, air, fire, and water). With either, energy emanates in all directions, filling its entire space.

Add a septarian sphere or cube to sacred space as a focal point in ritual, for meditation, or for spiritual work. For meditation, hold a septarian cube or sphere, close your eyes, and breathe deeply. Focus on your intentions as the collective energies of all directions and elements flow from sides of the cube (or curves of the sphere), imparting grounding, healing, protective, and transformative properties.

Transformation: Pillow Stone

Septarian stone is exceptional for healing and transformation. Healing from a painful experience often leads to transformation. Once a cycle or relationship ends, moving forward, sometimes without closure, may be challenging. Septarian stone's visible cracks represent the physical, emotional, and spiritual growth that occurs during the healing process. By honoring the "cracks" within yourself (all past experiences, positive and negative), you move toward self-acceptance and deeper inner wisdom: true transformation.

Septarian pillows resemble inflated, puffy palm stones but are less common. Like palm stones, pillows are used during deep meditation as they fit in the palm of your hand. Perform this ritual to embrace change. Face south during each of the following steps.

In sacred space, light a dark red or crimson candle—votive size is fine. Ask (out loud or silently) for the element of fire and energy of the dragon to join you in your sacred space, doing no harm. Ask fire and the dragon to incinerate what no longer benefits you, doing no harm. Thank them for their purification and strength.

Meditate in a comfortable position, holding a septarian pillow in your hand. Give yourself permission to discard what no longer serves your best interests. When you finish meditating, bid fire and the dragon farewell. Extinguish the candle.

Close the sacred space.

Communication: Palm Stone

As its name suggests, this septarian stone should fit within the palm of your hand. Unlike the "puffed" pillow, palm stones are round and flat. They're also a favorite of mine, perhaps because they're easy to carry.

The palm stone may serve as a "worry stone" or accompany you in a pocket, handbag, or bookbag. (I kept three in a small bowl in my former office.) They enhance clarity, self-confidence, optimism, and stability, all of which benefit individual and group communication.

When traveling, the compact palm stone is a practical companion for peaceful meditation or ancestral or spirit guide communication.

Self-Confidence in Public Speaking: Palm Stone

Wear or carry septarian if public speaking challenges you, as septarian increases self-confidence. At its foundation, septarian helps calm nerves and reduce anxiety before public speaking events, which is a fear many people share. Regarding speaking to groups, septarian stone will amplify your ability to hold an audience's attention, keep them engaged, and impact them on a personal level (i.e., retain the information you presented). In this context, septaria will encourage you to speak naturally, professionally, and eloquently and to articulate your message clearly and directly, without alienating or offending your audience.

Healing a Broken Heart: Heart Stone

Both druzy and "puffed" (smooth, uncracked) septarian hearts are associated with peaceful and graceful change, stability, acceptance, and healing of emotional wounds (recent or past).

What represents a failed romance better than a cracked, stone-cold heart?

After a relationship ends, it's often difficult to release the past and move forward. Harder still is having faith that things will get better. In sacred space, meditate with a druzy heart, drawing strength from its cracks. If you're overwhelmed, keep an uncracked heart on your nightstand, your altar, or carried in a velvet pouch. Know you will heal, emerging stronger and wiser than before.

Septarian Stone Care

Cleanse septarian pieces after each use and twice per year, under lukewarm, running water. Let druzy pieces air dry.

To recharge each septarian stone after meditation or ritual use, use one of two methods. The first method is to surround the septarian piece with a group of clear quartz crystals overnight. Under moonlight is preferred, but not required. The second method is to leave the septarian piece in direct sunlight for three hours. Outside is preferred, but not required. After recharging, return the clean, dry stone to a safe place (cabinet or display stand).

Moon phases haven't been relevant in cleansing or recharging my septaria. However, determine what works best for you.

Display stands keep septaria out of reach of young children or athletic pets. Decorating sacred space with septaria between activities

is a personal decision; I display heavier, Bengal-proofed pieces year-round.

Dracarys!

Like most *Game of Thrones* fans, I wasn't thrilled with the ultimate fate of Daenerys Stormborn, Mother of Dragons. I eventually accepted it, like the post-pandemic world in which we live. This Mother of Bengals hasn't deluded herself into thinking that protector dragon Drogon would swoop down to avenge my old life and those who took it from me. Profound grief and loss are as real as the dark and terror-filled nights. We cope with tools we trust, be they dragon glass, alcohol, or therapy. Whether direwolf or Bengal, *A Song of Ice and Fire* or Sirius XM, dragon stone or concretion stone, I'm eternally grateful to a cracked, glittering egg that once upon a time shared its peaceful wisdom that led to self-acceptance. Embrace your flaws and stand out. Be a flame in the land of icicles.

We all have cracks. We can celebrate them openly, like "Sir" Brienne of Tarth, Knight, or hide them in the shadows, like family secrets within House Stark. The decision is yours.

After all, winter is coming.

The Threefold Bread

Charlie Rainbow Wolf

Wait, isn't that supposed to be "the threefold braid"? In this case, they're one and the same. When a threefold bread is made, using three different grains or three different herbal inclusions, magic is being woven into something to be consumed on the physical as well as the esoteric level.

Triads are popular in many schools of mystery. Christianity has the Holy Trinity, Nordic traditions have the Three Norns, shamanism has the three worlds, the triquetra is a popular representation of the union of three, the threefold braid is a traditional pattern in Aran fisherman knitting, and there are the three faces of the Mother and the Maiden and the Crone. The list is seemingly endless—but why three?

In numerology, the number three is a blend of the characteristics of one and two. One is singular, two is plural, and three blends that into a trine that reaches out in all directions. Three has some kind of stability; a three-legged stool will balance on its own; a one- or two-legged stool will not. In astrology, the trine—a 120 degree angle—is usually considered to be a favorable and positive aspect.

The Wheel, the Wheat, and the Why

I'm an avid bread baker and don't need any excuse to break out the yeast, but my favorite time—and to me the most symbolic time—for baking bread is between Lughnasadh and Samhain. These are the harvest festivals, and my penchant for them goes back to when I lived on a farm in Lincolnshire, watching the first of the grain being harvested in August and the last of the potatoes and autumn fruits being gathered in by the beginning of November. This is also the season of my birth, the time running up to the thinning of the veil, and when I feel like my soul has come home, at least for a while.

When it comes to grains, I like to make my threefold bread mean something as well as look interesting. I start with a rye flour dough; it adds a dark color and robust flavor. Rye is a sister to wheat, both being members of the Triticeae tribe. It is a feminine grain, aligned with Venus, and it brings the magic of love, fidelity, and self-control to the loaf. Rye does not have as much gluten in it as wheat, so I make it first, giving the dough extra time to rise and adding two tablespoons of vital wheat gluten to help it along.

While the rye dough is proving, I start the second dough made from whole wheat—and before today I've even grown the wheat and milled it on an old cast-iron mill with a flywheel. I was taught that wheat is the most sacred of the seven grains—it's certainly the most used grain in my kitchen! Like rye, it is feminine and aligned with Venus, and it brings the magic of abundance, prosperity, and rebirth. Whole wheat absorbs more water than all-purpose flour, which is worth noting when following the recipes; I add an extra two tablespoons or more. Because this is a whole grain, I also add the vital wheat gluten to this dough, just to ensure that it will rise. When baked, this produces a dark and grainy textured loaf, although lighter in color than the rye.

The third of my doughs for the threefold loaf is made from unbleached bread flour. This is wheat, but it has had the germ and the bran removed. This is the basis for much commercial bread—in fact, the whole wheat flour sold in stores is this flour, with the bran and germ added back into it! Because it is from the same grain as whole wheat (usually hard red winter wheat berries), it has the same magical properties.

The Recipe

Bread is not something that can be rushed. When I make a threefold braided loaf, I give myself a day to do it. That way I know I can proceed at the bread's sense of timing rather than my own. The speed at which the bread rises and proves depends on many factors, including temperature and humidity. The loaves go a lot faster at Lughnasadh than they do at Samhain!

This recipe yields one large loaf, about twenty to twenty-four slices, or twelve to sixteen doorsteps if it's sliced my way!

The Basic Bread Recipe
1¼ cups warm water
1 tablespoon sugar
1 teaspoon salt
4 cups bread flour
1 teaspoon active dried yeast (or 1 small packet)

Place the flour in a large heavy mixing bowl (I prefer ceramic or glass to plastic and use my mum's old yellow Pyrex bowl). Measure

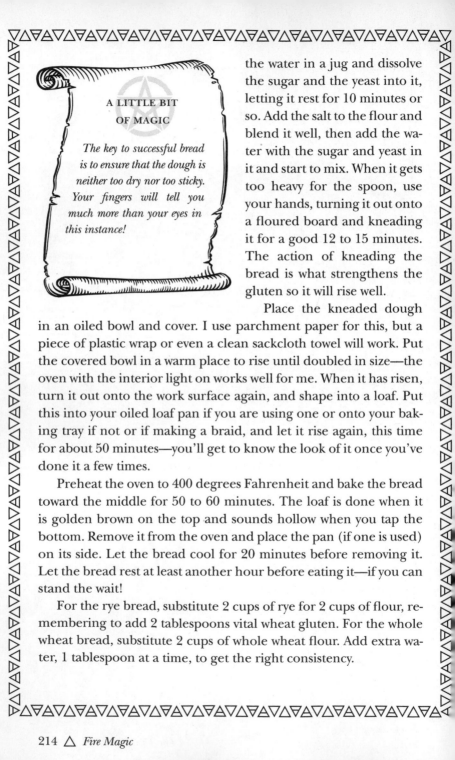

A LITTLE BIT OF MAGIC

The key to successful bread is to ensure that the dough is neither too dry nor too sticky. Your fingers will tell you much more than your eyes in this instance!

the water in a jug and dissolve the sugar and the yeast into it, letting it rest for 10 minutes or so. Add the salt to the flour and blend it well, then add the water with the sugar and yeast in it and start to mix. When it gets too heavy for the spoon, use your hands, turning it out onto a floured board and kneading it for a good 12 to 15 minutes. The action of kneading the bread is what strengthens the gluten so it will rise well.

Place the kneaded dough in an oiled bowl and cover. I use parchment paper for this, but a piece of plastic wrap or even a clean sackcloth towel will work. Put the covered bowl in a warm place to rise until doubled in size—the oven with the interior light on works well for me. When it has risen, turn it out onto the work surface again, and shape into a loaf. Put this into your oiled loaf pan if you are using one or onto your baking tray if not or if making a braid, and let it rise again, this time for about 50 minutes—you'll get to know the look of it once you've done it a few times.

Preheat the oven to 400 degrees Fahrenheit and bake the bread toward the middle for 50 to 60 minutes. The loaf is done when it is golden brown on the top and sounds hollow when you tap the bottom. Remove it from the oven and place the pan (if one is used) on its side. Let the bread cool for 20 minutes before removing it. Let the bread rest at least another hour before eating it—if you can stand the wait!

For the rye bread, substitute 2 cups of rye for 2 cups of flour, remembering to add 2 tablespoons vital wheat gluten. For the whole wheat bread, substitute 2 cups of whole wheat flour. Add extra water, 1 tablespoon at a time, to get the right consistency.

The Braid

The key to a successful plait lies in having all the dough proved adequately and to have all the strands the same size. Roll the dough until it is an even width and approximately 24 to 30 inches in length. Start the braid by laying the three strips of different dough side by side. Weave one over the other in the usual way until the end is reached. Pinch the ends together, then tuck them under the loaf; now go back and to the same to the start. This way the ends are hidden, and the plait seems to be neverending from start to finish. To make this really stand out, brush a bit of milk or a mixture of beaten egg and water over the top; this gives the baked loaf a glossy finish, as well as helping the plaits stick together.

Bake the bread on a bread stone or cookie sheet as described in the basic bread recipe. I judge doneness by the all-purpose strand: if that looks golden brown and done, then I do the tap test (seeing if it sounds hollow). It is often hard to tell when the darker strands have been adequately baked just by looking at them.

Additions

If you don't want to go to the trouble of mixing three doughs and making a giant loaf, a threefold braid can still be made by dividing the bread dough after the first proving, and rolling the different strands in herbs before braiding. Some of my favorite herbs are the traditional sage, rosemary, and thyme, but others will add flavor and magical properties to the loaf, making it stand out for ceremony just as nicely as if the three different flours had been used.

Rosemary: Depending who you ask, rosemary is either masculine or feminine and associated with the Sun or the Moon! I liken it to the Moon and believe it to be feminine. It brings the magic of remembrance and purification to the loaf.

Sage: Sage has long been used as a healing and protection herb. It's one we regularly have in the garden here at the Keep. It is masculine, is associated with Jupiter, and brings the magic of abundance and wishes granted to the loaf.

Thyme: Thyme is another feminine herb, associated with water and the planet Venus. It's believed that thyme enables communication with the fae and other earth spirits. It brings the magic of strength and courage to the loaf.

Conclusion

This is only the tip of the iceberg—well, the bread loaf. There are many other cereals that could be included, such as oats and rice. Other additions also make the bread interesting; we often add leftover mashed potatoes. The herbal seasonings and the magic they bring are numerous and unlimited in their potential combinations. The plait also works as a sweet loaf (think of raisins and brown sugar, with added nuts and cinnamon or nutmeg or cloves, for example). The main thing to remember is that this is a loaf that is symbolic as well as being "the staff of life." Bear that in mind and watch traditions come to life as the smell of freshly baked bread permeates the kitchen.

Further Reading

Alterman, Tabitha. *Whole Grain Baking Made Easy: Craft Delicious, Healthful Breads, Pastries, Desserts, and More.* Minneapolis, MN: Quarto, 2015.

Bateman, Michael, and Heather Maisner. *The Sunday Times Book of Real Bread.* Emmaus, PA: Rodale, 1982.

Forkish, Ken. *Flour Water Salt Yeast: The Fundamentals of Artisan Bread and Pizza.* Berkeley, CA: Ten Speed Press, 2012.

Luebberman, Mimi. *Bread Baking with Herbs: Breads, Muffins, Focaccia, and More.* New York: Prima Lifestyles, 1996.

Water Magic

The Mystical, Magical Frog

Blake Octavian Blair

The animal kingdom has some pretty captivating magical creatures, some whose magic is strong enough to be found across cultures. The mystical, magical amphibian that is the frog is one such creature. Frogs have entered our cultural folklore, magical and spiritual traditions, our fairy tales, and pop culture. From princes in disguise to purportedly ending droughts, frog lore pulls out all the stops. So let's hop right in!

By their very nature, frogs seem to perform a bit of natural magic, being the amphibious creatures that they are. As they traverse between the realms of land and water, it is no wonder that magic workers who work and travel between the worlds have a magical affinity for frogs. It is also no surprise that this makes them a wonderful ally to attune to the quality of adaptability. If we find ourselves needing a bit of assistance in adapting to different environments, perhaps a bit of time aligning ourselves with the energy of the frog could assist. The lessons of this creature can help us feel more at ease in varying conditions, which is useful for most persons as we navigate between our private home life, our work life, and oftentimes the homes of our family members, who may in fact have a very different lens on life than we do.

The frog is an ally of transformation. Born as the smallest of tadpoles and transforming through a series of phases into its fully realized adult frog self, it is the perfect symbol of the various progressions we go through in life along our own journeys. The frog's progression is literally termed *metamorphosis*. If that isn't empowering! Many of us would certainly describe our spiritual journey as an ongoing metamorphosis. Many magical people usually come to their path through quite a transformative process. This is especially true for people who were raised in a religious tradition very different from magical and earth-based paths. However, even once one is already on a magical path, magical traditions in themselves often set into motion a profound process of metamorphosis within the individual. This is a common experience among those in mystery traditions, and the frog itself is a mysterious creature indeed.

As frogs grow and undergo their transformation process, they shed their skins. Certain species of frog actually eat and consume the shed skins. This integration and processing of the old as we strive toward growth and the becoming of a new version of ourselves mirrors our process along our spiritual paths. Art created by the Olmec people of Mexico depicts the frog as a symbol of rebirth due to this fun fact, with the consumption of the skin viewed as mirroring the cycles of life, death, and rebirth.

When we visit the frog's presence in fairy tales, an extra step is often added to the process: the transformation to human form. This could potentially be viewed as one way that shamanic shape-shifting has made its way into popular culture by its inclusion into the fictional realm. This spiritual phenomenon is often coded into mythological stories and fairy tales. Of course, any shamanic practitioner knows that outwardly, a shape-shifting individual may not visually change form to onlookers. That does not mean the metaphysical merging and integration that true shape-shifting consists of isn't occurring. However, the fictional accounts of literal physical transformation help convey a story and better allow the message to unfold. One such tale is the classic fairy tale of "The Frog Prince." Over time as the story traveled, there have been many different versions. However, historians have traced its origin to a German version of the story from the thirteenth century. The general narrative of the tale involves a princess or young woman being courted by a charming frog. She then takes pity on the creature for making advances on an unobtainable human love interest and eventually grants the frog a kiss. This serves as the catalyst for the frog's transformation into a handsome human prince. History also provides many local variations of the story in which the genders are reversed and a young man plants a kiss onto a frog and is then presented with its transformation into a human princess. While it is unfortunate that most classical variations are limited to such heterosexual and cisgender pairings, the stories still offer the transformative allegory.

Cultural Significance

The frog has been seen as a harbinger of abundance and wealth in various forms in a number of cultures. This is certainly evident in the European fairy tale of "The Frog Prince," in which the frog in fact turns out to be royalty in disguise. However, even as we globetrot a bit, we see this link of the frog to abundance grow stronger. Chinese culture has a magical mythical frog figure referred to as either wealth-beckoning toad (*zhāocái chánchú*) or golden frog (*jīn chán*). Many of us are likely familiar with this creature and perhaps have seen statues of such spirits in Asian-owned businesses and grocery stores. Commonly, in the West it is referred to as the money frog. Lore says that if you're lucky enough, perhaps you just might spot this mythical creature perched outside the door of your home or business during a Full Moon, thus indicating an incoming windfall of wealth. The money frog is most commonly depicted as a very robust and squat bullfrog perched upon coins or ingots and holding a coin in its mouth. Also notably, it generally has three legs, two in the front and a single center hind leg. On a mythical creature, of course we aren't surprised to see featured in some form the magical number of three!

Why the money frog has but three legs is explained in one of the versions of the myth surrounding the creature's origins. Legend has it that the wife of one of the Eight Immortals (a group of figures from Chinese mythology) drank a potion that she had stolen from the Empress Mother of the West, Hsi Wang Mu. Well, as you can imagine, in mythology when someone commits a theft, especially of a potion, which they consume . . . something enchanted is about to happen. Oh, did I mention, she drank it on the Full Moon as well? One doesn't just go consuming potions on the Full Moon without repercussions! The stolen potion turned the woman into a frog. However, it is said that as an act of compassion, the gods allowed her to keep the tail of a tadpole at the hind end instead of the fully developed legs of an adult frog, thus leaving the magical frog with just three legs as depicted in its iconography.

Celtic traditions also hold the frog in high esteem. Evidence of the sacredness of water is abound in Celtic culture, and the frog is seen as representative of the water spirits. In fact, in Shropshire, England, the spirits of the well near an ancient healing spring would appear as frogs. In *The Druid Animal Oracle*, authors Philip and Stephanie Carr-Gomm write in their telling of the tale that the spirits of the well would appear as three frogs (there is that most magical number again!) and that the frogs were viewed as connected to the underworld. Therefore, the largest of the three frogs would be referred to as the Dark God. This bestows quite a large amount of power upon our amphibious friend!

The frog is also associated with purification and the bringing of rain. Some stories even tell of frog spirits bringing an end to droughts. Clearly, this is an extension of its healing associations.

With the frog's relationship to water, something so vital to life on our planet, it is not surprising the frog has far-reaching associations with abundance, healing, and fertility. To Scandinavians, Greeks, and Romans alike, the frog had associations with the uterus due to its presence surrounding the flooding of rivers, which are connected to water, life, and fertility. Of course, the frog's literal reproduction itself is an act of abundance. Although not all will survive to adulthood, a female frog can lay one to two thousand eggs for a male to fertilize!

Of course, the frog and its relative the toad have spent their fair share of time as maligned creatures as well. Their association as a magical companion, a familiar to Witches, and an associate of faeries and the misunderstanding of such relationships by outsiders is often the reason for their demonization. Some European traditions identify frogs as a sort of psychopomp, carrying dead children's souls. Due to its association with wise women, the fertile toad's reputation was a casualty of the witchcraft accusations and dangerous hysteria perpetrated by fearful patriarchal religious conservatives of bygone eras and so well documented in history. Many work to not let history repeat itself. Although, a fun fact: it is thought that the toxic secretions of toads might have been used in the fabled flying ointments of Witches. Friends, do not try that at home.

Abundance Magic with the Money Frog

Magical and earth-based spiritualities are lived spiritualities. Therefore, why don't we hop into this pool of frog wisdom and get our feet wet with some frog magic? Allow me to share with you a little spell that I worked in my college days to bring in a little more wealth and abundance with some frog magic! You will need to obtain a Chinese money frog like the ones discussed earlier in this article. You will also need a plate, dish, or saucer of some sort to set the frog on, with some space left around the frog. You can obtain money frogs from local Asian grocery stores; often they can be found for sale near the register (fitting!). If you live in a large city that has a Chinatown, head on over and surely a frog friend awaits. Otherwise, they can be found easily online. Now, you're ready for some frog magic.

You'll need to pick a location to set the spell up that both makes sense to you and fits your living situation. Upon your altar, dresser top, or a central location in your home is a good place to start. If you live in a dormitory-type situation with less privacy, you might like to do this inside a drawer. Put the money frog in the center of the dish on top of a $1 bill and a few coins. When I worked this spell during college, I'd add my loose pocket change to the

dish. Over time, the frog began to sit atop a pile of money. The frog is said to attract the energy of wealth, and like attracts like, so adding the money to his hoard puts the message into the ether. It's sympathetic magic. At the time I attended college, a fair number of transactions still required paper money and coins, not to mention coin-operated laundromats! Perhaps you still end up with physical change. If you don't as often, you can use other representative items, such as deposit slips from the bank or printed copies of a pay stub. The point is the frog sits atop a pile that represents accumulated wealth. At the end of a semester, I would then spend the money under the frog on something enjoyable. This too represented not just having enough to get by but also having a little extra. I can't tell you for certain how much this spell contributed to my financial situation, but I seemed to have enough money plus a little extra from time to time. Sympathetic magic plus a helpful animal spirit—it's worth a shot!

Journeying with the Frog

We've explored some of the various longstanding cultural associations and interpretations of the powers, energy, and lore surrounding frogs.

However, my shamanic and druidic traditions encourage practitioners to not simply take another's word for what an animal means or what their qualities are but rather to also find out for yourself. What is most important is what the frog (or other animal spirit) means to you. As you likely have guessed, I'm going to suggest that you do the same. I find one of the best ways to do this is to seek the frog spirit out in an altered state of consciousness. The two methods I recommend are shamanic journeying via sonic driving and meditation. Sonic driving is the use of repetitive rhythmic sound to enter an altered state such as in the shamanic drum journey. Instructional resources on the shamanic drum journey are widely available.

When framing your question for the spirits and your goal prior to embarking on the journey, center it around finding a frog spirit and asking it how it can help you and how you should work with it. Entering a meditative state via your favorite form of meditation is another accessible method for encountering the spirit of the frog, inquiring similarly, as mentioned, how and when to work with frog as an ally. Be sure to journal your findings and move forth accordingly if you wish to build a relationship with the frog as a helping spirit.

The frog is a powerhouse of magic: revered, misunderstood, a psychopomp of departed souls, and a symbol of rebirth and fertile abundance. I hope this little tour through frog lore has given you a leg up on this creature's mystical nature so that you can get a jumpstart on leaping in to working with these creatures!

Resources

Brown, Paul. "Specieswatch: The Common Frog." *The Guardian*, March 23, 2014. https://www.theguardian.com/environment/2014/mar/23/specieswatch-frog-spawn-tadpoles-ponds-gardens.

Carr-Gomm, Philip, and Stephanie Carr-Gomm. *The Druid Animal Oracle: Working with the Sacred Animals of the Druid Tradition.* New York: Simon & Schuster, 1994.

Illes, Judika. *The Element Encyclopedia of Witchcraft: The Complete A—Z for the Entire Magical World.* London: Harper Element, 2005.

Four Magical Waters for Power and Healing

Melissa Tipton

Water is a symbol of fluidity and adaptability, and in keeping with its shape-shifting nature, it can be deeply healing and magically useful in a variety of circumstances. The following meditation technique is designed to help you connect with the energy of water in a way that might be quite different from what you're used to, and you'll learn how to discern which type of magical water is most suitable for specific aims. We'll start with the basic meditation, and then we'll discuss the various waters and their unique properties.

You'll want to choose a place where you can sit undisturbed for fifteen minutes, and optionally, you can introduce a physical water element by turning on an indoor fountain if you have one or simply filling a pretty dish with water. Close your eyes and bring your awareness to your body. Do a gentle scan from head to toe. No need to change or fix anything; you're simply giving each area of your body a little love and attention. Then, bring your awareness to your breath. Again, without forcing or changing, simply be present with your breath and let this focus help you find more calm and inner repose.

Conjure a blank screen or empty room in your mind. This is simply a clean slate upon which you can project anything you need. Then, call up the image of a door on the screen or in the room. It might be an ornate metal door or a simple wooden plank; let it arise organically. Next, draw or simply see a symbol of water on the door, a triangle with a downward-facing point:

You might color it blue or even see animated waves inside the triangle. This is your doorway to the healing realm of water.

Each time you use this technique, you have the option of setting an intention to visit a specific type of water (more on those to come), or you can ask to visit the form of water that is correct and good for you at this time. Once you have your intention in mind, knock on the door three times and then enter, closing the door behind you. Take as much time as you need getting your bearings, and then seek out the water source. Sometimes this will be immediately apparent (e.g., you'll be standing on the shoreline), while other times you may have to travel through the landscape a bit to find the water. Keep your intention in mind (e.g., "I seek the healing River") as you search, and trust that you will find precisely what you need, even if it's not always what you expect.

When you reach the water, there are a number of ways to interact, and we'll cover a variety of possibilities when we discuss the unique types, but know that you can always follow your intuition and ask the water directly for guidance. For example, if you entered the meditation with a sense of overwhelm, as you're standing on the edge of the Ocean, you might receive the intuitive guidance that you need to pile your burdens on a raft and let it wash out to sea. Do so! If you ever feel stuck, you can always rely on the prompts outlined in this article.

When the experience feels complete, thank the water and any other beings who appeared to help, if applicable, and exit the way you returned, closing the water door behind you and allowing it to fade from the screen or room of your mind.

All forms of water share some common qualities. For starters, they're powerful gateways to the unconscious, meaning they can help you access parts of yourself that might otherwise remain hidden from conscious awareness, parts that may be seeking expression in your life and hold the power to ignite great satisfaction and creative passion if given an outlet to do so. Interaction with the unconscious also introduces us to new ideas and creative possibilities, which can be anything from the vision of a new painting to a way of phrasing something you've been struggling to express to your partner.

The unconscious is also our connection to Source. It's like an intimate portal to the Divine, and when we're overly caught up in the conscious mind, or ego, we can get disconnected from this Source and feel isolated and purposeless. Water is a conduit for plugging back into a larger sense of meaning and nourishment, giving us more energy and motivation in our day-to-day lives. And finally, water is cleansing and purifying. When we're feeling stuck or stagnant, it can help us dissolve blockages and get things moving again.

Now, we're going to cover four main types of water, each with specific strengths in terms of initiating healing, providing guidance, and improving your magical aims. Keep in mind that this is far from an exhaustive list, and by using this meditation technique, you

A Little Bit of Magic

USE THIS POTENT JOURNEY TECHNIQUE TO EXPLORE FOUR DIFFERENT MAGICAL WATERS, EACH WITH UNIQUE POWERS AND HEALING CAPABILITIES.

might well encounter different forms of water that are just what you need in your unique situation.

Ocean

The Ocean, in its vastness, is great for helping us put things into perspective, especially when we've built them up in our minds to overwhelming proportions. It's a bit like hitting the reset button by seeing that whatever you're experiencing, no matter how big, is still a drop in the immense cosmic Ocean of shared human experience. Guaranteed, no matter how uniquely specific your situation, you're not alone. Many (*many*) others have experienced—and survived—similar experiences, and you can too. For this reason, the Ocean is also great when you're feeling isolated and alone. It can help you tap into the beautiful web of interconnection of which you are always a part.

This theme of interconnection makes the Ocean ideal for shifting from an overly zoomed-in view to a larger perspective, which can be useful if you need to uncover new options, discern common threads, put yourself in another's shoes, or otherwise step out of your habitual way of approaching something and experiment with a different tack.

Generally, the Ocean imparts a sense of expansion and liberation, making it a wonderful ally when you feel stuck in a rut or constrained by seemingly insurmountable factors, and a sense of connection, bringing comfort and healing when you're feeling alone.

Some possible ways of interacting with the Ocean include releasing things into the water, diving deep in search of insights (perhaps in the form of an animal, mermaid, or other water-loving being), floating on the surface and feeling fully supported and part of something bigger than yourself, or standing at the shoreline to receive guidance when transitioning from one thing to another.

River

The River is all about movement, and it's a useful ally when you're feeling stuck and need to shake things up or when you're preparing to transition from A to B and could use some momentum and guidance. Rivers can be fast or slow moving, so you can choose to work at a watery pace that feels best for your unique situation; although, keep in mind that if you've been dragging your feet on something that's important to your growth, your inner wisdom might challenge you with a raging river of energy and possibility to help you break out of your comfort zone.

The theme of movement can be approached in different ways depending on your goals. If you're feeling blocked, you can ask for insights at the riverbank, uncover what it is you need to release, and then set that energy free into the water. If you have a goal—for example, you want to apply at three new companies by the end of the month—you can see yourself in a boat, launching from the present moment, and traveling, unobstructed, to your desired outcome by visualizing yourself emailing your résumé, nailing the interviews, and happily accepting your dream job as you move down the River, aided by the momentum of the current. This can be easily adapted for inner shifts as well, such as changing your mindset from trapped and pessimistic to inspired and motivated. Swim or boat from one experience to the next, allowing the water to facilitate your transition.

Generally, the River imparts a sense of progress and change, making it wonderful for situations that move through a series of steps, as well as a sense of clearing, bringing release and unburdening from unnecessary baggage.

Some possible ways of interacting with the River include releasing things into the water, traveling from place to place with the power of the current, noticing changes in the water and along the riverbanks as you progress from A to B (this gives you symbolic insights as to what you might expect along your journey), and getting a rush of energy and motivation by standing or swimming in the current.

Woodland Pond

The Woodland Pond is about nourishment and stages of growth, and it's a great place to visit for longer-term projects that require a sustainment of energy and effort. For example, if you're launching a new business, you can go to the Woodland Pond for initial ideas and guiding structure and then return on a regular basis to see how the water and landscape have changed, providing you with ever-evolving insights relevant to your project.

You might see a turtle at the water's edge, and by asking for messages, you learn that now is a phase when it pays to be methodical and take your time, even though you're wanting to charge full speed ahead. You go back in a couple of weeks, and this time a fox appears, advising you to trust your intuition and reach out to that intellectual property lawyer you were on the fence about. Alternatively, you might gaze into the water's mirror-like surface and receive messages from your reflection.

In addition to guidance, the Woodland Pond can serve as a source of nourishment, whether you're just starting a project or magical working, or you're midway and in need of a recharge. Just as the water sustains the plants and animals of the woods, you too can visit this safe haven to build up your energy stores, clear your mind, and help you stay the course.

Generally, the Woodland Pond imparts a sense of sanctuary and support, making it an ideal place to visit repeatedly when you need

a calming, helpful presence in your life. It can foster inner quiet when your monkey mind is achatter and leave you feeling more grounded and focused.

Ways of interacting with the Woodland Pond include meeting plant, animal, faery, and other guides; dialoguing with your reflection to expand self-awareness and increase partnership between your inner aspects; noting alterations in the inhabitants, seasons, and landscape features in recurring visits, which offer symbolic indicators of change; and releasing offerings into the water as thanks to guides, deities, and other benevolent forces in your life.

Cave-Fed Spring

The Cave-Fed Spring is all about finding deeper purpose and seeing underlying connections. While all forms of water help you dialogue with the unconscious, the Cave-Fed Spring is particularly well suited to initiating bubblings up from the more remote corners of your psyche. If you notice you're caught in an unhelpful pattern, such as unsatisfying relationship dynamics or frustration around food, the Cave-Fed Spring can aid in identifying what's fueling the pattern and how you can heal.

This is also a place that carries a sense of reverence and profound sacredness, and as such, it's useful to visit when you're feeling a little devoid of these energies. Perhaps you're burned out at work or you feel like you've been going through the motions with your spiritual practice. Traveling to the Cave-Fed Spring with the intention of renewing your connection to the things that truly feed you can be a wonderful way to feel more vibrant and purposeful again. While you can certainly do this at any of the Waters, I find the Cave-Fed Spring to be an especially magical spot for doing inner rituals, and within the meditation, I might visualize lighting candles, call upon guides and deities, cast a spell, and so on.

The Cave-Fed Spring imparts a feeling of devotion and sacred meaning, perfect for reviving lackluster practices and helping you reconnect with your passion and purpose. It also supports you in understanding underlying causes so you can heal at the root rather than playing whack-a-mole with symptoms.

Ways of interacting with the Cave-Fed Spring include holding an inner ritual near or in the water; requesting healing or guidance and drinking from the Spring; asking to see underlying patterns in your situation and the advised actions for change, then gazing into the water or swimming below the surface, following underwater passageways to your deepest inner chambers; and baptizing yourself with a submersion in the Spring, aligning yourself with the intention of your choosing.

• • • ☽ • • •

This meditation practice is meant to connect you with inner resources that, in the hustle and bustle of daily life, can be all too easy to overlook. You possess vast stores of strength, wisdom, and healing energy, and by working with the magic of water, you can channel these forces into your life to improve your problem solving and decision making, relationships, physical and mental health, and the success of your magical workings, among other things. By partnering with water, you will feel more in tune with the unconscious, which is the source of your intuition and creativity, and your magic—and your life—will be imbued with more fluidity, resilience, and flow.

Ritual Madness:
Communing with Dionysus

Charlynn Walls

Viticulture is a staple industry in the area where I live. Wineries abound and vineyards can be glimpsed while driving through the countryside. Families gather, celebrate milestones, and just enjoy being together. They are places of laughter, celebrations, and festivities.

The art of winemaking spans the seasons, from planting new vines, tending to the grapes, and to the harvest when the grapes are gathered. From there the grapes are pressed and made into wine. It is understandable that Dionysus, the god of the vine and wine, is often honored by those who practice winemaking through the region and around the world. He is also one who is honored by those who are seeking unique spiritual experiences.

Working with the God of the Vine

Dionysus is most often associated with wine and ecstasy, having given the gift of wine to humankind. He showed them how to grow the vines, how to manage them, and what to do with the fruit once harvested. However, Dionysus is also the god known for fruitfulness and vegetation. Through him the cultivation of the vines and good crops were ensured.

Even today there are wineries that use a biodynamic approach that embraces sustainability. It combines organic farming practices with the lunar calendar for planting, pruning, and harvesting (Denig 2018). These types of practices embrace the elements and set specific times for the care of the vineyard. Many of these now "modern" practices have long been used but are seeing a resurgence.

From the cultivation of the vines through the fermentation process, the life cycle of the plant was extremely important to those who followed Dionysus, as it was a physical embodiment of the deity on the mortal plane. Working closely with Dionysus would ensure the longevity of the vineyard and good harvests.

Harvest

Harvest comes in the fall in Missouri, where I live. From August through October, grapes are harvested and sent off for processing at various local wineries. Growing up, I often stayed with my grandparents, who rented a home surrounded by vineyards. As kids we would run through the rows and get lost in them. We all pitched in at harvest time. There were harvesting

machines, but to ensure that the bunches were not bruised, we would cut and pick them by hand.

Harvest festivals abound in the area as well. We always had a Grape and Fall Festival in our area. There were typical fair activities, such as a pageant, rides, and food. However, we also had a grape stomp, wine garden, and prizes for grape products like jellies, pies, wreaths, and more. Being able to celebrate the harvest is a community-building experience and sets the tone for the coming winter months.

Often during harvest, a libation made from the harvested grapes was poured back into the vineyard. This symbolized the cycle of life, death, and rebirth as everything had now come full circle. The libation would also be made with thanks to the god of the vine.

A simple devotion that could be used for this is as follows:

Oh, Dionysus, god of the vine. The fruit has ripened, the harvest is plentiful, and we give thanks. From what once was, we let it now return to nourish the soil and continue the cycle. Let this wine continue to provide us blessings as the seasons continue to turn.

At this point, pour some of the juice from the grapes or wine back into the ground.

Ritual Madness

The Dionysian mysteries played out as ritual madness and were a way to connect more deeply to deity. We may not know all the details, as they have been lost to time. However, they were typically associated with inducing an altered state of mind. Therefore, many of the followers of Dionysus were thought to be mad or drunk, as wine was a part of their rites.

There are many ways to induce an altered state, including drinking wine. It was thought that by drinking wine, one was taking the god Dionysus directly into oneself. In a way, it is similar to the rite of Drawing Down the Moon, as you draw down the goddess into yourself. Other ways that you can induce an altered state are through music or dance.

There are a couple of times when I witnessed or experienced an altered state during ritual that immediately come to mind. At one of my first festivals, we were preparing to be led to the ritual area. The participants all started off quite a distance out. The drumming started off in the distance and became a beckoning call. As we moved to the ritual space, we all danced our way there. It was intoxicating. The rhythm was hypnotic and even though rain started to fall, I never became wet during the ritual. It was like the energy of those gathered created a barrier, and it is a ritual I will never forget being a part of. It was truly a moving experience and was one of the most powerful rituals I had been involved in at the time.

In another ritual, I participated as a watcher. I would stay on the perimeter of the circle, close enough to step in should someone need me to help them ground when they started to come out of the ritual. The rite called for the participants to drink an elixir. The contents were not made privy to anyone and could have been anything from wine to water, though the organizer checked for allergies and possible drug interactions beforehand. However, the act of consuming the liquid helped the participants let go and become disinhibited. They were able to step outside of themselves and contact their spirit animals and learn from them. The changes the participants exhibited were incredible. They moved differently and acted differently. They were able to interact with one another, and when they were ready, the watchers would help them ground and step out of their trance state.

Both instances were ecstatic spiritual experiences that had profound impacts on the participants. That is what ritual madness is truly about.

Modern Ritual to Honor Dionysus

Gather all the tools you need prior to beginning your ritual. Items for the altar could include candles for the quarters, grapes, grapevines, pinecones, and a container of water. Also include some grape juice or wine and crackers or cake as an offering later in the ritual. You may want a small notebook or your Book of Shadows to write your experiences in after your ritual. You may also want a drum or a recording of some drumming that could be turned on during ritual.

The ritual should begin near dusk and run into the evening, as Dionysus enjoys merriment and a festival atmosphere. Adding some fairy lights around the ritual area would also add to the atmosphere.

This ritual can be done on your own or with others. It can be done inside or outside as weather permits. You should make sure that you have plenty of room to move within the circle, as you will be moving to the drumming or music that you chose for this ritual.

Prepare your ritual space and cleanse the area. There are a variety of ways to cleanse the area, and you can use any that works best for you. One suggestion that works well and is appropriate is the use of a bundled grapevine to asperge blessed or charged water. It is also a suitable alternative if you are unable to use something like sage because of an allergy, and it is what we will use in this ritual.

To begin, you will want to set up your altar area. Place the quarter candles in their corresponding directions. Put your notebook or Book of Shadows on the altar as well. Set your water near the bundle of grapevines for easy retrieval. You can include decorative items like grapes, grapevines, or a small wreath. You can include pinecones as well, as they are reminiscent of a thyrsus wand, which is made with a fennel stalk and a pinecone.

Bless the water before beginning. Hold your hands over the water and close your eyes. Feel the energy build up through your core, and as you feel it peak, say,

Water is life. From it comes all things. May the energy within sustain and cleanse. Blessed be!

Cast your circle by calling each quarter. As you move to each quarter, take the grapevine bundle, dip it into the blessed water, and sprinkle the water to create the circle.

Calling the Quarters

North: I call to the powers of the north, the guardians of the earth. Bless us with your grounding influences as we reach toward communion with the god. We welcome you to our circle!

East: I call to the powers of the east, the guardians of air. Bless us with the wind in our hair as we dance ecstatically. We welcome you to our circle!

South: I call to the powers of the south, the guardians of fire. Bless us with warmth as we move and dance with divinity. We welcome you to our circle!

West: I call to the powers of the west, the guardians of water. Bless us with cool waters to temper our emotions. We welcome you to our circle!

Invocation

Start your ritual music at this time, whether that is from you drumming to get into the right frame of mind or if you play a recording of drumming or some other music that speaks to you. Now will be the time to reach out directly to Dionysus and ask him to enlighten you with an ecstatic spiritual experience. You will be trying to get into a trancelike state so that you can be receptive to what Dionysus wants to share with you.

Pick up your glass of wine or juice and take a drink. Dionysus is the god of wine, and you are taking him into you so that
he can provide you "madness," or a unique way of seeing. Say,

*As I drink of you, Dionysus, grant me your presence so that I can be
moved. Let my mind and body be free to receive your messages this day.*

Set aside your cup. Get up and move. Feel the rhythm inside
of you. Lose yourself in the music and feel the weight of the
day slip off you as you open yourself up. Continue to move and

know that the elements and Dionysus are there dancing with you. Open yourself up to the messages as you dance in joy. Continue to do so until you need to rest, and then lie on the ground to help restore yourself before continuing. Be aware of what you are seeing and feeling. You may want to note these things after coming out of the trance, as not all messages given by deity are immediately clear.

Cakes and Ale

This is a time to renew your strength from the ecstatic, trance-like dancing and to acknowledge your honored guest. You should take a bit of the crackers or cake and drop it onto the ground near the altar or, if inside, drop it on a dish to be later taken outside, saying,

Dionysus, thank you for your presence. Your insight has been a blessing.

Next, take some of the wine or juice and pour the drink onto the ground or into the dish, saying,

This elixir has given me insight and visions that will sustain me. Thank you, Dionysus.

Once you have presented the cakes and ale to your guests, you can take some for yourself. Take the time you need to restore yourself and absorb what you learned during your trance before closing out the circle. This is an excellent time to make any notes on your observances during the ritual.

Releasing the Quarters

West: Powers of the west, I thank you for your time and tempering my emotions, keeping them in check. Hail and farewell!

South: Powers of the south, I thank you for your time and your subtle warmth while we communed. Hail and farewell!

East: Powers of the east, I thank you for your time and your gentle winds that danced with us. Hail and farewell!

North: Powers of the north, I thank you for your time and your strength to keep me grounded. Hail and farewell!

Closing the Circle

Take a moment to contemplate the rite and the visions that Dionysus gifted you with. Take time to again thank him and all who gathered with you. End by saying,

The circle is now open. Hail and farewell to you all!

Conclusions

As spiritual seekers, we are always hoping to deepen our awareness or connection to the Divine. Working with any deity takes a certain amount of trust. When you are taking a deity into yourself, there is also some risk. However, if you go in with an open mind and heart, it can be a life-changing experience. Dionysus invites us to let go of our inhibitions to see beyond what can sometimes be a stagnant worldview. He allows us to see what can be if we only let go and trust. Sometimes a little madness can be a good thing!

Resource

Denig, Vicki. "Biodynamic Wine, Explained." VinePair. July 5, 2018. https://vinepair.com/articles/biodynamic-wine-explained/.

New Moon Magic in the Houses of Your Birth Chart

Danielle Blackwood

I n my work as a professional astrologer, one of the most common questions I'm asked on social media is how to find what house a given New Moon will fall into for someone. Every month the New Moon occurs in a different house in your birth chart, highlighting a particular life area and showing you the most fruitful ground to set new intentions that will develop over the next six months, when the Full Moon occurs in the same sign. You will need a copy of your birth chart to find where each month's New Moon will occur for you. You can either consult an astrologer or obtain your chart in one of the many online chart generators.

Consult an astrological day planner such as *Llewellyn's Astrological Pocket Planner* to find out what degree and sign the next New Moon will be in. For example, the next New Moon may be at 7 degrees Libra. First, look at the outer circle of your chart and find the Libra glyph. The chart is read counterclockwise, beginning at the cusp of the first house (this is the rising sign, 9:00 if you were looking at a clock). The house (life area) you find 7 degrees of Libra is where this month's New Moon will occur for you. Remember that a birth chart is read counterclockwise, so when you're looking for that degree, that's the direction you want to be moving in.

The New Moon occurs when the Sun and the Moon are in the same astrological sign, between Earth and the Sun. At this time, the Sun, the Moon, and Earth are aligned, or *conjunct*. The Moon appears dark from our perspective here on Earth because the side that is facing away from us is the side illuminated by the Sun. The New Moon also rises and sets at the same time as the Sun, so it is submerged in the Sun's light and is invisible from our viewpoint. Although the night of the New Moon is dark, it's important to remember that although we can't see it, it begins waxing the moment it is new. Approximately one day after the New Moon, a sliver of a crescent can be seen in the night sky. The tides are at their most extreme at the New and Full Moons, referred to as a *king tide* or a *spring tide*. The New Moon signifies the beginning of a new lunar phase that will culminate at the Full Moon in two weeks' time, when the Sun and Moon are opposite of each other. Much the way the New Moon affects the ocean's tides, it also acts on the water table. Ground water rises, and seeds planted during the New Moon may absorb more water, which causes the seeds to swell, split open, and germinate. Gardening lore has it that seeds planted on a New Moon precipitates growth and produces sturdier plants. Aligning our energies and intent with the Moon's cycles can be a powerful catalyst for creating potent magic and bringing desired changes in our lives.

It's helpful to take into consideration both the sign the New Moon is in and what house it is landing in for you personally, so you can harness those energies for magical intent. Astrology and magic are inextricably entwined and have been used in conjunction for millennia. In the early modern period leading up to contemporary times, learned cunningfolk in the British Isles employed astrology in their everyday working magic with clients. Learning about the correspondences between astrology and magic will strengthen your practice and help you time your spells and workings for optimum results.

New Moon in the First House

This is the beginning of a brand-new personal cycle. Sow the seeds of your new intentions in the life areas of self, creative spark, and new beginnings. Create a ritual to mark the first steps toward a new chapter. Work magic to break new ground, set plans in motion, and heed the call to adventure. This is a time of growing self-awareness, enthusiasm, and self-actualization. You might feel a renewed sense of inspiration. Reactivate your inner spark, embark on an uncharted path, or unveil what you've been working on behind the scenes. Create spells to launch new projects, take the initiative, and be bold. This New Moon invites you to step into a position of leadership or take a stance.

New Moon in the Second House

Plant seeds today in the fertile earth of sacred sensuality, finances, and self-worth. Work magic to enhance your relationship with your body and commit to radical body acceptance. Give yourself permission to enjoy all your earthly senses and reclaim your right to pleasure on your own terms. Do an inventory of everything you appreciate about yourself to work spells for enhancing self-love and to cultivate tangible self-worth. Create a ritual to thank your body for all the pleasure it has brought you and all that it does on a daily basis. The second house is also aligned with manifesting, so work magic to move toward building financial security, attracting the right clients, and acquiring wealth that is aligned with your own values.

New Moon in the Third House

The most potent area to plant your seeds of intention is around learning and communication, both written and verbal. Now's the time to register for or plan to teach a course, webinar, workshop, or weekend retreat. Create spells that include chanting, writing, and weaving the magic of words. Pick up some fresh magical skills and knowledge. Work magic for networking and to get a message across. Here's your window to write that blog post, get cracking on social media, or update your website. Study, research, editing, and gathering information are highlighted. Connect with other Witches and exchange rituals, spells, and knowledge.

New Moon in the Fourth House

Plant your new seeds of intention in the life areas of family, home, and your sense of belonging. Work magic to make sure your foundation is sturdy and supportive and for emotional stability. Seek wisdom of older, more experienced Witches who can provide perspective.

Cast spells to find or create the perfect home. This is also a good time for emotional alchemy: turning lead into gold. Do a release ritual to let go of unhelpful patterns and apply healing balm to old wounds. Ancestral magic and connecting with traditional wisdom are beneficial now. You might feel pensive, melancholy, or nostalgic today. It's a good time to journal and dive deep for insight.

New Moon in the Fifth House

The most fertile ground to plant your seeds of intention is in the life areas connected to pleasure, play, romance, creativity, and self-expression. The fifth house is connected to our feeling of vitality, radiance, and life force and is also related to courtship and the feeling of falling in love. Work non-manipulative love spells and magic to connect with your creativity. Work magic to recharge your energy, tap into your vitality, boost your confidence, and reclaim your sovereignty. This New Moon is an opportunity to create a ritual to bring your unique brand of self-expression into the world. Make your life an extension of your magic.

New Moon in the Sixth House

It's time to plant seeds in the life areas of wellness, work, organization, and everyday life. Self-care rituals and magic focused on health and wellness are potent now. Set new intentions around your diet, lifestyle, and well-being. Today is the perfect opportunity to go on a cleanse, detox, and reset your body, mind, or spirit. Holistic healing, natural remedies, herbs, acupuncture, massage, TCM, and naturopathic medicine are sixth-house themes to lean into today. The sixth house is about creating rituals for everyday life. Use the energy of this New Moon to streamline your schedule, to make plans and lists, and to sift, sort, declutter, and organize your home and altar.

New Moon in the Seventh House

It's time to plant your seeds of intent around partnerships, relationships, balance, and beauty. Partner with other Witches for a mutually beneficial exchange of energy. Cast spells for diplomacy and peace. The seventh house is also about beauty, the arts, and sacred adornment. Create an altar to Aphrodite and revaluate how you show up in the world. Love spells to find the right partner or to deepen a commitment are beneficial now. Give yourself space and time to paint, dance, write, and work magic through art. Devote yourself to bringing more beauty and balance into your life in every aspect. Create a magically charged vision board of the kind of beauty you want more of in your life.

New Moon in the Eighth House

It's time to plant your seeds of intent around profound personal transformation. This New Moon can be a turning point, so crossroads magic is potent today. Shed old skins and shine a light on your deepest wounds and fears—now is the time for shadow work. Look closely at your emotional bonds with others. Do you find yourself giving your power away? Work magic for taking back your power, creating healthy boundaries and protection. Sex magic can be powerful today. Rituals for cord cutting, closure, grief, and rebirth are more potent during this New Moon. This is also an auspicious time to begin or deepen a study of magick, Witchcraft, shamanism, and other "hidden" paths to wisdom.

New Moon in the Ninth House

Today is the perfect time to plant new seeds of intention around the search for meaning, adventure, and wisdom. Explore new horizons and plan a pilgrimage to one of the world's sacred places. If you can't travel right now, get online and learn about somewhere you've always wanted to go. Respectfully explore spirituality, belief systems, and cultures that you are not familiar with. Work magic to hone your vision, begin your quest, and set out on the archetypal hero's journey. Refill your well and trust serendipity. Try to find time to be in nature today and connect with the magic of the wild world. Magic and ritual for reclaiming your inner wild can be powerful now.

New Moon in the Tenth House

The most fruitful ground to plant your new seeds of intention today is around your life's work and vocation. What are you willing to commit to? Use this energy to clarify your professional goals and take conscious steps toward manifesting them. Rituals to commit to your life's calling and reclaim your inner authority are beneficial now. If you're ready, cast spells to take on a position of leadership and more responsibility. You could become a mentor or find a mentor now. Re-evaluate your public image, website, and social media presence. This is the house connected to achievement, accomplishment, and milestones, but not without dedication, commitment, and a willingness to get out of your own way and do the work.

New Moon in the Eleventh House

Plant your seeds of intent around hopes, dreams, community, and social justice. Get ready for a paradigm shift. Step outside your comfort zone and connect with like-minded others for a meaningful cause. Work magic in groups, in covens, and for the collective. Cast spells for resistance and fighting all forms of oppression. The eleventh house is associated with game plans, friendships, and gathering for a common purpose. Reclaim your inspiration, reconsider where you are headed, look at the big picture, and ask yourself whether your goals and friendships are still in alignment with who you're becoming. Now is the time to wake up to your higher purpose and step into true authenticity.

New Moon in the Twelfth House

It's time to plant the seeds for a deep dive into the Mysteries. Set magical intention around your dreams, the collective unconscious, the numinous, and the intuitive realm. Witnessing the stories of your ancestors can begin to illuminate and heal old patterns and intersections of privilege and oppression. This is the perfect time to get a reading or delve into your own study of an intuitive practice, such as tarot or astrology. Plan a spiritual retreat, begin a meditation practice, or start a dream journal. Guided journeys and pathworkings are a powerful doorway to self-knowledge now. Work magic through writing, art, and other creative exploration. Create a closure ritual, and hold with compassion and nonjudgment the parts of you that need healing.

Spells of Restoration

Diana Rajchel

Illnesses, loss, death, pain, trauma—they all happen. Times of crisis can absorb us to the point that we no longer know what to do with ourselves when the emergencies finally stop. Facing this subconscious vacuum, we may hunt for a fresh crisis, or more emergencies somehow find their way to us no matter how often we scream, "Give me a break!" It's necessary, at times, to grab that pause in the storm to signal to the spiritual world that it's time to stop, now. Otherwise, the energy out there may not recognize that you mean it—you need the rest. Spells of restoration come in handy for that situation to help you create structure needed for recuperation from whatever life slammed at you.

As soon as you have anything that appears like a moment of calm or clarity, seize it. Turn off your phone and step away from all internet-connected devices. Ignore knocks on your door. Take that time to cleanse, ward, and re-establish personal protections. Open the path for any healing you need. The following rituals and practices prepare the way for restoration spells.

What to Expect from Restoration

Restoration brings back a sense of wholeness. It doesn't renew a relationship (reconciliation work is a different thing, burdened with consent complications). When it "takes," it brings a sense of grounded, connected calm. Ultimately, every restoration spell must be customized to the person who needs it.

This list of questions, meant for extended self-exploration, assists with that customization. Perform this self-examination through journaling, talking to a friend, or taking a physical accounting. While you may perform the later spells to the letter, you can set the intention of these spells to what you need to feel nourished and complete.

1. What have you lost?

Make a note of what you no longer have, physical and abstract. You might have had property stolen, or you may have lost a sense of trust, for example.

2. What changes are permanent as a result of the loss?

3. What do you need to feel whole again?

You can only regain a sense of completeness when you understand that your new wholeness differs from the old one.

4. What parts of you feel unbalanced?

Look for the parts of yourself that you stopped feeding, including hobbies and similar frivolities.

5. What do you need to feel nourished now?

Those frivolities matter. How can you get that sense of emotional fullness back? What activities can you engage in to help that?

Ingredients of Restoration

You thought through what you can restore and what you can't. Now gather and prepare ingredients for the rituals and spells necessary to return fully to yourself.

Restoration Oil Recipe

Soak rose leaves, rosemary, chaparral, rhodiola root, and ginger in a jar of olive oil for two weeks. At the end of the two weeks, strain the herbs, and discard, reserving the oil. Use the elixir to anoint spell tools such as candles and your body. You can also add a few drops to your shampoo if you want cumulative results.

Coins

Part of restoration involves going to Spirit and asking to have pieces of yourself returned. Even though those pieces belonged to you, the spirit world has a "finders keepers" mentality. Consequently, give something in exchange for what you take back. Mercury dimes, shiny pennies, modern dimes, and dollar coins work well. This exchange—a coin at the crossroads for a return of self—functions as a self-contained spell or as part of a larger, more complex ritual.

Baths

Ritual baths don't require immersion. For a restoration practice, bathe yourself in or apply a scrub made from Epsom salt, lemongrass, rosemary, coffee, and, if available, a little teasel leaf. Continue the self-cleansing ritual until you feel you completed all necessary spells of restoration.

Spells of Restoration

Now that you have ingredients and rituals prepared, you can move on to the spells most appropriate to what you want restored.

To Restore a Sense of Safety

Before beginning this spell, resolve for yourself what safety means to you. With that fixed in your mind, proceed with the working.

You will need:

Restoration Oil
Place for quiet reflection
Miniature lock and key, with a small chain that can fit around
    your wrist

First, take a ritual bath to clear random energies. After you dry, before you dress, anoint the crown of your head, your lips, your heart, the back of each hand, your belly, and the arch of each foot with restoration oil. When finished, stand with your legs and arms apart, Vitruvian-man style. Invite the Sun and stars to enter you until, in your mind's eye, you see yourself glowing from the inside out.

When you feel filled with that light, pick up the lock and chain. Wrap the chain around your nondominant hand. Slip the lock through the chain and snap shut. Wear the charm for a week to signify locking in that glowing repair. At the end of the week, unlock it and save it for future reinforcements of this spell.

To Restore Peace to a Home
Sometimes after you cleanse the home and establish wards, it still feels frayed. While some peace only happens after repairing relationships, resetting the ambient vibe to mellow can help.

You will need:
Restoration Oil
Blue 7-day candle
Bowl
Water
Orange peel
Stick of cinnamon
Vanilla bean

Rub a small amount of Restoration Oil on the wick of the candle and place it in the bowl. Fill the bowl with 1 inch of water for fire safety. Add the orange peel, cinnamon, and vanilla to the water. Light the candle, and if appropriate to your spirituality, request Psyche, archangel Gabriel, or an ancestor you have a relationship with to expand peace through the house. Imagine that energy evaporating from the bowl of water. Burn the candle for 1 hour a day until the wax is completely gone.

To Restore Peace to a Neighborhood
If your neighborhood has had frequent disturbances, this spell restores equanimity in the community. Gather the materials for the candle spell to restore peace to a home. Grab a marker. On the candle, write the name of the major intersections in your neighborhood. Add a little dirt from those cross streets, leaving a penny at each crossroads as payment for the energies. When the candle burns down completely, throw out the candle glass and reserve the water. Sprinkle the water in front of trouble spots and at the crossroads named on the candle.

To Restore Justice
Justice work differs from restoration but sometimes needs restoration spells beforehand to succeed. This spell restores the social structure that allows justice. It takes 3 to 7 days of spell sessions at a minimum because it requires contact with an assisting spirit.

Only perform this working outside, with adequate tools for putting out fires.

You will need:
Spirit (saint, deity, angel, daemon, etc.) associated with engineering or hard work, such as Hephaestus, Saint Patrick, Saint Joseph, Hestia, Aediculus, or Vishwakarma
Charcoal grill, safe for burning outdoors
Offering for the spirit
Pen

Paper
Bay leaves
Resin incense, something gum-based like frankincense
Liquid offering of thanks

First, establish a relationship with the spirit whose help you desire. Don't switch beings immediately if you don't feel like you got a response. Sometimes you have to let the entity turn you away a few times to prove that you're serious.

Open interaction by establishing a small altar, preferably outside near your grill. Give an offering appropriate to your chosen spirit. During this time, present a written petition asking for help in creating conditions that allow a path for the return of justice. Take the time to read it out loud, if possible. Much of this particular spell relies on the ancient Egyptian belief that smoke raised prayers and messages to the deities. Burn incense. Talk. Some may succumb to the temptation to burn a history book as a means of offering context.

Sit in front of the altar once a day. During these sessions, speak out loud, explaining what happened to undermine justice. Provide an offering to the spirit, speak its name and a prayer, and then assemble the petition, the bay leaves (for justice), and the resin incense (to repair gaps) on the grill and burn to ash. Allow to burn out, and then pour a liquid offering of thanks to your deity or spirit.

Allow 24 hours to elapse, and then commence with any justice work.

Try to be flexible and realistic in your expectations when you work these spells; recovery and restoration do not rush. You won't reverse time or get exactly your old self back—rather, you will get a new, recovered self. These spells help you muster a healthy enough version of yourself that you can do what you need to become a healed version of yourself.

Shadow Working with the Goddess Never Not Broken

Mickie Mueller

Yes, you read that right. It's a double negative and it's confusing for a reason: it's unsettling and makes you slow down, analyze, and question the meaning. That's the whole point. We humans are under pressure every day. Show me someone who hasn't experienced trauma at some point in their lives, and I'll scoff and remind you that the world is beautiful, magnificent, challenging, horrible, elating, devastating, uplifting, and terrifying. To think that we are required to always be in a state of being together, being happy, and emitting "good vibes only" all the time is unrealistic to the human condition. Through my own personal journey of shadow work and self-discovery, I recently stumbled upon a goddess named Akhilandeshwari (pronounced Ah-keel-lan-desh-vah-ree). Translated from the Sanskrit, her name is the "Goddess Never Not Broken." According to Shivali Bhammer, a writer for *Hinduism Today*, the Goddess Never Not Broken's name is translated as such: "*Akhila* means 'whole' or 'complete' but *akhilanda* means the double negative 'never not broken'; and *eshwari* comes from Ishwari, meaning the Supreme Ruler."

Wow! That means always broken, right? Are you picturing a goddess sobbing in the corner, devastated, unable to get up again? Guess again. This goddess rides down a river through the rapids of life on the back of a crocodile! Yes, she is "never not broken," but she is not a heap on the floor—she's a trauma and PTSD warrior! Yeah, I can say that: I'm in therapy for my own trauma and PTSD. I know a fellow traveler when I see them. The Goddess Never Not Broken exists in a constant state of flux, always falling apart and mending, using her own wounds to generate power, remaking herself, and

even embracing imperfection as a strength. I knew right away she was a goddess I wanted to get to know a little better.

Akhilandeshwari is a very old Vedic goddess. Some of her sacred imagery shows her as being literally in pieces, shattered like a broken piece of glass with beams of light streaming out of the edges. Armed with a trident, she stands or sits with a bewitching smile on the back of a fearsome crocodile that navigates through a rushing river. She is a goddess who helps us navigate through fear, trauma, grief, disasters, and transformation. She shines through the aftermath of all those things in life that can leave us feeling a little bit broken and whispers a simple message: "It's okay."

Goddess of Legend

To understand her better, we can look to her place of origin. She is often referred to as a incarnation of Parvati. Because she is also a Vedic goddess and very old, there are many stories, songs, ritual dance, and mantras about her. I'll share a few of my favorite with you.

Shivali Bhammer explains in *Hinduism Today* that Akhilandeshwari is the more formal name of Khodiyar Maa, which is more often used by the Gujarati people. Gujrat, India, is where we find this old story of this fearless goddess that goes back to 700 CE and is shared with travelers to Khodiyar Temple in Rajpara, Gujrat, India. The temple shares her origin on their website: Mamaniya Gadhv was a villager who was also best friends with the king, but the king's ministers were jealous and convinced the queen to keep Mamaniya out of the palace because he and his wife were childless. The heartbroken Mamaniya went to Shiva's temple to request Shiva grant him children. Shiva took him to meet Nagdev, king of the snakes, to see if he could help. Nagdev's seven daughters and one son told him to return home and make eight cradles. Soon eight snakes showed up and crawled into the cradles, transforming into eight human babies, seven daughters and one son. One daughter named Janbai performed several miracles as a baby. As a child, Janbai went into the sea and down to Naglock, the snake kingdom, to fetch the elixir of life to heal her brother from a deadly snake bite. She injured her foot on the sharp rocks and was rescued by a crocodile who gave her a ride. The word for a foot injury is *khodi*, so when they saw her heroically limping back with the cure, they called her Khodiyar Maa. According to Bhammer, this is the goddess who became more widely known as Akhilandeshwari, a more formal name for the Goddess Never Not Broken when her veneration spread from the region her story hails from.

There is another story about Akhilandeshwari in which all the raw power she manifested with was often misdirected, and her primordial anger and fear frightened the worshipers away from her temple, writes Naveen Sanagala of Hindupad. The philosopher Adi Shankara designed the *sri chakra,* also known as the *shri yantra,* which is a diagram of nine interlocking triangles and made the design into earrings. He pleaded with the goddess to wear them, allowing the raging energy to be transformed into a form of energy that was more productive. Transforming fear into creativity is another of Akhilandeshwari's powers.

In a beautiful Carnatic song asking for her protection, she is described as being "dark coloured," "the embodiment . . . of all arts," "resplendent . . . with pendulous curls," "a bestower of boons"; having "a smiling face"; and "rejoicing in the sound of musical instruments," translates Indian music blogger Suja.

Authenticity and Witchcraft

Shadow work is a concept first put forth by Carl Jung, but many Witches and magic workers have discovered that this very specific kind of self-introspection can help us harness our true power and potential. Part of shadow work is the kind of poking about the subconscious and looking at emotional triggers that is firmly in the wheelhouse of the Goddess Never Not Broken.

In modern society, we tend to hide our wounds. We paint a pretty picture on social media and even in person, allowing people to think we lead a perfect, shiny life. Maybe because others see these wounds as a sign of weakness, or perhaps that is just our perception of what others expect. I've noticed that many of us in spiritual communities—Pagans, Witches, Druids, and so on—believe that we must show a face of unwavering strength for others, but perhaps avoidance of our wounds is avoidance of our authentic selves. I've also noticed that many people who work with spiritual energy have either discovered their path as a coping mechanism for getting through tough times or have faced abuse from other people who don't understand their gifts. Why should we be ashamed of our wounds and hide them? That places blame on our wounds and ourselves and no one ever helped themselves this way. Akhilandeshwari reminds us that we have a choice in our states of brokenness to be a victim or a survivor. Does it help your broken parts to know that there is a Goddess Never Not Broken? If so, perhaps admitting to our own states of being "never not broken" will help us inspire others too.

You may hold fear of your wounds, afraid that acknowledging them equates to self-pity or weakness. That's something that society has taught us—"Don't cry," "Just rub some dirt on it; you'll be okay!" or the ever-damning "Just get over it; others have it worse than you!" But that is not how the mind or the spirit works. As magic users and Witches, we live outside of societal norms, so we can choose to discard those old outdated messages. We find inspiration for our magic in liminal spaces and states of mind, so let's find our deep power by embracing our liminal selves, our own never not broken-ness.

We can decide to look at wounds we've suffered without wallowing in suffering. Yes, it may hurt to look at these things, but when we do, we can reframe the initial wound and figure out a way to rebuild ourselves. Choosing to ignore our broken parts will not make them less broken. A broken vase swept under a rug will not mend itself. Look at it and grab the glue. So what if your mending isn't perfect or if it looks different when you're finished? It can still be beautiful and functional. Who cares if you can't put water and flowers in it anymore. Place a candle inside and see how beautifully the light shines through it! Don't hide the cracks—repair them using the Japanese art of *kintsugi* and fill the cracks with gold, turning it into art. So it won't hold its previous shape? Give it a new shape and create a beautiful mosaic. Don't give up, don't give in, reinvent! This is the power of being never not broken.

Our Witchcraft can grow so much stronger when we acknowledge our broken parts, scars, and wounds. We can stop saying, "When I'm healed, I can finally get a better job, fall in love, or climb a mountain." We can learn to put ourselves back together in the ways that we need to in order to accomplish those goals. The more often we pick our broken

A LITTLE BIT OF MAGIC

A great way to begin delving into shadow work is mirror gazing for five minutes every day using affirmations that resonate with you. Feel and accept whatever comes up for you and keep a journal.

selves up and put ourselves back together again, the less afraid we may be of breaking, and we develop resilience of spirit. We can choose to embody Akhilandeshwari and become never not broken—not defined by our broken parts, but stronger by acknowledging them and freer through reinvention. Akhilandeshwari does not teach us how to be broken, nor how to be healed, but to choose how we wish to frame both and truly live through reinvention.

The Lie of Attaining Static Wholeness

We think all we want to do is be whole, but being whole is a limited concept. Consider the avatar in a video game. At the beginning and the end of the game, you're whole. Either you're a clean slate, blinking on a blank background waiting to begin, or you've reached the achievement at the end of the game and the adventure is over. There's nothing to do now but take a bathroom break and grab a fresh bag of cheese curls. It's the rest of the game that's interesting and engaging, when you're learning and in a state of

flux. Your character takes hits and expends energy as you work to overcome the more difficult parts of the game, the bosses. Your character is constantly taking on damage but also healing; in this way, your video game avatar is also never not broken. It's during full play when the character is unlimited, reinventing itself with new skills, weapons, tools, and experience points. Never not broken means anything and everything is possible. Video games are designed this way because life is designed this way: we are never not broken, as we heal, shatter, mend, level up, and break a little bit again, but that makes us interesting, flexible, unlimited, and yes, human. There's a kind of freedom in it.

Playing a video game isn't the same as feeling the punches that life deals us. How can we learn to continually put ourselves back together again like Akhilandeshwari when that happens? First we have to admit that it happened at all, which can be harder than you think.

There's a well-known concept in metaphysics that when you can name a thing, you gain some power over it. So if you can't even acknowledge trauma that you've experienced or the resulting shadow part of yourself, that shadow works away at you in the background, quietly undermining your life, secretly steering your life from just beyond your perception. The actions you repeat can be self-destructive and not in your best interests. They hold you back. The lack of belief in your own power to manifest what you want—that's a shadow part of your psyche, born from past trauma. When you shine a light on it, look at it, name it, and acknowledge it, you can see that it's just like Akhilandeshwari and the crocodile in the river. Sure, it's got big teeth, and its nature is to drag you under the water and spin you around in the murky depths, leaving you discombobulated, but that's what it does when you haven't identified it. Once you've seen it and named it, you can have the upper hand. You travel together, but now you're the one in charge of the journey. Don't be afraid to treat it with compassion. After all, it's just being a crocodile, but you're the one who gets to steer now. Accepting and acknowledging our wounds can help us reach a state of recovery, reclaim our power and create bigger and more significant magic in our lives.

Ritual for Acceptance of Your Wounds

This ritual is layered and meant to be repeated many times; accepting our heartbreak, loss, grief, and trauma isn't easy, but it's always worth it. If you work this practice and feel that it's overwhelming, look for a licensed therapist who can assist you on your healing journey, like I have.

Find a quiet place where you will not be disturbed. You may play some soothing music and light a candle and some healing incense. You'll also need a jar with a lid (it can be plain or you may decorate it), a sheet of paper, and a fireproof dish. Write down a wound from your past and how it made you feel. It's okay to cry, scream, punch a pillow, and just let it all out. Now look at the wound and see it with new eyes. See the person you were at the time the injury took place. Send that person love and healing. Treat them with the same kindness you would treat a friend and let them know that you support them. Write a loving note of support to them on the other side of the paper, telling them how brave and strong they are because they made it through a hard time. Light the paper and let it burn in a fireproof dish, sending the message of love to your former self. Put the ashes into the jar. Mix in a pinch of chamomile, ground ginger, and sage from your kitchen. You may also add lemon balm, skullcap, and passionflower if you have it. Repeat this no more than once a week with as many wounds as you need to or the same wound multiple times as needed using the same jar.

Pieces of Us, Pieces of Time

I'm writing this to you in the future from me in the past. You may ask, "What past, exactly?" Publishing an almanac takes time; I'm at my computer and it's June 2020, a time of the COVID-19 global pandemic, a reckoning of systemic racism, and political unrest. You remember that year—global trauma on multiple levels. What changes have occurred personally, socially, and globally between the time I've written these words and the time of publication of the book you hold in your hands? I have no idea.

Has this year left me feeling broken? Yes, as it has left many, probably yourself included. Right now I'm working on embodying Akhilandeshwari by putting my broken bits back in different ways with the full realization that there are also ancient broken bits that I'm still working on, and yes, there will be more to come. I shall remain never not broken, I'll go with the flow with eyes wide open, and I'll meet you there on this page in the future. We'll be glued, taped, light shining through a few cracks, and with any luck at all we'll be riding our own darned crocodiles, embracing the life that we have in the time given to us. I thought about this driving home from the post office, masked, smelling of hand sanitizer, yet weirdly full of hope, the car radio jamming tunes. I wailed along with feeling, singing occasionally out of tune, a tear in my eye, to "Hand in My Pocket" by Alanis Morrissette. I thought to myself, "If the Goddess Never Not Broken had a theme song, this just might be it!"

Akhilandeshwari, Alanis, and I drove a few extra trips around the block just singing. After all, we're all of us never not broken, yet fine, fine, fine.

Resources

Bhammer, Shivali. "Worship: Learning from Akhilandeshwari Ma." *Hinduism Today,* web edition, July/August/September 2018. https://www.hinduismtoday.com/modules/smartsection/item.php?itemid=5880.

Khodiyar Maa Temple. "Birth of Khodiyar Maa." Shree Khodiyar Charitable Trust. Accessed November 11, 2020. http://www.khodiyarmandir.com/history.

Sanagala, Naveen. "Goddess Akhilandeshwari." Hindupad. Accessed November 11, 2020. https://hindupad.com/goddess-akilandeshwari/.

Suja. "Akhilandeshwari." *Music to My Ears* (blog), March 10, 2011. https://sujamusic.wordpress.com/2011/03/10/akhilandeshwari/.

Coloring Magic

Color Correspondences

C olor magic uses various hues to influence energy. It can attract or repel, strengthen or weaken. It expresses thoughts and feelings that don't fit easily into words. People choose colors of clothes, jewelry, walls, and carpet to create desired effects. In magic, we use altar cloths, candles, gemstones, bowls, and other altar tools to channel this energy. Coloring pages help people relax.

Different cultures may use different correspondences. Western cultures associate white with life and black with death; Eastern cultures tend to reverse those. It comes from interpretations. Red is the color of blood, which can suggest vitality or danger, depending on how you look at it. So there is no "right" or "wrong" meaning. Use the color associations that resonate with you.

Maroon: Crone, drama, respect, sensuality

Crimson: Determination, righteous anger, survival

Scarlet: Action, female sexuality, vitality

Red: Fire, strength, danger

Orange: Creativity, addiction, opportunity

Gold: God, Sun, justice

Topaz: Male sexuality, memory, fast effects

Yellow: Air, joy, charm

Lime Green: Growth, speed, end frustration

Green: Envy, money, health

Teal: Acceptance, abundance, happy home

Turquoise: Work-life balance, guilt, receiving

Blue: Water, truth, family

Indigo: Will, spirit, psychic

Purple: Wisdom, emotions, power

Lavender: Knowledge, intuition, divination

Violet: Calm, gratitude, tension

Coral: Mother, nurturing, emotional energy

Pink: Love, compassion, partnership

Fuchsia: Fight depression, self-direction, self-worth

Rose: Maiden, romance, friendship

Brown: Earth, stability, memory

Tan: Construction, food, past life

Black: Dark Moon, defense, grounding

Gray: Balance, loneliness, rest

Silver: Goddess, Moon, dreams

White: Crescent Moon, purity, peace

Ivory: Full Moon, luxury, animal magic

A Crow Spell

Kate Freuler

The crow is a symbol of occult wisdom and power. Long associated with Witches, crows have a mystical presence with their inky black feathers, uncanny intelligence, and portentous voices. The crow is thought to be a psychopomp, which means it can traverse between the realms of the living and the dead. A creature that is able to travel between worlds can access hidden knowledge and uncover esoteric secrets. Being able to exist equally in both light and darkness is an important part of spiritual awakening. The crow teaches us to embrace both our light and dark selves, to accept the shadows as well as the sunshine, and to fearlessly cross the space between endings and beginnings as our spiritual path unfolds.

This picture contains many symbols. As you color each one, you'll visualize and state your intentions to grow and transform on your chosen spiritual path.

You will need:
Black candle
Markers or colored pencils
Crow picture on page 269

Find a quiet spot where you can work uninterrupted, and light the black candle.

First, color the crow black. Notice the deep darkness of black and how it contains all the potential in the universe, because it is everything and nothing at the same time. State,

I gaze bravely into the unknown darkness, embracing all that is hidden within me.

Choose a color for the key in the crow's mouth. As you color the key, say,

I have the power to unlock the doors to my potential, my spiritual self, and all the wisdom of the cosmos.

For the jewel, choose your favorite color. As you color it in, contemplate the meaning of a jewel, its value, and its coveted status. Say,

My intuition is precious and worthwhile. I value and acknowledge my inner sense of knowing.

Find the heart hidden in the tree branch. Color it half black and half white. Say,

I fully accept the power of my light and dark sides as they work together in perfect harmony.

As you color the branches, think about how stable and strong wood is. Say,

I find stability on my chosen path and am anchored by my own strength and wisdom.

Color the leaves and acorns, symbols of growth. Say,

I welcome growth and new beginnings as I create my own future, finding knowledge and wisdom along the way.

There's a star on the crow's neck. Color it silver or gold. State,

I find the magic hidden in the mundane every day.

Notice the eye in the sky behind the crow. Color it the same color as your own eye and say,

I see the beauty and synchronicity in everything and everyone around me.

Color the beams emanating out from the eye in different colors of your choice, filling the background. These rays represent all the endless possibilities open to you on your magical journey and in life. While you fill in these rays, meditate on the things you wish to achieve.

Keep your drawing where you can see it for daily inspiration, and repeat the statements as needed.

Remembering Your Dreams Spell

Charlie Rainbow Wolf

Have you ever awoken from a deep sleep knowing you have dreamed something important but were unable to recall what it was? Perhaps you have heard others talking about their vivid dreams yet can't contribute to the conversation because you never seem to remember your dreams. Dreaming is an important part of the sleep pattern, although there are different schools of thought about why.

Some cultures believe dreaming is the time when your soul walks the other realms and visits with deceased loved ones and other spiritual beings. Others say dreaming is where your creative ideas originate. Psychologists might be divided about why you dream, but most of them believe dreams are important to your emotional and mental well-being.

This simple spell will help you to remember your dreams.

You'll need:
Coloring picture on page 273
Small bottle of water
Colored pencils, crayons, etc.
Pen or pencil
Notebook

I like to keep a specific notebook for my dream journal, but use what you have to hand. As you color your picture, think about what dreams you want to recall. I like to consider the chakra colors when doing this type of work.

- Red is linked with the root chakra. It brings a very stimulating energy. This is a good color to use to draw energy from the earth to help you meet your basic needs.
- Orange is associated with the sacral chakra. This is an excellent choice if you want to enhance your creativity and balance your emotions.

- Yellow resonates with the solar plexus chakra. Use this color if you're struggling to find your self-esteem or determine where your talents lie.
- Green is the color of the heart chakra. Shades of green are ideal if you want to cultivate compassion and understanding.
- Blue is associated with the throat chakra. Blues are great for helping you learn how to communicate efficiently—including learning to listen.
- Indigo corresponds with the brow, or third eye, chakra. This might be one of the best colors to use for this exercise, for it is coupled with clairvoyance, intuition, and seeing things clearly rather than through illusions or even deceptions.
- Purple and lilac are matched with the crown chakra. These colors will help you use your dreams to link to the ascended masters, the spiritual realms and the astral planes, and the higher levels of consciousness.

Once you have colored your picture, put it under the bottle of water on your nightstand and lay the pen and notebook beside it. As the last thing you do before you close your eyes to sleep, take a sip of the water. Upon waking from your slumber, immediately take another sip of the water and write down everything that you recall, before the day steals away the visions.

Regular practice of this will enable you to start to recall your dreams more easily. As you look back through your dream journal, you will start to see recurring patterns. These can be a valuable asset when it comes to connecting with your higher self and using your dreams as a tool toward your self-empowerment.

Discovering a New Path

James Kambos

Sometimes we get the feeling we need something new in our life. Perhaps you could just be bored. Or maybe you seriously need a new path in your life. But how do you find a new direction?

The goddess Hecate is a good deity to seek help from when trying to discover a new path in life. Hecate is known as the Triple Goddess, but she is more than just the Maiden, Mother, and Crone. Hecate is also the goddess of the sky, earth, and the underworld. She passes effortlessly through these three realms. Since she travels at ease through these worlds, she is associated with paths and crossroads. She's also a guardian of doors, gates, and boundaries. Her ability to unlock any blocked passageway also means keys are sacred to her. Owls and dogs are her special messengers.

Hecate is a protector, so the shield is one of her tools. As a deity associated with the night and the underworld, Hecate is frequently depicted carrying a torch. She will use her torch to illuminate your way to a new path of knowledge, or enlightenment. Remember, it was Hecate who, using her torch, helped the goddess Demeter search for her daughter, Persephone, after she was abducted by Hades and taken to the underworld.

Her numbers are three, six, nine, and thirteen. The Moon and stars, which have helped guide humans for centuries, are understandably sacred to her.

Considering Hecate's attributes, she'll make the perfect guide to help you discover a new path in life.

You will need:
Silver or purple candle
Lighter or matches
Crayons, colored pencils, or watercolor pencils with a brush
Image provided on page 277

A New Path Coloring Ritual

Since the night belongs to Hecate and the Moon is sacred to her, begin this coloring ritual after dark. Safely light your candle. The candle's flame represents Hecate's torch illuminating your path to a new goal or phase of your life. First meditate and divine into the flame. Can you "see" any symbols or messages from Hecate?

After your meditation, remove the image from the book. Begin by coloring the torch. Make it bright and warm, imagine you can feel its glow! Next, color the path on which Hecate is standing. Visualize her guiding you along this path to your goal.

As you color, do so with purpose. Color the night sky. When coloring the stars and Moon, think how they guided the ancients along a new path. Imagine the owl bringing you a message to help guide you. Decorate Hecate's gown with her sacred symbols. Visualize the key unlocking a new door leading you to a new path and a new day.

When done, safely extinguish the candle. Place the picture on your altar. Meditate on it each evening until your new path becomes clear to you. If you wish, frame the picture and keep it in a special place.

Let Hecate guide you to your new path or goal.

Contributors

H. BYRON BALLARD, MFA, is a teacher, folklorist, and writer who was born and raised in western North Carolina. She has served as a featured presenter at Sacred Space Conference, Southeast Wise Women's Herbal Conference, Glastonbury Goddess Conference, and other gatherings and has spoken at conferences at Harvard and the University of North Carolina. Ballard is senior priestess and cofounder of Mother Grove Goddess Temple and the Coalition of Earth Religions. She writes a regular column for *SageWoman* magazine and is the author of four previous books, including *Roots, Branches & Spirits*.

ELIZABETH BARRETTE has been involved with the Pagan community for more than twenty-seven years. She has served as managing editor of *PanGaia* and dean of studies at the Grey School of Wizardry. Her book *Composing Magic* explains how to combine writing and spirituality. She lives in central Illinois. Visit her blog *The Wordsmith's Forge* (ysabetwordsmith.livejournal.com) or website PenUltimate Productions (penultimateproductions.weebly.com).

STEPHANIE ROSE BIRD is an eclectic Pagan, a columnist for *Witches & Pagans* magazine, and contributor to many magazines and journals, including several Llewellyn annuals. She has written seven nonfiction books, including the award-winning *Sticks, Stones,*

Roots & Bones, 365 Days of Hoodoo, and *Light, Bright, and Damn Near White.*

MIREILLE BLACKE, MA, LADC, RD, CD-N, is a registered dietitian, licensed alcohol and drug counselor, and professor at the University of Saint Joseph in West Hartford, Connecticut. Mireille worked in rock radio for two decades before shifting her career to psychology, nutrition, and addiction counseling. She spends considerable time renovating her Victorian home, pining for New Orleans, and entertaining her beloved Bengal cats.

DANIELLE BLACKWOOD is the author of *The Twelve Faces of the Goddess: Transform Your Life with Astrology, Magick, and the Sacred Feminine* (Llewellyn, 2018). She is also a professional astrologer and registered counselor (RTC). Her passion is helping others through their rites of passage, finding meaning on their journey, and consciously reframing their stories through an archetypal lens. Danielle has been a priestess and educator since 1994 and lives in an enchanted cottage on magical Salt Spring Island, the original lands and unceded territory of xʷənenəč. You can reach her at www.danielleblackwood.com.

BLAKE OCTAVIAN BLAIR is a shamanic and Druidic practitioner, ordained minister, writer, Usui Reiki Master-Teacher, and musical artist. Blake blends mystical traditions from both the East and the West along with a reverence for the natural world into his own brand of spirituality. He is an avid reader, knitter, and pescatarian. Blake lives in New England with his beloved husband. Visit him on the web at blakeoctavianblair.com.

CHIC AND S. TABATHA CICERO are Chief Adepts of the Hermetic Order of the Golden Dawn as re-established by their mentor, Israel Regardie. The Ciceros have written numerous books, including *The Essential Golden Dawn, Self-Initiation into the Golden Dawn Tradition, The Golden Dawn Magical Tarot,* and *Tarot Talismans.* Both are prominent Rosicrucians: Chic is currently Chief Adept of the Florida College of the SRICF, and Tabatha is Imperatrix of the SRIA in America.

MONICA CROSSON is the author of *Wild Magical Soul, The Magickal Family,* and *Summer Sage.* She is a Master Gardener who lives in the beautiful Pacific Northwest, happily digging in the dirt and tending her raspberries with her family and their small menagerie of farm animals. She has been a practicing Witch for thirty years and is a member of Evergreen Coven.

KATE FREULER lives in Ontario, Canada, and is the author of *Of Blood and Bones: Working with Shadow Magick & the Dark Moon.* She has owned and operated the Witchcraft shop whitemoonwitch craft.com for ten years. When she's not writing or crafting items for clients, she is busy being creative with art or reading a huge stack of books.

MICHAEL FURIE (Northern California) is the author of *The Witch's Book of Potions, Supermarket Sabbats, Supermarket Magic, Spellcasting: Beyond the Basics,* and more, all from Llewellyn Publications. A practicing Witch for over twenty-five years, he is a priest of the Cailleach. He can be found online at www.michaelfurie.com.

SASHA GRAHAM is the author of *Tarot Diva, 365 Tarot Spreads, 365 Tarot Spells,* and *Llewellyn's Complete Book of the Rider-Waite-Smith Tarot.* She is the editor of and contributor to *Tarot Fundamentals, Tarot Experience,* and *Tarot Compendium.* Her tarot decks include the *Haunted House Tarot* and *Dark Wood Tarot.* Sasha hosts *The Enchanted Kitchen,* a short-form magical cooking series for YouTube and Heyou Media's *Mobile. Mini. Movies.*

RAECHEL HENDERSON (Chicago, IL) is the author of *Sew Witchy* and *The Scent of Lemon & Rosemary.* She has been sewing professionally since 2008 and has traveled around the Midwest selling her handmade bags, skirts, coats, and accessories at various events and conventions. She maintains a blog at idiorhythmic.com and is on Instagram and Facebook. She writes about magick, creativity, living by one's own life patterns, her family, and books.

JD HORTWORT resides in North Carolina. She is an avid student of herbology and gardening. She wrote a weekly garden column for

thirty years. She is an award-winning author, journalist and magazine editor and a frequent contributor to the Llewellyn annuals. Her new book, *A Witch's Guide to Wildcraft: Uncommon Magick with Common Plants,* was published by Llewellyn Publications in 2021. When not at the keyboard, she spends time in her own landscape, taking trips with friends, and with her nose buried in a book.

JAMES KAMBOS became interested in folk magic as a child. His mother and grandmother performed folk magic rituals from their native Greece. Today he is an artist and a writer. He lives in Ohio's Appalachian hill country.

KELDEN (Minnesota) has been practicing Traditional Witchcraft for more than a decade. He is the author of *The Crooked Path: An Introduction to Traditional Witchcraft,* and his writing has appeared in *The Witch's Altar, The New Aradia: A Witch's Handbook to Magical Resistance,* and *Modern Witch* magazine. Additionally, Kelden is the cocreator of the Traditional Witch's Deck, and he authors a blog on the Patheos Pagan channel called *By Athame and Stang.*

LUPA is a naturalist Pagan author and artist in the Pacific Northwest. She is the author of several books on nature-based Paganism, including *Nature Spirituality From the Ground Up: Connect with Totems in Your Ecosystem,* and the *Tarot of Bones* deck and book. More about Lupa and her works may be found at www.thegreenwolf.com.

DANIEL MOLER is a writer, artist, educator, and shamanic practitioner. He has published fiction and nonfiction works around the world in magazines, in journals, in gaming modules, and online, including *Positive Health Magazine, Cannabis Culture, The Tattooed Buddha, Sacred Hoop, Elephant Journal,* and *A Journal of Contemporary Shamanism.* He is the author of *Shamanic Qabalah, RED Mass,* and *Machine Elves 101.* Visit Daniel online at danielmolerweb.com.

MICKIE MUELLER is a Witch, author, illustrator, tarot creator, and YouTube content creator. She is the author/illustrator of multiple books, articles, and tarot decks for Llewellyn Publications and also has a jewelry line with Peter Stone and a statuary line with Sacred

Source. Her magical art is distributed internationally and has been seen as set dressing on SyFy's *The Magicians* and Bravo's *Girlfriends' Guide to Divorce*. She runs several Etsy shops with her husband and fellow author, Daniel Mueller, in their studio workshop.

DIANA RAJCHEL began her career planning to serve as clergy and write about all subjects spiritual. Her background includes Wicca, folk Witchcraft, conjure, and a whole lot of experience organizing people who don't like knowing that they're organized. Diana splits her time between San Francisco, California, where she co-owns Golden Apple Metaphysical, and southwestern Michigan, where she runs Earth and Sun spiritual coaching with her partner. Diana has twenty-five years of experience as a professional tarot reader and Western herbalist and twenty-nine years of experience as a professional writer.

SUZANNE RESS runs a small farm in the Alpine foothills of Italy, where she lives her husband. She has been a practicing Pagan for as long as she can remember and was featured in the exhibit "Worldwide Witches" at the Hexenmuseum of Switzerland. She is the author of *The Trial of Goody Gilbert*.

ASTREA TAYLOR is the author of *Air Magic: Elements of Witchcraft* and *Intuitive Witchcraft: How to Use Intuition to Elevate Your Practice*. She's an eclectic/intuitive Witch, Pagan, writer, and speaker who blogs as *Starlight Witch* on Patheos and whose writing has appeared in several anthologies. When she's not coleading Aurora Fire or writing for the Blessed Be Box, she leads workshops and rituals across the country. Learn more at www.AstreaTaylor.com.

MELISSA TIPTON is a Structural Integrator, Reiki Master, and founder of Jungian Magic, which uses potent psychological insights to radically increase the efficacy of your magic. You can find more inner-journey techniques and Jungian Magic courses to improve your magic and your life at www.realmagic.school.

CHARLYNN WALLS is an active member of her local community and a member of a local area coven. A practitioner of the Craft for

over twenty years, she currently resides in Central Missouri with her family. She continues to expand upon her Craft knowledge and practices daily. Charlynn shares her knowledge by teaching at local festivals and continuing to produce articles with Llewellyn Publications.

CHARLIE RAINBOW WOLF is happiest when she is creating something, especially if it can be made from items that others have cast aside. Pottery, writing, knitting, astrology, and tarot are her deepest interests. A recorded singer-songwriter and a published author, she is an advocate of organic gardening and cooking and lives in the Midwest with her husband and special-needs Great Danes. Visit www.charlierainbow.com.

STEPHANIE WOODFIELD has been a practicing Pagan for over twenty years. A devotional polytheist, teacher, and priestess of the Morrigan, she is an organizer for several Pagan gatherings. A longtime New Englander, she now resides in the Orlando area with her husband, a very pampered cat, and various reptiles. She is called to helping others forge meaningful experiences and relationships with the gods.

NATALIE ZAMAN is the author of *Color and Conjure* and *Magical Destinations of the Northeast*. A regular contributor to various Llewellyn annual publications, she also writes the recurring feature Wandering Witch for *Witches & Pagans* magazine. When not on the road, she's busy tending her magical back garden. Visit Natalie online at nataliezaman.blogspot.com.

© 2001 by Joe Musser
All rights reserved
Printed in the United States of America

0-8054-2480-6

Published by Broadman & Holman Publishers,
Nashville, Tennessee

Dewey Decimal Classification: 813
Subject Heading: JOHN NEWTON
Library of Congress Card Catalog Number: 2001035019

Library of Congress Cataloging-in-Publication Data
Musser, Joe.
        The infidel : a novel / Joe Musser
            p.   cm.
        ISBN 0-8054-2480-6
        1. Newton, John, 1725–1807—Fiction. 2. Anglican Communion—
Clergy—Fiction. 3. Church of England—Clergy—Fiction. 4. Slave
traders—Fiction. 5. Hymn writers—Fiction. 6. England—Fiction.
7. Clergy—Fiction. I. Title.

PS3563.U84 I5 2001
813'.54—dc21

                                                                    2001035019

1 2 3 4 5 6 7 8 9 10 05 04 03 02 01

To the memory of
Brandt Gustavson,
longtime friend and early mentor,
who helped teach me the virtues of
faith, perseverance, and diligence.

Chapter One

July 24, 1725

Reverend Alwyn Aimsley, the old vicar, was taking his morning stroll on the neighborhood London road when he thought he heard a scream. He hesitated for a moment, hoping it might be just the cry of a crow or hawk. His hearing was not all that good, but he was convinced that he had heard the sound of a woman screaming.

While such a sound might be common in the more seedy areas of the city, it was unusual in this area. Following the Great Fire of the last century, the people of London had spent sixty years rebuilding their city. This part of London was a well-to-do area with newly built stone cottages, and to hear a woman scream here was uncommon.

It was only four hours past dawn, but the hot July sun was already unbearable. As he paused, the vicar took out a large handkerchief and wiped his forehead, still listening. The countryside was quiet except for the birds, a distant sound of a dog barking, and several children

laughing at play. As he cupped his hand by his ears, he even heard the rustling of the leaves in the towering oak trees overhead.

Then he heard it again. "That truly is a woman screaming," he observed to no one in particular. Puzzled, he listened more intently. The screams were not the sound of terror, as with someone being attacked or hurt. Rather, he reckoned they were more measured—as if giving vocal expression to some intense physical effort.

The screams were coming from the tiny home of John Newton, just ahead. Newton, a sea captain, was almost always at sea—and as was the custom in 1725, neighbors and friends took the responsibility of looking after the safety or other needs of Newton's young wife, Elizabeth, especially now that she was pregnant.

Reverend Aimsley strode quickly toward the sound of the screams. A flock of chickens in the yard scattered noisily as he came closer to them. Alongside the Newton cottage, he noticed an unfamiliar horse and buggy tied to a tree.

As the vicar approached the front door, he heard a commotion inside and excited voices. At first his knocks went unnoticed, then a young child whom he did not recognize came to answer the door, which was already open to let in some air. The boy did not speak, so the vicar did.

"Hello," he said, "Is Mrs. Newton in?" The lad did not respond.

Impatiently, Reverend Aimsley called out, "Mrs. Newton? Are you all right?"

"Who is it?" a woman called from inside.

The vicar squinted. He did not know the voice of the woman who had answered him. He shuffled nervously outside then answered, "Uh . . . it's me—the vicar, Reverend Aimsley. Is Mrs. Newton all right? I thought I heard her cry out—"

"Mrs. Newton is doing quite well under the circumstances, Vicar," the woman called out. "Her baby is coming, and I'm acting as her mid-

wife. I'm dreadfully sorry, but you'll understand if we can't receive you just now."

"Ah, yes. I see. Might I be of any help?" the vicar inquired.

"Thank you, no," the woman inside answered. "It's all in the Lord's hands now. I've had experience in this kind of thing. I'll take good care of Mrs. Newton. I dare say it won't be too much longer 'til her baby comes."

The vicar wiped his brow once again; then he shrugged, nodded, and resumed his leisurely stroll.

Inside the cottage, Elizabeth Newton was lying in her bed, damp from sweat and from her ruptured "bag of waters." Her contractions were coming more frequently now and were growing more intense. Her hands gripped the headboard so tightly that her nails dug into its hard wood.

Elizabeth Newton was young, barely out of her teens. She was beautiful despite her condition. Her auburn hair was disheveled but healthy and lustrous. Her brown eyes were clear and soft, and as a window into her soul, they revealed intelligence as well as a warm, loving young woman who embodied grace, piety, learning, and laughter.

Standing beside the bed was her cousin and closest friend, Abigail* Catlett. The vicar had correctly assumed that it was her horse and buggy tied outside. She had come all the way from her own village, Chatham in Kent, some distance from the Newton home in London. Charles, the boy whom the vicar had seen at the door, was her son.

Abigail dipped a washcloth into the porcelain water basin and wiped Elizabeth's face with its wet coolness, and the pregnant woman's breathing became more even.

Abigail felt a sympathetic twinge in her own stomach for Elizabeth who, by now, had been in labor for at least twenty-four hours.

---

*Her name was also Elizabeth but is changed here to avoid confusion.

"Charles," she said to the small boy. "Why don't you go outside and feed the chickens. After that, you can play with the neighbor children."

The young boy did as he was told, happy to retire from the odd commotion inside the cottage.

"I'm not sure I can keep this up," Elizabeth moaned softly. "The cramps nearly make me faint."

"I know, dear," Abigail said to console her cousin. She lifted the sheet and checked the opening to the birth canal. The contractions were closer together now, and the opening was stretched to nearly the size of a small woman's fist.

Abigail used both her hands to massage Elizabeth's abdomen to feel where the baby was in its journey through the birth canal. The next five inches would be the most difficult. "It'll soon be over," Abigail said quietly to reassure Elizabeth.

She wished for a cool breeze to come through the window as she raised Elizabeth and helped her take off her nightgown, damp with perspiration. With the attention and skill of a real nurse, she wiped Elizabeth's arms, breasts, and swollen belly with the damp washcloth, which again seemed to soothe her for awhile. Then a cool breeze wafted in and blew over the young woman's nude body, relaxing her for a few moments—as an unexpected answer for Abigail's wish of a moment ago.

Just as Abigail finished cooling her off, Elizabeth caught her breath and grabbed her stomach as another contraction engulfed her body. She screamed, louder than before, her fingers again digging into the wooden headboards.

"It's coming!" Elizabeth shouted. "I feel it pushing out. Can you see?"

Abigail lifted the bedsheet once more to look. Elizabeth had her knees up and bent outward to maximize the opening in the birth canal. Her friend knelt by the side of the bed to examine her.

"Yes!" Abigail said. "I see the head! And the opening is bigger. I think you're ready. When you feel the next cramp, Elizabeth, take a deep breath and push hard!"

Elizabeth did as she was instructed. With a deep gasp of air, she pushed hard over the next several contractions to try and expel the miraculous little life from her womb. Nearly an hour passed as she pushed every time the contractions came.

Then a mixture of bright, dark red blood, water, and a thin waxy film gushed away as the baby's head pushed its way out of the womb after another half hour of this intense struggle had elapsed. Next came the baby's shoulders. Then, as if the most difficult part of the transit was over, the rest of the small infant's body slid out quickly, along with the afterbirth. The baby began to thrust its arms and legs into the air as if declaring its appearance and triumph with its struggle to be born.

Abigail saw that the baby's mouth and nose were still filled with mucous and fluid, preventing it from breathing. She took clean water and squeezed it from the washcloth onto the baby's face, and then she bent down and with her mouth sucked the mucous that was obstructing the nasal passages, spitting it out into a nearby pan. She repeated the step until the baby coughed and began crying lustily.

Even though she had been present at a number of births, Abigail was still amazed at the mystery and wonder of the birth process. She picked up the tiny baby when it began to cry. "It's a boy, Elizabeth! And he's perfect in every way."

Abigail wiped the remaining fluids away from the baby's nose and mouth and made sure his breathing was unobstructed. Then, after carefully bathing the baby, she cut and tied the umbilical cord. Finally Abigail gently dried him, then wrapped the tiny bundle in a clean, white cloth and nestled him onto the soft, round breasts of its mother who was weeping quietly, her eyes radiant with joy.

"He's beautiful!" Elizabeth crooned softly. "I wish Captain Newton could have been here to see his new son born."

"He'll be back before you know it, Elizabeth. Four months isn't such a long time. He's been away for much longer periods than that." Abigail changed the subject. "What will you name him?"

"He'll be John, named after his father."

At Sea . . .

Captain John Newton stood on deck and gazed at landfall on the horizon. The sea was calm, and the weather was perfect. He began his usual routine of giving the pilot deck its daily inspection. He ran his hand over the polished mahogany rail and made a mental note to have the crew give it another coat of varnish. This time, everything else within view met with his approval.

A sailor on watch kept his eyes on the captain. He knew firsthand what wrath might be dispensed if anything was less than shipshape. Captain John Newton ran a tight ship, and everyone made certain to stay just one step ahead of his critical inspections.

The ship was just off the western coast of Portugal, and would make landing in Lisbon harbor in three hours or so. Already sea gulls from the coast were swooping down from the skies, looking for handouts from the galley whenever the cook threw garbage overboard. The loud, raucous calling of the birds somehow invigorated Captain Newton, and he looked forward to spending some time on land. His crew was even more eager to have an overnight shore leave.

Captain Newton still felt a little strange and unsettled, having been awakened from sleep just before dawn. No weather anomaly or trouble had arisen; yet he awoke, sitting bolt upright in bed with his face soaked in sweat.

While trying to go back to sleep, he had collected his thoughts, contemplated how his wife was, and wondered about her health. He spoke

a silent prayer for her and the child she was carrying. Tossing and turning, he was unable to go back to sleep, so he'd gotten dressed and went topside for his early inspection.

"Mornin', Cap'n," the first mate smiled. "Up kinda early?"

"Good morning, Mr. Cooke."

That would be the end of the conversation; Cooke knew better than to try and force small talk with his captain.

Captain Newton was only thirty-two, a few years older than his first mate, but he gave the appearance of one from another generation altogether. Newton was captain of a merchant vessel that plied the trade from England to the Mediterranean, then back to England.

It was about this time that England, Wales, and Scotland had been brought together to form Great Britain, giving rise to a great new world power. Captain Newton took full benefit of the opportunities presented by this new entrepreneurial force to now make his living.

Trade with Europe and North Africa had been in vogue for hundreds of years, but trading with the New World had been introduced only within the last century, and it had energized the entire shipping industry. It was this more traditional shipping route between England and Africa that Newton had sought and served during his career at sea.

However, profitable routes were now being established not just between Britain and Europe but also between the West African coast, India, the Far East, and colonial America. Ships made a circuit from Britain to Europe to Africa and then on to the American and West Indies colonies. From the colonies they returned to Britain.

A typical tour at sea might include shipments of grain, textiles and other dry goods, gunpowder, and furniture from Britain to Portugal, Spain, Italy, or Africa. That was the way it was for Captain Newton's ship. Some of the merchant ships that continued on to Africa, after unloading their remaining cargo, might be outfitted to carry slaves as cargo from West Africa to the mainland or to the West Indies colonies.

This human cargo was jammed into filthy, cramped, and stifling quarters in the bowels of the ships. Every few days or so, the slaves would be brought up on deck, not out of compassion, but to extinguish the stench. Below deck, in chains, the slaves were forced to lie in their own waste.

When the slaves were brought naked to topside, they were splashed with buckets of water. It was a brief respite that also provided some semblance of a bath. These cleansing times were necessary for another reason. If the slaves contracted dysentery from the terrible and filthy conditions, lives would be lost, which would result in a loss of revenue in the colonies.

Some slaves tried to escape or lash out at their captors during these cleaning times. But the sailors were ready, and before things got out of hand, they cut them down swiftly with a musket or axe. Their bodies were tossed overboard, along with other slaves who had died from heat, disease, or the terrors of being confined for weeks at a time during the passage to the colonies.

Once in the colonial port, the slaves who survived were auctioned or bartered for goods. After a brief shore leave and time for the crew to reload cargo, the ships headed back to England with their holds filled with a manifest of full cargo—usually lumber, sugar, molasses, and beeswax.

Such slave ships were not for captains with any real sensitivity. Actually, Captain Newton seemed to have the perfect disposition for the slave trade, but for some reason he never considered it. To his shipmates, this may have seemed especially strange. Newton had the exact nature for the work. He was a stern ship's master and ruled with severe discipline. Never bothered by any twinge of compassion or sympathy, he ran his ship by strict regulations, logic, and discipline and could do so with a complete sense of detachment.

Captain John Newton was not a particularly commanding presence in person; he wasn't tall or otherwise imposing. Still, aboard his ship, no

one dared dispute his authority. It was quite common for one or more of the sailors to be flogged or otherwise disciplined for even the most minor infraction.

Newton was well known among those in the British merchant sailing industry. His toughness and harsh ways gave him a reputation that everyone seemed to fear. Unfortunately, he was unable to separate his personality from his position. At sea he was the feared sea captain. At home, it was the same. Even his wife, Elizabeth, often dreaded his return from sea duty.

At home he was restless and irritable. If his wife annoyed him with too many questions, if she took too long to prepare his meals, or if she did not do her housework with the efficiency he expected, it was not altogether uncommon for her husband to treat her almost as harshly as one of his deckhands.

His scoldings were abusive enough, but if he was really angry, a hard slap or violent shove might send his young wife reeling across the room. Yet, Captain Newton never thought of himself as cruel or abusive. And now, as he stood on deck, his thoughts of Elizabeth were surprisingly tender. He even felt a little afraid for her, knowing that many women actually died in childbirth. But there was nothing he could do for her so far away.

It'll be any day now, he mused. *The child will probably be several months old by the time we return to England. Hopefully, all will go well.*

That was the extent of his reverie, however. He wouldn't allow himself the luxury of such simple daydreaming, wondering about whether the child would be a boy or girl, what he or she might look like, or anything having to do with planning for his or her future. None of that fit into his provincial ideas of parenthood. It would be his wife's responsibility to rear the child. Only if it were a boy would he be involved, but not for many years.

Newton turned sharply and came back to the present.

"Mr. Cooke!" he called out.

"Yessir, Cap'n," the first mate replied.

"Get some men on the rigging. Let's open up some sail. I'd like to make landfall before the sun gets too high in the sky."

"Aye, sir!"

Chapter Two

London, 1730

✝

Elizabeth was doing a remarkable job at rearing her son, now four years old. As her only child, and because her husband was almost always at sea, she devoted most of her time to young John.

Captain Newton (even his wife addressed him so formally) was lately at home, taking advantage of a rare furlough.

He had been with his family for several weeks but was now getting quite restless. At breakfast, little Johnny was noisily crunching some toasted bread and homemade jam. The boy accidentally dropped the toast, and it landed jam side down on the floor.

His father suddenly rose and slapped him. The boy fell from his chair and began crying.

Elizabeth jumped up quickly to clean up the mess.

"Leave it!" the captain commanded. "He will clean it up. The boy must be taught proper manners and discipline."

"B-but surely you saw it was an accident," Elizabeth stammered.

"Are you contradicting me?"

"No, sir," his wife replied meekly. She did not intervene but wished she could wrap her boy in her arms and soothe his tears.

"All right, young man," his father said sternly, "after you've cleaned that up, you will stand at attention at the other end of the table, eyes forward and backbone straight. Do you hear me?"

"Uh-huh," the boy sniffed.

"What did you say?!"

"Aye, aye, sir!" the four-year-old answered, jumping to attention.

The next days were even more tense while Elizabeth anxiously awaited her husband's return to sea duty. She felt guilty for feeling such joy at his leaving and asked God's forgiveness in her evening prayers for such wicked thoughts and feelings.

Somehow, though, when her husband was at sea, their lives were easier, less stressful, and more filled with laughter than when he was home.

✛ ✛ ✛

It was nearly a month after Captain Newton's departure, and Elizabeth was happier than she had been in a long time, not so much because of his leaving, but for another reason. Today she was looking forward to something special. Abigail Catlett was coming for a visit. It had been a long time since the two best friends had seen each other, and Abigail's letter indicated she would visit, arriving this very day.

Elizabeth had scrubbed and dusted the small cottage and arranged flowers from her garden in a small bowl on the table.

Johnny sat quietly on a stool reading a book. He had even impressed the vicar with his ability, at age four, to read from the Bible. His mother had taught him the ABCs when he was only three. He was reciting memorized hymns, Bible verses, and poems at two, so this was not that big a leap.

"Mother?" The little boy's face looked up at her quizzically. "What does this word mean?"

She looked at the page where he pointed. "That's pronounced affection—and affection is when we have certain feelings or show feelings of love for something or someone."

"Affection," the boy repeated. His face clouded for an instant.

She was quick to pick it up. "What is it, darling?"

"Um . . ." he stammered, "I wish that Father had affection for me."

"Oh, Johnny. Your father loves you. It's just that he doesn't do well in expressing his affection. Do you understand?" She could see by his look that he did not.

"Your father is a good man. He works hard and is gone much. Sometimes he appears to be stern, but—" Elizabeth stopped herself since she, too, was unconvinced of her husband's love and affection.

"Why don't you put your book away for awhile and get ready for Aunt Abigail to come. She'll bring her little boy for you to play with."

Johnny did as he was asked, and Elizabeth was grateful for the change in the direction of their conversation.

Less than an hour later, Abigail arrived. Her son, now eleven, drove the horse and buggy. Abigail had more important matters to attend to. Several months earlier she had given birth to a daughter, Mary, whom she carried safely nestled in her lap.

Now it was Elizabeth's turn to look after the needs of her friend. She had drawn water from the well and heated it in the big kettle hanging in the fireplace for Abigail to take a sponge bath and wipe the road dirt from her face and arms. Then, while Abigail attended to her baby, Elizabeth prepared tea and small cakes. The new mother held her baby who nursed quietly while the two of them ate and chatted. Their boys were heard playing noisily outside in the nearby meadow.

"She's such a beautiful child," Elizabeth cooed as she lightly touched the baby's face.

"Do you ever wish for some more children, Elizabeth?" Abigail asked her friend.

Elizabeth looked away. It was obviously not a topic she expected to discuss.

"I'm sorry," Abigail said softly. "Did I say something wrong?"

"Of course not," Elizabeth answered. "It—it's just, well—" Her eyes began to fill with tears.

"Elizabeth, what's wrong?"

"I'm sorry. I didn't mean to spoil your visit by my foolishness," Elizabeth said wiping her eyes.

Then she continued. "My little boy asked me just before you came why his father didn't love him. He's only four and already perceives his father's lack of affection. And his lack of affection isn't only for the boy—" Her words trailed off.

"I'm sorry, Elizabeth, but it's probably just his life. You know, being a sea captain and all that. He has to be stern and such. It must be terribly hard to come home and become gentle and loving."

"Maybe. But to answer your question, I truly would like more children."

Abigail obligingly changed the subject. "Tell me about Johnny. I can really see that he's grown."

Elizabeth was happy to discuss her little son. "He has a wonderful mind. He knows how to read and is even learning how to write. He soaks up Bible verses and memorizes hymns almost better than I can. My prayer is that he'll become a minister one day."

Then her expression grew dark again. "But his father wants him to follow in his steps and take to the sea."

"Well, plenty of time to worry about that later," said Abigail. "Maybe by that time your boy will marry my daughter. Wouldn't that be something?" she laughed.

Elizabeth suddenly moved closer to her friend. "Oh, Abigail, there's nothing I'd like better. But there's something else I want to talk to you about. I've been thinking about being with you for so long, and I've grown more excited every day. I hope that I am not being presumptuous about this, but it's quite important."

Abigail sensed Elizabeth's serious mood. She rose with her baby and laid her carefully on the bed, then came back to the table.

"What is it, Elizabeth?" she asked.

"I dare not impose on you, but what I have to say, what I am about to ask you, can be the same for both of us."

Abigail cocked her head quizzically. "I don't understand."

"I've been thinking and praying for young John ever since he was born. And it frightens me to think what would happen if something ever happened to me—with his father always away."

Elizabeth took her friend's hands in her own and knelt beside her chair. Tears filled the eyes that looked up at her friend. "Abigail, if anything happens to me, I want you to raise my son. And, God forbid, if anything ever happens to you, I'll do the same for your children."

"Of course," Abigail whispered. "You can count on me. It's agreed. We needn't say any more about it."

Chapter Three

1732—A Twig Is Bent

By the time he was six, young John Newton had mastered the basics of reading and writing as taught him by Elizabeth, and he was already studying Latin and mathematics. She had also instilled in him the essential Christian virtues and instructed him in religion, temperance, character, goodness, morality, integrity, and other values.

John's mind was like a sponge, and he thirsted for more and more knowledge. At times he would pull his mother into his studies with probing questions and comments. It seemed incredible to Elizabeth that he was still only a boy—John was so much more mature than the other youngsters his age. He seemed to have mature questions about her teaching and often asked questions to follow up a particular point.

Elizabeth told John what a terrible thing it would be to be called before the judgment seat of Christ. If someone were to die in his sins, he'd be cast into hell without any hope or second chances. She also

taught him to revere the Bible as the source of God's truth. As such, the Bible was never to be doubted or disobeyed.

Their conversations and discussions about his reading and learning expanded her own mind and soul as she tried to stay ahead of his seeking mind. Through this investigation of life and its meaning, their bond became one of mutual love, trust, and enrichment.

While the captain was away at sea, Elizabeth took John to her church, a Dissenter chapel where Dr. David Jennings was the minister. He was the role model for Elizabeth's wish to have her son become a minister.

On the other hand, her husband wanted John to follow in his seafaring shoes. Perhaps her religious instruction was to instill in John virtue and values that would deter the temptations to sin that seem almost to be a part of a sailor's job description.

When Captain Newton was in London, he took John to his place of worship, a Church of England service where the boy always fought to stay awake. A choir performed all the music, and the sermons, prayers, and psalms seemed incredibly dull and boring.

The captain liked the more liturgical style of worship, having been raised a Catholic and educated in Spain by Jesuits. It was only later in life that he converted to Protestantism.

John did not like the more formal worship at his father's church. True, he also found the sermons boring in his mother's church, but at least there the music was lively and it engaged him and the congregation.

When Captain Newton returned from sea, he always brought gifts for his wife and son. Their gracious home was furnished with small treasures from all over the world, which he acquired on tours of duty—rugs from Turkey, exquisite porcelain from Spain, great carved furniture from Italy, warm colorful quilts from Portugal, and all kinds of fabrics and souvenir trinkets.

Knowing of his son's thirst for knowledge, the captain often brought books and pamphlets for him to read. When he came home to London, sometimes Captain Newton wished he could enter into those rich learning and sharing experiences that John was having with his mother. It was at times such as these that he felt more keenly the terrible loneliness that also troubled him while he was at sea.

With certain satisfaction he watched the two of them engaging each other in the excitement of learning. Yet he felt awkward to be there. This was one of those troubling times when he felt completely shut out of both their lives. As the sun died in the western skies, he lit an oil lamp and took it to them to illumine their books.

Elizabeth looked up and smiled gratefully to her husband. She was sprawled out on the rug and seemed almost childlike herself. John sat with his back against the wall and his chin resting on his knees, reading aloud.

"This book says that the Hundred Year War lasted from 1377 until 1453. That's not a hundred years, it's only 76!" he laughed. To John, even history lessons could be fun.

Elizabeth also laughed at his joke. "Maybe the soldiers fought their battles in a hurry."

Captain Newton sat in his chair watching the two of them across the room—angry with himself that he felt some measure of jealousy at their affinity for each other and for their enjoyment of learning. To him it all seemed so remarkable, and it generated a special kind of gnawing hurt that he could not quite understand. He truly envied the bond they had.

He recalled a recent interaction of his own with his young son. When he came home on this furlough, he had scolded the boy for not saluting when he and the other officers came down the gangway from the ship. Never mind that the seven-year-old boy was simply so glad to see his father that he ran excitedly up the gangway to greet him, nearly

knocking his father down in his enthusiasm. Such a lapse in decorum had been too much for the captain, who grabbed John by his shoulders and shook him, making him go back to the dock and stand at attention and "do it by the manual."

The captain winced at what now seemed to him a terrible mistake. Yet he lacked the ability, the ease, of going to the boy and apologizing or repairing the rift he had created by his brutish insistence upon his stilted protocol over the boy's evident affection.

The captain sighed deeply, picked up his clay pipe, pushed a pinch of tobacco into it, and tamped it down with his thumb. He rose from his chair and pulled a thick splinter away from a log near the fireplace, ignited it from the fire, lit the pipe, and strolled back to his chair to watch his wife and son some more. They'd never know what bittersweet pleasure it brought to him, for he could never bring himself to share such personal feelings.

Elizabeth, laughing at another one of her son's jokes, suddenly started to cough. It grew into a spasm of coughing that took her breath away. It sounded husky and serious, coming from deep inside her.

The captain frowned. She had been getting these coughing fits nightly ever since he'd arrived several weeks ago. Now, looking at her more closely, it seemed to him that she looked thinner, more frail. He hadn't noticed before. While he wasn't trained in medicine by any means, he did have firsthand experience with that coughing sound. More than once he had heard sailors with a cough that had that deep, harsh sound, and they always got worse.

"How long have you had that cough?"

Elizabeth got up, drew a dipper of water from the bucket, and swallowed it gratefully. It checked the coughing spell briefly so she could at least talk.

She shrugged it off. "Oh, it's been hanging on for awhile. It's probably just a cold and will eventually go away," she said.

"Perhaps we ought to go tomorrow and see the physician," Captain Newton advised. "Ask him to give you a tonic or something for it."

"Yes, all right."

✝ ✝ ✝

Elizabeth lay in bed that night dreading her visit to the physician. She, like her husband, already knew the sound of that cough. Enough friends and relatives had contracted what was commonly called consumption (which in later years would be diagnosed as tuberculosis) and marked by that kind of cough. No one Elizabeth knew had ever survived consumption. The disease invariably did as its name implies—consumed the life and breath of the one who contracted it.

Elizabeth had not told her husband that she had been afflicted by this cough for some time—or that she'd already seen the physician. The doctor had treated her a few times by bleeding—a common practice for treating illnesses of that day. He had also prescribed hot soup and instructed her on how to make and apply poultices and bags of raw onions to sew to her nightdress. These treatments, along with other equally innocuous and ineffective doctoring, did nothing. She was losing weight and her daily strength. Her household chores were getting to be much more difficult.

Elizabeth first took notice of the cough when Abigail had visited her two years earlier. It had been more of an annoying tickle in her throat and occasional cough. But when Abigail asked about it, she thought more seriously about it. Then, as it grew worse, she began to have concerns. Perhaps her intuition caused her to ask her friend, during that visit, to promise to care for John if anything ever happened to her.

The captain's last several leaves had been so brief that he'd never really noticed the cough or her weight loss—or if he did, he never mentioned it.

Elizabeth had been growing worse and getting weaker. She knew that it was only a matter of time. But how much time? Elizabeth couldn't bring herself to consider the extreme eventual consequences of her terrible illness.

As she lay there in the dark, the single awful thought concerning her condition was the appalling future it presented for her son. How could he continue to grow and excel in his learning without her? What would happen to him if she died? Then she checked herself—not *if* she died, but *when* she died. Elizabeth felt tears roll down her cheeks and her emotions give way.

Captain Newton had not yet fallen asleep either. He heard his wife weeping softly, but he resisted the impulse to turn toward her and close his arms around her, to comfort her. She was only inches away; he could even feel the bed shaking slightly as she sobbed quietly. But if he held her, consoled her, he'd be admitting to her that he knew. She had bravely tried to downplay her illness, and he understood that action to mean that she did not want to talk about it or to dwell on its inevitability.

The captain decided he would help her by being optimistic about her condition and by not admitting its seriousness. Besides, *maybe it truly is just a simple cold,* he thought.

He decided to wait for providence to reveal their fate.

✞ ✞ ✞

Two days later Captain Newton received word that his ship was soon ready to sail. He greeted the news with mixed feelings. For the first time in his memory, he was reluctant to leave. As he looked at his wife and son, each seemed to have a terrible vulnerability that he'd never before seen in them.

The boy, of course, knew nothing about his mother's condition, and he was only seven—hardly old enough for the captain to take with him

to sea. He should be at least eleven or twelve. Perhaps providence will keep his mother alive until then, Newton hoped. It was his unspoken prayer.

The next day the captain took John with him to the London docks to watch the longshoremen hoist cargo aboard his father's ship. John loved the excursion. He always looked forward to it whenever his father prepared to go to sea. The two of them walked the dirty, noisy street toward the docks, and the various sights and sounds captivated John.

It was still early in the morning, but already some sailors were engaged in drunken storytelling outside a nearby pub. Their loud, ribald tales were laced with foul profanity. As they passed the pub, John smelled the sour, almost nauseous odor of rank ale that had been spilled on the floor of the pub and now hung in the air along with the stale tobacco smells. The captain ignored it all as he marched along the street, John running to keep up with his great strides.

As they came to the dockside where the captain's merchant ship lay anchored in the harbor, it pleased John to see how much respect the sailors showed for his father. He was impressed to learn that his father was obviously an important man.

Captain Newton took John down the slippery stone steps from the seawall to the water's edge where a small longboat was tied. John had to tread carefully and step over the piles of fish entrails spilled onto the steps by a grizzled old fisherman who was cleaning his catch. Two sailors jumped to attention as the captain and John climbed into the waiting boat.

Without instructions, the sailors began rowing the longboat toward the sailing ship. When they reached the ship, the sailors held the boat steady alongside as their two passengers stood up to leave.

"Follow me, John," the captain told his son. He grabbed a rope ladder hanging over the edge of the rails and began pulling himself up to the deck.

John, although he had done this before, was always a bit fearful and unsteady.

"Come on, boy. Don't dally. Just follow me and don't look down. You'll be just fine."

The boy did as he was told but was scared, despite his father's assurances. It was, after all, nearly a three-story drop from where he was on the ladder into the cold, dark sea. Finally, after what seemed to be an eternity for John, he reached the deck. It took him a few moments to get his "sea legs" on the swaying ship. Then he looked across the harbor to the city of London.

The boy's eyes widened in pleasure. It was a fantastic sight. Tall buildings and factories loomed into the sky. Black, sooty smoke belched from chimneys and smokestacks. He could see people everywhere—working, walking, some simply sitting on the seawall. Horses and wagons, swift carriages, pushcarts, and street vendors were everywhere, but they were not common sights for the boy.

While his father checked out the cargo and manifests, John worked up the courage to explore the ship's quarterdeck, with its huge wheel and mast. Sailors were busy tying off the rope rigging and noisily rolling heavy barrels toward the hold.

John looked heavenward to follow the lines of the mast and sails. Nearby, he saw a rope ladder like the one he'd used to board the ship. By now he had enough confidence to climb it in order to get an even higher view of the city. He climbed about twenty feet and peered across the harbor. It was a striking sight. He climbed a bit higher and was now more conscious of the swaying of the ship. For several minutes he stood there transfixed by the whole visual scene and the sounds and smells.

As he climbed down, his father came back on deck. "I can't wait, Father."

"Can't wait for what?"

"For the day when I can go to sea with you. Do you think it will be soon? I promise not to get homesick or get in the way. Will you let me come next time?"

"The sea is a rough life for anyone, son, let alone a child. Ordinarily they say a boy isn't ready for sea until he's twelve," Captain Newton told his son. But after noticing the cloud that came over his face, he added, "Still, some boys are more mature than others and can adapt well. We'll see."

✝ ✝ ✝

It was time for Captain Newton to leave. He had hired a hackney carriage to help him get his things to the dock, and the horse and carriage had already arrived.

As he picked up his sea chest and put it onto the carriage rack, the captain watched young John. The boy, fascinated by the horse, jumped up and down in excitement. As John glanced at his father, he suddenly stopped his boyish antics, stood tall, and saluted his father who, in turn, smiled and returned the salute. Then, uncharacteristically, the captain strode over to John, swept the boy up into his arms, and hugged him tightly.

Elizabeth, watching from the door, felt a catch in her throat. This was such an amazing scene to her that she ran to her husband and threw her arms around him, kissing him with great love and excitement, oblivious to the usual rules of formality demanded by their relationship.

The captain surprised his wife by putting down the boy, wrapping his arms around Elizabeth, and kissing her in return. She was crying, and even the captain's eyes blinked back tears.

Captain Newton never utterly lost his composure, however, and slowly pulled away from her before he did. "I must go now," he whispered simply. "But see to it that you visit the physician. I am concerned about your health." With that, he climbed into the carriage and slapped the side of the door to tell the driver to move on.

The boy and his mother watched the horse and carriage move quickly down the lane and become lost among the trees, curving the road at Simpson's Corners.

Elizabeth wondered—would this be the last time she'd ever see her husband? If so, the sweet memory of this final good-bye would be the perfect way for them to part. Her heart was at peace at his remarkable show of affection.

She watched as John and his dog ran after the carriage until it outpaced them. Then the boy ran to the nearby meadow to play with friends.

After a few moments, Elizabeth went inside and took out parchment, a small bottle of ink, and a pen to write a letter:

My dearest friend, Abigail,

How I have grieved about this day. Today my husband has left for sea. Our parting was sad, but he greatly lifted my spirits with his fond farewell. I shall treasure how he expressed his affection to me as never before.

Somehow I believe he has guessed the secret that I have shared only with you and God. Still, he has not talked of it, except to say that I must see a physician. Perhaps he still does not know, which is my preference. I do not wish him to be worried for me.

Abigail, I shall impose upon our friendship once again. I find that I am growing weaker daily. Soon I will not be able to care for John. Dare I presume that you might visit me, and stay until the end, which I suspect, is near? Please ask your dear husband if it is at all possible for you to come to London.

Yours affectionately,
Elizabeth Newton

Chapter Four

Angel of Mercy, Angel of Death

✟

Abigail Catlett had wrestled with the contents of Elizabeth's letter for several days before replying. It was true; she had given her word that she would look after John. But in practical terms, that was difficult now that she had more children of her own—Mary, now three, Elizabeth who was one and barely walking, plus a new baby boy.

She conferred with her husband, George, who was a customs officer in Chatham. He helped her respond to Elizabeth's letter with logic as well as compassion. Instead of going to London to care for Elizabeth, Abigail could bring Elizabeth and John to Chatham where it would be easier for her to take care of her friend.

Abigail left her children in the care of a friend and took a carriage to London where she found Elizabeth sick in bed. Seven-year-old John was trying to care for her, and women from the Dissenter Chapel came by often to help.

"Elizabeth," Abigail said shortly after her arrival, "I cannot stay, but George and I have talked it over, and we believe the best thing is for you to come back with me to Chatham. You must get away from the smoke and soot of London and get some fresh air into your lungs. You'll be able to rest and recuperate. After two or three months of rest, perhaps you'll have regained enough strength to resume your life."

Abigail began at once to pack Elizabeth's clothes and things into a small trunk. She then fixed tea and some food and took her a tray in bed. "I want you to eat something. You must try and fight this to regain your strength."

Elizabeth forced herself into a sitting position and took the tray. As Abigail looked at her, she nearly began to cry. Her dear cousin and closest friend looked like an old woman. Her pale skin was dry, gray, and wrinkled. There were bags and dark circles under the eyes that no longer shined with the excitement and enthusiasm of life. Elizabeth was dying.

"I'll be back shortly, Elizabeth," Abigail said as she wrapped a shawl around her shoulders. "I am going to see Dr. Jennings, your minister, to let him know that you will be coming to stay with me for awhile."

Elizabeth simply nodded and sipped her tea.

Dr. Jennings received Abigail following her short walk to the church. As she explained to him the situation, he seemed to understand.

"But you say that you have three small children at home?" he asked.

"Yes."

"I see." He paused thoughtfully. "Then allow me to make a suggestion. I know you have given Mrs. Newton your commitment to care for John in the event, God forbid, something dire happens to her. But you will certainly have your hands full."

"But I promised Elizabeth—"

"Yes, I know," Dr. Jennings replied. "But why not let a family from our church look after the boy while his mother is away? It would be best for him in the long run. If his mother takes a turn for the worse while she's away, he won't have to look on as she suffers. I know of a very loving family who'd love to take care of him."

They talked for nearly a half hour longer while the parson took notes and copied the Catlett's address in Chatham so the boy could write his mother letters. He promised to make the necessary arrangements for John's care.

"Now you go, take Elizabeth, and nurse her back to health, God willing. I'll see to the care of the boy. Don't worry. You are doing the right thing."

Abigail reached out and shook the pastor's hand and whispered, "Thank you, Dr. Jennings. And if anything should happen to Elizabeth, be sure to tell Captain Newton and the family caring for John that my husband and I will come and get him and take him to live in our home."

Dr. Jennings nodded and ushered her to the parsonage door.

When she came back, Abigail told Elizabeth of the change in plans—namely that John would stay with a family from the church. Elizabeth knew the family and felt reassured. She had been concerned about John having to watch her die and felt relieved that she would not have to see him suffer. This way he'd come to the Catlett home afterwards and avoid being caught up in her conflict with death.

When John came back and saw that his mother was leaving in the carriage with Abigail, he began to cry.

"Don't cry, John," his mother soothed. "I must go away to rest. You know that I have been sick for a long time. I shall try and get better. I need you to be brave and pray for me."

"Let us all pray for your mother," said Dr. Jennings, who had come to say good-bye and ask God to watch over this frail, saintly young woman. His deep baritone voice asked heaven to intercede for her and for God

to send his angels to watch over Elizabeth and her son. He also prayed for Captain Newton.

The boy stood by the tall preacher as the carriage took his mother away. John knew now that his mother was terribly sick and wondered if she was going to die, but he didn't share that fear with the minister. Rather, he decided that he would pray for her and told Dr. Jennings, "I'll pray every hour, whenever I hear the steeple clock chime, until God answers my prayers."

"There's a good boy," said the pastor, patting the boy on the head. "God delights in hearing prayers of children. Be assured, he'll hear you."

Angel of Death . . .

Never had Captain Newton experienced such storms as struck his ship off the coast of North Africa on his way to Barcelona. Hurricane-strength winds battered the sturdy craft and crippled the main mast. In addition, they had glanced off a coral reef in the Straits of Gibraltar and tore an eight-inch hole in the cargo hold, just below the waterline. The crew managed to stuff it with some hemp and tar, but it still leaked badly.

For two weeks the ship was tossed about in the angry seas. When the weather cleared, they turned northeast and headed for the Balearic Islands for repairs. The ship's pilot reckoned they were still several days out of Palma on the major island of Mallorca of the Balearics.

Their store of fresh food and water was running low. The captain had ordered his men to collect rainwater for drinking. Adding to their predicament, much of their flour had been soaked by rain coming into the galley, so the cook and cook's helpers were forced to provide more and more meals of fish—fried fish, dried fish, fish stew, fish broth—and the men soon wearied of such monotonous fare.

Captain Newton ordered the ship to track close along the Spanish

coast on their way to Mallorca to see if they could find a harbor where they could lay in a store of fresh water, flour, and meat.

They found such a spot one Sunday morning. It was about forty miles north of Valencia on the east coast. The captain sent a dozen crewmen ashore in a longboat, with muskets, to hunt for wild game. They returned with a deer and a half dozen quail.

Upon their return, the lieutenant, Hiram Bishop, pulled the captain aside.

"Captain, I think we'd better hoist anchor and be on our way," he said quietly.

"Why? We haven't found fresh water yet."

"To be sure, Captain. But we have a fairly good supply, what with the rainwater. The reason is, I saw another ship laying at anchor opposite that cliff that juts out into the water, over there." He pointed to the peninsula that hid the other bay.

"I went to scout for water when I saw it. It's maybe Turkish or some other registry. But it doesn't matter because it's full of pirates!"

"Pirates?" The word made the hair on the captain's neck stand up. Pirates were the plague of the shipping industry. Only two other times had Captain Newton encountered them directly—both times he was given strong winds and was able to outrun their ships. This time his ship was crippled and could barely sail.

"How do you know they're pirates?" the captain asked.

"A small ship was nearby. They were loading cargo from the smaller to the bigger ship—"

"But that doesn't necessarily mean they're pirates."

"I took my telescope with me and watched. I saw them take the crew members of the small ship to shore, and they were tied up. A few had been wounded. They'll probably leave them stranded on land and scuttle their ship once they've plundered it."

"Did anyone see you?" Newton asked.

"No, sir. They were too busy getting ready to set fire to the small ship. There—you can see the smoke now, rising above the cliff." He pointed to the spot about a mile or two away.

The proof was convincing enough for Captain Newton. "Tell the men to get those supplies stowed and prepare to sail," he ordered his officer. "Make sure they keep their voices down. Sound carries for miles at sea, and we don't want to alert them."

Captain Newton reviewed his defenses. His ship was outfitted with only a few cannons, and in their condition, they were highly vulnerable to attack and boarding. As his men were preparing to sail, the captain excused himself and hurried to his cabin.

He reviewed the maps and charts on the desk for a few moments. Then, pushing them aside, he took out paper and pen to write. He wrote a letter to Elizabeth, in case they were unlucky in their attempts to avoid capture—or worse:

> My dearest wife,
>
> I have only time to write you this brief letter, and I pray that it gets into your hands. We are at the mercy of providence or perhaps the angel of death, having lost our main mast and taking in seawater in the hold. We have managed to keep ahead of the flooding, but we now face a terrible threat that I fear even providence cannot keep us from.
>
> If we do not survive, I want you to know that I hold you and John in highest affection, that you are both dearer to me than my own life. My regret is that I may never see you again to express my love for you. I pray that God will deliver us. If that is not possible, please tell John that his father died valiantly with no regrets.
>
> Your devoted husband,
> Capt. John Newton

He folded the letter, sealed it with candle wax, and put it in a small metal box on the desk, on top of the copy of his last will and testament. Then he strapped on his sword and went back on deck.

Lieutenant Bishop was standing on the quarterdeck, his eye steadfast on the cove where the pirate vessel lay at anchor. Their ship had gotten underway and was now about to cross into the pirates' line of vision. The officer focused the telescope and caught sight of the pirate ship just as their own ship reached the outer banks. The pirate frigate was three miles astern, and so far, no one had seen them.

Suddenly, they heard several gunshots in the distance.

"They're signaling the shore party! They must have spotted us! They must have been looking for fresh food and water as we were," called out Lieutenant Bishop. "They have two or three longboats with crew ashore. It'll take them awhile to get the men back to the beach and then to the ship. We might have a chance."

"Let's get every square inch of canvas into those sails that work! Run with the wind as fast as we can," the captain shouted. "And if any of you are God-fearing men, pray as though your very lives depend on it. For they do!"

Captain Newton watched the pirates through the telescope. He reckoned they had a crew of fifty or more, which was a mixed blessing. As such, they outnumbered his crew. But because so many of them were on shore, they were having difficulty rounding them up from the nearby woods. Newton's ship was many miles away by the time the pirate ship finally weighed anchor and set sail, but the pirate ship was faster and not crippled.

As if to add to Captain Newton's misery, it began to storm again. His beleaguered crew toiled despite the roaring wind and downpour.

"Lieutenant Bishop!" the captain called out.

"Aye, sir!" The officer ran over to Newton.

"Can you see the enemy?" he asked.

"We can't see the pirate ship through the rain," he replied, and then grinned broadly.

The captain looked puzzled. Why was this good news?

As if anticipating the question, Lieutenant Bishop said, "If we can't see them, they can't see us."

The captain responded quickly. "Tell the men to turn hard to port!"

"But sir, won't we get away faster if we keep the wind at our back?"

"Yes, and that's just what they expect. We can't outrun their ship with its full sails. If we go hard to port, at right angles to our present course, we'll be harder to find when the storm ends and when they start looking for us again."

"Aye, sir!" Lieutenant Bishop ran to carry out the orders.

It was as if providence had prevailed over the angel of death. Captain Newton's crew worked far into the night to elude their captors. Just before dawn on Monday, the storm finally subsided, and the ship's pilot reckoned that they were some sixty miles south of the pirate ship.

Before sunrise Captain Newton called the crew on deck and asked one of his officers to offer a prayer of thanksgiving to God for their deliverance. Then he went to his cabin, found the letter to his wife that he'd written earlier, took it, and tore it up, tossing the pieces out the porthole into the sea.

✝ ✝ ✝

It had been nearly four months since John had last seen his mother. He could remember the woman who took her away, but he had almost forgotten how his mother looked.

Four months is a long time in the life of a seven-year-old boy. Sometimes his father would be gone for that long, but he was used to it, and when his father returned, he was expected.

Now Dr. Jennings not only told him that there was no telling when he'd see his mother again, he also told him that his father had sent word

by way of another merchant ship that he was in Spain where his ship was being repaired. It would be another two or three months before he could return to London.

When John had persisted and asked the minister about his mother's return, Dr. Jennings was vague and added, "You must be brave, my son, and remember to pray."

"I pray every hour when I hear the church clock chime," John reminded him. "But I don't think God hears me," he said, discouraged.

"Well, your father will be home in a few weeks or so. When he comes, perhaps he'll take you to visit your mother."

When John was returned to the home of the family caring for him, he sat in the corner, thinking about the day and his concerns.

He was so engrossed in his thoughts that he began to daydream about the old days when his mother played with him, read to him, and sang to him. He recalled her youthful beauty, not the sickly frame that housed her soul when Abigail had taken her away. He remembered their fond times together, reading, singing, and playing. His reverie was pleasant, and he held onto the memories for a long time.

Suddenly it occurred to him that he must have missed hearing the clock chime at four o'clock, and as a result, had forgotten to pray. He felt a sense of panic. After all, he had promised God to pray every waking hour. Now he had broken his promise. He hadn't meant to, of course, but what if God broke his end of the supposed agreement?

John thought, *What if God doesn't keep his end of the bargain because I failed to pray?* And for the first time, this thought, *What if my mother dies? It will be my fault!*

✝ ✝ ✝

Abigail held her baby in her arms while four-year-old Mary (who somehow got nicknamed Polly) stood nearby, holding her father's hand. George Catlett held their toddler, Elizabeth (namesake of her aunt). The

entire family was together, dressed as for church, but it was midweek and not the Sabbath. Nor were they in the sanctuary of their church.

A few onlookers stood nearby out of respect for their neighbors, the Catletts. Everyone was outside the church, in the back, in the grave-yard. Elizabeth had finally lost her struggle and expired on Sunday, just after midnight.

She had tried to be valiant, but she was devastated because she was not able to see her son before she died. She wasn't bitter about dying. She'd even come to welcome it when her body began to give out completely. Elizabeth was an inspiration to Abigail and her family. Her faith left each of them eager to find such peace and hope for themselves.

Elizabeth had written letters to her husband and son, to be given to them after her death. Abigail did not know exactly what was in them, but they were no doubt expressions of the love Elizabeth had for each of them—love that sustained her to the end.

As the vicar stood beside the open grave, he prayed as Abigail's eyes looked over the scene. The grave was situated beneath a giant oak tree that promised a place of peace and tranquility for Elizabeth's remains. Since summer was at its height, flowers were in bloom throughout the cemetery, and thick green ivy covered the stone walls of the church. It was all too lovely. In light of her grief, Abigail thought the surroundings should be bleak and dreary, raining and cold—not as it was, pleasant to the eyes and soul.

The vicar concluded the service, pronounced the benediction, and stood aside as the caretaker and his assistant lowered a plain wooden coffin into the newly dug ground. Abigail walked over to it, holding a beautiful long-stemmed yellow rose from her garden. She lightly kissed the rose and dropped it onto the coffin below.

One by one, the others drifted away and back to their homes. George had taken the children and walked slowly back to their home as Abigail

stood for several minutes by Elizabeth's fresh grave, weeping with heartfelt grief. For many months Abigail had held back her tears in an attempt to bolster Elizabeth's spirits, but now she could not hold them back. Her body shook violently with great sobbing.

She thought of John and wondered how she could ever tell the boy that his mother was dead. Perhaps George was right. Maybe it was best just to leave such things until Captain Newton returned.

Elizabeth's husband didn't even know she was dead. Abigail decided to leave to Dr. Jennings the task of telling him and to let the vicar and the boy's father decide how to break the news to John.

Chapter Five

1733 — The Captain Returns

✠

It had been several months since young John had been told of his mother's death. Dr. Jennings felt it best not to wait until the captain's return. As it turned out, his instincts were correct. The boy would have been kept waiting for nearly a year—the actual time Captain Newton was delayed at sea.

In the simplicity of his childlike faith, John could not understand why God did not answer his prayers and restore his mother's health. He even feared that he had caused it to happen—that by sometimes forgetting to pray "every time the steeple clock chimed" as he'd promised, maybe God had punished him for his lack of diligence. It troubled the boy greatly, and he wondered if it was so—was God that demanding and unloving?

Young John had been having nightmares that his father was also dead, leaving him an orphan. He reckoned that since no one had told him about his mother's death until well after its occurrence that maybe

he wasn't being told the full story about his father. First he'd been told that his father's ship was damaged and that he was delayed in Spain for repairs. Then he didn't get word for months. After that he received occasional snatches of news but could tell from his guardians' whispered conversations after a visit by someone from the admiralty office that his father was more than a little overdue. John suspected that he wasn't the only one who feared for his father's life.

Dr. Jennings and John's guardian family had been kind and supportive during his time of grief, but there was no way they could fill the void left by the loss of his mother. John even missed the presence of his stern father.

Dr. Jennings received a letter from the Catletts with word that John was welcome to come and live with them. As nearest kin they were prepared to look after him while his father was at sea. Dr. Jennings replied that such a decision should wait until John's father returned or until word of his loss at sea.

✝ ✝ ✝

The captain's wife had died almost a year earlier, and he was still unaware of it. Captain Newton had missed his expected return by many months. He was supposed to return just after John's seventh birthday in July of the previous year but didn't. He finally returned in the spring of 1733, a full year after he'd left.

A neighbor met the captain at the London docks when his ship entered into the harbor. The neighbor had no real details for him, except the news that Captain Newton's wife had died in the care of her cousin, Mrs. Catlett, the previous summer. The captain learned that her death was caused by consumption—which, of course, was no real surprise.

Captain Newton received the news without emotion and displayed no outward grief. He hired a carriage and rode to his home. By now John

had been fetched and ran to greet his father as the carriage pulled up in front of their home.

The meeting was awkward for each of them, but for different reasons. John, who was so relieved to see that his father was still alive, wept with joy and smothered him with hugs and kisses. His father, helpless to find words to comfort the boy at his mother's death, simply said nothing.

The two of them went into their house. John's guardian and his wife had taken the boy to meet his father there. They had also taken him there right after Elizabeth's death and had draped black crepe ribbon in the windows and on the door. This, the couple had explained to John, was done to let everyone know that a death had occurred and that this house was in mourning.

The captain stared sullenly at the crepe. Then he strode across the room, savagely pulled down the black crepe, rolled it into a ball, and threw it into the fireplace. Breathing heavily, the captain stood silent for a moment.

"I'm glad you have come back, Papa," John whispered to his father. "I was afraid you were dead too."

Captain Newton still said nothing.

✝ ✝ ✝

Abigail had received word that the captain had returned from his sea voyage, so she sent him a letter extending her consolation and her offer to take in the boy. She invited him to bring John to Chatham when it was convenient, before he had to go back to sea. Several weeks passed, and she heard nothing.

"You'd think he'd want to talk to us about her death, to learn the details of Elizabeth's passing," Abigail had told her husband.

"Um . . . maybe," George had replied. "But you have to remember, he's just found out about it himself. For him, it's like it just happened.

Give him time to get used to it, time to grieve. Also, I expect he needs time to be with the boy. Just wait awhile. He'll come around."

Three weeks after that conversation, the Catletts still had not heard from the captain. Abigail was getting impatient. She asked her husband if the family could take a holiday and visit London where she could talk with Captain Newton and bring John back to Chatham. He agreed. When they got to London, they stopped at the Newton home, only to find it all shuttered.

A neighbor told them that Captain Newton and his son had recently moved everything to Avely, some fifteen miles away, in Essex.

"They've moved? Why?" asked Abigail.

"That's where his new wife lives, with her father," the neighbor answered simply.

"Wife!?" Abigail stammered, "H-he has a *wife?* When—how?"

"Well, Captain Newton weren't much for tellin' his feelings. I expect he felt sorry for his first wife dyin', but he has a boy who needs a mother, and I s'pose he wanted to find himself a wife before he went back to sea. Comes from a good family, the new wife. It'll be good for the boy—havin' a mother."

Abigail looked at her husband incredulously. As soon as the neighbor was out of earshot, she sputtered, "I can't believe it! How could anyone be so cruel to his wife's memory?"

"It does seem surprising," George answered. "But then, it has been about a year—that's a decent amount of time."

"But not for *him*. He's only known about her death for weeks, not the whole year. He hasn't had time to grieve, let alone mourn her decently. The man is absolutely heartless!" she fumed. "It's as if one of his crew died, so he just goes down to the docks and recruits another man to take his place! No feelings—no emotion. Just 'hire' a new wife so he can go back to sea without having to worry about what'll happen to John!"

Her husband tried to be more positive. "Well, the neighbor says the

new wife comes from a good family. Maybe the captain made the only decision that seemed right to him. The boy needs somebody to care for him. The captain found someone to marry him, so we'll have to trust providence that it'll all work out."

Abigail was not as sure as her husband, but she said nothing more about it during their ride back to Chatham.

✛ ✛ ✛

John was confused. His father came home one day and said simply, "Your mother has died, and she's buried. We must get on with our lives. I don't want you to speak of her again. You must get over it. She's gone. You'll have to forget her. Don't ever mention her again in my presence."

That did not make sense to John and neither did what happened the next day. His father came home with a woman about the same age as his mother. She was attractive and well-dressed, but she seemed quite nervous.

With the utmost economy of words, his father introduced them to each other and defined the future. "John, may I present Thomasin. She and I were married this morning. She's your stepmother, but you may call her 'Mother.' We'll be moving today to her father's farm in Essex. We must leave right away for I sail in three days."

Then, as the shocked boy watched, most of their belongings were brought from the house and loaded on a large livery wagon, and the men who helped load the wagon got aboard and drove off.

Some of the things that didn't go on the wagon were put into the family carriage. John was lifted onto the seat to sit between his father and his new wife. The three of them then drove east for four hours until they arrived at the farm.

That night, in a strange house, John watched as Thomasin unpacked his mother's fine porcelain and other precious things and arranged them on shelves in her home.

John was told that he would sleep in the bed used by Thomasin's father, a widower. The boy undressed in the dark and climbed into the bed. It had old, matted feather pillows that smelled sour and musty. He lay on his back to avoid the smell and cried himself to sleep, only to be awakened awhile later as Thomasin's father crawled into the bed with him. The old man smelled of sweat and onions. His breath reeked of whiskey—the same sour smell in the pillows.

"Good-night, boy. Rest well," said the man.

Chapter Six

1735—Learning to Hate

✠

Nine-year-old John had a great deal of trouble adjusting to his new situation. Thomasin, his stepmother, had absolutely no experience with children and decided not to even try. She was nervous enough as a new bride living in the same home as her father.

She hadn't consciously rejected John; rather, she ignored him. She let the boy have free rein and seldom had any conversation or involvement with him, except for common meals and his chores. And since he made such a fuss about doing his chores, his stepmother found it easier and less aggravating to ignore the missed chores than to constantly nag him. John was glad for that and learned quickly that if he argued loud and long enough, Thomasin usually gave in.

Much of the time he was unsupervised and left to himself. Often he ran down to the marshes where he could see the tall ships coming from the sea into the inlet that was the water path into the docks at London.

As he lay quietly on a grassy knoll watching the big ships slowly make passage through the inlet, he wished he were aboard and could go to London with them. He also wished for a way to turn back time and go to his old house, to be with his mother, laughing and learning. He also missed being with her in church, the two of them singing the hymns that they both loved.

Here in Avely, he neither went to church (except for the rare occasions when his father was on leave and took him to services) nor kept up his schooling.

He'd found another source for his "education," however. Since Thomasin had no interest in what he did each day, he ran with a motley gang of neighborhood children, most of them several years older than John. These local teens and adolescents did not have the benefit of an upbringing by a mother like Elizabeth. They had no sense of morality or virtues. As a result, John spent most of his time with these unruly neighborhood boys. They were mostly unschooled but were knowledgeable in fighting, stealing, and other lawbreaking activities. From them he learned even more ways to irk his stepmother and get into trouble.

In contrast to Elizabeth's godly influence, the only time John heard anything about God these days was when his name was used as profanity. The gang he ran with taught John lessons from the street. At first he learned a few petty crimes—how to pinch fruit and other items from the marketplace, how to swipe clothes from clotheslines, and other kinds of mischief. Then John graduated to more serious offenses. In that day it was a capital crime to poach on private land; even children were sometimes hanged for killing game on private land. John's companions taught him how to stay away from the game warden and hunt without being caught. John killed pheasants, rabbits, and deer but never kept any of the game for himself, realizing that Thomasin's father would know at once that it was taken by poaching.

The gang also taught John how to stand up to authority, which he practiced to perfection at home. Many times, however, his insolence was met with punishment. If he talked back to his stepmother, Thomasin's father intervened. He'd take a wide belt and beat John until he raised welts and bruises. That only made the boy more impertinent, triggering more outbursts, which led to more beatings. It never occurred to John that he could control that cycle of punishment and pain with his behavior. Instead, the beatings only inflamed the feelings of hatred he had for both his stepmother and her father.

The matter of John's unruliness was given to Captain Newton when he came home on leave. His wife suggested that they enroll John in a boarding school where he could be disciplined and educated.

The idea was attractive to the captain. After all, he had been sent away at that age and was taught the rigors and disciplines of life through formal education.

The methods of instruction had not changed since the Jesuits had taught the captain as a boy. Intimidation and harshness governed the process. Classes were held during the daylight hours. Homework was to be done later, requiring work in dim light by oil lamp or candlelight. Any infractions were dealt with quickly and harshly. No recesses or breaks for recreation or relaxation were given, and only a few holidays were observed, mainly Christmas and one or two other religious days.

John Newton hated the boarding school. His disobedience and rebellion were not tolerated at all. Yet, even a question, if not phrased in the right way, could be interpreted as insolence. He was constantly in trouble and being punished. John quickly made the observation that he had merely traded the beatings of Thomasin's father for those of his teachers. But now it was worse—there were more adults to punish him and treat him harshly! The headmaster who organized and ran the school was a true sadist. John's hatred of the headmaster and other emotionally warped, abusive teachers grew fervent.

Soon John's circle of hatred widened to include his headmaster and teachers, his stepmother and her father. He also hated Mrs. Catlett, the woman who took his mother away to die. In a strange, perverse way he even hated his mother for deserting him through death and his father for deserting him as well, although on more regularly scheduled occasions. And of course, he hated God for ignoring his prayers and allowing his mother to die in the first place.

Perhaps more than anything, he hated himself worst of all. He felt he had betrayed all the goodness and moral decency his mother had taught him, that he had let her down through his terrible behavior and disobedience. He knew better. He had a grasp of moral good—the difference between right and wrong—yet he seemed unable to act on that knowledge.

John struggled for nearly two intolerable years at the boys' school. On more than one occasion he had pleaded with his father to reconsider and allow him to return home, but Thomasin resisted that idea. She was now pregnant and would soon have her hands full caring for a new baby.

Despite the punishing hardships, John stayed in school, and he did learn. He also found a new teacher, younger and more sympathetic, who encouraged the students rather than punishing them as part of the process of learning.

This young teacher used positive means to inspire his students. He saw in John an ability to learn. The boy also had an advantageous bent toward language, so he encouraged John to study Latin, Greek, and algebra. With this encouragement, John was soon reading the classics of Western literature and quickly outpaced the other students—and even some of his teachers. This proved to be a problem. When he asked questions his teachers couldn't answer, they often rebuked him—as if he was disparaging them by pointing out their ignorance.

John got great satisfaction in thinking that his learning might be on a par with some of his instructors. That satisfaction was tempered, how-

ever, by having to endure canings and constant verbal abuse. The basic atmosphere and activities at the school did not change.

Finally, after two terrible, trying years of this nightmare experience, John could bear it no longer. When his father came home the next time, he went to him, showed him the welts from a recent beating, and told him of the horrors of the place. The captain tried to explain that it was all a part of growing up, that discipline was part of the process of learning.

"I understand discipline, sir. But these people aren't interested in learning. Many of them barely know what they're talking about. It's not like the university where the instructors are qualified. Some of them are immature, and many don't even have formal schooling. They don't care about honest inquiry, sir, but only in having students recite answers by rote."

His father seemed to be listening, so John was encouraged to continue. "When I ask questions they can't answer, they say I'm being insolent, and they beat me. Sir, I tell you that if you don't take me away from there I shall run away as soon as you take me back!" John declared defiantly.

Speaking to his father in such a way was the most insubordinate act he'd ever shown to his father. Never had he stood up to him and stated his feelings so forcefully. Instinctively, Captain Newton's hand came up to slap the boy for his insolence, but at the last instant, he held it in check. The captain blinked and at first did not know how to respond. Then he turned his back to John for a long moment.

"All right," he said finally, "I will take you out of the school, but you can't come home. Your stepmother has her hands full caring for William."

John's half-brother, born six months earlier, was a joyous event for the family. However, he took all of Thomasin's attention, time, and energy. Thomasin and her father were so focused on the new baby that

they totally ignored John. Both Captain Newton and John knew that he'd be unwelcome at home.

"I think maybe it's time for you to go to sea with me," his father said.

"Really? That sounds like a great idea!" John said enthusiastically.

"You've had enough education. You can read and write well enough to serve you. What you need now is some experience at sea. You need to learn the value of hard work and the merchant trade. Normally a boy should be twelve to go to sea, as I've told you many times. But you're almost eleven now, and perhaps you are ready."

"Oh, I *am,* I really am ready!"

✛ ✛ ✛

John could hardly believe his good fortune. On July 24, 1736, his eleventh birthday, he boarded the ship with his father and sailed. He soon mastered his chores aboard ship and was also quick to learn the basic skills of a seaman. His father had not put him in the crew quarters with the other deckhands but allowed him to stay in his quarters.

This was a mixed blessing, however. John appreciated the better accommodations, but in order to justify the "favoritism" to his crew, Captain Newton was unjustly harsh with John. He made more demands and expected a higher standard from his son than any of the other crew, despite John's youth and inexperience.

The other members of the crew noticed the captain's harsh treatment and felt sorry for John, but the boy did not seem to mind. After all, he had never known anything except the strict and brusque ways of his father, so he simply accepted the discipline without complaint.

For John, this regimen was better than the boarding school. In fact, he enjoyed the fresh air, the feel of salt spray, and all the sights, sounds, and smells of the sea.

Eventually the captain no longer felt compelled to make such an effort to avoid any crew accusations of favoritism. Actually, many of

them had even volunteered to the captain how well John was doing. It was true. He *was* doing well.

The captain, trying to be objective concerning his son, was nevertheless forced to conclude that John was not only doing a good job—he also had a natural ability as a seaman.

John had been at sea for nearly a month and still hadn't shown any signs of seasickness. And he was fearless at climbing the rigging. He always pulled his own weight as part of a crew. For the first time in his life, the captain had feelings of pride and affection for his son. Gratefully, John sensed that his father was showing him more respect and was all the more determined to please him. He put his full energy into becoming a real sailor.

The men respected John too. Ordinarily, young boys who went to sea were teased and hazed by the crew members during their initiation. However, John got little of this torment. Instead, the crew welcomed him into their off-duty gatherings. He listened to their ribald stories and picked up their foul-mouthed language (which the boy often used to their amusement, but never within the captain's hearing).

It was in their company that he learned about their sexual excursions—times they looked forward to when in port. John listened attentively as each man bragged of personal experiences and lied about sexual prowess. But much of their talk went naively over young John's head.

On Sundays Captain Newton held church services aboard ship. Not much of a religious man himself, apart from his occasional visits to church while on shore leave, the captain took Sunday services aboard his ship quite seriously. The men were required to attend, but they showed little interest or respect for the service.

As Captain Newton read a psalm or led them in a hymn, he did so perfunctorily and without passion, and he read the Book of Common Prayer with a droll and pompous voice. The men snickered and whispered when the captain wasn't looking and mocked him behind his back.

John picked up on this disrespect, and because he knew the captain better than anyone, he was uncannily accurate in exaggerating his speech as well as all his mannerisms and quirks.

After they were at sea several weeks, John was on deck one night studying the constellations in order to get his bearings. The night was warm and muggy, the sea was calm, and he couldn't sleep. Several other crew members were also still up. A couple stood quietly talking near the ship's wheel. Two others were on watch. A lone sailor sat on a coil of rope beneath the rigging and sang softly.

Most of the men, like John, had shed most of their clothes in the heat—the near nakedness of the men was common at such times, and no one seemed to be perturbed.

"Can't sleep, Johnny?" a voice from behind him asked.

John turned to see Nivens, the cook and ship's doctor. "Just restless, I suppose," the boy replied.

"Yeah, me too. But I know just what you need. Come with me," Nivens said as he led the boy along the rail corridor to the stairway below deck. They walked to the galley where Nivens worked and slept. Nivens went to the unkempt cot at the edge of the quarters and motioned for John to come and sit beside him.

✝ ✝ ✝

An hour later John was back on deck. This time, however, he shivered in the night air. Sick to his stomach, he shook with fear and shame. He didn't know what had just happened to him, but he knew that something terrible had taken place.

Nivens had reassured him that what happened was appropriate—just a part of growing up, but John had not believed him. He felt that what Nivens had done was wrong. Then, when the man had threatened him, he knew it was wrong. Nivens had smiled, but his words had a sinister

ring. "This is just between us. If you ever tell anybody, I'll slit your throat—so help me God!"

On deck, John felt tears of shame and anger roll down his cheeks. His distress impelled him to want to run to his father and tell him everything, but he checked himself. What if his father didn't believe him? What would he say? John knew that his father was more than likely to punish him even more.

He wasn't sure exactly what had happened, so for some moments he just sat there, shivering. Then he began to sob softly as the feelings of hurt and revulsion overwhelmed him. He suddenly bent over the rail, retching violently, and in the silence he heard his vomit hit the water below.

After awhile, John regained control and went to the bow of the ship. He felt like throwing himself overboard into the shiny wake below but didn't have the courage. Instead, he took the rope bucket, lowered it over the side, and brought up a full bucket of seawater. He found the brush for scrubbing the deck and used it to scour his body in a rough attempt to be clean once more.

The next day no one noticed the scratches on his skin made by the harsh brush, and Nivens was nowhere to be seen. He had kept close to the ship's galley all day, wondering if John would reveal what had happened.

I'll just tell 'em I was drunk, Nivens thought to himself. He hated himself for what he'd done to the boy the previous night. He tried to ease his conscience by reminding himself that another sailor who said he was teaching young Nivens the facts of life had similarly abused him at that age.

Nivens muttered to himself, *He'll get over it. I did.*

Chapter Seven

1739-42—the Boy Becoming a Man

During the next several years at sea, serving as a sailor aboard his father's ship, John Newton grew into maturity. He started living in the crew quarters, sleeping in his own hammock instead of in the captain's quarters. The crew had come to respect the young man who received no favoritism from Captain Newton.

John had shown a natural inclination to the sea. It would not be long before he could apprentice aboard another ship and learn how to become a sea captain himself. He looked forward to this time. However, he also felt a kinship with the ordinary men and relished the time he still had to be a youth and to be as rowdy as the best of the men.

When he was fourteen, his father had him stay home for a year, hoping that he'd settle down. Instead, he fell into the company of a rough crowd in the Essex region and got into a number of skirmishes with local authorities.

Three particular incidents had a dramatic impact upon John. The first took place at the farm owned by the father of Thomasin, his step-mother. John loved to ride horses and always rode at breakneck speeds across the countryside.

One day, while racing across a meadow, his horse stopped suddenly. The momentum threw John from the horse, and he fell onto the ground. He shook his head, clearing his focus. His eyes widened in horror as he got up. The farmer had pruned his hedgerows into stubby, twelve-inch spikes. If he had landed farther to one side, his back and head would have been pierced and he'd have been killed instantly!

Immediately John thought of his mother's teaching of God, whom he was quite convinced had saved him from death. For awhile he became very sober and dedicated to prayer and devotions.

Another time, a British man-of-war was anchored in Long Reach harbor near his home. One Friday evening, he and a friend went down to the beach to check it out. They watched as a longboat from the ship made its way toward shore.

"What are our chances of getting a closer look at the man-of-war?" John called out to one of the sailors beaching the longboat.

The sailor recognized John as the son of Captain Newton whom he respected greatly. "Sure, I can take you over to see the ship," he replied. "But I can't take you until Sunday. Come back early Sunday afternoon, and I'll take you aboard."

John ran back home excitedly. When Sunday came, he could hardly wait. Captain Newton decided to take John and the family to church, but the Sabbath service ran unusually long and the Sunday meal seemed to drag on and on. He knew better than leave the table before his father dismissed them, so John merely shifted nervously, looking at the clock on the mantle click by the minutes.

The meal finally ended and John leaped up to run to the barn where he saddled a horse and rode it quickly to Long Reach harbor.

By the time he got to the beach and dismounted, he saw the longboat had already left without him. He watched from shore as his friend, along with a number of other village boys inside the longboat, yelled and jeered at his misfortune.

John cursed loudly and stomped his feet in anger. Then the laughing, teasing voices in the boat changed pitch. John looked back and watched in horror as the longboat pitched over, having struck an underwater obstacle and throwing its occupants into the swirling tide, swallowing their screams.

Within a minute every one of them drowned, even the experienced sailor at the oars. John stood there motionless for a long while, expecting and hoping that heads would bob up out of the water and tease him for being frightened. But it never happened. All hands were lost. At their funerals over the next several days, John was again troubled of soul. He thought, *That could have been me! I would have died with them.*

On a third occasion, John was drawn into a mad plan dreamed up by local rowdies he ran with. They got muskets and were poaching on lands that could get them into serious trouble. It was a capital offense to be caught poaching.

While hunting, they were spotted by a game warden. The boys took off running as fast as they could. They ran for what seemed like miles and then separated. John ran through the woods, branches of the trees slapping him in the face. Running down a steep slope out of breath and with his legs out of control, he stumbled.

His musket was underneath him as he fell. Just as he landed, the hammer fell, igniting the gunpowder. He was nearly blinded by the terrifying flash in front of his face, feeling the powder burning his cheeks and eyes. The explosion nearly deafened him. Finally, in the completion of that split second, the fiery lead shot roared past his face, grazing and searing his throat and chin.

For the next few minutes, John lay where he fell, unable to move and shaking uncontrollably. As he felt his face and checked for blood, he saw that the musket ball had only grazed him. Yet, if he had not instinctively thrown his head back at the last instant, the musket blast would have taken much of his head off. He had just managed to stay alive.

Once more, he wondered why God had given him another chance. He had been saved three times—by inches and minutes. He vowed not to squander his good fortune and sincerely revisited his devotions and prayers. But his piety disappeared when he went back to sea in the companionship of his fellow sailors and was introduced to more revelry.

Sometimes, as he thought of how far he'd strayed from his mother's virtues and teaching, he'd be convicted by guilt, would try to reform his ways, but soon fell back into the wild lifestyle of his companions.

His father sometimes showed his disapproval of John's unrestrained habits, but Captain Newton eventually stopped scolding him, thinking his son's wild ways were merely a rite of passage.

Instead of reprimands, Captain Newton had a different idea. He decided to have John spend a year in Spain, where he might learn a trade and become a rich merchant upon returning to London. It would get him away from his crewmates and their unrestrained escapades.

The idea sounded rather exciting to John, who at first was glad to be free of his father's constant presence. When they landed in Alicante, Spain, some weeks later, John was still enthused about this venture. But after awhile, in a strange land where he didn't understand the language—learning a trade that was dull and uninteresting—John began to sorely regret the idea.

After his son's year-and-a-half of service in Alicante, Captain Newton sailed back to Spain to check on him. The merchant met the captain with great relief and gave him back his "useless, stubborn, and daydreaming" son.

Perhaps the captain was privately pleased that his son was not interested in business. He no doubt held out hope that John would become a
sea captain like himself. So, contrary to his nature, he never rebuked his
son. In fact, they never discussed the matter at all.

John returned with his father to England on what turned out to be
Captain Newton's last voyage. He was retiring from the sea, having
taken a position with the Royal Africa Company. This company had the
sole rights to engage British shipping merchants in order to provide
three thousand black slaves annually to the plantations in the West
Indies.

The new land job meant the captain was unable to take John to sea
with him, so he decided to apprentice his son to a friend, this time
another merchant sea captain. John sailed with him on a tour as third
mate. The ship took a route similar to those he'd already traveled with
his father around the Mediterranean.

Captain Newton was pleased. At last someone would teach his son
the merchant ship business. John was also pleased; this time he'd have
some rank aboard ship and, perhaps, a little more respect than he had
gotten while serving aboard his father's ship. Of course, his fellow
sailors respected him, and even his father was treating him less harshly
out of respect for John's efforts.

The trouble was, John took advantage of his father's friendships as
well as his new rank aboard ship. He proved to be shiftless (as the
Alicante merchant had observed) and a daydreamer.

John also was an embarrassment to the new captain. Whenever the
ship was in port in a city, the youthful third mate led his shipmates in all
kinds of revelry. By the time they came back aboard for duty, they were
often drunk, disorderly, and brawling. On more than one occasion the
local authorities threatened to have them jailed for their rowdy high jinks.

When at sea, John sometimes was another person. He kept to himself and read a great deal. Many of the sailors couldn't read, so they had

no idea what John read, but they were amazed when they learned that they were devotional books and the Bible.

Tom, a friend who could read for himself, recognized John's reading material and said, "I wouldn't have taken you for a pious man."

"Ah, that's my trouble. I'm constantly torn between temptation and my mother's teachings. I know that if I keep on sinning I'll go to hell. But my trouble, Tom, is that I *enjoy* those things—it's great fun to do all those things people say are wrong. I can't give them up because *I don't want to*. But I keep reading to see if there's something I haven't learned that will get me off the hook as far as hell is concerned."

"Well, let me know too. I expect everyone wants to hang on to his sinning ways but not have to go to hell," Tom observed.

"I think I have found it," John replied. He held up a book titled *Characteristics*.

"The author, Lord Shaftsbury, says our 'deformity of soul'—which we call sin—is only the result of what Shaftsbury calls 'weak bodies and pervertable organs.'"

"Yeah, I know—I've got one of them pervertable organs," Tom said with a laugh.

John tried to be serious. "He says that misconduct is merely poor taste in morals or manners." He read a passage from the book that described religious leaders as "starched and gruff gentlemen" and dismissed their authority. That anarchistic statement appealed to the teens' youthful rebellious spirits.

"I don't think this fellow is saying that we ought not to believe in God—I'm sure he's a religious man," John said. "But maybe he has a different concept of God—where he's remote, at work somewhere else in the universe on other issues. Maybe he's not really all that concerned with inconsequential moral choices of humanity."

"What's that mean?" asked Tom.

"The author says each of us is responsible enough to make our own choices of right and wrong, that we all can decide for ourselves what's good or bad," John answered.

"Is he saying the Bible is wrong to say sin is wrong and we'll go to hell?"

"No, not really," John explained. "I think he's just saying that the Bible is probably outdated. With our modern knowledge, we don't need all those rules and commandments. We're enlightened enough to know right and wrong for ourselves. Besides, morals and customs change over the years. After all, in our day we don't go around stoning adulterers and fornicators."

"Yeah. Good for us they don't, eh?" Tom said, chuckling.

John tried to be serious. "Don't you see—man is basically an animal. We have natural appetites, lusts even. Satisfying these appetites is enjoyable, pleasurable. Why go around with a sour disposition and be shackled by those obscure commandments? From now on, I won't resist my own natural passions—the door has been opened for me!" John told his friend.

By taking the element of judgment out of the equation of how to live, John found the worldview that could ease his conscience.

"I can tell that the captain is unhappy with me," John confided to Tom. "He's told me many times that I'm lazy and a troublemaker. But I'm not, really. I just like to read and think. I guess I was born to be a philosopher, not a sailor."

Although the captain was not within earshot, he would have agreed wholeheartedly. By the time John's tour of duty ended, the captain was more than eager to give his third mate back to Captain Newton.

Chapter Eight

Polly

By now Captain Newton had almost run out of ideas on how to prepare his wayward, shiftless son for life. Then he ran into an old friend. They sat in a tea shop and leisurely reminisced about the old days. Joseph Manesty, like Captain Newton, had come from modest origins, but unlike the captain, Manesty was substantially more successful.

Captain Newton, who still wore his uniform and officer's cap although officially retired from the sea, went out of his way to impress people. Never mind that most people mocked him and imitated his pompous, pretentious walk. He even worked into their conversation the news of the new town house he'd just purchased in London for Thomasin and their son, William.

Manesty smiled graciously. His own success was a thousand times greater than the captain's, yet he was not ostentatious. He changed the subject of their conversation.

"And how is your son John? I've heard that he's been to sea since he was eleven. Is he going to follow in your footsteps?"

The captain winced. This time he dropped his pretensions. He sighed, "I'm afraid he's not cut out for the seafaring life. He's a thinker. Reads a lot."

Manesty seemed interested. "Reminds me of myself at that age. Wasn't sure what I wanted to do in life. My father wanted me to apprentice and learn a trade, but after some rather aimless excursions on my part, I finally found something I liked."

The captain listened attentively as Manesty told him how he went to the West Indies, worked for a plantation owner who took him under his wing, and eventually acquired plantations and wealth of his own.

This gave Captain Newton an idea. "I wonder if I can prevail upon our friendship, Joseph. Do you think you can help me find such an opportunity for my son?"

"Of course," Manesty smiled. "I'm sure we'd get along famously. I think I know him already by what you've told me about him. The trick is to work with his interests, not against them. If he likes to read and think, give him challenges that relate to the work. He'll soon be so wrapped up in the work that he'll spend less and less time daydreaming."

"I hope so," the captain said.

"Tell you what," Manesty offered, "I leave for Jamaica just after the first of the year. You have John meet me in Liverpool before we sail, and I'll work it all out. If he spends ten or fifteen years working with me, he'll end up with his own plantations, slaves, and untold wealth. I tell you, John, he'll be so rich you won't be fast enough to count all his money!"

Later that day the captain told his son about the meeting. "He told me that slaves do all the work, that you'll live like a king, and in a few years you'll be a rich man."

"Sounds great," John grinned. "And Jamaica. That sounds good too. I've had enough of these cold, damp English winters."

"I wish I were your age," the captain said wistfully. "If I'd have done that when I was your age, I'd have been a rich man at thirty. Can you imagine?"

"I've never been one to turn down riches," John smiled.

"Good. I've told Mr. Manesty that you'll be here in London for the next several weeks. I believe he said the ship sails the second or third week of January—right after the Christmas holidays. You'll have plenty of time to meet him and make ready."

For the next two weeks, John had great relations with his father. The captain seemed to be investing everything into his son and the promise of a new and prosperous career. He took John to some of the best tailors and had an entire wardrobe made for every possible use in the New World. Thomasin helped pack his clothes and books into brand-new luggage trunks.

Two weeks before Christmas, the captain needed John to care for an important matter in Kent. He'd have to ride all day by horseback, probably stay overnight, and return by horseback. John didn't really want to do this. Winter had already frozen the countryside and waterways. Snow was banked in drifts, making the roads and trails all but invisible, but John felt obligated. After all, his father had done so much in providing him with goods and passage to Jamaica and the "dream" job. It hadn't occurred to him that his father might only be insuring his own future by investing in his son's success. Regardless, John decided to do as his father had asked. Then he remembered the strange letter he'd gotten a week earlier. By coincidence, it was from someone in Kent.

✝ ✝ ✝

Abigail Catlett, whom John had not seen since his mother's death ten years earlier, had written to John. Although the two families were

estranged, she had somehow kept track of him through the years. Abigail had also heard that Captain Newton had retired from the sea and taken a land job.

Abigail remembered that awful vision of the pathetic little boy watching the carriage take his poor mother away forever. That scene was indelibly etched in her mind and haunted her dreams. For years she had suffered because she'd been unable to keep her promise to Elizabeth and take John to rear as one of her own family. However, lately she had entertained other thoughts. Was it providence who kept that from happening? After all, if the little boy had come into their home, he'd be as a brother to little Polly, and as a "brother" it would be impossible for him to have romantic feelings for her daughter.

Abigail did not have quite the strength of religious belief as her late cousin and friend, but she was still a person of devout prayer. She always prayed for the safety and well-being of her children and family. Suddenly, one day in the midst of her prayers for them, it came to her that perhaps it was still possible for God to grant the casual wish that she and Elizabeth had shared before her death—that their children might one day marry.

Over supper that evening, she told George, "I've been thinking about John. He's already seventeen, and I wonder if he might now be out on his own, free from his father's influence," she mused.

George shrugged. "It might be best for John if he is. That man was truly strange."

Abigail reminded him how the captain had impulsively and contemptuously severed all contact with them. George agreed that his actions seemed most un-Christian.

That night Abigail decided to write to John and try to restore relations. Recalling the forlorn little boy that she'd left behind, she also remembered clearly that John's mother had prepared him for life with moral and character virtues that would make him an ideal husband. And

after all, Polly was now fourteen—old enough to start thinking about whom she might marry.

She wrote:

> Dear Mr. Newton,
>
> This letter is to simply inquire as to your welfare. It has been quite some time since we have had occasion to see you and have often wondered about you.
>
> Kindly accept our invitation to visit us at your convenience. You will be most welcome. No doubt you will want to learn of the details of your mother's passing, which we did not have the opportunity to share with you at the time—

Abigail took her quill and drew a line through the last sentence, then copied the letter over again. After that, she sealed it, sending it on its way.

✝ ✝ ✝

John read the letter again. The name meant nothing to him, and when he asked his father who sent it, the captain told him simply, "a relative of your dead mother."

Then his memory retrieved the information. Of course—she was the woman in whose home his mother had died. Suddenly his mind was flooded with all kinds of questions about her death that were never resolved for him. John stuck the letter in his breast pocket and prepared for his trip.

The first few miles were uneventful, but as time wore on, both he and the horse tired. The wind was brutally cold, and John pulled a woolen muffler around his head and neck. When the snow stopped swirling, he stopped.

John sought shelter under a bridge and broke the ice on the edge of the stream so his horse could drink and he could get water to boil.

He found some firewood and built a fire to make some tea and warm his hands and feet. After half an hour of rest, he kicked snow onto the blaze and listened to the hiss of dying flames as the fire was smothered.

By late afternoon John arrived in Kent and went directly to his appointment, taking care of his father's business. The man he went to see seemed preoccupied and did not offer any hospitality other than a cup of tea. When John left his office, it was almost dark. He did not relish going any farther without a warm meal. In fact, he knew that he did not want to travel back home until the next day. He'd find a place to stay for the night and leave in the morning.

Then he remembered the letter. Taking it out, he squinted at the writing, holding it at an angle to catch the last rays of the dusky sunset so he could see the address of the writer.

He asked directions of the man lighting the streetlamp and rode his horse to a house at the edge of Chatham. As he looked at the house, its windows glowed with reddish warmth. Tiny bright sparks rose from the chimney, and he could smell the wood smoke—tinged with smells of roast chicken and potatoes inside.

His mouth watering, he nudged his horse and rode up to the door. Tying his horse, he stomped the snow from his feet and knocked.

Inside he heard voices, and then finally the door opened. A pretty teenage girl looked up at him and saw it was a stranger.

"Yes?" she inquired.

He stood there, ill at ease, not knowing quite what to say. Then the moment of awkwardness ended as Abigail turned to look at the stranger and her face brightened. She saw the handsome features of Elizabeth in his face.

"John!" she called out and ran to kiss his cheek. "I'm so glad to see you! Come in, come in."

As she introduced him to her husband and children, John's memory of Mr. and Mrs. Catlett came back to him. He took off his coat and was welcomed to their supper table. He ate with great gusto but throughout most of the meal did not take his eyes off of the girl who sat across the table. Nor did she ignore him. Polly laughed at his jokes, looked shyly away when he smiled at her, and blushed when her mother asked her to escort John to a chair when the meal was over. This was the first time she was asked to take part in the "adult" conversation and she felt quite grown up.

After an hour of conversation, George Catlett asked, "John, do you have any plans? Can you stay the night?"

"No, sir. I mean, yes, sir," he stammered. "I mean, no—I don't have plans, and yes—I'd be pleased to stay the night, if it doesn't impose—"

"Nonsense," Abigail interrupted. "There's so much more I want to hear about what you've been doing these past ten years—"

This time John interrupted. "Yes, Mrs. Catlett, and if you wouldn't mind, I have some questions about my mother I thought you might be able to help me with."

Tears welled up in Abigail's eyes, and she turned away. George picked up the cue and said, "We'd be happy to tell you all about it, son. But now, you must be exhausted from your travels. Let's find you a bed."

The Catlett house had many beds. John counted three children, besides Polly, who were still awake. The others were put to bed early. Two of the boys doubled up in one bed and gave John the other bed in their attic bedroom.

John's head was spinning as he undressed for bed and finally settled his head on the pillow. In a few minutes he was sound asleep.

He awoke the next morning to the sounds of children noisily scurrying around the kitchen below. He eased out of the bed, lifting the heavy comforter aside. Although some heat from the fireplace rose to the attic, it was still not much warmer than the barn where he left his

horse. John could see his breath as he dressed quickly and went to wash his hands at the small bedside washbowl. A thin layer of ice had formed on the water, and he washed his face hurriedly and went downstairs.

Polly waited on him at breakfast, bringing him a bowl of hot boiled oatmeal, followed by fried potatoes and rabbit. He talked energetically and with animated gestures as he ate.

Abigail and her husband were impressed by his friendliness and good manners. He regaled Polly and her brothers with his tales of the sea—of storms, skirmishes with thieves and pirates, foreign ports and cultures. It was all very fascinating.

Polly was amazed to hear his stories. He was only a few years older than she was, but already he'd done so much in his life. It staggered her imagination to think of it all.

John looked at Polly sitting across the table from him. When she looked at him and smiled, he had a strange flutter in his stomach and his mouth suddenly went dry. As he gazed at her, she blushed self-consciously and looked down.

Polly wasn't as educated as John but had gone to a "school for young ladies" where she learned the skills to make her a good wife—singing, dancing, cooking, and household care. Her mother had taught her from the Bible and hymnbook, just as Elizabeth had instructed John. Polly was an excellent singer, and her parents called upon her to sing for John, who applauded the girl's efforts with enthusiasm.

Before long it was nightfall again. John accepted their invitation to stay another night. He told them that he had no plans or duties and could stay as long as he was welcome.

They assured him that he was most welcome, so John stayed and celebrated Christmas with them. Those days were high-spirited for John and Polly. The spark between them was evident to each of them by now, and her parents even encouraged them to take walks in the snowy woods by themselves to get to know each other better.

As they walked along the path, they laughed and talked excitedly. John playfully tossed some snow at her, which landed on her bonnet and fell down the back of her coat. She squealed and threw some snow at him—squarely in the face. He pretended to be angry and walked toward her with a double handful of snow to rub on her face.

Polly laughed and ran. John caught up with her and feigned an attack with the snow, then lobbed it aside, grabbing her instead. Pushing her body against a tree, he lowered his face directly into hers. Her laughter suddenly dissolved, and she looked up at John. She blinked several times, her dark lashes fluttering, shaking off some snowflakes. John drew his arms around the trunk of the tree, with Polly between him and the tree trunk.

He felt her body next to his, and everything grew silent. Polly was elated but confused. She had always enjoyed such horseplay, but this time it was different. Wonderful, extraordinary warmth came over her as John's arms enveloped her and his body pressed against hers.

John was also affected. He felt aroused, playful, and eager. As Polly gazed up at him, her breath came in quick gasps, with little clouds of steam freezing in the cold air as it escaped from her lungs. John bent to her, bringing his face next to hers and finding her lips with his in a lingering, tentative kiss.

Polly's heart quickened. No one had ever kissed her before, and it excited her. John's kiss wasn't simply adolescent playfulness, and it created a much different quickening inside her. She responded by pressing her lips more firmly against John's.

The kiss was absolutely enjoyable, like nothing either of them had experienced before. John smiled and kissed her again. Polly felt the joy and pleasure inside her and returned his kiss.

Then, as John held her in his arms and put his hands inside her coat to caress her, she pulled away nervously.

"I-I'm sorry," he stammered. "I shouldn't have done that."

Polly giggled nervously and ran from him. Nothing more was said about their show of affection during the walk back to the house. The subject turned to John's agenda.

"When do you have to go back to London?" she asked.

John didn't tell her what was waiting for him in London. In fact, Joseph Manesty was probably making final arrangements for the ship's passage to Jamaica.

As John reflected over the past few days, the idea of leaving for Jamaica—where he'd spend the next five years without seeing Polly—didn't appeal to him at all. Impulsively, he decided he wouldn't be sailing with Manesty.

✛ ✛ ✛

Captain Newton and Thomasin were beside themselves with worry. What could have happened to John? The inexperienced traveler could encounter many dangers—he could lose his way and be marooned in a snowdrift and die of exposure; highwaymen, as happened all too frequently, could kill him; or, roving gangs looking for "recruits" to be pressed into military service could kidnap him. It was a common practice for able young men to be "press ganged" into service and put aboard a ship for two or more years.

The captain and his wife considered other fates, many worse than the more common ones. It had been almost a month since John had left to complete some business for his father. Joseph Manesty had waited in Liverpool as long as he could but sailed without him.

Then one day, the errant young man returned and simply apologized for his delay without going into any details. Captain Newton was furious. Not only had John lost a "dream" appointment with a superb financial future offered by Joseph Manesty in Jamaica, but worse—at least for the father—Captain Newton had lost face with Manesty, and that infuriated him even more.

In the days that followed, the captain tried to make arrangements for John to go back to sea. He hoped to find another ship sailing for Jamaica and to sign John aboard as a sailor. Once he got to Jamaica, John could seek out Manesty and plead his case for another chance. However, Captain Newton already knew that most of the ships to the New World were trading vessels and were committed to a trade route. It wasn't likely that he'd find a ship.

He decided to give up on the boy. After all, he was seventeen, old enough to be out on his own. The captain angrily told John that he was throwing him out of the house and would have nothing more to do with him—that he was through trying to help him.

However, Thomasin interceded on John's behalf. Before Captain Newton could act on his threat, he relented. "All right," he conceded, "you can stay, but I expect you to go and look for gainful employment."

Chapter Nine

The Seeds of Rebellion

✠

Seventeen-year-old John Newton contemplated his situation. The last thing in the world he wanted to do was go to sea in a merchant ship, especially now that he'd met and fallen in love with Polly Catlett.

He now regretted his impulsive actions of staying in Kent and missing Manesty's ship. Not only that, but John saw a ferocity in his father's actions that he'd never seen before. He decided this time not to further antagonize the situation.

John went to the London docks and looked for work. England and France were at war, and a number of military ships were in the harbor, but John didn't want to go to sea aboard a British man-of-war. Finally, just as he despaired of finding work, he found a merchant captain who needed a sailor. However, this time, instead of being an officer, John would have to serve again as third mate, but this time with more common and difficult duties.

To John, that was the least disagreeable part of the job. It was a fair trade—giving up a five-year journey to one that might allow him to see Polly sooner. But even that troubled him—he would be at sea for at least a year and wouldn't see Polly for all that time.

John felt ill at the entire situation. He considered running away, but where could he go? He had no money and no job. He had no real work experience, despite his service in Alicante where he had worked for the Spanish merchant. He had no skills other than those of a seaman. Reluctantly, John resigned himself to the inevitable. He signed the papers obligating him to a year's service on the merchant ship.

The ship sailed at once. When it got under way, the rigors of sailing took John's mind off his situation. He had plenty of shipboard duties to keep him busy day and night. In fact, seldom did he even think of Polly, except when she visited him in his daydreams.

Several grueling weeks later, the ship anchored in Lisbon. The crew members went ashore for liberty, and John joined them. He took several letters he had written to Polly and posted them before joining his mates.

It was here that John got drunk for the first time. His thoughts of Polly had kept him focused on the straight and narrow but now grew dim as he took part in the revelry of his shipmates on shore leave. Their influence upon him was greater than his distant memories of virtue that his mother had instilled in him ten years earlier. Here, in this unknown city, his conscience was useless.

However, as it turned out, it may have been best that he was drunk and not able to be with the rest of the men that night. Several of them bought the services of two women before heading back to the ship. When John woke up from his stupor, he was still a virgin, and his relationship with Polly was untarnished by prostitutes. Months later, however, after his eighteenth birthday, in a brothel in Spain, John slept with a woman for the first time.

Lisbon, Amsterdam, and London could each vie for the honor of

being the site of John's first brawl—since in each fracas he'd earned that reputation from various crew members who were with him, but he was too drunk to remember any details of the altercations.

The ship lay at anchor in Venice. After the cargo was unloaded and hoisted ashore, John went with the crew to let off steam before they sailed again.

When he returned to his bunk, he fell into a fitful sleep. As his head spun from the effects of the rum, he thought of Polly. He settled comfortably into his bed and anticipated sweet dreams of her. Instead, he dreamed of Venice Harbor.

In his dream he was strolling on deck alone. A stranger came up to him with his hand outstretched. John could see that he held a beautiful ring with a large stone that reflected the moonlight as the man held it out to him.

"Take this," the man instructed.

John took the ring from the man and thanked him, holding it up in the moonlight.

The stranger said, "Take good care of it. If you do, you'll be happy and successful. But be warned," he added, "if you lose it or give it up, you will have nothing but misery and trouble."

John nodded solemnly and examined the ring more closely. When he looked up, the man was gone.

An instant later in his dream, another man materialized, just as mysteriously as the first one. He asked to see the ring, and John held it out for him to see, telling the second stranger what he'd been told about its unusual properties.

"That's ridiculous!" the man scoffed. "You're too old to believe in magic. You say it's supposed to make you happy and successful? Well, are you happy right now?"

John didn't answer right away. Then he muttered, "I suppose it's too soon to tell."

"Put it to the test," the man said. "Throw it overboard. You'll see that nothing changes. It's nothing but superstition. Get rid of it—it'll cause you nothing but grief."

John argued with the man. He used all his reasoning to argue for believing the man who gave him the ring, while the second stranger used doubt, mockery, half-truths, and innuendo to sway the young man's mind to his own point of view.

Finally, embarrassed for having believed the first stranger, John took the ring from his finger and tossed it into the sea.

Instantly, a distant mountain exploded with volcanic fury. Molten lava, a livid red-orange, glowed with intensity. Flames shot high into the sky. The man beside John erupted with cynical, mocking laughter.

"The mercy that God had in store for you has been thrown away with that ring. You willfully threw away that which could have kept you happy, safe, and secure. Instead, now you must go to that inferno you see. Those flames have been kindled for *you!*" he said contemptuously.

Horror-stricken, John stood on deck as the vision of the terrible stranger receded. He wondered how he would be transported to the hellish flames in the distance.

Suddenly another figure appeared. It may have been the first stranger—perhaps another visitor—he couldn't tell. "Why are you so afraid?" the man asked John.

Assuming it was the one who gave him the ring, John fell to his knees and cried, "I'm sorry! I was stupid. I listened to that man, and he convinced me that the ring had no power—that it had no value, so I threw it away."

The dream was so real to John, and he did not wake up. The man seemed to be willing to give him another chance. "Tell me," he said, "do you think you have learned your lesson? Would you be wiser if you had the ring again?"

"Oh, yes!" John cried.

The man suddenly turned and jumped overboard and sank beneath the water. Before long, he surfaced and held the ring in his hand, gleaming in the moonlight. He swam to the ship, climbed the rope ladder, stood on deck before John, and held out the ring.

The fiery volcano was instantly extinguished, and the flames were gone. Only the moon and stars lit up the sky. With tearful gratitude John reached out for the ring in the man's hand, but the stranger quickly pulled his hand back.

"No!" he told John. "If you were to have the ring, the same thing would happen again. You can't be trusted with it. You'll get yourself into the same predicament right away."

The stranger smiled and said, "You cannot keep it, but I will keep it for you. I'll take care of it so it is never lost or thrown away. Whenever you need it, I'll produce it for you."

The next morning the dream was still vivid in John's mind. He pondered its meaning, if it had one. One thing was certain. There was no escaping the meaning of those flames and the words of the tempter, the second man in his dream. John resolved to try and live a more virtuous life after that.

John's resolve never lasted, however. As the ship sailed around the "boot heel" of Italy on its way to Spain, he would have many opportunities to visit port cities and throw away his virtue, without even planning to do so.

✢ ✢ ✢

When ashore in Cadiz, John went to a pub with three of his friends. They longed for a good home-cooked meal and ale. His friends ordered chickens baked on a spit, and he ordered lamb stew. A young girl brought them the meals and several tankards of ale and set them on the table. Joseph Brooks, the oldest of the sailors and ship's cook, slapped the girl good-naturedly on the backside as she waited on them.

"Hey, girlie," he said, "you're the prettiest thing I've laid eyes on since I left London. Got a kiss for your ol' Uncle Joseph?"

The girl smiled and tried to remain courteous, but it was obvious that this game was boring to her, having heard it in one variation or another every night. She managed to stay out of reach as she placed their food on the table. Brooks, a rough man of forty, seemed older despite his athletic frame.

Tommy Churchill, second mate, was the physical opposite of Brooks. He was ten years younger but much heavier. He'd lost most of his hair, and his clothes seemed too small for him. He was already drinking heavily.

The table was long enough for more than a dozen men to sit without crowding each other as they ate. The large wide planks of the table had gaps of an inch or so where the scraps could be scraped onto the floor, and when some of the men had too much to drink, their forks and knives also disappeared through the gaps.

The men were grateful for the delicious food and wolfed it down quickly. Their stomachs satisfied, the men looked to other satisfaction. Churchill waved at the tavern keeper who came over to the table.

"Do you speak English, señor?" he asked. The man nodded. Churchill motioned for him to bend down for a private conversation. "Me and m' friends are lookin' for some whores."

John looked down at the table. He had come only for food and ale. He still held out hope that he could maintain the discipline of will that would keep him away from the brothel.

Churchill wasn't getting much response from the tavern keeper. "You know, prostitu-*tay,*" he said, trying his limited Spanish. "Is that a business sideline you're able to offer?"

The proprietor shook his head. "No, señor. But maybe you ask some other sailors. Sailors know how to find whores," he said with unmasked contempt in his voice.

"What's the matter? You got somethin' against women who try to earn an honest livin' on their backsides?" He laughed at his own joke and looked for support from his friends.

The man merely shrugged. *"No comprende,"* he said as he walked away.

"Yeah, right. You *comprende* all right," Churchill yelled, throwing a chicken bone at the tavern keeper.

John watched as several men turned to see the unruly commotion. They were local Spanish dockworkers who had come in for a few drinks before going home. Rivalries between the local dockworkers and foreign sailors were commonplace, so the two groups were easily provoked.

The Spaniards outnumbered John and his fellow crewmen by a margin of three to five. The men ambled over to the sailors' table, and one of them began talking in Spanish.

"I don't understand your gibberish," Churchill muttered. Don't you know that the wonderful language of commerce, the speech of the world, is the beautiful mother tongue of the King of England, you savages! Speak English!"

The five dockworkers looked at each other and shook their heads. They didn't understand all that the British sailor was telling them, especially since his speech was slurred by ale, but they fully understood his tone. One burly man, well over six feet tall, grabbed Churchill by the collar and lifted him off the bench. Suddenly the entire room erupted as men from both groups lunged at each other, fists flying.

John jumped up and ran headlong into the man closest to him, knocking the wind from him. The man hadn't expected someone so young and much smaller than he was to come at him. This surprise helped John take immediate advantage. The force of his running lunge knocked the man against the wall. Grabbing the man's ears, John slammed his head against the door's frame where it tore a deep gash in the man's brow. Blood from the cut ran down the man's face, and he seemed dazed.

"Look out, John!" called Brooks. "Behind you!" John turned in time to see someone rushing at him with a stool. He took hold of the man he was fighting, spun him around to use as a shield, and shoved him into the other man. Both fell to the floor clumsily.

Churchill, despite his alcoholic haze, was handling himself quite well. He had decked the man who had started the fracas and took on one of the others. Brooks had grabbed another man and slammed his head down onto the heavy plank table, breaking his nose and rendering him unconscious. The entire brawl had lasted less than two minutes.

Brooks took some coins from his purse and handed them to the tavern keeper. "This should cover the cost of the dinners, the ale, and pay for the damage to your place." The money was generous enough to keep the man from calling the local constable.

The three sailors then left and walked down the cobblestone street. It was getting dark, and the streetlights were being lit.

On one of the street corners two women loitered outside another tavern. The taller one, with dark hair and brown eyes, was attractive but hard looking. The second was probably in her teens and still looked somewhat fresh and pretty. John smiled at her, and she waved and smiled back. The taller woman beckoned the three men to come over, asking them a question in Spanish.

Having spent over a year in Alicante, John knew the language well. He translated for the other two men.

"She wants to know if we want them. She and her friend work here. It's a brothel—upstairs, over the tavern. There's another girl inside, and she says they can make all three of us happy and satisfied," John explained.

"Ask her, how much?" Brooks said. "They always try and get more afterwards. It's always best to agree on a price beforehand."

John translated for the negotiations.

"Then it's done. Let's go inside, mates," Churchill grinned.

"Uh—I'll wait here for you," John told them. He still intended to stay away from temptation. He had earlier told his friends about Polly, using her as his excuse for staying away from the brothel.

"Look, Johnny. It ain't right for a man to go without. It's unhealthy. Women understand that their men need—uh—the comfort of other women sometimes," Brooks said.

Churchill added, "It don't mean anything. You ain't married, or even engaged. Besides, you don't have to tell her," he added with a laugh.

John looked at the pretty girl beside him and was immediately captured by her soft curls and beguiling smile.

"Come," she said softly in English. The girl took John's hand and moved close to him.

John licked his lips and in his imagination wondered what the girl looked like without clothes, lying in bed.

Brooks nodded. "C'mon, John. It won't do to go back to the ship with your mind dwellin' on what Churchill and me will be doin' upstairs. You *have* thought about what it'll be like to lay with that pretty woman there, ain't you?"

John grinned. "Yes, I have thought about it, but I'm trying to get it out of my mind."

"It's too late," Brooks said. "Jesus said that anybody who even *thinks* about havin' his way with a woman has committed adultery in his heart. The way I see it, you've already sinned, so you might as well go all the way."

Perhaps it was the ale, but that weird logic made sense to John. He put his arm around the young girl and let her lead the way inside.

✝ ✝ ✝

The next few days aboard ship, John felt the consequences of his drinking and fighting. His shoulder was sore where he had strained a muscle in the fight, and his head ached from drinking too much ale and rum.

He remembered the pleasure of being drunk and the good feelings of besting someone in a fight. But these fleeting pleasures brought regret the next day. Curiously, he seemed to have no such consequences for having sex with the Spanish girl. In fact, he recalled the experience with satisfaction and wonderful memories. It seemed strange to him that the other pleasurable actions brought eventual feelings of regret, but somehow he was glad he had given in to the last temptation.

As he remembered the experience, he savored the physical pleasure of it. Even now he could almost feel the girl's soft skin and the urgency and energy they shared.

He thought, as he was with her, that it might be more honoring to Polly if he closed his eyes and imagined he was making love to her. But it did not work. The girl he was with was pretty and exciting, and she made no demands. He didn't think about Polly at all.

Curiously, though, on several more occasions, John had the recurrent dream about the ring and the strange visitors. For the rest of the journey, he resolved to "practice the orderly pursuit of virtue," as he wrote in his journal.

The weeks passed uneventfully, and the ship was on its way back to London. With good weather and luck, he'd be home for Christmas. He thought of Polly and had fantasies of making love to her but checked these thoughts. *I can't declare my love for her yet,* he said to himself. *Before I ask her father to give his permission for us to marry, I'll have to wait until I get a commission as an officer so I can support her.*

It was the custom of his day that no young man of eighteen would consider proposing marriage—especially to one as young as Polly—before making appropriate financial preparations. He still looked forward to going home to England and seeing his family—but most of all, seeing Polly.

Chapter Ten

The Seeds of Defiance

John's ship docked in London Harbor in early December 1743. After receiving his pay for his year at sea, he rented a horse and rode to the home of Captain Newton and Thomasin.

The captain seemed to be another person—not at all the stern authoritarian that John remembered. He was genuinely pleased to see his son again.

At dinner several days after his son's homecoming, he said, "Ah, it's good to have you back, John. I ran into your captain at the Admiralty Office today. He gives you good marks for your service. I am pleased to see that you have purged yourself of the disobedience that caused you to miss the ship to Jamaica. I think you've learned your lesson."

"Yes, Captain," John replied. "You're right. I won't do anything as foolish as that again. I *have* learned my lesson."

His father nodded and said, "That's why I checked around for another assignment. I wanted to find you an officer's berth so that you won't have to serve as an ordinary hand when you go back to sea."

"Really? And did you find anything?"

The captain smiled broadly, proud of his accomplishment. "Yes! Yes, indeed. I found you a berth aboard a merchant ship. If you do well, after a few years you could have your own ship!"

John smiled in appreciation for his father's efforts on his behalf. By this time next year, having saved most of the pay from his recent voyage and his officer's salary, he'd be in a position to ask for Polly's hand in marriage. Things were truly looking up.

"The only thing is," Captain Newton added, "the ship sails in January. I'm afraid you won't have much shore leave this time."

"I understand. I'll be ready when it's time."

After a few days at home, John became restless. It had been nearly a year since he had seen Polly and her family, and he was anxious to make the trip, especially since he had so little time until he had to sail again.

His father noticed John's restlessness but said nothing. Finally, after dinner one evening, John approached the captain. He stood at attention in front of the captain—knowing how to win a favorable hearing.

"Sir, if you have the time, may I speak to you?" he asked.

The captain nodded, and the two of them went into the parlor where Captain Newton sat in his favorite leather chair and lit up his pipe. John did not sit. He stood straight with his arms folded behind him in the "at ease" position.

"Captain," he began, "I have a matter of . . . um . . . personal business that I'd like to attend to before the ship sails."

The captain said nothing but nodded for John to continue.

"With your permission, I'd like to visit Miss Catlett," he said in a jumble of words that tumbled out so quickly it was hard to understand him.

The captain still did not answer.

"As you have noticed yourself, sir," John reminded him, "I have learned my lesson. I will not stay too long this time. You have my word. With your permission, I'd like to leave tomorrow so I can return in plenty of time."

Captain Newton drew on his pipe and blew a cloud of smoke toward the ceiling before replying. He was savoring this moment of contrition and appreciated the respectful way that John had approached him.

John's brain, meanwhile, was spinning with all kinds of other remarks to strengthen his argument. Wisely, he said nothing more.

"You're asking *my* permission to go?" the captain asked.

"Oh, yes, sir."

"I see," observed the captain. He puffed at his pipe once more.

John held his tongue. He didn't tell his father that he'd leave in the morning whether he had his permission or not. He knew that his father was a man who lived by the chain of command and authority. Even if he had no real hold over John, the son manipulated the moment to let him feel in command.

"Well, as you seemed to have learned your lesson, I'll grant my permission," Captain Newton said at last.

John smiled broadly. "You won't regret it, sir. I won't disappoint you this time." He then excused himself to go pack a few things for the trip.

"Just a moment," his father said. "There's something else. I want you to be careful on the highway. Since England and France are talking up war, His Majesty's navy is looking for men and boys they can impress into service.

"Check around before you leave to make sure there are no press gangs in the area. Most of our neighbors are already on the lookout for them."

Press gangs were squads of men given the task of drafting men into the navy. These squads consisted of either marines from a British naval ship led by one of her officers or men hired by the navy. These gangs had the authority to fill a quota of able-bodied men into the ranks of sailors for a naval ship. Especially prevalent during times of war, men—and even boys who were big enough to do the work—were drafted into service on the spot where they were taken.

"You'll be in danger of capture because you haven't been given your certificate of protection. You won't get that until you've signed aboard your own ship. If you don't have papers, you can be taken," the captain reminded John. "And if you are snatched, it'll be for *five years,* not one!"

"I'll be careful, sir."

✝ ✝ ✝

The Catletts were delighted to see John again. Their warmth and friendliness made him feel as if he belonged with them. Polly was especially happy to see John, and the two of them spent long hours together, talking and walking in the snowy fields and woods.

John remembered how they had aroused each other's passion the year before and had thought about it many times. This time he vowed not to get too close to her. His recollections of being with the Spanish prostitute also weighed heavily on his mind and made him feel guilty for his infidelity to Polly.

He made a personal vow not to take advantage of Polly, although he was convinced that he could probably seduce her and make love to her before he left, if he wanted to.

Instead, he kept his kisses light on her cheek rather than full on the mouth. When Abigail saw them outside a window in the trees, they were walking and holding hands. When she saw him kiss her, it seemed to her to be a chaste, brotherly token of affection, so she did not feel the need to caution her daughter.

That night John's pledge was put to the test. The family had gone to visit another family, and the couple was left alone in the house. John had gone outside to chop some firewood.

The late afternoon sun was going down, and the air was getting cold. John picked up a log and set it on the chopping stump. With a wide arc of the axe, he split the log in two, then split each one again. He took other logs and repeated the process.

All the while, his mind was on Polly and his desire for her. His thoughts became fantasies of kissing her and making love to her. He knew that her parents would not be home for some time. His body acted independently of his conscious mind, and he had soon chopped much more wood than was needed. He chuckled out loud to himself and stacked the wood neatly by the door.

After stomping the snow off his feet, John carried an armload of firewood inside to put by the hearth. His mind was still on the fantasy he had outdoors while chopping wood. After putting the wood down, he hung his coat by the door. He returned to stand beside the fireplace. Polly came into the room from the kitchen.

She walked over by him, so close that she brushed him as she bent down to stoke the coals in the fireplace. The firelight reflected off her face and created a halo around her soft, dark hair. John was even more entranced by her loveliness in the firelight.

Polly placed a couple of fresh logs onto the fire. Some of the snow still lodged in the bark fell into the coals and hissed, and the sparks rose up the chimney. Polly used the andiron to push the coals underneath the wood to help it burn better. As Polly leaned in closer to the fire, the loose bustline of her dress accidentally fell open—just enough for John, who was still standing above her, to catch a glimpse of the girl's breast.

John caught his breath as he stared at her and felt a flush of arousal. Polly was oblivious to the fact that she was baring her rounded,

developing bosom to his lustful eyes until she looked up and caught him staring at her. She blushed when she realized what had happened.

John's imagination was running wild. The opportunity to act on his thoughts was taking over his consciousness and pushing him to respond to his desires. He had fantasized about taking Polly in his arms and kissing her, holding her, caressing her, undressing her, and making love to her.

Polly stood up quickly and brushed the ashes and pine needles from her hands before smoothing her dress and regaining her composure.

John wrestled with the promise of chastity he had made to himself, but now he was willing to set aside his pledge not to seduce Polly—it was suddenly no longer important to him. In fact, he now felt compelled to take advantage of this wonderful, special opportunity.

Then his reverie was interrupted.

"Shall we go for a walk?" Polly asked him. "We can go and meet my parents—they should be coming back home soon."

"Uh, yes. All right," John replied. They put on their coats and walked outside into the cold evening air. They walked hand in hand, but his fantasy was fading. Strangely though, his disappointment was tempered by the unusual reality that he was keeping his promise to himself not to take advantage of Polly and seduce her—for now, at least.

✝ ✝ ✝

As the days went by, John felt the pressure of a deadline approaching. He knew that he had to be aboard the ship when it sailed. He dare not break faith with his father again. Yet, the pleasure of being with Polly and staying with the Catletts was a stronger pull on his emotions, so he put the deadline out of his mind and stayed another week. By the time he returned to London, the ship had sailed and his father was furious.

Thomasin took her children into a bedroom as far from the parlor as she could get. Still, the captain's angry voice could be heard. She could

not understand everything being said, but the words "irresponsible," "ungrateful," and "stupid" were used quite frequently.

Then the captain raised his voice and began using profanity—words she'd never heard him use before. Thomasin started singing to her children to drown out the angry dialogue in the other room.

John stood at attention in front of his father, unable to give a coherent defense of his actions. This only infuriated his father more.

"I've a good notion to throw you out of the house!" the captain shouted. "After all I've done to help you, this is how you respond. I won't have it! And I won't have you here to lead my other children astray with your disobedience and ungratefulness. I've had enough of you!"

"I'm sorry . . ." was all that John could manage to say.

"Well, you'll be sorry, that's for sure," his father snarled. "Tomorrow you'll go and find your own ship. I'm through helping you. You'll soon see what you've thrown away!"

"Yes, sir. I'll leave first thing in the morning. I'll find something, I promise. I won't let you down."

"I've heard that before," his father said with a voice filled with cynicism. John thought he'd better keep quiet.

Finally the captain dismissed his son.

The next morning things had calmed down. Thomasin tried to keep things cheerful at breakfast. The captain was subdued by her serenity. By the time he talked to John, all his anger was spent.

"You go to the docks and ask around," he told John. "Meanwhile, I'll go to the Admiralty Office and check. Maybe together we can find you a ship soon."

Chapter Eleven

His Majesty's Navy

✠

Captain Newton had no luck in finding another opportunity for his son. Neither did John. For several weeks they both tried every possible lead, but nothing materialized.

One day John decided to make a quick trip to Chatham to briefly see Polly once more. He was about two hours away when he reached the ferry. But John had been careless. He had forgotten to ask whether any press gangs were in the area. By the time it occurred to him, it was too late—he was already waylaid by a press gang. They had come over a hill behind him, and he hadn't seen them. They had seen him, however. There was no mistaking John's gait. After a year at sea, he still hadn't recovered his "land legs," and they immediately recognized him as a sailor. They came up so quickly that he had no time to avoid them.

John saw them and thought about running but did not think he could outrun their musket fire. So he decided to try and bluff them.

"Good day, gentlemen. Are you heading to the ferry?"

"My name is Second Lieutenant Loggie of His Majesty's navy. By authority of the king, we are taking you into custody for naval service," the leader said tersely.

"I'm sorry, but you're making a mistake. You see, I'm an *officer* myself," John responded to him.

"Then let me see your papers," Lieutenant Loggie ordered.

"Uh, I don't have them. I was just now on my way to fetch them."

"What's the name of your ship?"

John could only think of the name of the ship on which he'd recently served, and he told the lieutenant that name.

"That ship sailed in January. Looks like you're our man, all right!" he said gloating.

John protested, but they took him anyway. The press gang marched him into the village where he was locked into a small shed at the rear of an inn. Before they locked him up, however, John managed to get the attention of a small boy. He scribbled a note to his father and gave the boy a few coins to deliver the message right away.

It was late morning when John was grabbed, so he languished in the shed while the press gang sought more "recruits."

Within several hours, they had more men and boys inside the shed. One man had escaped while they were taking him and two others to the shed for safekeeping. The captors took their frustration out on the two men still in custody as if it were their fault that the other man had escaped. They hit the captured men with batons and shoved them roughly through the doorway of the small shed.

Several captives were boys. One claimed to be only twelve years old—two years too young—and he began to cry. "Your deep voice tells me you're older than twelve. You're old enough," he said.

One man complained that his wife had just given birth, and he was on his way to find her a doctor, pleading for mercy. The lieutenant offered to have someone fetch the doctor and tell his wife that he'd been taken.

"You'll have time to write a letter to your families when we get to the Plymouth docks. We won't sail for several days yet," he explained. The problem, however, was that half of the men and boys couldn't write, and their families couldn't read, so a letter would be pointless.

It was getting dark outside when John heard the unmistakable voice of Captain Newton. He was talking to Lieutenant Loggie in a fairly subdued voice, and John could not hear what they were saying. Still, John could make out a persuasiveness in his father's voice and knew that he was doing his best to have John freed. The lieutenant was unmoved, however. No doubt his quota, minus the one who escaped, kept him from changing his mind.

After awhile the door to the shed was unlocked and opened. In the dim light John saw his father, dressed in his uniform (no doubt to impress and convince the lieutenant). He seemed to slump as he entered the door, his expression a bit forlorn.

He looked around the room until his eyes found his son. Then he walked quickly over to John and put his hand on his shoulder. "I'm sorry, John. There was nothing I could do. Lieutenant Loggie tells me that France has fired on English ships. That probably means that war will be announced any day now. Even if he wanted to release you, the lieutenant feels he has a patriotic duty to the king. I must agree. You can't turn your back on your king and country."

John sighed deeply. "Yes, I was afraid of that. If—if only . . ." He didn't finish the thought.

The men and boys were kept inside the shed for the night since it was too dark to march to Plymouth. They took turns lying down on the floor of the shed to sleep—it was too crowded for them all to lie down at the same time.

At daybreak they were lined up in a rag-tag line and told to march to a waiting boat, which ferried them to a British man-of-war lying at anchor in the Plymouth harbor.

The H.M.S. *Harwich* had been launched two years earlier and was used primarily for escort duty in the North Sea.

John climbed up the rope ladder with the ease of an experienced sailor and watched while most of the others struggled. One of the youths panicked and couldn't move up or down until he was prodded upwards by the whip of one of the marines aboard the *Harwich*.

Once aboard, the captives were roughly led down a steep ladder into the hold, well below the waterline. There were no portholes, so escape was impossible. If they had been locked up in quarters above the waterline, some of them would have taken a chance, diving into the cold, dark water to swim ashore.

They were housed with scores of other captured men. John made a rough count and guessed that several hundred had been press-ganged into service. The actual count was 300 of the 350 men aboard. Fifty were seasoned marines who had signed up for duty; most of these men were from the educated elite who had hopes of eventually becoming officers in the British navy.

The impressed sailors consisted of whatever able-bodied men the press gangs could capture. Some others were indentured servants sold into service by their masters who no longer wanted them. Many were boys brought by fathers who could no longer control them and felt that the military experience might discipline and "make men of them."

The rest of them were criminals who chose the chance to go to sea in order to escape the gallows for their crimes. Perhaps a third of the crew were from the jails and prisons—thieves, murderers, rapists, or military deserters.

They had simply exchanged one jail for another. No one with any sense, if given a chance, would actually choose this life for himself. In

fact, one person had said that a sailor has a worse jail—that at least on land you had better food, better companions, and more room—but on ship, you also had a good chance of drowning.

The accommodations for the newly arrived crew were terrible. Without portholes the men had very little fresh air to breathe, and the smells were unbearable. Many of the captives became seasick in the harbor and vomited. Many of the drunken captives (who awoke from their stupor in irons) also got sick.

The latrines were filthy and smelly. Many never made it to the latrines and soiled the areas where they were expected to also eat and sleep.

John had never experienced anything quite as dreadful as this.

After two days of imprisonment, John and the others who were captured with him were brought on deck where they were ordered to strip.

A blustery March wind blew across the deck, and the temperature was near freezing as they stood for almost an hour, waiting for the ship's surgeon. Finally he came, and after a quick, superficial look at each of them, pronounced them all able-bodied.

The recruits were told to get dressed and report to the captain. Captain Phillip Carteret read the articles that gave him the authority to seize them and "impress" them into service.

Once the men were impressed into service, they could be hung as deserters if they tried to escape. The dockyards had gallows as a means of deterrent, although it was hardly a deterrent. It seemed that someone was always being hanged.

Captain Carteret took time to briefly interview each of the impressed recruits. When he got to John he asked him if he had any previous seafaring experience. Taking a cue from how he tried to convince his father, John stood at attention and spoke firmly. "Yes, sir. My father, a merchant sea captain, trained me. I served with him for several years

before signing aboard a merchant ship and being appointed to the rate of Able Seaman. And then I was made a Third Mate," he added proudly.

"I see," remarked the captain. He made a note in his log. Later, after interviewing the others, Captain Carteret told John and two others who were taken with him by the press gang that they would be given a higher standing than the others would. "You'll be Able Seamen," he told them.

The others had no experience and were signed up as Ordinary Seamen. All of them would be given some basic training to outfit them for sea duty. It was conventional wisdom of the day that all recruits had to be "seasoned" and broken before they could be trusted to serve. They had to be so afraid of authority that they would obey every command without question or hint of disobedience.

Several of the junior officers carried whips or batons, and they used them for any real or imagined infractions. Even for John, who was an experienced sailor, the rigor of this training was terrible. The master of arms, bosun, and noncommissioned officers were even more brutal than the officers.

Within the first few weeks, the men became acquainted with floggings, beatings, running the gauntlet, and even hanging—although killing crew was thought to be counterproductive since a ship needed every able-bodied man. Despite the common belief that His Majesty's navy also practiced keelhauling, such punishment was never ordered. However, some more sadistic captains of the merchant vessels did practice keelhauling on occasion.

Rest was only permitted long after sundown when the men were allowed to go back to their quarters to eat and sleep. The rations were a bit better when the ship was in port because there they had access to fresh food and water.

One of the seasoned sailors who had served aboard the *Harwich* since her launching told John how things changed at sea. "You'll like the bread with maggots," he observed. "It at least has some flavor and meat,

but when the worms change into weevils, the bread gets bitter and all dusty."

Fresh water was also a luxury they could enjoy only while in port. After weeks at sea, the water in wooden barrels became brackish and sometimes had a slimy, green scum. No one knew about bacteria, but many were aware that bad water could make a man sick. They often diluted it with their daily ration of rum or just drank coffee. Somehow boiled water didn't make the men sick.

The *Harwich* finally set sail for its escort duty on March 8, 1744. The ship was only 140 feet long and 40 feet wide at the center, so the 350 crew members were packed belowdecks like cargo.

Ironically, the conditions aboard the ship caused John to reform to some degree. He thought himself better and above the kind of people who surrounded him on the ship. He hoped by clean living and careful attention to duty that the captain might notice him as a respected member of society.

Just as he had charmed his father by acting like a dutiful sailor, showing proper respect and obedience, he tried buttering up the officers and manipulating them to avoid hard work. However, it seemed to have little effect, and Seaman Newton was often the object of the first mate's wrath and whip.

A month into their escort duty, John was called out of his duty belowdecks. "Report to Captain Carteret," he was ordered.

John was nervous and felt a little queasy as he hurried to the captain's cabin. Sailors usually felt deep dread when asked to report to the captain. He knocked tentatively and entered when Captain Carteret told him to. The captain was seated at a massive desk in his cabin, surrounded by maps and other papers.

"Seaman Newton reporting as ordered, sir!" John said smartly.

"At ease, Newton," the captain answered. He added, "Well, at least you've helped me clear up one mystery."

"Sir?"

"Your name is John Newton—we've had it on the ship's list as John Newtown. I've been trying to locate John *Newton* ever since we sailed."

John looked at the captain quizzically.

Captain Carteret continued. "I have a friend in the Admiralty Office who gave me a letter. He asked me to do a favor for one of his friends, Captain Newton."

John felt relief, and his feelings of dread relaxed somewhat.

"Your father thought you might make fine officer material," the captain told John. "But I'll have to find out for myself, won't I?" He stood up and walked over to look at the sailor who stood in front of him. "I'm promoting you to midshipman and letting you serve on the quarterdeck where I can keep an eye on you. If you do well, we might find something better for you."

"Thank you, sir!" John replied. "I won't let you down."

"I should hope not," Captain Carteret replied and dismissed John.

The promotion led to an immediate improvement in John's life. For one thing, he moved from the terribly cramped belowdecks quarters to the gunroom.

Chapter Twelve

Spoils of War

After living like a criminal in a common cell, Midshipman John Newton enjoyed his new accommodations. He also had a new measure of authority. John soon forgot how exploited and miserable he had been as Seaman Newton. His new rank went to his head, and he became one of the tormentors.

Before, he had resented the regimented discipline of the military, but now—in a strange contradiction—he despised the rigid structure of the quarterdeck even more. Yet, he was smart enough to take advantage of that structure when it benefited him. When it didn't, he took out his frustrations on the lowly recruits, three of whom had been captured with him.

These three had shared the misery of being impressed into naval duty together with John. Their initial capture and subsequent beatings had given them all a special bond and camaraderie, but John's impudent

and hostile manner toward them now was hard to stomach. He yelled at them continually and punished them for even the most trivial failing at their work. They were doing their best at a new way of life that they hardly understood, and they had to learn complex duties and skills. Midshipman Newton would cut them no slack, and he pushed them incessantly. They could not understand John's change of personality. Before long, all the crew members avoided him when they could.

Strangely, John did not gravitate toward the captain and other officers as he distanced himself from the enlisted men. He was defiant and insubordinate, but not too openly—for fear of punishment—and he simply kept to himself.

Captain Carteret usually made it a point to speak to John when he saw him on the quarterdeck. John should have responded with at least some civility. After all, he owed the captain some measure of respect and gratitude for his intervention and for giving him his promotion. Instead, John was sullen, ungrateful, and rebellious. As far as his work was concerned, he did only as much as he could get by with and no more.

As the spring months became warmer, the sailors on deck found the work more tolerable. They were not as likely to lose their grip on the icy riggings and fall, or get sick from working in cold, wet clothes. The warm sun lifted the spirits of just about everyone.

During April and May the *Harwich* continued its escort duty in the North Sea, always on the alert for French warships.

Another midshipman, James Mitchell, had noticed John's disposition and tried to befriend him. One night, while off duty in the gunroom, he saw John reading from his favorite book.

"Shaftsbury, eh?" he observed. "I read his book, but—"

"You've read *Characteristics?*" John interrupted. His face brightened. "Tell me what you think of it."

"Well, why don't you tell me what you think of him before I tell you."

John was only too happy to explain his ideas to Mitchell. After a half hour his friend interrupted John with an insight of his own. "I don't think Shaftsbury was saying that every new age has to reinvent God. I think he was subtly telling us to throw out the idea of God—period—for those of us intelligent enough to catch the meaning. After all, he was really a free thinker and an atheist. But knowing the religious and political climate at the time, he probably didn't want to put his neck in the gallows for his ideas."

Mitchell had John's undivided attention. He had struggled with his understanding of what the writer meant. This new interpretation made much more sense.

"Think about it," Mitchell told him. "You were probably taught religion as a boy. Those were grand ideas meant to take you through life, but men can't live with contradictions. You've no doubt noticed that even the most religious persons on board still struggle with their consciences.

"Life is so much more simple and enjoyable when you get rid of that tension between pleasure and conscience. If you eliminate conscience, you have no such thing as sin. And if you don't have any sin, why do you need a God to point it out? And if there is no God, there is certainly no eternal damnation."

John listened attentively. It seemed true. Most of his grief and miserable feelings were due to his struggles with his conscience and guilt.

"I see by your eyes that you understand," said Mitchell in a low voice. "Maybe I can persuade you to become a free thinker like me."

John was shocked to hear him speak such words. Just years earlier men and women had been burned at the stake for such admissions.

"Think about it, John," Mitchell continued. "Are you happier or more successful if you submit to a God? Or are you happier, have greater pleasure, and live a fuller life when you *disobey* what religion tells you?"

"Yes! Some of the greatest pleasures of my life have been those I've experienced when I willfully disobeyed God's rules," John admitted. He told Mitchell about the times when he had given in to temptation.

Mitchell shook his head and continued. "Any desire you can think of ought to be expressed. Those things that religion calls temptations are not wrong for someone who is intelligent and mature. A mature person does what he thinks is right. There is no such thing as sin. If you give up the ideas of conscience, sin, God, and hell, then what do you have to fear?"

"Death?" offered John.

"What's to fear? It's just a life being extinguished. Like a candle flame. Poof—it's gone. No judgment day and hell fires. Just *nothingness.*"

John felt strangely attracted to these ideas. For one thing, they gave him the liberty he needed to act upon his desires and fantasies. To him they were simple pleasures compared with actions he believed to be truly sinful, such as murder, rape, or robbery. (In the several years to come, John would even be able to justify those.)

Over the next weeks Mitchell and John talked more about these ideas. One night, while standing at the stern of the ship watching its wake in the moonlight, John was troubled. He found himself indecisive about the matter. As he reflected upon his dilemma, he realized that his mother's religious instruction had made a profound impact upon his mind and soul.

He thought, *If I'm ever to be completely free, I must get rid of those ideas.* In a conscious effort John did just that—by figuratively throwing his mother's teaching of sin and salvation, along with his conscience, into the dark water below.

✝ ✝ ✝

During the days and nights that followed, John and his friend James Mitchell were always together. John had been soundly converted to

Mitchell's philosophy. The two of them, in turn, began to look for other converts. They enjoyed the debates and intellectual exchanges of talking to some of the junior officers and others who had similar doubts and ideas. One young, educated midshipman became a focus of their intellectual energy. Job Lewis was younger than the two of them and was a devout believer.

Job looked at the two older sailors with a mixture of admiration and fear. He had heard about their arguments against God and religion from other crew members but never pursued the subject with them.

Meanwhile, John and Mitchell had ridiculed Job's faith, but not to his face. Together they decided to put it to the test. "I'll wager I can get this boy to give up his religion," boasted John one day.

"A month's pay says you can't," countered Mitchell.

"It's a bet! I say that within two months I can change him from a hymn-singer to a rum-swigger—from sermonizer to a womanizer and whoremonger," John said, laughing loudly at his own joke.

The two of them agreed on the wager, with John insisting that the boy could not be told or in any way warned about what he was planning to do with him.

John went about his task of "converting" Job Lewis with extreme subtlety. He made friends with him and appeared to be eager to discuss religion with him. He asked Job to tell him why he held some particular viewpoint, whether about God, Christ, or a doctrine. Then, after Job explained it to him, John would quietly but powerfully demolish the doctrine with his own logic or counterpoint. If he had no logical opposing view, he simply introduced the element of doubt as to why Job's viewpoint was flawed.

In less than half of the sixty days he had allotted for the wager, John had convinced Job to throw away his religious faith in favor of the free-thinking ways of his two older friends.

INFIDEL

John and Mitchell then introduced Job Lewis to the pleasures of shore leave. It did not take long. The *Harwich* had escorted a merchant ship across the North Sea to Norway and docked in Oslo.

Planning their shore leave in Oslo, Job Lewis had suggested that the three of them go hiking. It was summer, but snow still covered the distant mountain peaks. This fascinated Job, not having such scenery near his home in Liverpool.

Instead, John convinced Job to accompany them to a wharf-side tavern—which conveniently had a brothel upstairs. John offered to take Job there for his initiation. By the time they took Job upstairs, he had been well furnished with rum and ale and could hardly stagger up the stairs—but somehow he did, laughing loudly at his stumbling efforts.

"Pretend it's your birthday, Lewis," John told him. "Choose your present and prove your manhood!"

A half dozen prostitutes sat in the small parlor at the top of the stairs in various stages of undress. Swaying from the effects of the liquor, Job put one hand over his eyes and spun around dizzily, then stopped and pointed while still covering his eyes.

Several of the women giggled as Job opened his eyes to see which one he was pointing to. He went over to a young woman in her early twenties, a few years older than Job. She took his still outstretched hand and led him into a nearby room. John and Mitchell chose two of the others and followed to separate rooms.

By the time the three of them were heading back to the ship, the effects of the liquor were wearing off, and John and Mitchell were kidding Job about his actions. But Job seemed depressed.

"I feel awful," he moaned.

"Yeah," Mitchell said, laughing again, "me too."

"Ah, but the pleasures we enjoyed tonight will carry us back to England. And we can sleep off our drunkenness before sailing tomorrow afternoon," John told them.

"That's *not* what I meant about feeling awful," Job said.

"What do you mean?" Mitchell inquired.

"Well, I've done everything tonight that a month ago I found repugnant. I don't even remember how many of the commandments I broke *just tonight!* I-I guess I'm feeling a bit guilty about what I've done," he muttered, almost in a whisper.

"Forget it, Lewis," John said to encourage him. "You've been enlightened. You don't have to feel guilty. That's all religion is about—making a person feel guilty. You take away the guilt and there is no such thing as God, and because there's no God, there's no such thing as sin. And if there's no sin, there's no need of hell. So, you see, Job, you're free to live your life any way you please. That's what intellectual liberty is all about."

"I-I'm not so sure," Job answered.

Chapter
Thirteen

Battles and Deserters

The convoy duty turned out to be quite dull for the crew of the *Harwich* during the summer of 1744, but the benefits outweighed the negatives. The ship was in port much of the time between its escort duties to Scotland and Norway, protecting British merchant ships now that war had erupted between England and France. Being in port so much should have given the crew more shore leave than usual, but not so. Captain Carteret never knew when orders would come and the fleet would have to sail at a day's notice.

When given, shore leave lasted twelve hours. That wasn't a problem for John when the *Harwich* was anchored off Plymouth or Bristol. However, when the ship lay offshore from Rochester, Chatham, or Sheerness—almost within sight of Polly's home, he was restless and sullen. She was so near—yet so far.

In one respect it did not matter. Polly's father had learned that John had, on at least two occasions, thrown away important opportunities by overstaying his visits with them in Chatham.

Her father had second thoughts about his daughter's future with such an unreliable prospect. On one occasion when the *Harwich* was anchored offshore near Chatham, John went to visit Polly. George and Abigail Catlett met him at the door and forbade John to visit their home or even write to their daughter without their permission.

John threw himself upon their mercy, but George Catlett was firm. Abigail, however, was not as rigid as her husband seemed to be, and as John was leaving, she went to him.

"John, you must be serious about your responsibilities," she told him. "I am afraid that Mr. Catlett's mind is quite made up on this matter."

"But he won't even let me write to Polly," John complained.

"Yes, I know," Abigail said. Then she brightened. Looking over her shoulder to make sure they were not overheard, she whispered. "Polly is going to attend a girl's seminary near here. It's a boarding school. Perhaps if you were to write her there—" She smiled and put a piece of paper in his hand as she shook it when they said their good-byes. As he turned to go, she added, "Remember all your dear mother taught you, John."

He turned back to her with a quizzical expression on his face. But Abigail did not add anything to her benediction.

When he was out of sight, John opened his hand to read the paper Abigail had pressed into it. It was Polly's address at the girls' school. His spirits lifted a little, and he hurried back to his ship. He was several hours late, but Captain Carteret did not make an issue of his tardiness.

Over the next few months John and Polly wrote to one another. He enjoyed hearing from her but felt at a disadvantage by not being able to see her. He worried that some local suitor might meet and win her simply because of his availability. As a result, John began to take every

advantage of a twelve-hour liberty whenever the *Harwich* was anchored within a day's travel. He'd usually rent a horse and return late after his visit with her, always overstaying his twelve-hour shore leave.

Captain Carteret noticed that John was taking advantage of his generosity in promoting him to midshipman. Not only that, he was also disappointed in the quality of John's work. As with the merchant in Alicante, John had become lazy and worthless, going out of his way to avoid hard work. He shifted the hard work onto poor recruits with no rank.

Captain Carteret decided that he had done enough for the son of another sea captain. From now on, John Newton would have to carry his own weight and obey orders.

✝ ✝ ✝

In September the *Harwich* had been sailing off the east coast of Scotland but was now on her way back to England, near the coast of Yorkshire. Two hours after sunrise, John was drinking coffee from a battered pewter cup when he heard the lookout call to the wheel deck below.

"Sail ho! Starboard bow!"

Captain Carteret reached for the telescope held by his first mate. He looked in the general direction of the lookout's call.

"It's a privateer—and flying no colors. Call all hands on deck!" the captain ordered.

"All hands on deck!" the first mate echoed.

Immediate chaos arose aboard the *Harwich* as some marines hurried to their battle stations. Some ran to the gunroom for muskets while others went directly to the various cannons protruding from some fifty different openings around the ship.

John and the other sailors on the quarterdeck and the forward stations ran to their posts and concentrated on running the ship while the marines got ready for battle. He looked across the starboard bow but

could barely make out a speck on the horizon. He was unable to tell that it was even a ship, let alone see if she was flying French colors. He watched as the captain looked through the telescope—and occasionally looked up at the *Harwich* sails and checked the wind.

The captain had ordered *full sails,* which meant that he intended to chase down the other ship. The other ship had been tacking at a right angle course to the *Harwich.* The British man-of-war had the advantage—she was in the "wind's eye" and was making twice the distance of the other ship over the same time. After a half hour of full speed, the speck on the horizon began to look more like a sailing ship.

Soon the *Harwich* had closed the distance, and the two ships were less than a mile apart. A half hour later the privateer was just a few hundred yards away and began raising her colors.

"Just as I suspected," Captain Carteret said. "She's French. Fire port bow cannons!"

The first mate shouted the command, and several loud explosions erupted just below deck from the front of the *Harwich.* John watched as smoke traced the arcs of the cannon shot. One grazed the stern mast of the French ship, but the others fell harmlessly into the sea.

Captain Carteret, still looking through his telescope, could now read the name on the stern of the privateer. "It's the *Soldide,* and she's getting ready to fire back at us. Stand ready!"

"All hands steady!" the first mate called.

The cannon shot from the *Soldide* fell far short. Meanwhile, the *Harwich* gunners had made adjustments on the range of its cannons. Captain Carteret shouted, "Bow chase cannon and starboard cannon, fire!"

A volley of cannon fire was released with an incredible, unremitting sound. John's ears were ringing, and he could smell the sulfurous odor of gunpowder. At least six of the *Harwich* guns had fired, and two found their mark. One hit the *Soldide* above deck and splintered part of the

coamings. A second shot struck the rigging of the main mast, and a top-sail fluttered clumsily to the deck. A loud cheer rose from the *Harwich*.

The *Soldide* immediately went into a defensive maneuver, putting her stern to face the guns of the *Harwich* in order to present a smaller target. This gave her an advantage while Captain Carteret ordered the helmsman to turn about so the *Harwich* might try for another broadside at the frigate.

The skirmish went on for another two hours, until noon, with each ship jockeying for an advantageous position without firing any more shots. The French ship was well helmed and continued to extend her stern toward the *Harwich* as Captain Carteret circled.

As the *Harwich* circled, she also closed the distance between the two ships and sent another volley of cannon fire at the stern of the *Soldide*. However, from the angle of the British ship it was difficult to see if any damage was done.

About three o'clock in the afternoon, the *Harwich* was close enough to fire another broadside volley. This time, instead of positioning her stern facing the *Harwich,* the *Soldide* maintained her broadside position. This surprising change in tactics gave her the opportunity to send her own broadside against the *Harwich*. Most of the shots whistled harmlessly overhead and dropped into the ocean. Only two shots struck the ship, and neither did much damage.

Captain Carteret still stood near the wheel where he had been for some eight hours. He glanced over his shoulder at the sun, estimating that he had only another four or five hours of daylight for the battle. If the *Soldide* somehow managed to survive until then, she might easily slip away under the cover of darkness. He resolved to finish her before then.

He barked out orders to maintain position for another broadside cannon volley at the *Soldide.* When the guns were fired, some of the shots found their mark, increasing the damage to the *Soldide*. As soon as the

port broadside was fired at the *Soldide,* the captain ordered the *Harwich* to tack about and quickly present her starboard broadside cannons. This added to the *Soldide*'s damage.

The *Soldide* tried to elude the *Harwich,* and because of the skill of her helmsman, was able to do so for another two hours. But Captain Carteret stayed with her just out of cannon range.

It was now nearly seven o'clock, and the sun was beginning to set. The captain and his crew had been at their battle stations for nearly twelve hours. Captain Carteret decided to make a dramatic offensive maneuver and get the *Harwich* even closer to the *Soldide* than she had been all day.

"Make steady those guns!" he ordered. "We're going to go get them!"

The men, eager for a finish to the marathon battle, cheered.

The *Soldide* was not able to outrun the *Harwich,* probably the result of taking on water from cannon fire striking below the waterline. The *Harwich* nearly rammed the stern of the French ship, turning away only at the final instant. Now the ships were broadside to each other, and both opened up with cannons at point-blank range. The *Harwich* was the faster of the two, however, and escaped with only a little damage.

The *Soldide* was not as lucky. She caught the full fury of the *Harwich* guns. At the close range, the marines aboard the *Harwich* also opened up with musket fire and tossed hand grenades aboard her, thus inflicting more damage.

The *Harwich* turned quickly and made another run close to the *Soldide*. This move was unexpected by the French captain who thought he had some time before the port broadside cannon crew of the *Harwich* would be ready to fire again. He had overlooked the starboard cannon crew—they were ready and fired their guns point-blank at the *Soldide* again, even while the frigate's crew was trying to put out the fires and repair the damage done by the earlier volley.

Then the *Harwich* port broadside crew readied for another attack. This time the aim was even better. The cannons blasted point-blank. One explosion hit the wheel deck, striking several crewmen and officers. Another shot split one of the masts, which crashed down onto the deck with massive force.

As the *Harwich* prepared for yet another attack, Captain Carteret saw the colors being struck aboard the French ship.

"She's surrendering!" he shouted excitedly. "Hold your fire! Lieutenant—take your marines and prepare to board!"

Once again, cheers rose from the deck of the *Harwich.*

A half hour later the marines from the *Harwich* boarded the *Soldide* and were met by her commander, Captain Sourbert. The French captain was immediately taken aboard the *Harwich,* where he surrendered his sword, his men, and his ship. The French ship suffered many casualties and much damage. The *Harwich* suffered little damage, mainly to the rigging, and only one man was wounded.

The marines from the *Harwich* disarmed the crew of the *Soldide,* and the two ships sailed to a British port. The *Soldide* would be sold to the British Admiralty, which would repair it and outfit it as a British naval vessel. The price paid for the ship would go to its captors and would be shared among the officers and crew of the *Harwich* as spoils of war. The prize money was divided in eighths. One-eighth of the prize money went to the admiral. A quarter share went to Captain Carteret; the officers, ship's surgeon, and marine officers shared one-eighth of the prize; warrant officers split another one-eighth share. Likewise, midshipmen like John, his mates, and the marine sergeants shared another one-eighth, and the rest of the crew split the final quarter share.

The officers and crew did much better on the "head money," which was given for the men they had captured. The Royal Navy paid five pounds per captured enemy on board the *Soldide.* This money was divided evenly among all the officers and crew.

John was excited when he got his share. It made the prospect of a five-year duty (at half the wages of merchant shipping) seem less difficult. *If the Harwich could capture more ships and share the prize money, this might not be such a bad enterprise after all,* he thought.

✝ ✝ ✝

John had learned that the next major voyage of the *Harwich* would take them to the Mediterranean rather than the usual escort route to Scotland or Norway. They were to be at sea for a year this time. However, they were ordered to continue their convoy duty in the North Sea during the autumn months.

Back in port before Christmas, John wrote to Polly and told her that he hoped they'd be able to capture more prizes of war so he'd have enough money and a promotion in rank to improve his standing in the eyes of her father. In fact, he told Polly, he was planning on asking her father for permission to visit the family at Christmas.

The *Harwich* was at anchor in the Downs, a sea anchorage north of the straits of Dover, just before Christmas. John was frustrated. He had hoped his ship would anchor closer to Chatham because he wanted permission to visit the Catlett family.

Not only would this location change complicate his plans for a brief shore leave, but the *Harwich* crew had just received some truly bad news. Originally the *Harwich* had been scheduled for a year of sea duty in the Mediterranean. The orders had been changed, and now the *Harwich* was scheduled to sail around the Cape of Good Hope at the southern tip of Africa and on to the Far East, thus traveling some twelve thousand miles more than originally planned.

To make matters worse, instead of being gone a year, the *Harwich* would be gone for *five* years! The news all but crushed John as he was planning his trip to Chatham.

All he could think of was the terrible impact of five long years away

from Polly. Much could happen in five years. She might even find another suitor, closer to home, and—with her father as the judge—someone more qualified to be her husband.

Most of the other sailors were upset too. Some of the older sailors told tales of their tours in the Far East. The odds were such that he might not even return. Battles, pirates, storms, and strange diseases posed all kinds of fatal possibilities.

Then came another setback. When John asked Captain Carteret for permission to visit Polly at Christmas, he denied his request. The captain reasonably believed that John could not visit Chatham and return to the ship within the space of a twelve-hour shore leave. In fact, due to the change in plans, the captain had restricted all liberty for the entire crew, half expecting some would take the news about the Far East duty badly enough to desert.

Although deserters were usually shot or hung during wartime, Captain Carteret didn't know what he'd do if—as he expected—too many of his men deserted. So he decided to clamp down on the men's liberty and not give them the opportunity to act on thoughts of desertion.

John stewed over the situation for nearly a week. The ship was awaiting favorable weather in order to sail off to duty, but the December skies were uncooperative. The *Harwich* sat at anchor for several weeks, leaving the men to sit around, grumbling and morose.

Finally John got up the nerve to visit the captain. He knocked on the cabin door and was invited to enter.

"Sir, due to the change in our orders, I respectfully ask you to reconsider your restrictions on leaves. Since we will be gone for five years, I'd like twelve hours to say good-bye to the young woman I plan to marry. I must meet with her father and let him know of my desire to ask for his daughter's hand in marriage. I thought these things could wait since we were going to be back in a year's time. But now—"

"Twelve-hour pass, you say?" the captain asked, sounding somewhat sympathetic.

"Yes, sir. That's all I ask," John replied hopefully.

Captain Carteret sat for a moment and looked at the young midshipman who stood before him. He sighed. Perhaps he had misjudged John. As he stood before him, he saw something of himself and the youthful impetuosity that had driven him at that age.

"All right," he said finally. "I'll give you a twelve-hour pass, but I don't want this to set a precedent and have every other love-struck sailor at my door begging for a pass. Keep it to yourself. Go aboard with the crew that goes for supplies in the morning."

John's face brightened. "Thank you, sir. Thank you very much!"

✝ ✝ ✝

Getting the pass was excellent fortune for John, but as usual, he had not thought far enough ahead. He had rented a horse and pushed the animal as fast as he could toward Chatham.

As he rode, John did some computations. It was eighty miles round-trip to Chatham and back. Even if the horse made the entire trip at breakneck speed and did the same for the return trip, John would have only minutes with Polly. And that was assuming that the snow was not drifted too high or the roads too muddy as to prevent the horse from maintaining its speed.

He should have told his captain that such a trip was impossible to make in December within twelve hours. Instead, he decided to place himself at the captain's mercy when he got back. Besides, if he got back six or eight hours late, maybe he could sneak aboard with the help of a friendly officer of the day—before the captain woke up.

When John arrived at the Catlett house, they were still celebrating Christmas and welcomed him warmly. Mr. Catlett was more reserved and wary of John's tricks—he recalled their last visit and shook hands

but was cool toward John. The rest of the family invited him to church for a worship service the next day. John mentally calculated that he could never make it back to the ship before the daily roll call. If he left immediately, he'd already be late and subject to the captain's wrath when he returned. He decided that as long as he was late anyway, he might as well be a little later.

Two days later he walked aboard ship. The captain saw him before he got to his quarters and vented his anger on him. John didn't know what kind of punishment to expect but was surprised that the captain merely confined him to quarters until they sailed.

The captain, although he never told John, made a distinction between being absent without leave and deserting. A deserter would not have fared well.

The storms of winter kept the *Harwich* at anchor for nearly two more months. On February 23, 1745, she finally sailed with a British fleet of other ships but ran into more storms. Several of the merchant ships being escorted by the *Harwich* ran aground. The fleet and its floundering ships were forced to limp back to Plymouth for repairs, which took most of March.

The weeks in port with no liberty made the men restless, and several deserted. Captain Carteret increased the guard around the longboats tied to the ship to keep deserting sailors from getting ashore.

As the time passed, the weather improved and repairs were near completion. John learned that his father was in nearby Dartmouth as part of his duties for the Royal Africa Company that employed him after he had retired from active sea duty. Captain Newton had been called to come and inspect storm damage to his company's ships that, like the *Harwich* and the fleet, were being repaired.

John got an idea. Perhaps these delays were providential—maybe it was a way of getting him out of the five-year tour of duty that faced him and his companions. His father did have some influence. Maybe he

could find a way of exchanging John from the *Harwich* onto another ship. If only he could talk with his father and discuss the matter.

John asked Captain Carteret if he could be given a short leave to see his father. The captain simply shouted, "No! And that's the end of it!"

John was seething inside but gave no outward response to the captain. He started to walk away when Captain Carteret called him back.

"I've got an assignment for you," he said. "Maybe it'll keep your mind busy so you won't have time to think up all these diversions. I want you to take charge of the longboat party that's going ashore. You'll supervise the men getting water, fresh vegetables, and other supplies. But mind you, I want you to take extra precautions. Some of the men are restless, and a few are even ready to desert. I'm putting you in charge to make sure that no one deserts."

"Me, sir?"

"Yes. You're not the kind of person who'll desert. If you were, you never would have come back when you overstayed your leave at Christmas. I know I can depend on you," Captain Carteret told him.

John could understand his captain's concern about the men deserting. Under cover of darkness, quite a number of men—and some officers—had slipped overboard during the night, trying to escape. A few drowned, not able to make it to shore in the icy water. The rest apparently did make it—temporarily. Some were later recaptured by press gangs and brought back aboard ship where they were placed in irons, awaiting the sentence of the captain who was the supreme authority at sea.

John was at least grateful for the captain's confidence in him, but still he wished for a way to see his father before they were to sail.

When John and the longboat party landed at the Plymouth dockside, he had already made up his mind to try to contact his father. He put another man in charge of the party, told him that he had another assignment, and warned him, "Mr. Oliver, I'm putting you in charge. Take care

that no one leaves the party or tries to desert. If anyone runs away, I'll see to it personally that you are hung for it!"

John had no such authority, but the sailor didn't know that. He gulped and turned and nodded. The sailor would do exactly as he was told.

John then took off.

✝ ✝ ✝

Meanwhile, in Dartmouth, Captain Newton had just finished a damage appraisal on one of the vessels owned by the Royal Africa Company and was sitting down to tea with an old friend.

"Admiral Nadeley, how good of you to see me," he began.

"Nonsense, John," the older man replied, "It's always good to see you. How are you adjusting to your land job?"

Captain Newton smiled. "Probably as well as you, Admiral. I'll wager you miss the sea as much as I do."

"Yes. Some days more than others," the admiral observed. "But I'm not sure I'd be up to serving in wartime again. You have to put in pretty long days and have one more enemy to deal with besides the sea and the weather."

"True enough," said Captain Newton. Then he put his cup down and leaned across the table in the small tea shop. Clearing his throat, he got down to business. "Admiral, I've come for your help. I hope I'm not being presumptuous, but I don't know anyone else who can help me."

"What is it? I'll do anything I can for a friend," the older man said.

"Well, it's about my son, John. You see, he trained with me for six years at sea, and then took a tour with a merchant ship on his own. I made arrangements last year for him to get an officer's berth aboard another merchant ship, but—uh—he wasn't able to sign the papers before the ship sailed. And while we were looking for another ship, John was taken by a press gang and impressed into service aboard a British

man-of-war. He was put in with the common criminals and other riffraff as an ordinary seaman."

"I see," the admiral said, nodding. "That can be a rather rude change of plans for a young man who has his eyes set on being an officer like his father."

Captain Newton continued. "I've just learned that his ship has been given new orders. She's to sail to the Far East for a tour of five years' duration," he said. His concern for his son showed in his eyes.

"Five years," the admiral said, shaking his head soberly. "A lot of good, healthy men never survive a tour to the Far East."

"Exactly," Captain Newton replied. "That's why I've come to you. Is it possible that you can get him exchanged?"

"Well, it's sort of difficult now that we're at war," the admiral answered. "But in this case, I doubt whether the exchange of one man will decide the balance of power in Europe." He took another long sip of his tea and thought for awhile. Then his eyes brightened. "I know. I've got a friend who has a merchant ship leaving in a month. With the war, I know there's a shortage of able-bodied men to man the merchant ships. He'll be most willing to exchange one of his press gang recruits for a man the likes of your son!"

"Can you make the arrangements?" Captain Newton asked.

"I'll do it today. I'll let you know right away, before your son's ship sails."

"Yes. Good!" the captain replied. He reached across the table and shook his friend's hand with gratitude and enthusiasm. "The ship is in for storm repairs to the fleet, like so many others all along the South Coast. But the *Harwich* herself had no damage, so once she's outfitted for the Far East journey, she'll sail. We must act at once!"

"Consider it done, my friend," the admiral assured Captain Newton. John's father was so happy he almost wept.

✝ ✝ ✝

John was careful as he left the longboat party and made his way to the road to Dartmouth where he could meet his father. The last thing he wanted was to be taken by another press gang. He knew he would be delayed past the time that the longboat party had to return to the ship. In fact, the trip to Dartmouth would take a full day and night on foot, but he could not take the chance of renting a horse or being stopped on a main road.

He was sure, based on Captain Carteret's reaction to the last time he overstayed his leave, that the old man's bark was worse than his bite. John felt he had learned a maxim about his captain—that it was easier to get forgiveness than permission. He would deal with that part of his problem when he got back from Dartmouth.

John slept under a bridge that night, shivering in the frosty air. He woke up after a fitful sleep with hands and feet that were numb with cold. Without the makings of a fire, he started walking and soon felt a little warmer.

He noticed a signpost after several hours of walking: *Dartmouth 2 miles*. John could even see the town just over the next hill. His spirits improved as he thought of warm food and the chance to see his father.

His reverie had made him careless. John had not noticed the party of marines who had been patrolling the coastline, looking for deserters. He saw them too late. He was too tired to run. He had no papers. There was no way he could bluff his way out of the situation.

The press gang stopped him and demanded to see his papers.

"I don't have them with me," he told them. "I have urgent business in Dartmouth. I must see my father, Captain John Newton."

"Not without your papers. You know that," the marine in charge told him. "Come on, you're going to march back to Plymouth. It's twenty-five miles, and if we hurry, you'll be back aboard your ship by nightfall."

John was one of a rag-tag band of actual deserters and was being force-marched to Plymouth with them. As they walked, John grew increasingly worried. He listened as the marine told the deserters not to expect any leniency. "We're at war, and you men deserted. That's a capital offense in wartime. You'll all face court martial charges. Your captain will decide your fate. I'm afraid it'll be hanging for many of you."

With that pronouncement, one of the captured deserters decided that if he was to be hung anyway, he'd take his chances at escape. He took off running across a newly plowed field. The marine in charge seemed to hesitate. If he sent men after the escapee, others might also run—without enough men to guard them.

The escapee was running with incredible speed and getting away. The marine in charge took a rifle from one of his men and braced its strap around his left wrist for stability and aimed. Following the man's course across the field through the gunsight, he cocked the hammer, lining up the sights allowing for distance and wind. Then he squeezed the trigger. The blast of the muzzle gave them all a ringing in the ears.

A split second after the blast, John watched as the running man suddenly arched, his arms flailing outward. The bullet had caught him squarely in the back and splintered his spine. His running momentum carried him several feet further, and then he fell facedown in the muddy field and didn't move.

"Go check it out," the marine in charge told one of the others. If he's dead, have that farmer yonder get the constable to bury him. If he's not dead, have him get a doctor. Catch up with us after you've attended to things."

The marine ran toward the place where the deserter had fallen while the others resumed their march. For the rest of the trip no one made any effort to escape. Some time later the marine sent to check on the shot deserter caught up with the rest of his patrol and reported to his leader.

They talked in such quiet tones that none of the deserters could hear whether the man was killed or not.

When the group reached Plymouth, John and the other prisoners were put in irons—shackles around their ankles and handcuffs around wrists—held by chains. They were locked up in the local jail for two days until finally John was pulled aside to be taken back to his ship. He was the only prisoner taken; none of the other deserters had been from the *Harwich*.

Aboard the *Harwich* the marines shoved him into a small smelly, dank room. He had never seen the brig before but had heard about it. Only the most hardened cases were generally put into the brig while awaiting their punishment.

John knew nothing of what was going on. He had no visitors, and the guards were out of earshot so he could not find out what was going on.

A few days after his capture, John's father came aboard the *Harwich* to meet with Captain Carteret. He presented the *Harwich* captain with papers for an exchange of men—an experienced seaman in exchange for John.

"A week ago I could have done this," Captain Carteret said. "But now I can't. I wouldn't be able to maintain any discipline at all if my crew found out that their captain winked at your son's folly. I don't know if he was simply absent without permission or if he really deserted, but I have to assume the worst in order to protect my ship's discipline. I'm sorry, Captain, but I can't help you. Your son betrayed my trust. He must stay and face the punishment."

"Then let me plead for mercy," Captain Newton interceded. "The boy's not a deserter. His brain isn't always thinking. Sometimes he—"

"Yes, I know. I'll give him the benefit of the doubt," interrupted Captain Carteret. And the meeting ended. Captain Newton was escorted from the *Harwich*.

A few days later the ship sailed. John could tell by the movement of the deck planking in the brig. Preparations were being made to get underway. He then heard the faint sounds of deck activity above him and, finally, the sound of the splashing wake as the ship moved through the water. John's spirit was utterly broken now. The ship was on its way! He had no way of escaping five years of duty to the Far East.

The next morning John was brought up on deck. The bright sun made him squint, and it took him a moment or two to get his bearings. The marine guards who fetched him brought him to stand in a prescribed place.

John suddenly noticed that all hands were in parade formation. The marines stood in ranks on the quarterdeck facing him. Behind him on the lower deck were the sailors.

Captain Carteret called the troops and crew to attention. There was a ceremonial drum roll, and the captain began reading from the *Articles of War*. The hair on the back of John's neck rose as he suddenly realized how serious the matter had become.

John didn't know whether this was a formal court martial or not— nor if he was being tried for desertion or being absent without leave. The worst case, desertion, could mean death by hanging. John's eyes darted fitfully to the yardarm where a noose would be placed. He was somewhat relieved when he saw none.

The captain's voice echoed across the decks of the *Harwich*. "Every person in or belonging to the fleet," he read aloud, "who shall desert or entice others to do so, shall suffer death—" and here he paused dramatically. He cleared his throat and continued reading from the *Articles of War*—"shall suffer death, or such other punishment as the circumstances of the offense shall deserve."

He continued reading the rest of Article Fifteen and gave a brief speech on the importance of discipline and order aboard a warship and why Newton had to be punished.

The captain had the keys to life or death in the matter, and he made it a point to let his officers and men know it.

"This is a serious matter, but in the case of Mr. Newton, not a capital crime. In your captain's opinion, this case deserves a mercy. We wish to be benevolent but must be sure that the punishment fits the crime. Therefore, I order that a severe flogging be imposed as sentence in this matter."

John didn't know how to respond. The captain was not going to hang him, but what did he mean by "a severe flogging"? The prescribed number of lashes was ordinarily twelve, but an officer who went by the book might quote Article Fifteen: " . . . *or such other punishment as the circumstances of the offense shall deserve.*"

John had desperately hoped that Captain Carteret would deal with him as one of the midshipmen (who were treated as junior officers). John already knew from experience that captains dealt more favorably with midshipmen than ordinary members of the crew.

The usual punishment for a midshipman might be "kissing the gunner's daughter." This colloquial name came from the position of the man forced to prostrate himself over a cannon with his back and buttocks ready to receive blows from a cane administered by the master of arms or someone else.

If he was charged as a midshipman for desertion, or "only" charged with being absent, he could still expect a severe beating, but a "caning" would be preferable to the other punishment. He had been caned before—it was painful, but it left only bruises rather than torn and lacerated flesh.

The commanding officer of the ship could use his own guidelines in imposing the sentence, and Captain Carteret was ready to make his own judgment. His voice was loud and angry as he finished reading from the charges. "I hereby strip you from your rank as midshipman and reduce you to the lowest rank of ordinary seaman. I want you brought down to

the lowest position aboard my ship and open to the insults of your fellow crew members."

John had expected the demotion, but he hoped the captain would delay stripping him of his rank and grant him some leniency.

He was so caught up in thinking about his situation that he wasn't paying attention to Captain Carteret's sentence. Then he heard his words, "You shall be given one hundred lashes with the cat-o'-nine-tails."

One hundred lashes with a cat-o'-nine-tails! That's what the captain meant by a *severe* flogging. John saw little mercy or benevolence in that. Such a sentence could accomplish the same thing as a hanging but might make the commanding officer seem more merciful. Many of the more seasoned officers and sailors knew that such a flogging could easily result in death.

John had no friends aboard ship, but even the sailors who had no use for him felt some sympathy at this judgment.

On hearing the sentence, the prisoner slumped to the deck on his knees. Inwardly John suspected that Captain Carteret wanted him dead. John would die a slow death of a hundred lashes. He had seen men lashed with the cat-o'-nine-tails. Two of them had died; the others wished they had. The metal-tipped leather strips were designed to beat the back, buttocks, arms, and shoulders of the prisoner. That was a horrible enough punishment in itself. However, the metal pieces imbedded in the nine leather "tails" each ripped into the flesh, tore open the skin, and cut into muscle tissue. The lacerations were deep—sometimes cutting to the bone—and excruciatingly painful.

John had little time to think, however. Two marines had already pulled him up to a standing position and dragged him to "the gratings"—the place (below the quarterdeck where Captain Carteret stood) where such punishment was generally carried out.

Horizontal and vertical bands of pressed iron about three inches

wide formed a grate in the side of the wheel deck. It was a large opening that let fresh air into the ship.

The marines removed John's handcuffs and chains then tied his wrists wide and apart, high on the grating. He stood at an already uncomfortable forced position. His arms had been stretched out so far that his face was pushed against the rough metal. Any movement of his head rubbed his face against the coarse iron—rasping skin from his face.

One of the marines ripped off John's shirt and pulled his trousers down around his ankles. He could hear the subdued chuckles and cat-calls from the sailors as he stood there utterly humiliated.

The drum roll sounded. There was a snap of the cat-o'-nine-tails and the whistle of leather. It struck across the middle of his back. He lurched upward in reaction to the pain.

"One!" Captain Carteret called out.

Another drum roll.

The second lash hit him mostly on the right shoulder, and one of the metal tips cut into his chin, which he had pressed against his shoulder in an effort to avoid rubbing against the grate.

"Two!"

Out of the corner of his eye, John saw that the sailor administering the blows was the bosun's mate. He and John were always at odds with each other, and it was obvious that he was getting some satisfaction out of beating John.

"Three!" The third lash cut deeply into John's buttocks where one of the metal tips buried itself in his flesh. The bosun's mate had to walk over and dig it out before going on with the punishment. John was shaking and could feel blood trickling down his back.

Another drum roll was performed, followed by a fourth lash. John cried out in pain as this one cut into his neck and shoulder. It felt like the bosun's mate was trying to cover every square inch of skin exposed to him.

"Four!" the captain intoned, adding, "Keep it on his back, Bosun."

John groaned and gritted his teeth.

"Five!" He still had ninety-five blows to endure. He didn't think he could last that long.

"Six!"

The pain was so intolerable that John began to cry out with every lash. Yet he was shown no mercy.

"Seven!"

The beating continued for nearly twenty minutes. After twenty-four lashes, John passed out. The bosun's mate waited, but the prisoner did not revive. A marine threw water from a wooden bucket at John, but he remained unconscious.

The ship's surgeon came over to look at John. He checked for a pulse and found a slow, weak beat. Then he lifted John's head and made sure he was breathing.

"The prisoner is unconscious, Captain. I fear for his life if we continue." The surgeon pursed his lips and looked up to Captain Carteret for direction.

The captain looked down at the prisoner whose back was shredded and bleeding profusely.

"That's enough," he said softly. "Cut him down and take him below." Then, turning to his second officer, he commanded, "Dismiss the troops and get the crew back to duty. We have plenty more to do before we call it a day."

Chapter
Fourteen

Seething Resentment

When he was cut down and taken below deck by the ship's surgeon, John's terribly lacerated wounds were washed, but no salve or healing balm was permitted on orders of Captain Carteret.

"Don't wrap him or put a shirt on him," the surgeon told the guards. "He's endured enough pain—let's not add to it by having cloth bind with the scabs. We'd torture him again just pulling off the dressing." The guard nodded and left the prisoner to sleep off the pain.

It took more than a month for John's wounds to heal. He was expected to be back on duty the day after the flogging but could hardly pull himself to a standing position. When he finally did return to duty, he felt like a leper. Everyone went out of the way to avoid him.

A few of the sailors among the ordinary seamen had previously served under John when he was on the quarterdeck. Now he was as low in rank as they were, and they seemed to relish the chance to get even

with him for his harsh treatment of them earlier. One sailor slapped John on the back, and the pain sent him reeling. He snarled sarcastically, "Hello, John, my 'friend'—how's my ol' mate today?" The action drew many guffaws. John's back hurt terrifically from the slap, but he said nothing.

As the days passed, John became the object of cruel pranks and nasty jokes.

At night, after a grueling day of duty, he all but crawled back to his quarters. He had to sleep on his stomach while the wounds healed, so he made a bed for himself on the dirty, rough floor.

As the days progressed, John's wounds were getting better. He had learned to wash the pus-filled scabs with seawater to curb infection. He stood one morning at the stern of the ship and dropped a wooden bucket on a rope into the wake behind the ship. He pulled it up and used an old rag to wash his wounds. It was difficult to reach his back, and he wished one of his former friends would help him, but no one did. Even James Mitchell and Job Lewis, who had been his friends, stayed away.

The salt water burned as he washed it into the wounds but he knew it would help them heal. As he looked out across the stern, his heart felt heavy and terribly sad. They were so far from England—far from Polly and his family. Soon the ship would stop in Spain, then the West Coast of Africa. From there they'd travel the long journey around the Cape of Good Hope to the Far East.

His life was thoroughly miserable. As he washed his wounds and later went about his duties, he fantasized about various ways to kill Captain Carteret. The method he liked most (and wondered if he had the nerve to follow through with it) required him to wait until they were in port. He'd take his knife and slit the captain's throat from ear to ear; then he'd stick the blade into the tyrant's heart and throw him overboard into shallow water.

Whether he survived was not important to him. He probably wouldn't survive this trip anyway. Beside, what was it that Mitchell told him? *Death is just extinguishing life. There's nothing more—no heaven, no hell.* Actually, if death was an end to it all, John thought that the experience might not be so bad after all.

To an atheist, death was even something to look forward to—it would be extinction. All his problems would be over—his pain would be gone.

Then a sudden thought gripped him. *No, death is not the end of it. Judgment and hell follow.* Where did *that* thought come from? He tried to push it from his mind but couldn't. Had a remnant of his mother's faith surfaced in his own mind to rebuke him? Was it true? Was there an afterlife? If so, there'd have to be a God.

John did not want to pursue those thoughts. Angrily, he continued to hone the edge of his knife, working the soapstone until the blade had an edge like a razor. Then he carefully wiped it with his shirt and slipped it back into the sheath hanging from his belt.

In early May the *Harwich* finally sailed into Madeira harbor. The tiny island off the northwest coast of Africa was a place where international ships could retire for rest, repairs, fresh water, and supplies. Captain Carteret decided to bring the ship into shallow waters to repair some damage that had not been detected when the *Harwich* was in Plymouth. The work would have to be done swiftly because the captain wished to sail no later than the tenth of May.

The repairs consisted of sealing some loose planking with hot tar. The acrid smell of boiling tar filled the air aboard the *Harwich* and reminded the men that hard work lay ahead. The captain had reluctantly agreed to let some of the men go ashore on a brief liberty as soon as they had heeled the *Harwich* halfway on her side so that the others could make repair from the keel up. With such an incentive, the men made quick work of the heeling.

The bosun's mate who had flogged John came up to him and grinned broadly. "Well, Newton, how'd you like to get off of this ship?"

John wasn't sure he heard him right. "Me? Really?" he asked.

The burly old sailor nodded. "That's right, you," he said. "You're gonna get off the ship."

"But I thought—" John stammered.

"You're gonna get off easy—by swingin' from a bosun's chair over the side—brushin' tar in the planks," he said, laughing loudly.

Once again, John's disappointment overwhelmed him. He had already expected that he'd be part of the work crew but hoped that he wouldn't have to hang precariously in the hot sun working on the hull.

However, without giving the sadistic bosun the benefit of seeing his anger and dismay, he tied himself into the rope chair and grabbed a bucket of hot tar. He was lowered over the side and began the assigned task.

Lying almost on its side in shallow water, the sun beat down mercilessly on the *Harwich* and on John's already tender back. He had forgotten how hot the sun could be when no breeze was made by the moving ship. It wasn't long before he could feel sunburn developing. His only respite came when he went back on deck to get more tar, but that didn't happen often enough.

By nightfall it was too dark to work, so he was allowed to go to his quarters with the warning that he needed to be back at sunrise to finish the job. By the time he crawled onto the floor where he'd set out his sleeping area, sunburn blisters were already forming on his back, so he tried sleeping in his hammock. He still felt sore, but it was better than sleeping on the hard floor.

As he waited to fall asleep, he fantasized now about slitting the throat of the bosun's mate. Then he got an idea. Tomorrow he would use his knife, not to kill anyone, but to cut the rope of the bosun's chair once he was lowered to brush tar. Then he could drop into the shallow water and get ashore. (No one knew that the reason John had never tried jumping

ship before was that he could not swim, a common predicament among sailors.)

The water was only six to ten feet deep. He figured he could tread water long enough to get to where he could stand. Then he could walk ashore and mix with locals and escape. Maybe he'd disguise himself to avoid capture.

The next morning his spirits were high as he anticipated his planned escape. As soon as the *Harwich* crew finished the arduous chore of heeling the ship all the way over on her other side so the starboard side could be tarred, he grabbed the tar bucket and was ready to lower himself over the side. However, the bosun's mate seemed to be reading his mind.

"Hold up, Newton," he ordered. "I'm sending Hutchins in your place today. You'll stay on deck and keep the fires going under the tar kettle. And you, Hutchins, don't try jumpin' into the water to try and escape. I forgot to tell Newton yesterday, but I posted a marine up there on the stern deck with a musket with orders to kill any man who tries to make a break for it." He motioned with a thumb over his left shoulder toward the stern.

John looked in that direction and saw the marine with his rifle. He was grateful that he had not attempted to get away yesterday.

Yet, as he thought about this change in events, John reckoned that his escape plans had to be changed. He made a vow to himself to have a plan, a sure plan, before they got to Africa's Cape of Good Hope. If not, he would jump into the ocean after effectively slitting his captain's throat.

✝ ✝ ✝

After nearly a week, the tarring and other repairs were made and supplies were laid in. John fell asleep as soon as he got to his hammock in the crew quarters that night.

The next morning he slept through the sound of the bosun's whistle at reveille. If he were still asleep when the men assembled on deck, he'd have hell to pay. Ordinarily, no one cared—in fact, many of the men got

a perverse pleasure in seeing John punished. This time, however, his former friend, Job Lewis, tried to rouse him so that he would not get into trouble. John groaned and turned away—now fully awake but not doing anything about getting up.

"Why, you lazy son-of-a-wench!" Job yelled at John. "I try and do you a favor, and you just lay there and mock me!" Then Job took out his knife and cut the rope holding the hammock. It collapsed, dropping John to the floor. He landed on his back, enduring the pain as well as the humiliating laughs of the other men.

John was almost ready to retaliate but thought better of it—Job had too many of his friends nearby.

The other sailors drifted outside to get their work assignments from the bosun and go get breakfast. Meanwhile, John dressed and folded up his hammock—he'd fix it later.

On deck, the day was a bright precursor of summer. The sun was just rising, but it was already quite balmy.

No sense going to the mess hall for breakfast, John thought to himself. He wasn't up to dealing with another likely fight. Instead, he looked out across the bay to see the other ships, each one coming to life with crews busy with preparation for sailing and loading or unloading cargo. He overheard one of the men telling another that the captain announced they would sail tomorrow, right on schedule.

As he watched the other ships, he noticed a small boat approaching the *Harwich* with two sailors sitting on the center seat while other sailors rowed. The two men had canvas duffel bags containing their belongings, and each of them carried carpenter's tools. John knew from this that Captain Carteret must have made an exchange with another captain for the two "chippies" (as the carpenters were called).

As the small boat came up to the rope ladder, John watched as a former friend, with his own duffel bag slung over his shoulders, stood on deck. He was to be one of the sailors exchanged.

"I wish that were me," John muttered to himself. He walked closer to the place where the exchange was to be made. A junior officer from the boat came aboard with the two carpenters and presented himself to an officer of the *Harwich*.

"Here are your two exchanges," the officer from the merchant ship said. "My captain sends his regards, but he sends these men most reluctantly."

"Yes," Lieutenant Boone said, "I quite understand. He'd never have agreed to the exchange, but the commodore has ordered it. The British navy has the right to impress any men it needs, but we have agreed to give you this sailor in exchange."

"You're giving us one miserable recruit for two experienced carpenters?" the other officer said angrily.

"Well, it's all we can do. We're getting ready to sail tomorrow, and we need all hands."

"You can't do this! The commodore told our captain that it was to be an exchange—two men for two men. You only have one man here," the officer barked. "We'll be undermanned. This can't be! Where is your captain? I must speak to him."

John's heart leaped with an idea. "I'll go get the captain, Lieutenant Boone," he cried and was off like a deer.

He was out of breath when he came to the captain's cabin and knocked insistently. When he went in he blurted out his thoughts in a tumble of words. "Captain, the two men you requisitioned from the merchant ship are here and are raising hell because they're only getting one man in exchange. The officer is threatening to take it directly to the commodore, sir!"

He let that information soak into the captain's mind—with special emphasis on the latter part of his statement. He knew that no officer wanted a problem to go to over his head to his commanding officer.

John continued. "Sir, you know that things haven't worked out for me aboard the *Harwich*. Might I be the second man? You'll be rid of me and save this problem from getting out of hand."

For the first time since I've known young Newton, Captain Carteret thought, *it's the first time he's made any sense.* It was true; he could be rid of this troublemaker once and for all. *And good riddance!*

The captain did not deliberate. "All right, Newton," he answered sharply. "Get your things. You can go."

John took little time in complying with that order. He ran back to his quarters, grabbed his things, and stuffed them into his duffel. Then he ran back to the boarding area of the deck. By this time Captain Carteret had come to explain to the other officers. He apologized to them for the mistake—that he was sending two men after all.

In another few minutes John had clambered down the rope ladder into the small boat and was now making his way back to the merchant ship. His spirits were higher than they had been in months. In a space of a half an hour he had gone from being sound asleep to being on his way to another ship. He was no longer a sailor in the Royal British Navy! His five-year tour to the Far East no longer hung over him like a guillotine blade.

In an amazing sequence of events, John had been taken off the man-of-war. As he reflected on these events, he couldn't help but be impressed by the odd coincidences. If he had slept only minutes longer, he never would have noticed the boat coming to the *Harwich*. If Job had not cut down his hammock, he'd never have dressed in time to talk to the merchant ship officer.

If I believed in God, I'd think it was an act of his providence, he thought. *Yet, it's too uncanny to have happened as random chance. Maybe I still do believe in God.* Again, he was a believer in spite of himself. This was a troubling thought.

He tried to force such ideas from his mind. Still, it was almost as if the events were staged solely for him. It had all happened so quickly that John didn't even know the name of the ship to which he was now assigned.

He asked the officer in charge of the exchange as the boat approached the ship. "I can tell your ship is a merchant vessel. But I'm afraid I don't know anything about it."

The officer nodded. "We're a Guinea ship working the West Coast of Africa. Our ship is called *Pegasus*."

John chuckled to himself. *How appropriate,* he thought. *I feel exactly like that winged horse of mythology. If I could, I'd fly aboard the* Pegasus.

Chapter Fifteen

The Slave Ship

✠

As John boarded the *Pegasus,* he was already more at home than he had been on the *Harwich.* The *Pegasus* was a smaller ship with fewer men, and as a merchant ship, would be more like the ships John served aboard before being impressed into the Royal Navy.

He met the captain, who seemed genial. When John told him of his background, the old man shouted, "Newton? You're Captain Newton's son? Well, praise be! I know him well."

John smiled in appreciation. He nodded respectfully at the other officers.

John was surprised that the captain was older than his father but still active at sea. He also got the sense that he was a God-fearing man—his language was peppered with homilies and quotations from the Scriptures. These quirks irritated John, but he figured they could not be as bad as the traits of Captain Carteret.

One of the *Pegasus* crew members was assigned to show John the ship and familiarize him with the details of the routine. Belowdecks they went to the cargo hold. Before his eyes adjusted to the darkness, he was struck by the awful smell. "Whew," he said. "That's terribly foul! Smells like part of your cargo is rotten." The odor had the smell of decay and the pungency of putrid fecal matter and urine.

The sailor with him laughed. "You should have smelled it before the crew swabbed it down with sea water and cleaned it up.

The sailor carried a small oil lamp, but John saw no barrels or trunks. "Where's your cargo?" he asked.

The sailor laughed again. "We off-loaded most of the cargo we brought from England in Spain. The only cargo left is back there." He pointed to some bales of wool and a number of wooden crates. "Wool, cutlery, and guns. We'll trade them for some gold and ivory, but mostly we'll trade for the new cargo and take it to the Colonies."

"Where are you going to buy new cargo?" John asked.

The sailor was amazed at John's naïveté. "Why, Africa, of course. This is a slave ship."

John was intrigued. He'd never been aboard a slaver before. "May I?" he asked, taking the lamp from the sailor.

He held it over his head and looked down into what seemed to be a dark cavern. Upon closer inspection he saw benches—or shelves—laid out along the inside of the hull. He figured that these must be some kind of quarters for the slaves. The center of the hold was outfitted with more wooden planking and low dividers. Chains with shackles and handcuffs hung from the bulkheads. The chains clinked softly as the ship swayed at anchor. Similar shackles and restraints covered the flooring.

"This is where you keep them?" John asked.

"Yes," the sailor replied quietly.

"It looks like it can get pretty crowded in here," John observed.

"That's the way my first quarters were on the *Harwich*. It wasn't as bad when I was a midshipman on the quarterdeck."

"Well, the 'cargo' won't appreciate it no matter how much room they've got. They don't take kindly to being moved from their land and taken away," the sailor said. "You better learn to be careful around them. They'll just as soon kill you as look at you."

"All right," John told him, "I've seen enough. Let's go back up on deck."

The concept of slavery meant nothing to John. True, his father worked for one of the largest slave shipping fleets in Great Britain, but the economics of slavery had evaded him.

Slavery had created a new leisure class in England. By shipping blacks to the West Indies and American colonies, Britain enjoyed the economic benefits of cheaper and more accessible raw materials and manufacturing from those areas than goods coming all the way from the East Indies.

Also, less risk was involved. Merchant ships took much longer to travel to India, Java, and other Asian ports for trade, and that route presented many more dangers—pirates, tropical disease, long distances, typhoons, and uncertain labor pools. Furthermore, trade in the East Indies was unpredictable and more costly. By transporting slaves to the New World, much of that uncertainty had been eliminated. Not only that, the routes were safer, quicker, and cheaper.

Slavery made many people rich, but at the same time, it sparked a holocaust of anguish, suffering, and death for the Africans who were uprooted, captured, separated from their families, and treated as animals (and worse), all for the sake of a better life for the privileged few in Britain.

✝ ✝ ✝

John was truly happy aboard the *Pegasus*. No one knew of his record aboard the British man-of-war, so everyone was ready to give him the

benefit of the doubt. He made new friends right away. During the warm summer evenings after duty, a group of sailors would sit around listening to John spin tales of the *Harwich*.

The men became as friendly to John as his former crew had hated him. The night before the *Pegasus* was to sail, the captain made arrangements to sleep ashore in an inn. He had done so because he knew his officers had planned to bring prostitutes aboard the ship for the pleasure of the men before they left for sea.

John watched as the men hooted and laughed at the prospect of a night of revelry and pleasure. One sailor played a flute and another had a battered fiddle. The men were singing bawdy songs and drinking their extra allotment of rum.

At first John resolved not to participate. He reasoned that as long as he was starting a new life aboard the *Pegasus* he might want to control his appetites. Then, seeing the fun around him, he thought, *Why should I worry? Nobody on board knows me. The captain isn't here. What's to keep me from enjoying myself?*

Taking one young girl by the hand, he twirled her around in a mock dance as the sailors played a lively tune. She giggled and took both his hands, letting John twirl her and dance some more before having a more intimate and passionate embrace with him.

✝ ✝ ✝

Over the next month, John learned the slave trade. The *Pegasus* sailed along the West Coast of Africa mainly around Liberia, Guinea, Sierra Leone, and the Ivory Coast. There the crew members bartered goods for slaves.

The ship anchored at Conakry where two crews in longboats went ashore. John went with Lieutenant Whitney's crew to help in the exchange of axes and gunpowder for fifteen Africans.

"If the trader asks you to test the gunpowder," Lieutenant Whitney

told John, "be sure you draw it from the keg with the dab of white paint on the side. The rest is salted with charcoal. It may not burn as fast."

John learned how goods were altered in other ways in order to take advantage of the traders. Whiskey from Scotland was watered; bolts of cloth had large sections cut out of the middle before they were rolled up. "You'll always find traders who'll deal with you. If one of them gets burned, no matter. We won't see him for at least another year—if ever. If we do run into one we've cheated, he just avoids us."

The boat was dragged ashore, and the crew assembled in close formation. Most of the men carried some kind of a gun—a long rifle or flintlock pistol. John had a rifle slung over his shoulder and marched along with the others. They had landed at a place where a muddy river spilled into the ocean. A small assortment of huts stood inside a cleared space far enough away from the water to escape flooding.

A grizzled white trader waved from just outside one of the huts. He motioned for several blacks, dressed in Western garb, to follow him to meet the ship's crew.

"Hello, Vander, nice to see you again," called Lieutenant Whitney.

"Hrumph," the old man snorted. "You've got nerve coming back here. You sold me flour filled with worms last time."

"I assure you, the worms were not in the barrels when we gave them to you," argued the lieutenant. "I understand you need axes and gunpowder this time."

"Aye. But I won't fall for your tricks. I want to test them myself."

"Of course," the lieutenant said, nodding to John. "Open a keg for Mr. Vander, Newton."

John reached for the one keg he knew would pass the test, but the trader was wise. "No, not that one. Let me choose," he told them, lifting one from the midst of the dozen kegs.

He took his knife and dug a splintery opening in the top of the keg, then reached inside, took a handful of gunpowder, and poured it onto

the ground nearby. Then he walked over to a nearby open fire and picked up a twig with a glowing coal at the end of it.

Holding it at arm's length away from him, he touched the spark to the black powder on the ground. It flashed brightly with a loud *poof,* and a cloud of bluish-black smoke rose from what had been the pile of powder.

John looked out of the corner of his eye at the lieutenant.

Vander smiled appreciatively. "One more test," he said. Grabbing another keg he repeated the routine. When that powder also flashed in a similar fashion, the trader was satisfied.

As the Africans carried the kegs into a small building with mud walls, John whispered to the lieutenant, "How did you do that? He didn't pick the right keg."

Lieutenant Whitney smiled and said softly, "I guessed we might run into Vander again. I just put a tankard of good gunpowder on the top of the other so that when he opened any of the kegs the gunpowder would work. I didn't tell you because I knew you'd give him the marked one, and he'd know it. So he thinks he outsmarted us."

When all the kegs and boxes were unloaded, Vander and his men went into one of the larger huts. In a few moments they came out with slaves—six men, four women, and five boys. The youngsters were about ten or eleven years old.

The slaves were chained together, and every two had a wooden yoke tied to their necks to keep them in line and from escaping.

In many cases African chiefs had captured the slaves in battle or kidnapped them when they encroached onto their lands. They then sold these slaves to the traders. Some had been marched hundreds of miles from their homelands and sold. Incredibly, a handful of them were from tribes more than a thousand miles inland. In any group of fifty, up to a dozen or more tribes could be represented, each speaking a different dialect. They had no idea what the African captors or the white men were saying.

The white men took satisfaction from the fact that the Africans were selling the slaves. Somehow that seemed to legitimatize the awful activities. However, if the Africans did not have enough captives to fill their quotas, it was not at all uncommon for the crew of a slave ship to attack a tribal village and capture men, women, and children as slaves.

John watched as Vander's men half pulled and half dragged the recent captives from the building in which they were being held. The traders had handcuffed the male slaves in line and had chained them to a long and heavy chain. The men were spaced between the women and children whose hands were tied but not handcuffed.

The women were wailing loudly, and most of them were naked. They were covered with the dust of traveling many days over scores (if not hundreds) of miles. One woman's breasts were swollen and leaking.

"That slave is a nursing mother," Lieutenant Whitney complained. "What is she doing here? What happened to her child?"

"Who knows? Those are all the slaves we have. Take her or leave her," Vander said.

The lieutenant decided that he did not want to go back to the ship without a full consignment. "All right. I'll take her," he muttered.

John looked into the eyes of the boys. They were so frightened that they seemed almost catatonic. They responded to the tugs of the chain and moved in the direction of the others.

The slaves—after some serious prodding, whipping, and pulling— were somehow put into one of the longboats. Two sailors sat at the bow of the boat with pistols at the ready. The rest of the crew members crowded into the second boat and pulled at the oars. As the second boat rowed toward the *Pegasus,* it pulled a towline attached to the boat that carried the slaves.

More struggles ensued as the crew tried to get the slaves on board the *Pegasus.* Once on deck, the black men were taken from the long,

heavy chain and were shackled to individual iron braces anchored to the deck. The women were kept in a group, as were the children.

Screams of pain filled the air as the slaves were branded. John could smell the burning flesh as the searing iron left an indelible scarred mark on the shoulder or arm of each slave.

At last they were taken to the cargo hold where they were chained.

John was breathing heavily when they left the cargo hold. Lieutenant Whitney was standing on deck as John climbed the ladder from below. "First time, eh? It can be a bit difficult the day you get your first slaves, but it'll become common enough. We've still got more than a hundred and twenty to buy before we head to the West Indies."

After supper later that night, John rested on deck. Several of the crew members were sitting around, enjoying the evening, smoking pipes, and singing softly. But as a backdrop to this peaceful scene, John could hear wailing from below.

Chapter Sixteen

Descent into Deeper Darkness

✝

John sailed aboard the *Pegasus* for the next several months. Slave trading was a time of hectic (and sometimes dangerous) activity. The crew was always kept busy—or was supposed to be.

It didn't take long for John to take advantage of his situation and fall back into the lazy and disrespectful ways that had gotten him into trouble in the past. First Mate Daniel Collins, in particular, became irritated with him.

"Just because you've been aboard a man-of-war for a year doesn't give you any rank here. Why aren't you done with your work?" Collins demanded.

John tried his charm. "I'm sorry, sir. I'm doing my best. It's just that everything aboard the *Pegasus* is different. I can't seem to get used to where things are and how they're done."

Collins gave John a kick in the seat of his britches, sending him sprawling. "Just what is there to know about painting an anchor chain? Don't try your fancy words and lies on me! I know a lazy horse's rear when I see one. Now get that work done!"

When the first mate was out of earshot, John mimicked his voice and actions for the benefit of the sailors nearby, then added, "If I'm a horse's rear, then what is Mr. Collins? I'd say *he's* a horse's rear—unless he's an ass's rear, or—"

Just then the first mate came down the stairs leading to the top deck. He had overheard John and strode directly to him. Collins took a small billy club from the back of his belt and swung it hard against John's head. He fell in a heap onto the deck. He was smart enough to feign unconsciousness in order to avoid further blows.

"Take him below and lock him in irons until he can find some more respect!" Collins shouted to two nearby sailors.

John was confined for nearly a week with only bread and water rations and had plenty of time to reflect on his situation. When the first mate released him, he told John that he was giving him double duty to make up for the work he didn't do while he was confined.

The punishment was not enough to prevent John from continuing in his laziness and mockery of the officers and first mate. He was just careful not to carry on where he'd be overheard.

During the mandated worship services on Sundays, the crew members daydreamed. A few of them even fell asleep and had to be nudged before their snoring caught the ear of the captain who led the service. However, John gave the appearance of giving the captain his full attention, and he sang the hymns loudly. What the captain couldn't hear, though, were the words John sang. He had created new lines with the most outrageous and blasphemous words, mocking God and Christ. The superstitious sailors who heard his disreputable lyrics usually sat some distance from him, imagining that if

lightening fell from heaven to strike Newton, they'd want to be sitting far away.

The captain, who had originally given John some slack because of his own friendship with Captain Newton, was nonetheless becoming more and more disgusted with John's antics. Yet he did nothing about them—although he flirted with the idea of exchanging John for another sailor at his first opportunity.

During the six months of sailing up and down the northwest coast of Africa buying slaves, John's lifestyle and demeanor also disgusted even some of the most disreputable crew members. He fought with officers and crew alike. His angry temper often set off a dispute over the most trivial matters.

Most of the crew members left him fairly much to himself. John tried to keep himself occupied with his duties just to avoid being harassed by the captain and first mate.

John noticed that as the hold of the ship was filled with more and more slaves, another difference between the *Pegasus* and other sailing ships became apparent. The fatality rate was higher—not just among the Africans but also among the crew. Unaccustomed to the tropics, the crew came down with all manner of illnesses—malaria, yellow fever, jaundice, and other strange malevolent diseases of the "Dark Continent" (as well as the more traditional European diseases of scurvy, pneumonia, tuberculosis, and influenza).

Every week at least one crew member died. After six months of sailing the African waters, the *Pegasus* was becoming seriously undermanned. Because of this, the slaves were a constant threat. The crew members were warned to be on the lookout for possible uprisings. The slaves were almost always chained, belowdecks at night and during bad weather, and topside during the day. A few of the males had to be constantly kept chained below—it was too dangerous to try and move them.

The women and children were not as dangerous and were therefore allowed to be together sometimes. However, the women and older girls were often kept in an area the crew called "the harem." The captain and other officers usually looked the other way when a sailor pulled aside one of the females.

None of the crew members knew how to speak any African dialect, and the captives could not understand the white men's words. However, the women knew by their leers and gestures what they were ordering them to do.

Terrified, naked, and shivering from the horror of their situation, they were forced into depraved sex. Some of the women were so numb from their capture and so weak from hunger and thirst and subsequent events that they submitted without a fuss. Other women and many of the girls fought desperately not to be raped.

At night the guards below deck in the slave hold usually walked around naked. It was unbearably hot, and any clothes they wore would soon be drenched with sweat.

Thus, both the crew members and the slaves were naked. This made for easy accommodation of forced copulation. Sometimes another sailor would have to guard or hold down or beat back a black male so that the other sailor could rape his wife, sister, or mother.

After awhile many of the crew members had more or less picked out their own favorites from among the women and girls. Some men, however—like John—enjoyed the variety of impregnating as many females as possible.

The licentiousness and violence of the whites caused more than emotional scars. Several of the female slaves who tried to avoid their sexual predators were severely beaten. Others even tried to kill themselves. At least two or three died, although their deaths were officially blamed on disease.

The sailors were always careful to make certain that they could not

be held responsible for the death of a slave. The captain would have made their lives miserable (or worse) if he thought that they had anything to do with the death of a slave—not for any humanitarian reason, but because it meant lost profit at the other end of the journey.

None of the sailors, including John, had any guilt or misgivings about treating the female slaves as sexual "pets" for their own loathsome satisfaction. It did not matter that some of the females, little girls not even old enough to have menstruated, were raped along with the teenage and adult females. Some of the sailors took matters even further than that. Little boys—aged only four to ten—were molested and sodomized by sailors "just to see what it was like." Teenage boys were raped for the same reason.

John thought that many—if not most—of these female slaves would likely arrive in the New World carrying babies fathered by their captors.

He smiled at the idea that some of them could be carrying *his* child— that a black baby, or many babies, born in the West Indies or American colonies might have Newton blood coursing in their veins. Why, he might have sired as many as a dozen offspring, at the young age of twenty.

Other female slaves—the ones not pregnant—were likely to bring something else with them to the New World. Many of the sailors had virulent cases of syphilis or gonorrhea that they quickly passed on to many of the slaves.

All the men on the ship were like John. They exercised no moral restraints at all. Even if they had, conventional standards of the day held that it was all right to have sex with a slave because, technically, a slave was not even a person.

✞ ✞ ✞

While John did not make any friends aboard the *Pegasus,* he did strike up something of a friendship with a man who was part owner of the ship. He resided in Africa and was a resident trader. John knew him

only as Mr. Clow. He never used a first name, and no one seemed to know it.

Clow personally helped the captain make slave buys. It was Clow who actually purchased the slaves at the various trading posts where the ship stopped. Clow acted as intermediary for the slave ship captains who only wanted to load their precious cargo and be off to the New World as soon as possible. Not many slave ship captains had the stomach to be so intimately involved in the actual buying and selling of human flesh. It was easier on their consciences if all they did was to transport them.

John respected Clow because he had grown up in poverty and was a self-made man. Yet he was also something of an enigma. John learned that he had built a number of fortified trading posts from Conakry to Pendembu on the coast of Sierra Leone. Heavily armed men guarded each of these "fortresses." Usually a white trader hired by Clow was in charge. Clow had his own "army" of Africans to defend the gold, ivory, gems, and slaves he had accumulated on inland trade incursions, which were stored in these fortresses.

"When I first landed on these coasts," Clow told John one day, "I was as poor as a man could be, but I learned how to trade. Before long I became wealthy. Maybe that's the life for you, Newton."

Clow also told John about a woman he called his wife—although John suspected she might have been a mistress. "Her name is Peh'eye. It's spelled funny, but it sounds like the initials P.I. She's a beautiful woman, and she's a princess. Yeah, really. Her father is an African king, and she's a princess."

John and Clow often conversed. Clow found Newton to be good company. He was educated, and they could converse in meaningful dialogue and not just about ordinary things.

John sometimes asked the captain's permission to go ashore with Clow. He wanted to observe him as he traded. *Maybe I can learn something of the trade and improve my lot,* John thought.

The ship always anchored just offshore from the mouth of a river. One of Clow's fortresses would always be located nearby. The shore party would meet with a band of twenty or so of Clow's private guards to accompany the traders as they traveled upriver.

John was surprised to see that Clow never abducted blacks from their tribal homes to sell as slaves. He let that dubious and detestable distinction go to other Africans who didn't mind selling their neighbors to the white men. John also thought it strange that men of the same race would carry out such acts against their own.

✝ ✝ ✝

As the *Pegasus* filled its hold with slaves, the duties increased. Many of the crew members were sent ashore to make arrangements for the slaves, while others guarded the rest and attended to normal duties.

Soon, however, the tropics brought fever and disease aboard the ship. Several sailors and a number of slaves died. Sickness became commonplace. Sometimes only ten or twelve men were available to watch over some two hundred slaves and to do their ship duties. It became necessary to chain the slaves below deck all the time. Only rarely were they allowed to come up for fresh air and washing.

John was assigned double-shift duty and could no longer go ashore. He argued with the captain and first mate. The captain, who had a touch of fever himself, refused to argue with John and turned the matter over to First Mate Collins.

Collins only had to pull out his small billy club and tap it into his hand for John to get the message. Although Newton said nothing, his glare at Collins told the first mate volumes. Things only got worse as the days grew closer to the time when the *Pegasus* was to sail.

The plan was to take the middle passage from the West Coast of Africa due west to the New World. The word was passed along that the ship would sail in a week.

One night, while waiting to sail, the captain was awakened by the sound of a baby crying. The child was hysterical, and its slave mother could not seem to quiet her.

"Mr. Collins," the captain called out to his first mate, "I cannot sleep with all that crying. Can't you do something about it?"

"Yes, sir!" Collins answered. He went below to where the slaves were kept and had no trouble finding the source of the noise. A young mother was trying to nurse her baby, but in the terror of capture and transportation, her milk supply had dried up. The baby was screaming with hunger.

Collins pulled the baby from the mother's arms. She tried to protect her baby, but he pushed her brutally back onto the floor. The first mate carried the still-screaming baby up the stairs to the deck. Then he strode quickly to the rail and threw the baby over the side. The crying stopped instantly as the sound of a small splash was heard.

John saw what had taken place and shuddered at the extent of cold-blooded malice in the heart of Collins.

Newton remembered this scene when, on New Year's Day 1746, the captain died suddenly. A fever had overtaken him and ravaged his system in just a day or two. His death, just before setting sail, caused a great deal of confusion.

The natural order of succession was for the first mate to take over the ship. Collins talked with Mr. Clow who—on behalf of the shipping line—conferred the necessary authority on Collins.

John felt sick when he heard the news. He knew that Collins would likely make his life even more miserable now that he was appointed acting captain.

Before long Collins confronted John and said, "Newton, I want you to know that you're the most disrespectful, mutinous, and worthless man who ever served under me. I plan to exchange you to another ship, but not one of these easy slavers you see. No. By God—I'm going to wait

until I can exchange you to serve on another navy ship! I'll see to it that you serve out every day of the next five years aboard a military ship where they know how to deal with your kind."

Terrified, John began to panic. He had become almost suicidal when he had served aboard the *Harwich*. He said nothing to Collins but inwardly vowed that he would never go back onto a military ship—he'd die first.

John decided to approach Clow and beg the trader to take him with him. Clow had already made plans to stay in Africa and had taken his things ashore. *It may already be too late,* John thought to himself. He was desperately worried.

To his great relief, Clow came back aboard the *Pegasus* that evening to have a farewell dinner with Collins and toast the crew to a good journey.

John cornered him and pled his case. Clow listened politely and thought about the request for a long moment. He recalled that the ship was already shorthanded. Yet, he also knew Collins wanted to get rid of Newton, maybe because he was jealous of John's education. Clow had always enjoyed John's company. He also figured Newton would be someone he could use, and he knew how to profit from John's predicament.

"If you leave the ship now," Clow said, "Collins can dispute your claim for wages. I'll get him to release you to me, and I'll give you a voucher for the six months' pay you've got coming, plus whatever wages you earn with me. What do you say?"

John did not even have to think about it. He was jubilant and ran to his quarters to get his things. In the excitement, he never thought to ask Clow to put their understanding in writing. This oversight would haunt him when he eventually returned to England and found the "vouchers" worthless.

In fact, his eagerness to leave the *Pegasus* was about to cost him dearly. He was being cast ashore penniless and wholly dependent upon

the resident trader whom he trusted. Before long, it would dawn on him that he was marooned in Africa, subject to the smallest whim of Mr. Clow.

Chapter Seventeen

Slave of Slaves

✝

Clow did not start out with entirely bad intentions. He reasoned that twenty-year-old John Newton had great potential. He was educated, experienced, and fearless and had the essential qualities of becoming a trader. After some experience John might become a person to whom Clow could entrust the day-to-day operations and enterprises.

During the first several weeks, Clow took John with him to visit a number of plantations and slave fortresses. The trader took a real interest in Newton and wanted him to learn as much as he could.

John was amazed that all these holdings belonged to Clow. Here in Africa, Clow had the respect of a general or a prince. He had his own armies guarding thousands of acres of land. He kept hundreds of slaves working dozens of plantations and farms. He employed mercenaries, traders, miners, and highly skilled tradesmen—mostly from England and Europe. It was an odd assortment of thugs and

artisans, all of them giving Mr. Clow the respect and obedience he demanded.

John learned from one of the mercenaries that Clow was a man to be feared as well as respected. "He is no longer English. He has become one of the savages. I've seen him kill men just because he felt like it—white men as well as black. Don't ever cross him. You'll die if you do," the mercenary warned.

It was a side to the man that John had never really seen while he was aboard the *Pegasus*. On the ship, Clow's true status was always understated.

They discussed John's first project a month after their arrival in Sierra Leone. The region got its name (Lion Mountain) from the high bluffs overlooking the river. Most of the land was, by now, uninhabited—its population having been carried off by slave ships. Clow took the land and built a fortress to protect it. Then he took over several of the immense islands just offshore. On the largest, about two miles across, he had the slaves clear away the jungle growth in order to build a new compound of factory and plantation. John figured that Clow was going to establish this other plantation to grow bananas or coconuts, as he had done on his other land holdings.

"Not this time, Newton," Clow told him. "This time I'm going to start a lime plantation."

"Lime plantation? What's a lime?" asked John.

"It's a fruit, like a lemon or orange. They say that it can prevent scurvy. If that's so, I'll make a fortune selling limes to all the ships that come here for trade."

John wasn't sure how a strange fruit could prevent scurvy but assumed that Mr. Clow knew what he was talking about.

"What do you want me to do?" he asked Clow.

"Well, you've watched me for a month. If you follow my instructions, I'll put you in charge of the project. But be warned—I'm a hard

man to please. You'll have to work hard, and you'll have to do things right."

John began his duties by taking charge of the construction crew. He directed their work as they felled and dragged coconut trees to a cleared area in order to build several log buildings. Once the laborers raised the log walls, the carpenters came to frame the roof beams. The roof coverings were made from banana fronds.

When completed, there were eight different buildings, the largest of which was Clow's residence. This building was also used for meetings and discussing business. A few of the other buildings were sleeping quarters for the workers, and one of the smaller buildings was set aside for John. Clow gave him some furniture and some slaves to plant a vegetable garden.

Other buildings were used for storage and housing Clow's trade inventory—gunpowder, axes, knives, rum, and whisky. An area was set aside for chickens and other livestock. Off to one side was a long narrow room where captive Africans were held until the slave ships came.

Mr. Clow was pleased with John's work, but not nearly as much as John was himself. The young protégé found great satisfaction in the efforts he put forth. But more than this, John wanted to make amends for his miserable past efforts at work.

Clow also gave John the chance to pick a female slave from the compound for his own. "She'll care for your living quarters, cook, and provide you with everything you need," Clow told him. "And I mean *everything,"* he said with a wink, "so choose wisely."

✝ ✝ ✝

After six months of hard work, the new facilities began to take shape, and John felt he was proving himself to his employer.

One day Clow looked into the face of the younger man and grew serious. "John, let me tell you something. I see something of myself in

you. I never married and don't have any children—that I know of, any-way," he added laughing.

"You can kind of be the son I wish I'd have had," he continued. "I'll adopt you as my own, and when I die some day, this will all be yours."

John found it difficult to process this new information. He wasn't sure if Clow really meant it or if he was simply trying to get greater produc-tivity out of his new protégé.

Not long after that exchange, Clow sailed north in one of his small ships to pick up his African mistress, Peh'eye, while John completed the construction of their house.

While Clow was gone, John had time to daydream about inheriting his enterprises. It sounded like an excellent proposition to him.

He continued to work hard by day, but at night he relaxed in bed where he lay beside the naked young slave girl he had chosen and eagerly enjoyed sex with her. The girl had no name—at least no one seemed to know it or know enough of her language to understand it. She was grateful that John did not treat her as cruelly as other white men.

At first he had tried to communicate with her by sign language, with some success. She was strikingly pretty, with expressive eyes and a smiling mouth. She wore only a loincloth, a leather necklace, and a pair of wooden bracelets. Her hair was black as ebony and so close to her head that it looked like a cap. Her hips were narrow, and John judged by this that she was probably in her teens (about Polly's age) and had never had children.

During pauses in the work when the noon sun made it too hot for construction, he tried to get the girl to talk. He pointed to a tree, naming it in English. He motioned for her to tell him her word for the tree. Once she understood the game, they were able to learn quite a few words in each other's language.

Then he asked for her name. He explained that his name was John, but she did not respond when he asked what people called her. The girl was confused.

"I am John," he told her. "John," he repeated, thumping his chest.

"John," the girl echoed. But she didn't respond when he asked for her name. Finally he resolved to settle the matter by naming her himself. "You are Ruby," he said. "I'm going to call you Ruby until I learn your real name."

"*Roo*-bee," she repeated slowly.

"Yes. I am John," he said, pointing again to his chest. "You are Ruby." He pointed at her.

She responded to his kindness by doing everything he asked, including submission to his nightly sexual demands. Sometimes he felt guilty—not for how he was treating the African girl, but that maybe he was being unfaithful to Polly. He'd then argue with himself—first, that he was an atheist, so it didn't matter what he did. And second, sex with a slave did not matter. He believed, as he had been told, that Africans were somehow subhuman and unable to have the same emotional and intellectual capacity as the "superior" Europeans.

One day Ruby was working in the garden planting some yams. John sat on a bench and enjoyed watching her work. Her graceful, naked body reminded him of the beautiful statues he had seen in Venice. He truly liked Ruby, and she gave him pleasure. She was his mistress, but he began to think of her as more than a mistress, perhaps even a wife.

Several other slaves were working nearby by the time Ruby finished planting. She noticed someone out of the corner of her eye and appeared startled. She checked herself and then looked cautiously toward John, who was still sitting on the bench by his house and appearing to be asleep.

Ruby stood up and backed away slowly. Puzzled, John sat still but tilted his head back in order to see where she was going. She went over

to where a male slave was working, and they began talking excitedly but quietly in their own language. John saw that he was a young African about his own age. He watched as the two embraced each other as if being reunited in some way.

The male slave and Ruby engaged in animated whispered conversation as John watched them. The two of them were talking excitedly and gesturing wildly but tried not to make any noise. Ruby looked up to see if anyone could see them, then quickly led the young black man into the nearby foliage where the shadows almost hid them.

John watched as Ruby tenderly embraced the young man and held on to him as he wrapped her in his arms. John felt a rush of jealousy as they embraced and held each other for what seemed to be a long time. The naked slave pressed harder against Ruby, who was leaning on a tree.

Jumping up, John grabbed a nearby hoe and ran toward the two slaves. Cursing and screaming, he struck the male across the back with the handle with such force that he broke the hoe. The slave lost his balance and fell. Ruby also fell to the ground. She screamed the few English words she had learned, "No! *No!* Master John, please!"

As the male slave looked up from the ground, John picked up part of the broken hoe and swung it angrily. The metal blade caught the black man just above his eyebrow and sent him backwards. The hoe blade had sliced his scalp away from the skull, and his head began to bleed profusely. More angry blows followed as John lost control of his senses.

Ruby tried to stop John from beating the slave senseless. He pushed her away twice. The third time Ruby tried to intervene, John swung his left arm and smashed her full in the face with his hand. She fell in a crumpled heap, crying hysterically.

Several of the white tradesmen watched the commotion but did nothing. Finally John threw the broken hoe away and stalked back to his hut, dragging Ruby with him.

He learned later, after overhearing the tradesmen talking, that the male slave was Ruby's husband and that they had not seen each other since their capture over two months earlier.

John felt somewhat chagrined that he had beaten them so severely. He tried to make it up to Ruby by showing her affection and kindness as before, but it was too late—her spirit had already vanished. It was as if she no longer lived in that beautiful body.

Ruby went about doing her work without feeling, without life. John was troubled to see the injured male slave around the compound and ordered that he be assigned to one of the other Clow plantations where Ruby would not see him again.

It was no surprise that Ruby no longer satisfied John in bed. He decided to give her time to get over the incident and banished her to the servants' hut to work with the kitchen slaves. After that, he slept alone.

✝ ✝ ✝

After more than a week away, Clow returned with his mistress, Peh'eye. She came with her own entourage of maids and slaves. John watched as the woman walked toward her new home. She was tall and regal and had all the poise and bearing of the princess that she claimed to be.

Peh'eye was a beautiful woman with round, dark brown eyes and lustrous black hair that was elaborately braided. Peh'eye was dressed in Western clothing—an expensive dress and hat that looked as though she might have just come from the opera instead of a several-hundred-mile journey by Clow's ship. She wore a great deal of jewelry, much of it heavy gold. Her earrings were gold with diamond pendants and matched her necklace.

Clow introduced Peh'eye to John, who nodded to her. "Pleased to meet you," he said.

She did not reply to him at all. Turning to Clow, she asked, "What is this white man doing here? You did not tell me about him."

"My dear," Clow told his mistress, "it's nothing for you to concern your pretty head about. John is a good lad. I've taken a liking to him. I look at him as a son," Clow said soothingly.

Peh'eye suddenly seemed filled with rage. "A son!? I will give you a son if you want a son," she shouted. Clow rolled his eyes toward John apologetically and escorted Peh'eye inside. "Come, my dear. Let's go and see your new house. I had them build the very best for you."

Despite his nonchalance at the rudeness of his mistress, Clow could not hide the fact of who was really in charge. John smiled. For a month he had watched as Clow gave orders and drew fear and respect from all his men. Now he seemed to only be another henpecked husband.

Clow invited John to share dinner with them that evening. John accepted and showed up promptly as he was instructed. When he arrived at the main house, a slave dressed in Western-style coat and trousers greeted him.

As he was ushered into the house, John saw that his hosts were wearing fine, formal dress clothes. Whenever he and Clow had eaten together before, neither of them bothered to change from whatever clothes they had worn during the day.

John suddenly felt ill at ease. No one had warned him to dress for the occasion, and he immediately saw Peh'eye's displeasure.

"John, I'm sorry. I should have told you that we enjoy a more formal time at dinner," Clow apologized. "Come. Wear one of my dinner coats. I realize you have not had the opportunity to acquire one since coming to Africa."

All through the meal Clow talked to John about the plans for the new plantation. His mistress barely spoke. John tried to break the ice and asked her about her trip, but she said little. He was grateful when the dinner and conversation ended and he retired to his own small hut.

As the two white men worked together over the next several days, Clow's mistress seethed. She knew that even though she was African royalty, and even if she did give Clow a son, there was no way that his culture would permit him to make that son a successor. Such a son would always be a bastard in the eyes of the English. And no matter how much Clow appeared to disdain his countrymen, he would never permit an African to be given the inheritance he had already planned for John.

Peh'eye knew her position was weak. When she was no longer young and beautiful, Clow would tire of her. She had hoped that before that happened she would secure her position and make certain that Clow would never throw her out. She had *her* eyes on his wealth and holdings. Now, unless something was done with this new white man, she would never have a sense of security about the future.

The next day Clow called John to his house to discuss an important change of plans. "I want you to accompany me upriver. Some men came to me today with news of gold found near Makeni. It's a two-week trip there, fighting the current, and a little more than a week to return. We'll take goods to barter for the gold. Whisky, I think, will be well appreciated. And gunpowder. Take a crew and load up everything onto the ship tomorrow. We'll set out on Tuesday."

"Yes, sir," John replied while making notes on some paper.

On Monday night the inventory had been loaded, and the ship was made ready. To celebrate, Clow invited John to dinner. He tried to beg off, remembering the last time he dined with Clow and his mistress.

"Nonsense," Clow argued. "I want you to dine with us tonight. I won't take no for an answer."

The evening was one of good conversation, fine wine, and a wonderful dinner. Yet, there was an uneasy chill in the air as Peh'eye stared at John. Then her demeanor toward John suddenly changed. After dessert she brought each of the men a glass of fine brandy and made a point of giving John a glass first before offering one to Clow.

John felt the warmth of the liquor as he sipped it. Never having tasted brandy before, he was unsure whether he liked it. Yet, not to offend his host, he finished the glass. Not long afterwards, he began to feel queasy.

"I think I should be going, sir," he told his employer. "I want to be ready to leave by dawn. If you'll excuse me—"

"Of course. Thank you for your company, John. I'll see you in the morning," Clow said.

John thanked his host and Peh'eye, then got up to leave. By now his head was spinning, and he had a little trouble keeping his balance. Once outside, he breathed the night air deeply to clear his head. He walked hurriedly toward his hut but on the way got terribly sick. He vomited and felt faint. Weak, he struggled to make it home. Once inside, he flopped onto the bed. Soon he was overwhelmed with nausea, tremors, and a raging fever. He was so sick all night that he could hardly be roused by morning and couldn't even get out of bed. Clow sent someone to check on him and went to see John when the slave reported finding him ill.

"It's probably one of the tropical fevers," Clow said, his voice trying to hide his concern. He ordered a house slave to fetch cool water and wipe John's forehead with it.

"You're too sick to go with me, and I can't stay. I have to meet this fellow in Makeni," he said. "That's all right. Don't worry. We'll have other opportunities. Just stay here and take it easy 'til you get better. You'll be well taken care of. I'll have you moved into my house where Peh'eye and her servants can watch over you."

Within the hour Clow was gone and John was lying in a bedroom inside Clow's big house. His employer would be away nearly a month, and John wondered if Clow's mistress would be as attentive to his needs as her husband had indicated she would.

John's suspicions were confirmed as soon as Clow's small ship was out of sight. The black princess came into his room and laughed, mock-

ing his illness. "So, you are like all white men? Weak. Helpless. Africans
are not afraid of fevers. You should have died in the night," she said
cryptically. "Still, maybe you will die today. That will be fine with me,"
she told him frankly.

Peh'eye then had John carried from her house to his own hut and
reversed all of the orders that Clow had given for John's care.

"Leave him alone!" she commanded the slaves. "If you disobey me, I
will have you beaten!"

Alone and desperately sick, his fever got worse. John became even
more weak and delirious. Late at night he awoke to see someone standing over him. His eyes could hardly focus.

"Am you wake?" The voice was Ruby's. She was wiping his forehead
with a wet cloth and tried to help his fever. He felt shame that she would
treat him so well after the way he had treated her.

After awhile John began to shiver with chills. Ruby covered him with
an animal skin robe and lay beside him to help give him warmth. By daybreak Ruby was still there trying to help prevent the alternate chills and
fever. "I be back when I can. Mistress have jobs for Ruby in her house.
I must go," she explained.

John assumed from her imperfect English and the way she sneaked
away that she wasn't even supposed to be with him. Peh'eye had taken
her back as a house slave, and she was ordered to have nothing to do
with him. John was too sick to worry about it though. His head ached,
and he was terribly weak. He wasn't even sure how many days he had
been lying in his bed sick.

For awhile he seemed to have some lucid moments and took time to
think about his symptoms. He had seen many men come down with a
tropical fever. Usually they got sick and simply became better or
worse—they either got well, or the fever killed them. As John thought
about it, his fever seemed strange. When other whites had contracted
tropical fevers, their symptoms were different.

John had never been this ill before. Once in Venice he had eaten some undercooked meat and got food poisoning—and this was similar in some ways. He tried to recall if he ate or drank anything suspicious before getting sick, but he couldn't think of anything. Then he suddenly had a flash of insight. *Maybe I have been poisoned!* he thought and remembered the strange-tasting brandy. *She might have poisoned me! Peh'eye told me that if I died it would be fine with her.*

He wondered about the possibility that she would really take such overt action and try to kill him. He decided to keep his guard up and not eat or drink anything she sent to him. Then he fell into a fitful sleep once more. He had terrible nightmares as he slept.

Ruby did not come back the following night. Someone else had brought food and water. He assumed it came from Peh'eye, so he didn't touch it. His fever still raged, and John became incoherent. He thrashed in his bed and cried out at the demons in his nightmares.

The next day Peh'eye came to see him. "Why do you not eat and drink what I sent?" she demanded.

"Why? So you can poison me?" John asked weakly.

She seemed startled to hear these words. She stepped back and looked around to see if anyone had heard him. Then Peh'eye called two of the slaves. "Come. Take this man to the slave quarters. He is my slave now. He is not good enough to have this house. I will use it for my servants. Take him away!"

The slaves carried John to the slave quarters and laid him on a reed mat with a log for a pillow. There he lay for several more days. He would have died of thirst if Ruby had not sneaked out at night to sponge a few drops of water into his parched mouth. The next several nights, Ruby brought him some broth.

He gradually began to feel better, much to Peh'eye's chagrin. She began to think that magic protected this white man from death. She ordered the slaves, especially Ruby, not to take John any food or water.

When Peh'eye visited him the next day, he pleaded with her for water and a little food. "But don't you remember? I am trying to poison you!" she laughed. "You don't want anything from me. It might kill you!"

After nightfall, a servant came to him with a platter and goblet. "Mistress tell me to bring you," he said. "She say you not worry that it be poison. She already taste it and it be all right."

John looked at the platter. It was the remains of Peh'eye's dinner consisting of a fish head, some bones and skin, yam peelings, husks, and other remains of her dinner. The water in the goblet was murky and smelled as if Peh'eye had urinated in it. But John was too hungry and thirsty to turn the food and drink away. He ate the scraps of food still clinging to the bones, the fish head, and the husks, and forced himself to drink from the fetid goblet.

Later that night, when everyone was asleep, he was still weak but tried to stand. It was impossible. John forced himself up from the mat and crawled outside into the clearing. He went to the place where the slaves cleaned their plates and looked for more scraps of food among the reeking, putrid garbage. Furtively he rummaged through the scraps for something edible and tore at it with his fingers, cramming it into his mouth.

John then crawled to a mud puddle where he lapped water from it like a dog. It was enough to sustain him for the night, so he struggled back to his sleeping mat in the slave hut.

Peh'eye ordered the slaves to continue to ignore his cries for food and water. No one but Ruby would have responded anyway, but even she was prevented from helping him. He was utterly on his own. The next night he resorted to his scavenger hunts. Not finding much to eat among the garbage scraps, he dug up roots and some of the vegetables that Ruby had planted many weeks earlier. Since it rained almost every day in the tropics, he had no trouble finding more mud puddles.

By now the fever had gone, and John fought to regain his strength. Yet, without proper food it would be impossible.

The word got out that the princess of the island had her own slave— *a white man*—and it became a curiosity. People paid secret nighttime visits to the Clow plantation to see for themselves. They were entranced at this strange situation and watched John as he dug roots and lapped water from mud puddles. They laughed and threw pieces of bread or fruit at him like some weird pet. John grabbed the pieces of food from the dirt and ate them hastily.

Word somehow got back to Peh'eye, and she came by John's quarters. "So, you like to have us throw food at you?" she asked. "Well, I have brought you something to eat." She picked out some rotten fruit and putrid, spoiled meat from a basket and she threw them at him, spattering the garbage on his face and chest. When she ran out of garbage, she reached for rocks and began pelting him with them. "Why don't you die, you devil? Why don't you die?"

John was beginning to feel a little stronger by the time he heard that Clow had returned. He was glad because he knew that now things would change for the better.

✝ ✝ ✝

"Where's John?" Clow had asked Peh'eye on his return, wondering why he was not there to greet him.

She began to weep loudly and wail with pretended feeling. "Oh, how glad I am that you have returned! You will not believe what happened while you were gone."

Peh'eye began to weave tales of John trying to abuse her, of stealing from Clow's treasury, of taking things from the house and making them his own. She brought one of Clow's supervisors to the house. This man was also jealous of John and resented the fact that Clow had given Newton prominence over him in the business. The supervisor gave a

similar version of Peh'eye's story—even elaborating on her stories of John's irresponsibility. "Why, he hasn't worked a day since you left," he told Clow.

"You'll see for yourself," Peh'eye told him. "All you have to do is search his hut. You'll find the things he has stolen from you—if he hasn't already sold them."

Angrily, Clow went to John's hut to see for himself. He upended the furniture and tore open trunks, finding silver from the house and some money from the treasury.

Then he went to find John. He found him lying on the reed mat in the slave's quarters.

"Mr. Clow," John cried out. "Oh, am I glad to see you!"

"Are you really?" Clow replied sarcastically. "Is this how you treat my generosity and hospitality? By abusing my wife, stealing from me, and by not doing any of your work?"

"I don't know what you're talking about, sir," John stuttered. "I have been sick all the while you were away."

Clow snarled, "Oh, yes. You were sick all right. Sick in your mind. I leave you comfortable in my own home, and you take advantage of my wife and me. And I suppose you thought I would not miss the things you stole from me and hid in your hut?"

"Mr. Clow, your mistress had me taken out of your home right after you left. Then she had them move me out of my hut. I haven't been there at all. I don't know how those things got in my hut, but I didn't take them," John said sincerely.

"Don't lie to me, Newton," Clow barked. "I know when somebody is lying." Then he told John how the supervisor had corroborated Peh'eye's story in every detail.

"But sir," John pleaded, "they're making it all up. It's not true."

For a moment Clow was ready to believe him but strode off without saying anything more.

For several days relations were strained between John and Clow. John hoped that his employer would be convinced of the truth and that things could be put back as they had been. Then Clow called him to the house.

"We're going to start planting the lime trees today," he said. Earlier he had talked about John being the overseer of the slaves on the new lime plantation. "But there's been a change," Clow said. "Newton, you'll join the slaves and plant limes with the rest of them. You'll be a field hand until I determine that you can be trusted with other responsibility."

"Well, sir," John replied, "if it's all the same to you, I think I'll leave. I'll see about working with another trader. One who'll believe me."

"Leave!?" Clow yelled. "You're going nowhere! You owe me. There's still money you took that I can't account for. And there's the matter of the food and shelter you owe me for—more than six months' room and board. When you can pay me for that, plus interest, you can leave. But not until then!"

Clow then shoved John in the direction of the slaves. "Now get out there and get busy."

John toiled in the blazing African sun with the other slaves, trying to avoid the whip of the black overseer who took sadistic pleasure in beating a white man. His back and joints ached from stooping all day— digging, planting, cultivating. He staggered under the weight of the huge jars of water that were carried to the fields to water the new shoots.

This work went on for many weeks. Then the weeks turned to months. John's rations and quarters were the same as the other slaves, and he began to look like one of them. The fierce sun blackened his skin, and his hair and beard grew long and unkempt. His clothes rotted, and he worked naked like the others. He looked more like a savage than the educated son of a British sea captain.

Things began to look a bit better when Clow called him one day and gave him some new clothes. "Get cleaned up and put these on," he told

John. "I have to go on another trading trip upriver. Since Peh'eye doesn't feel safe with you here, I'm taking you. We leave at dawn. Be ready."

John almost enjoyed the trip by boat. The boat was small by seafaring standards. Only some twenty feet long and about eight feet wide, it had a small cabin that Clow and John shared.

Two blacks made up the crew, and they had to use rafting poles to move the ship upriver when the sails were useless. Even though he had to row along with the slaves, John was grateful for the overhanging jungle growth that provided shade.

The trip began in August, one of the hottest months. Torrential tropical rains added to the discomfort of any journey. Traveling upriver was especially dangerous this time of year. The heavy rains caused the rivers to swell by fifteen or twenty feet, and the currents were often treacherous. This was also the breeding season for mosquitoes, and the swarms were known to drive men insane.

As if the mosquitoes were not bad enough, flies also swarmed in fury. Their bites sometimes stung as badly as a wasp, and it seemed that they had an agreement with the mosquitoes—the flies tormented in the daylight and the mosquitoes tortured at night.

Snakes and crocodiles were also dangers to avoid. The Africans jokingly referred to these trips as "the graveyard of the whites," and with good reason. However, none of these distresses seemed to bother John. He was just glad to be away from Clow's mistress.

Because Clow was so busy on this trading trip, he let John help him. John took some of the goods and traded with one trader while Clow and the others went to another.

John had done well with his assignment, and Clow began to wonder if he had misjudged the young man. His trust in John began to improve.

One of the traders resented Clow who always seemed to be encroaching into his territory and cheating those with whom he dealt.

Clow seemed to know intuitively when the inland traders would be coming with slaves to trade. He was always there first, and by the time the other traders got there, there were no more slaves to buy.

This infuriated one trader so much that he wanted to kill Clow, but he realized that Clow's army would never permit it. Instead, he devised a plan to upset the equilibrium of Clow's organization. He stuffed a small bag of silver coins in John's backpack when the men were busy. Then he went over to Clow and said, "I see that your partner sold some of the slaves I sold him."

"What are you talking about?" Clow asked.

"When you were in the other territory buying slaves, your man Newton bought fifteen slaves from me for gunpowder and knives. Now he's only got ten slaves. I saw him sell five slaves to another trader. I just wondered if you knew what he was doing," the trader said.

"Newton!" Clow called.

When John joined the other two men, Clow asked him if the man's story was true.

"Of course not!" asserted John.

"Then he won't mind if you search him for the money they gave him for the slaves," the trader said.

"I don't have any money," John told him.

"You said you bought ten slaves? What did you pay for them?"

John told Clow what he had given for the slaves. Clow shook his head, "This man says he sold you fifteen slaves for the goods you gave him," Clow said.

"It's not true. You know the going rate for a slave. What I gave him is what you'd have to pay to get ten slaves, not fifteen."

"Turn your pockets inside out," Clow ordered. John complied, having nothing to hide. "Now open your supply sack." John reached down and picked up his backpack. The bag of coins dropped noisily to the ground.

"That's not mine," John said nervously.

Clow picked it up and counted the coins. "It's exactly what you'd expect to get for five slaves," he muttered. His big fist slammed into John's face, knocking him to the ground.

"But I swear," John pleaded, "I didn't do it."

"And I was just beginning to trust you again," Clow snarled. "I can see that you're nothing but a thief."

Chapter Eighteen

A Prisoner

✠

John had thought of running away but knew that Clow's army would find him and probably execute him on the spot. He decided to wait and reason with Clow when things settled down a bit. Clow's temper was well known—he did not want to test it.

Clow did not take the time to deal with Newton as he had wanted to. He had more pressing matters to take care of. Instead, he chained John by his ankle to the deck of the boat that had taken them upriver.

The two black crewmen accompanied Clow on the inland trading incursions while John was left padlocked in leg irons on the boat. Before the first excursion, one of the blacks felt some sympathy for John and left a small dish of rice within his reach.

John managed to reach a small slop bucket near the cabin entry and pulled it to him. Taking a rope from one of the sail lines, he tied it to the

bucket and lowered it into the murky, muddy river. It tasted awful, but it slaked his thirst.

The sun, beating down onto the dark wooden deck, absorbed the worst of the heat. Even so, John felt like a pig on a roasting spit. Late in the afternoon it began to rain. At first it refreshed him after the heat of the sun. Then the rain turned cold. Soon it stopped, and a breeze blew in from the ocean some miles away. John breathed deeply. The salt air made him wistful for the life of a sailor again.

When sun set, John's clothes were still soaked by the rain, and he began to shiver, as the night seemed extra cold. Mosquitoes attacked him fiercely as he tried to sleep. Miserable and cold, he slept only a little that night.

The next day was a repeat of the first. By nightfall, though, Clow and the crew returned. They built a campfire on the riverbank and began to roast a large bird. The smell of the roasting meat blew across the deck of the ship, and John's mouth began to water. He could see and hear Clow and the other men enjoying a meal on shore. It was obvious that they were not going to share any of it with him.

A few hours later one of the crew members came aboard the boat. "Master Clow say to bring you some quail."

John's spirits lifted immediately, but something in the man's voice made him question the gift. He was right to be cynical. The slave had placed the offering on a banana leaf and set it down on the deck in front of Newton. On the leaf were the head and feet of the bird used for the meal, along with its entrails. John was repulsed and gagged at the thought of eating the waste matter, but wisely he said nothing.

The slave looked away with an expression of shame. Then he reached surreptitiously into the folds of his shirt and pulled out another, smaller leaf. He handed it to John and left.

John opened the gift and found a handful of cooked rice, which he quickly devoured. He was about to throw the bird entrails overboard

when he got an idea. When the men left in the morning for another trip, he'd use the remains for bait and try to catch a fish.

The next day was hot like the previous ones. Again the broiling sun beat down. However, on this day no rain came to grant John relief.

John kept his mind off of his trouble by preparing a line for fishing, no small task for a chained man. He made use of a variety of "tools"—including a rafting pole, the bucket, a coil of rope, and his knife (thankfully Clow had left it with him). He pried off a metal grommet from the sail and pulled it apart. Then he painstakingly used his knife to whittle away enough of the metal to make a curved thin hook, complete with a barb and small hole to thread the fishing line through.

For the line he unraveled a piece of rope and braided a ten-foot length of fibers to use to hold the hook and bait. After several hours of constructing his "tackle," he was ready to fish.

It was another several hours before he had any luck. At first he was unsuccessful. Small fish nibbled at the bait until it was gone. They were too small to get the oversized hook into their mouths. John stayed with it though. Finally, when it was almost time for the sun to set, he felt a tug on the line. John pulled quickly to set the hook and began pulling the line from the water. Flopping on the end of the makeshift line was a silver fish at least nine inches long. John was elated and grabbed the slippery creature before it flopped free of the hook.

John tossed the fish triumphantly onto the deck but had to perform one last task before he could enjoy feasting on it. He had to reach the brazier to see if it still contained some coal. He used the rafting pole to drag it slowly across the deck to where he was chained. Thankfully, it contained some coal.

He took his knife and cut small pieces of the rope into a ball of fuzz for tinder, and after a great deal of effort, with the flints in his pocket he started a fire.

The fish was half raw and half burned, but no meal ever tasted so good. John kept the fish guts to use for more bait over the next days.

John lost track of time but suspected he was chained to the deck for at least two months. Actually, it was closer to three months. John was greatly emaciated by the time Clow ended his trading trip. The sympathetic crewman tried to leave John a little rice, at least every other day, but Clow would tolerate no other "kindness" for the prisoner.

Finally, to John's great joy, they left the mosquito-infested jungle rivers for the island. He was hoping he had served his sentence and that Clow might begin to show some human kindness toward him.

However, the first thing Clow did upon their return was to take John to the blacksmith's forge. There they fashioned ankle cuffs with an eighteen-inch chain between them. John's spirits really sank at this point. It was one thing to be in chains aboard the ship where a padlock held his ankle cuff. A padlock gave him hope that his confinement was temporary.

Now, as he shuffled back from the forge, he felt helpless and hopeless.

Peh'eye walked toward them as Clow pushed John along toward the fields. She smiled broadly at the sight of John in ankle chains.

"Hello, my dear," Clow said, greeting his mistress. "I trust all went well during our absence."

"Yes, all is well, my husband," she cooed.

"Well, Newton," Clow said with sarcasm, "I've brought you home. You can go finish planting and cultivating the lime trees. It looks as though you'll outlive all of us. Who knows, if you do live that long, you'll be around to see these trees bear fruit. I'll tell you what—when these trees bear fruit, I'll set you free. You can go back to England, maybe get yourself a ship, and sail back here to buy fruit from these very trees you planted!"

Clow laughed at his own preposterous joke.

As John shuffled to the field to work, he felt the irony of the fact that he now had something in common with many of the other slaves who also wore leg irons.

John continued to work in the plantation fields day after unrelenting day. Clow and his mistress did their best to kill him without actually raising a weapon to do so. By sheer willpower, though, Newton took their abuse and managed to survive.

Some time later, a white man visited the Clow compound. He introduced himself as Mr. Barker and told Clow that he, too, was a trader.

Clow had heard of Barker. He was younger and more skillful than Clow. The other traders and merchant shippers respected him more than Clow, who by now was losing favor because of his cheating and other indiscretions.

In the minds of Clow's fellow traders and his competitors, Barker was thought to be even richer than Clow. No one knew if it was true or not, but because Barker had white servants instead of black slaves, he gave the impression of ultimate affluence. Barker commented on Newton toiling in the fields nearby.

"I see you have a white slave. I have only white servants—I don't make the whites work with the slaves. It's not dignified," Barker observed.

"Yes, well—he's really a servant, but I am punishing him for a misdemeanor," Clow explained.

"I see. Would you want to sell him to me?"

"No," Clow barked. "He's not for sale."

Barker left with two of his men, tipping his hat politely to Clow.

During the weeks that followed, some of the slaves felt sympathy for John and began to smuggle leftover food and other treats for him from the house. One of the special gifts was pen and ink. He wrote a letter to his father, laying out the full panoply of his plight. Another letter was

addressed to Polly, in which he expressed his devotion and hope that he might soon return to England to see her.

A house slave charged with taking mail to outgoing ships took Clow's overseas correspondence in a pouch, under his seal. John pleaded with the slave to put his letters in the pouch after Clow gave him his mail but before the pouch was sealed.

John hoped that his smuggled letters would find safe passage and not be found before the ship sailed. If the ships did get through, he had a chance. It required several months for the journey, first to the New World, then back to Great Britain, where the captain and Polly might actually receive his letters.

Just to make sure, John wrote two or three more times—as infrequent word came of a European ship at anchor nearby—and he was able to smuggle these letters into the mail pouch as well.

✝ ✝ ✝

Months later, the first of the letters arrived at the home of Captain John Newton. Thomasin gave him the letter when he returned home from the shipping offices. He was overjoyed to see his son was still alive. However, that joy was dampened by the account his son gave in the letter.

The captain read the letter to Thomasin, whose eyes filled with tears as she listened: "Father, I am the lowest of the low. I am a prisoner and a slave. I am starved and abused and have no hope of rescue. I have many times barely escaped death through fevers and other sickness. My tormentor refuses to release me, and I have lost all hope. If there is any way under heaven that you get this letter and can help me, I pray for your urgent intervention. Your obedient son, John." Captain Newton choked back tears as he read the final words.

"What can you do?" Thomasin asked.

"I don't know. I'll check with my friends and see if any ships will be

anywhere near the western coast of Africa in the near future," the captain replied. "I just pray we aren't already too late."

The next day Captain Newton sent word from London to his friend, Joseph Manesty. Ruefully, he thought how different things would have been if John had gone with Manesty to Jamaica years earlier instead of acting irresponsibly.

In Liverpool, Manesty recalled the same incident when he received the letter from Captain Newton. However, by now he had gotten over the matter and saw an immediate need in his friend's plea.

He agreed to help and wrote Captain Newton to tell him of the plan. However, as he thought of the "plan," he wasn't so sure that it was an effective one. Manesty had a ship—the *Greyhound*—that was about to sail along the West Coast of Africa and trade, then catch the trade winds for the colonies.

He told the captain of the *Greyhound* about the son of another sea captain who was marooned somewhere in Africa. Manesty told the captain to make inquiries up and down the coast, taking a few extra days if need be, and see if John might be found and rescued.

"And Captain," Manesty added, "I recall that this young man can be quite undependable. If you do find him and he resists coming back, I want you to use any means necessary to get him aboard and bring him back to England."

✝ ✝ ✝

John was grateful that Clow gave his slaves a little time off during the hottest part of each day to eat. It was at this time that John also washed his clothes, which were now his only earthly possessions. He washed them at the beach, then put them on to dry. On such days, he took his mind off his situation by using data from the one book he had brought ashore when he landed in Africa almost a year earlier, *Euclid's Elements of Geometry.*

John had memorized the theorems and used a stick to sketch them in the damp sand. One day he was drawing in the sand when he became aware of someone watching him.

"Hello, my name is Barker," said the well-dressed man. John backed up, ashamed to be seen in public as he was. The chains of his leg irons rattled as he tried to leave.

"Wait," Barker ordered. "I wish to talk with you. What's your name?"

"Newton, sir. John Newton," he answered quietly, looking at his feet.

"Did you do these geometry equations?" Barker asked.

"Yes. It helps take my mind off . . . uh . . . it's a good distraction," John answered.

"I'm impressed. You're obviously an educated man. I can't imagine why you're here. You're the one I see working in the fields for Clow, aren't you?"

"Yes."

"But why? He told me the first time I asked about you that you weren't really a slave but a servant who was being punished. But every time I go to Clow's plantation, I see you there. That must be some punishment that he's imposed upon you."

John did not reply and kept looking down. He had seen Barker talking with Clow before—this could be a trick—maybe Clow was using this man to test him about complaining to others about his situation.

"Look, Newton," Barker said, "the purpose of my recent visits to Clow has been to ask him to sell your indenture to me. But he refuses. It makes me wonder why."

He had a softness in his voice and a quality that seemed sympathetic, and John decided to take a chance and talk with Barker. "I was aboard a ship in which Mr. Clow was part owner. He agreed to take me on and teach me the slave trade. For awhile everything went quite well. I served him faithfully and was learning from him. He even trusted me with his business. Then he went away, and his mistress—"

"You mean Peh'eye, the one who acts like a queen?"

"Yes. Peh'eye—for some reason—was jealous of me. Mr. Clow had promised me that I would take over his business and inherit his holdings. I think she felt threatened that he might throw her out," John observed.

"But what got you into trouble?"

"She poisoned me, or maybe drugged me. Anyway, I got terribly sick. Then, while I was delirious, she had someone—I think it was the former supervisor of the plantation, or maybe one of the slaves—hide some of Mr. Clow's things and some money in my hut to make it look like I stole from him. When he came back, Mr. Clow believed Peh'eye and not me," John said quietly. "Then he went back on his word. He claimed I owed him money for food and shelter while I was working. He also said I had to work to repay the money that he claims I 'stole,' plus interest. That's why I have to work in the fields—to work off a debt he says I owe."

"But you can get around. Why don't you hail a passing ship and escape? Couldn't you earn your way back home as a sailor?" Barker asked.

John grinned sardonically. "If a man in leg irons came to you and asked for asylum, and you checked with the man who was holding him prisoner for the other side of the story, whom would you believe?"

"Yes," Barker said. "I see what you mean. I can appreciate your fear. But even Clow is not above the law. He can't do this."

John shook his head sadly. "Yes . . . he *can*. I've been here long enough to know that English law has no power in Africa. Clow is the law here."

With that thought John suddenly became more nervous about talking with Barker. He stood to leave. "I must get back to work now," he said.

Barker watched him shuffle away toward the Clow fields.

The next day Barker showed up at Clow's plantation again. "Look, Clow," he told the trader, "I've been thinking about that poor white you've got working out there with the blacks. You say you're punishing him. Well, I think it's something else that's making you treat him like that. I believe that white man is educated, and he's being wasted here. I want you to sell him to me."

Clow said nothing. He took a moment to consider Newton and the extremes he had taken to make John's life miserable. There was no way he could make him more miserable than he was already.

As Clow thought about it, he figured it might be time to consider selling his indenture. He was constantly defending his actions to other traders who stopped by (like Barker) and asked why he had a white slave. He also didn't want to face the social implications of killing John. Perhaps he was tiring of this sadistic game after all. Clow then named an outrageous price for Newton.

Barker snickered. "Well, for someone you treat like dung, you certainly have placed a high value on him."

"It's a fair price. That's only what he owes me," Clow snapped.

"Yes, I'm sure," Barker said. "All right. I'll give you your price. Now take off those leg irons and bring him here."

✝ ✝ ✝

John could not believe his good fortune. With the weights taken from his ankles, he felt revived. On the way to Barker's plantation, he sobbed his gratitude to his benefactor.

"You can thank me by using your mind and talents to help me in my business. When we get home, I'll give you some new clothes, some decent food, and a room of your own. You get cleaned up, eat, and rest. Later tonight I'll draw up a contract. You can work for me to pay back what I had to pay that bloodsucker.

"But unlike him, I'm not going to exploit you. I learned long ago that

a man will serve you with loyalty and productivity when he's well paid and is treated fairly and with dignity. With the wages I'm going to pay you, you'll be able to pay me back in a few months and have your full freedom. If you'd like to stretch it out over a year, you can pay me a tenth every month from your wages until your debt is paid. Either way is fine with me, but I'm hoping you'll enjoy working for me and want to stay on as a partner."

Barker proved true to his word. Later that night John read over the contract his new employer had prepared. It was exactly as Barker had said—all the terms of employment were spelled out clearly and fairly. How John regretted not having the initial arrangement with Clow in writing—not that it would have helped, but it would have made him feel better.

In his own hut later that first evening, John looked over his spartan accommodations. They were simple, but compared to the terrible conditions Clow had kept him in for almost a year, they seemed to him to be luxurious.

On one wall was a small dresser with a porcelain washbasin and pitcher, and beside them a small dish with soap. John picked up the soap and breathed its fragrance. It had been so long since he had used soap that he had almost forgotten what it was like.

Replacing the soap, he was startled by some movement out of the corner of his eye. Before him stood a man who seemed scarcely human. His hair was unkempt and his beard overgrown, both bleached by an unrelenting sun. The man was European, but his skin was parched and almost black. His eyes were yellow from jaundice, and his cheeks sunken to match his gaunt frame. It took some time for Newton to realize that he was looking at himself in a mirror.

The first thing he did was bathe, cut his hair, and shave. The white skin on the back of his neck and lower face, hidden by hair for so long, was a startling contrast to the rest of his appearance. A good meal filled

his belly with a feeling of great satisfaction. That night, for the first time in many months, John Newton slept well.

Over the next weeks, John flourished in the new environment. He already knew much about trading and plantation work. Barker was impressed with the skills of his new employee. He left John in charge of his business when he traveled inland. Whenever his employer left, John busied himself so that when Mr. Barker returned he would be pleased with his accomplishments.

The trader repaid this loyalty by entrusting John with greater and greater responsibilities. In Barker's absence, John took care of the slaves and brokered deals with the goods and money his employer left with him to use.

The only thing that still bothered John was the fact that the business was located on one of the Plantain Islands where Clow's plantation was based. It made him nervous to think that his old nemesis was less than a mile away.

That issue was resolved when Barker told him about his newest venture. "I've started a new factory about a hundred miles up the Kittam River but still near the coast. The river actually runs parallel to the coast for the last hundred miles of its course. I want you to help run it for me, John. I have another Englishman named Edwards who has managed some of my other factories, but he'll need some help. What do you say?"

John was delighted at such an opportunity. He had worked long and hard to prove his loyalty and gratitude to Mr. Barker. Now he'd have an even better position.

Thomas Edwards was not much older than John and was less formal than his employer, Barker. Edwards had not been a sailor prior to accepting this position but was recruited by Barker from one of his other factories. Curiously, John and Edwards complemented each other's personalities and skills. They made a perfect team, and the business prospered. Edwards stayed back at the compound and supervised

all the activities there. He was in charge of overall planting of vegetables, melons, and squash. The captured slaves worked as planters while they awaited the slave ships.

Edwards had them harvest plantains and coconuts as well as other cash crops. He was also responsible for the actual trading with European ships that sailed up and down the coast. Since the slave factory was only a bit more than a mile from the seacoast, they had almost immediate access to any passing ship.

John proved to be the best inland trader and slave dealer. He took the goods received from the ships to use in trading for captive blacks. He followed the shady practices of Clow and other successful European slave traders by cheating on the quality or amount of goods offered for trade. The gunpowder was either diluted or shorted by placing rocks in the kegs. The bolts of cloth were also shorted or had large sections cut from the middle. Goods were weighed with false balances or incredibly overpriced. The African chiefs and warlords who brought them slaves were routinely cheated.

Ironically, the blacks had a code of fairness and honesty that should have shamed the "Christian" whites. Many times John was alone on his trading trips, yet was never robbed of his goods. Often he stayed overnight in a village hut with his goods on the floor beside him. There were no doors to lock or windows to latch—only the open doorway stood between a thief and his goods. Yet no one ever disturbed his sleep. It occurred to John that this was an unusual phenomenon. He would never think of sleeping in a London house without locking the doors and windows.

The white men thought of themselves as shrewd, not dishonest, in their trading. The Africans thought the Europeans were demons who would rob you in broad daylight. In fact, when charged with dishonesty or unfairness, the Africans would often bristle and declare defensively, "How can you think such a thing of me!? Do you think that I am a white man that I would cheat you?"

Chapter Nineteen

Witchcraft

✝

Edwards and Newton showed some measure of kindness to the slaves at the Kittam factory. Barker's slaves were fed well and kept in a fortified building. Barker discovered that healthy slaves garnered higher prices from the slave ships—prices that more than covered the small increase in rations. Likewise, slaves kept out of the hot sun during the worst time of the day and during the torrential rains were less likely to get sick and die. There was certainly no profit in a sick or dead slave.

John had his own quarters, a small hut built for him—similar to the one he had on Clow's land. He also took advantage of the opportunity to choose from among the female slaves for nighttime companionship.

Edwards, who likewise used the slaves for sex, joked with John about it one day. "Imagine when these females get to the New World.

Some will be pregnant by us. Wouldn't it be funny to be there when the plantation owner sees the baby when it's born and it's half white? Wouldn't you like to see his face?"

John laughed. "Yes, but I think it'll be funnier to see the plantation owner's *wife*—who do you think *she'll* think fathered that child?"

The African girls and women that he slept with satisfied his lusty sexual appetite to such an extent that he thought it would be impossible for him to ever lie with Polly. She would never want him now, having moved so far away from her genteel Christian ways and prim and proper London society.

John's memories of England were faint now. He rarely thought about his homeland. After awhile, he even decided against returning.

John enjoyed learning about the African culture. The customs of this unusual people were colorful, intense, and mysterious. At night, under the moon, they would beat drums, then dance until they were put into a trance. Wild-eyed and sensuous, the men and women twirled in nearly naked abandon.

A number of times John would go among them, naked as they were, and dance to the beat of incessant drums. He drank heavily, and the combination of alcohol and voodoo was overpowering. Sometimes he used native drugs to take him into unspeakable levels of intoxication and possession. He let himself be possessed by "the spirits of the undead" and went into trances where he had no conscious memory of his actions. These were only some of the dark practices John experienced and witnessed when he went inland to trade.

When he stayed in their villages, strange rites in which animal sacrifice took place mesmerized John. One time a bull was tethered at the center of the village, and a frenzied dance took place around it, after which the animal was killed. A witch doctor took a knife and slit the bull's throat. A stream of blood spurted across the clearing and splat-

tered many of the frenzied dancers. They rubbed it on their faces and bodies and seemed energized by it.

John entered into the mood of the mysterious occultish event and was completely taken over by evil spirits. Once captured, he returned again and again to these depraved ceremonies. Sometimes it took several hours—and once even several days—for him to regain his own personality and sanity.

On one occasion John was present at an African ceremony of a human sacrifice. A mother had given birth to a baby without a left hand and foot. This, he was told, was a child of a demon—the mother may have had intercourse with a devil while in a trance. The child was killed to appease the spirits, and the mother was banished from the tribe.

Unlike the other sacrificial ritual with the bull, a tribal elder carried out this act of sacrifice. (It may even have been the child's father or grandfather.) He placed the baby on the ground beside a fire. It was crying vigorously and pumping its diminutive arms and legs in a display of otherwise good health.

The elder chanted and sprinkled some kind of potion or powder onto the baby, then suddenly smashed its tiny head with a stone axe in a quick, unemotional but violent act.

As he reflected on what he had just witnessed, John wondered if he had the willpower to kill such a defenseless little one if such a practice were common in his society. In Western cultures, a baby born with a birth defect would often grow up and learn to compensate with other skills and abilities. *But here, if the child grows up unable to take care of itself, maybe it is best for it to die now,* John thought. *After all,* he reasoned, *there is no god who would take care of the child.*

He learned later that Africans sometimes sacrificed twins in this way too. It was thought the firstborn twin was good and the second was evil. They reasoned that if no one could tell which was the firstborn, the best thing to do was to kill them both.

From one African who spoke a little English, Newton learned how to cast a spell. He chose Clow and called down all kinds of evil spirits to ravage Clow and his jealous mistress.

John also followed African customs relating to the phases of the moon and wore protective amulets of animal claws and teeth to give him strength and to ward off demons. He also drank special potions to ward off evil spirits and make him powerful against his enemies.

Tribal deities, idols, and magic potions filled the shelves in John's hut. Despite his education and upbringing, he grew superstitious and began to trust in the charms and in witchcraft. In his white world these superstitions would be considered crazy. Yet, here, Newton was completely at ease with the customs.

Once when Mr. Barker returned to visit the factory, he was astonished to see what John had gotten involved in and confronted him at once. "Newton, I fear for you," he exclaimed. "I think they have you in a spell. You've become 'black' since I left. They've made you one of them."

"Don't worry, sir," John replied. "It's just a way of passing time."

"If you need a distraction, I'll bring you some books when I return. Don't go pagan on me, John. You might not come back," Barker warned.

John smiled to reassure his employer.

Later that night John had a nightmare. He dreamed he was back at Clow's plantation, chained to a whipping post in the yard. Peh'eye came over to Clow who was standing beside John. She was pushing and dragging someone who didn't want to come. As the reluctant figure approached, John saw that it was Ruby who was pregnant and about to deliver.

"Here is the witch, my husband," Peh'eye said to Clow.

"Give her to the slaves. They'll know how to deal with her," Clow snarled.

John flexed his muscles and broke the chains, but in his dream he could not intervene. Somehow he was able to follow Peh'eye as she took

Ruby to a clearing at the center of an African village but was incapable
of helping her. Clow's mistress pushed Ruby down in the center of the
clearing. "This woman has been with a devil. She is an evil witch! Her
child is the child of the devil and must be sacrificed!" Peh'eye screamed.

A small man whom John took to be an elder of the tribe came from
the shadows and stood over Ruby with a knife. Several others held her
arms and legs down. John tried to go to her aid but couldn't move. He
was still paralyzed.

The man with the knife cut along the bottom of Ruby's belly. John's
eyes widened in fear and rage. He tried to scream, but no sound came
from his throat. Blood ran down Ruby's thighs as she screamed in pain.
The old African dropped his knife and pulled a baby from the abdomen
of the hysterical girl. He held up the crying infant for all to see.

John stared at the baby in his dream. Although it was a baby, it had
the face of an adult—*his face!* He tried to scream at them to stop, but
again no sound came from his throat.

The elder took the baby and picked up the knife and plunged the
blade deep into the tiny chest, strangulating the infant's cry and cutting
its heart in half.

John woke up with a loud cry, shaking. He was perspiring and
breathing heavily. The horrific nightmare was still fresh in his mind, and
it was as if it had just taken place. He got up from bed and looked outside. All was tranquil and quiet.

A nightmare! John said to himself. *It was only a nightmare.* But was
it? He began to wonder about Ruby—where she was, and—as the hair
on his neck stood up—he wondered if she was expecting a child.

✛ ✛ ✛

The captain of the *Greyhound* had all but exhausted his efforts to
locate John Newton. His employer, Joseph Manesty, had ordered him to
look for the son of a friend. Manesty had even promised a reward for

bringing him back to London. Captain Newton had indicated he would pay dearly for his son's safe return.

For several months the *Greyhound* had inquired at every shipping way station along the African coast. No one seemed to have heard of John Newton.

Finally, at a post near the Plantain Islands, his hopes were lifted.

"Aye," said an old, battered trader. "I know him. He was set ashore near here—more than a year ago. He worked for Mr. Clow on a plantation on that island," he told them, pointing to the nearby island.

Just as the captain was about to give the orders for a boat to be sent to the island, the man continued talking. "But he ain't there anymore."

"Where is he?" the captain asked.

"I dunno. I heard Clow made a deal with another trader who took Newton with him inland. I heard they went a hundred miles upriver," the trader answered.

The captain didn't know that a hundred miles upriver still placed Barker's factory almost within sight of the sea because the river ran parallel to the coast.

The *Greyhound* could not afford the time to search so far inland, its captain reasoned. The ship would leave now and sail south along the coast. He figured on finding a few traders looking for goods they could purchase in order to buy more slaves.

✝ ✝ ✝

John Newton was preparing to go inland on another trading trip. His associate, Edwards, asked him to wait.

"But I'm ready to go now," John argued.

"Yes, I know," Edwards responded, "but if you had some more goods, you could make your trip more productive. I'm going to the seashore to build a signal fire. If there's a trading ship anywhere near, she'll stop. Then I'll take a boat out to trade for some more goods."

John shrugged. No ships ever stopped along the shore parallel to the Kittam River. Just to the north, the trading with ships ended. But John was willing to consider Edward's idea.

He said, "Yes, you might be right. Our inventory is pretty slim. I'll wait here until late afternoon. If I don't hear from you, we'll start out, but we won't be far away—we can come back if you're lucky enough to see a ship. If not, we'll set off in my boat by tomorrow morning."

Edwards had some of the black men carry some fresh meat, vegetables, fruit, and coconuts. Merchant shippers valued fresh foods for their crews—it helped morale and kept the crew healthier. It took Edwards and his men just over an hour to trek the two miles to the beach.

Just as they got there, Edwards spotted the sails of an English merchant ship sailing south. It had already passed by. Still, if they hurried, someone on the crew might see a signal fire before they were out of sight.

Edwards quickly built a huge fire on the beach, which was soon burning fiercely. He threw green banana leaves onto it to create the signal smoke. The smoke rose skyward, dark and thick. Any ship within sight of the coast could see it and return, unless it was already into the wind and eager to make distance.

Edwards watched the English ship continue south. He cursed quietly and kicked at the sand. A few minutes later one of the slaves called out. Edwards turned to see him pointing to the ocean. The ship had tacked about and was sailing back!

An hour later the vessel anchored in deep water offshore. Edwards took a boat loaded with supplies and started for the ship. As the ship turned slightly into the current, he read her name: *Greyhound.*

Edwards and his slaves rowed out to the merchant ship with the goods and climbed aboard. The captain was a tall, thin man, about fifty, who looked older than his years. He introduced himself and welcomed Edwards aboard for trading. "I am Captain Josiah Hiram, in command of

the *Greyhound,*" he said. After a little preliminary small talk and some petty haggling, they struck a trade deal.

Edwards said, "You almost missed us. If we'd have been ten or fifteen minutes later, you'd have sailed out of range."

"We saw your signal smoke right away," Captain Hiram said, "but I was reluctant to turn back. We had a good wind, and we're behind schedule. My first officer reminded me that we have been so busy with our other duties that we didn't take time to put aboard some stores for the next leg of our journey. That's why we stopped."

"Lucky for both of us, I guess," Edwards smiled. When all the goods had been exchanged, Edwards motioned to his slaves that it was time to leave, and they began climbing over the rail ladder to their boat. Edwards was the last to climb over.

"Oh, by the way," the captain called to him, "do you by any chance know of a castaway sailor named Newton?"

Edwards stopped in his tracks. "Newton?"

"Yes. John Newton," Captain Hiram replied. "I'm told that he used to work for a man named Clow some leagues north of here, but no one there seems to know that happened to him."

"Why do you ask?" Edwards asked cautiously.

"I've been commissioned by the owner of my fleet to search for him," Captain Hiram replied.

"Why?" Edwards asked again.

Now the captain was cautious. This man seemed to know something. "Seems the lad wrote to his father about the terrible plight he was in and asked for help. We were sent to help," Captain Hiram explained.

Edwards seemed satisfied with the answer. "Well, Captain, your search has ended. John Newton is less than a mile from that bonfire you see on shore, but I'm not sure he wants to be rescued. He says he wants to stay in Africa," he told the astonished captain.

Captain Hiram saw his reward turning to dust. How could he convince the young man to leave? When Captain Newton in England offered a reward to find his son, Mr. Manesty had said that young Newton might not be dependable. Captain Hiram recalled that Manesty had told him to use any means to bring him back. He thought quickly. "Bring him back to talk with me," he said. "I have other news. He—uh—he is to come back to England to claim a great inheritance. A relative has died and left him a fortune."

"Really?" Edwards answered. "Well, even if he does want to stay, no one will pass up a fortune. John can always go back, collect his money, and come back to Africa. I suppose I could get along on my own for a few months."

"Then you'll bring him back to us?" the captain asked excitedly.

"I'll tell him what you told me. It's up to him if he comes," Edwards said.

That response was not positive enough for Captain Hiram. He said, "Well, let me come with you. If he's that close, I cannot take the chance of coming all this way and not talking to him."

Edwards nodded and helped the captain into the small boat beside the *Greyhound*. "We may already be too late. He was to wait until late afternoon before starting out on a trip, but he may have already started out. If so, we'll never catch his boat."

When the party got back to the factory, a slave told Edwards that John was almost ready to leave but was still there. "He be in the dining room, sir," the slave said.

John had reasoned that this would be the last time before leaving on a primitive and dangerous trading trip that he could enjoy good food and other pleasures, so he decided to indulge himself before leaving. A table was set with sumptuous food and wine. John sat back in his chair with his feet on the table. Several slaves waited on him as if he were royalty. His mistress was massaging his bare chest and shoulders sensuously.

Edwards stood in the doorway and cleared his throat. He introduced Captain Hiram, who strode toward John and pumped his hand vigorously. "I've just come a quarter way round the world to find you, lad," he said. "I bring you warm wishes from your father and my employer, Mr. Joseph Manesty. Your father received your letter, and he asked Mr. Manesty to help bring about your rescue from Africa."

The captain backed up a step. He looked again at John and his surroundings. He did not look at all like someone in need of rescue.

As if reading his mind, John laughed. "Well, Captain, as you can see, I no longer want to be rescued. I'm not going back to England."

Once again Captain Hiram saw his reward slipping away. He decided to take the other tack that had worked with Edwards. "Yes. I can see you do not need rescuing, but your father began the search for you and was making plans for your rescue even before your letter arrived," the captain told John. This news touched him deeply because it showed a rare sensitive side to his father that he deeply appreciated.

Captain Hiram continued. "But the real reason I have come is to tell you that your father has asked that you come back to England—uh—temporarily. A relative has died and left you an annuity. But you must come and claim it."

"A relative of mine has died? Who?" John asked suspiciously.

"I don't know," the captain answered.

John tried to think of anyone who might fit that picture. He had an aunt, quite well-to-do, who had been in ill health for a long time. She had never married. Perhaps she had left him an inheritance.

"How much is it?" John asked.

Captain Hiram had to think quickly. How much would it take to get Newton to return to England? "Four hundred pounds," he suggested.

John's face turned to a frown. "Four hundred pounds?" That truly was a fortune, but by John's expression, the captain did not know if John thought so.

"—four hundred pounds per year," Captain Hiram added quickly.

That sounded even better to John, but he still wasn't convinced. "I no longer need help. I have repaid my debt. I'm free to stay or go as I please. I'm no longer obligated to anyone. I choose to stay," he said.

The captain was getting desperate. He began to embellish his original story with possibilities of even greater wealth awaiting John in England. "You do not have to stay in England," he told John. "Merely come back for the settlement of the estate. The inheritance must be even greater than I told you. Mr. Manesty said that if necessary, I was to sell half my cargo to redeem you if you were still in obligation to that man Clow. Obviously he would not have offered so great a price without some collateral in England. Surely the inheritance must be a princely sum. I'm certain that it's a fortune. Don't throw it away. Just come back for the settlement. You can come back to Africa after that if you like."

Edwards encouraged John to return to England, saying, "I can get along for a few months on my own. You should go—collect your inheritance—and return a rich man. You might even get enough capital to start your own factory and become even richer," he said to his friend.

The captain had one last card to play. "I also bring a letter from a young woman," he said.

"Polly?" John asked excitedly. Something about the sound of her name still made his heart flutter. "You have a letter from Polly?"

"Yes," the captain lied. He had only assumed that John had left a love in his homeland—but it was a logical guess.

"Come back with us. You'll be treated as royally as you are here. You can share my cabin, my food, and my wine. I have books to keep you company, and you won't be expected to do anything in return."

The deal was beginning to sound better to John. He was still hesitant but thought about his father's concern for him. He wanted to personally thank him for his valiant efforts to rescue him. And Polly—he surely

wanted to read that letter! Finally he agreed to go back with the captain on the *Greyhound*.

John made hasty arrangements with Edwards to explain the situation to Mr. Barker. He also asked his friend to make provisions for his African mistress—insuring that she was not to be sold—then took the small boat back out to the *Greyhound*. Several hours of daylight remained for the ship to sail, and the crew immediately weighed anchor and put the wind behind them.

Chapter
Twenty

Homeward Bound

✠

John felt at home aboard the *Greyhound*. True to his word, the captain moved Newton's few belongings into his cabin—John was to stay there for the journey back to England.

However, the trip would be rather roundabout. Unlike European slave ships that quickly and routinely received their cargo from a single area and sailed immediately for the colonies or West Indies, the *Greyhound* and other merchant ships often took a year or more to acquire cargo.

The *Greyhound* had to sail another thousand miles along the southwest coast of middle Africa for the rest of its cargo, then faced the next long leg of the journey—a trip of seven thousand miles across the Atlantic, catching the trade winds to Brazil. From South America the *Greyhound* planned to follow the New World coastline to the north, to

Newfoundland. From there it was a fairly straight line to England and home.

The long journey was determined to be the best route, taking full advantage of the trade winds and avoiding French warships in the Atlantic waters off the coast of Europe.

The *Greyhound*'s first destination was Gabon, located directly on the equator, where the crew would load its cargo of lightweight camwood (used in making dyes) and beeswax. Crew and captain alike appreciated this cargo. The crew had an easier time loading this kind of cargo—it was dry and fairly light. That very lightness in the hold permitted the ship to sit higher in the water and wring more speed from the sails while it cut through the water.

Africa's coastline was at the eastern horizon by sunset when John sat down to an evening meal with Captain Hiram.

"I'm sorry," the captain said after some preliminary conversation. "I'm afraid I was mistaken when I told you about a letter from a woman. I must have heard wrong. I do have a letter from your father, and he must have told Mr. Manesty about the girl's letter. I thought he was sending it along, but I fear it is not in the packet that was sent."

John's heart fell. He was glad for the letter from his father but had counted on a letter from Polly. Captain Hiram busied himself with an after-dinner brandy, hoping that his lie had not been detected, but John was too preoccupied with his father's letter to sense the deceit. He took it, excused himself, and went to a quiet corner of the cabin to read it alone.

John felt a new, strange warmth toward his father. His past relationship with him had always been distant, harsh, and demanding. Now he sensed a softened tone, almost affectionate, in his father's words. John read the letter several times before retiring for the night.

The next day the *Greyhound* headed for Gabon, and within the week, had anchored just offshore from Port Gentil some thirty miles south of

the Gabon River. The crew spent the next nine months in that area trying to fill the ship with cargo.

Despite the lighter cargo, the crew members were almost overwhelmed by heat exhaustion. Captain Hiram was concerned and did not
drive them hard, even though the ship was shorthanded. They had
already lost several men to tropical fever and other illnesses and would
have appreciated John's help in supervising the loading of cargo.

John seemed oblivious to the need, however. He reminded the captain that he was a passenger and not part of the crew.

The crew did not want him anyway. They were glad he *was* a passenger. True, only twelve crew members remained (from an original
roster of twenty), but none of them wanted Newton to be the unlucky
thirteenth man.

Although they didn't want Newton to work, the crew members nevertheless resented his laziness and crude manners. His presence
aboard began to make even the most seasoned sailors frown at his foul
mouth and habits.

John seemed unable to utter the most simple or inane sentence without using an expletive. This foul language particularly irritated the captain, who confronted him.

"Newton," he said sharply, "I personally find your conversation particularly unpleasant and offensive. I must remind you that you are breaking His Majesty's law."

"Really?" John grinned. "How is that?"

Captain Hiram said, "While you've been away, the English Parliament
passed a 'profane oaths act' to go along with the 'blasphemy act' that was
passed earlier. Your words, sir, are in violation of both acts, and I forbid
you to use such language aboard my ship."

"Well, sir," John answered with a chuckle, "I cannot believe the members of the English parliament have no serious business and spend their
time inventing such petty laws. But I remind you, Captain Hiram, this is

not England. As captain you may make these demands of your crew, but I am a passenger, and as such, I am exempt from your 'swearing act,' at least until we return to England."

The captain refused to let the matter lie. He said, "I wonder how that young woman you plan to see in England will take to your swearing with every other word. Why don't you think of her and reform your speech before you completely overwhelm her with your sacrilegious and vulgar talk. Surely she is not a whore that you should fill her ears with your blasphemy!"

That argument made Newton try to redeem himself. He was careful about his tongue for awhile, but it didn't last—his habits were too ingrained to be changed. John reasoned that he would have plenty of time to work on bad habits before they returned to England.

Meanwhile, John decided to treat everyone to drinks when the last day's cargo had been taken aboard, hoping that his generosity would also buy him some friendship.

John seldom had enough alcohol to make him drunk, but he enjoyed getting others drunk. When they lost control of their senses and inhibitions, he was entertained by their foolishness.

Only a handful of crew members (minus the captain) showed up on deck for John's offer. After a few healthy swigs of strong Geneva spirits (gin) with rum, they were all inebriated. Even John, who ordinarily kept himself from drinking too much, was drunk.

In his drunkenness, John demonstrated a voodoo dance he had learned in Africa and twirled aimlessly across the deck of the ship. Near the rail, his hat blew off and into the harbor below. John, thinking the longboat was beneath him, climbed over the rail to jump into the boat and retrieve his hat. The longboat was some distance away, however. John was about to plunge into sixty feet of pitch-black ocean water— drunk and unable to swim. A crew member grabbed him just before he fell overboard. John was suddenly sober, shaking with fear. If he had

dropped into the sea, he'd have been lost. Even if he'd survived the plunge into the deep, dark water, he surely would have drowned in the force of the riptide. No one on deck was sober enough to have jumped in to save him.

The next day several of the crew members congratulated John on his good luck. Someone joked that he had a guardian angel to protect him from dying. John smiled wryly but said nothing. He was reminded of the many times his life had been spared. Was it really just "good luck" or chance?

John could almost hear his former minister, Dr. Jennings, reminding him that it was the hand of providence that saved him each time. John had a difficult time getting that thought out of his mind for a long time after that.

✝ ✝ ✝

It was January 1748 before the *Greyhound* was finally ready to sail to South America. It had been nearly four years since John had left England aboard the *H.M.S. Harwich* and nine long months since he had first boarded the *Greyhound* on the African shore near the Kittam River.

The ship was put on a westerly course, some five degrees south of the equator. The winds had taken the *Greyhound* a bit north and seven hundred miles from Africa by the end of the second day.

John was sitting on deck reading a book. He had grown weary of the dog-eared copies of Euclid's *Geometry* and Lord Shaftsbury's *Characteristics,* and he asked the captain if he could borrow something else from the ship's library to read.

The captain enthusiastically told John to help himself. When John looked at the books, he understood why Captain Hiram was so anxious to lend them—nearly all of them were religious books. However, John was so bored by now that he was willing to read anything. He found an English translation of *Imitation of Christ* by Thomas á Kempis.

Thinking the book might have some inspirational value, he began reading in the first chapter:

> "He who follows Me, walks not in darkness," says the Lord. By these words of Christ we are advised to imitate His life and habits, if we wish to be truly enlightened. . . . Now, there are many who hear the Gospel often but care little for it because they have not the spirit of Christ. . . . It is vanity to follow the lusts of the body and to desire things for which severe punishment later must come. . . . For they who follow their own evil passions stain their consciences and lose the grace of God.

John was riveted to the pages. The writer seemed to be addressing him personally although the book was written two centuries earlier. He continued reading. More truths leaped from the pages:

> An unmortified man is quickly tempted and overcome in small, trifling evils; his spirit is weak, in a measure carnal and inclined to sensual things; he can hardly abstain from earthly desires. Hence it makes him sad to forego them; he is quick to anger if reproved. Yet if he satisfies his desires, remorse of conscience overwhelms him because he followed his passions and they did not lead to the peace he sought. . . . True peace of heart, then, is found in resisting passions, not in satisfying them. There is no peace in the carnal man.

John was sitting near the captain, who was taking sextant readings before sunset; his reading was interrupted by Captain Hiram's comments.

"Well, here we are, Newton," he said to John. "Right now you're either at the absolute center of the world or nowhere—depending on how you read the chart."

John looked up from the book he was reading. "Where are we?" he asked.

"We're at zero degrees longitude and zero degrees latitude—where the equator and the Greenwich Meridian intersect. Interesting, don't you think?" the captain commented.

John smiled and went back to the book that he was reading, but he was struck by the captain's metaphor. It suddenly had meaning that Captain Hiram had probably not intended, but John was even more awed by the coincidence of the words on the page before him: "I find myself nothing but zero and zero, O substance that cannot be weighed! O sea that cannot be sailed! . . . I find that my substance is nothing and above all, nothing."

He read essay after essay, each fully describing his own life and inner turmoil. Alone with his thoughts, John could not fool himself. It was one thing to put forth bravado and demolish the fledgling faith of another but quite a different matter to confront the issues of faith and doubt, of good and evil, of eternity, judgment, and the existence of God.

As hard as he tried, John was unable, intellectually, to dismiss the idea of a real God at work in the universe. He rehearsed the tired ideas of Shaftsbury and other agnostics and atheists. He even considered himself an atheist. Yet, despite all of his silver-tongued arguments and intellectual rationalizations, he was unable to shake the deep conviction of his soul—*God exists*.

He reasoned that if God exists, then he would one day face judgment for his sinful practices. He could not even control his own thoughts anymore. It was as if God were relentless—hounding him as prey. John closed the book, stood up, and paced the decks for a long time.

In addition to the accusing words from the book, John was assailed by his own memories. He recalled the peace of mind and soul he had as a child. It all seemed so simple and easy to believe then. He tried to argue with himself that it was illogical to believe. Then he thought of how many *did* believe. Could so many be wrong? Was he wrong?

A strange attraction kept him reading the book over the next few weeks. After finishing it once, he started reading it again.

✠ ✠ ✠

Not long after that, in January 1748, the coast of South America was sighted, and the *Greyhound* circumnavigated Brazil, heading north.

The captain briefly toyed with the idea of laying over in the West Indies for repairs. The *Greyhound* had been at sea for some two years, and the ship was beginning to show some serious wear and tear. In fact, the sails had been patched so many times that they were really in poor condition. The tropical climate and salt air had also damaged the rigging and other ropes. Most of them had been spliced many times and were quite rotted. More serious, however, was the damage of the climate and salt water on the ship's hull. The planking had alternately expanded and shrunk, and had, with each occurrence, given up some of the oakum filler.

It was late February by the time the *Greyhound* reached the West Indies. Captain Hiram carefully inspected the ship and considered whether or not to do repairs. In the month it would take them to reach Newfoundland, it would be spring. The winter storms of the North Atlantic would probably be over by then.

"If we stop for repairs, it is quite likely that we will be laid over for a month or two," the captain told John. "If we don't stop, we could be in England in five or six weeks. Otherwise, it may be summer by the time we get there."

"Well, if you ask me," John responded, "I am for getting back to England. The *Greyhound* has been at sea for two years—I'm sure the

men are eager to get home. And as for me, I haven't been back for four years."

"I've inspected the ship, and though it does need work, I think we can hold off until we get home," Captain Hiram said.

They discussed the matter some more over dinner that night, and Captain Hiram decided that the *Greyhound* would continue its voyage.

John excused himself after dinner and retired to the cabin to read again from *The Imitation of Christ*. He was troubled by a passage that haunted him all through the night as he tried to sleep: "Wherever you are, wherever you go, you are miserable unless you turn to God. . . . If you seek your Lord Jesus in all things you will truly find Him, but if you seek yourself you will find yourself, and that will be to your own great loss."

As he paced the deck in the middle of the night, unable to sleep, he thought about that line. "But I haven't been seeking Christ," he said out loud to himself. "It's as if he is seeking me."

Over the next few days, John tried to erase what had been written on his mind. He returned to his old ways of cursing and blaspheming God. The crew and Captain Hiram were getting increasingly weary of Newton and his corrupt ways, and the gulf between them continued to widen.

Soon, however, other things began to occupy their conversations. The *Greyhound* reached the Newfoundland outer banks by early March. Captain Hiram had mixed feelings about the strong westerly winds that pushed the ship toward England. Though he was grateful for the almost gale-force wind that filled their sails, these same winds made him a bit uncomfortable and left him wondering whether he should have made repairs to the *Greyhound* while they were in the West Indies.

Chapter
Twenty-one

Nights of Terror

The ship was being tossed by high waves, and the winds roared furiously on the night of March 9. John had not ventured out of the cabin all day. At dinner he noticed that Captain Hiram was quiet and preoccupied.

After dinner the captain excused himself, put on his heavy wool coat and oilskin overcoat, and ventured out to check on the weather. He had been unable to take a reliable reading of the ship's position because the skies were so heavily overcast and the sun was obscured. Captain Hiram hoped that enough clouds had cleared and that he'd be able to get an accurate reading of their position from the stars.

He was gone for a long time, and John was grateful for the quiet in the cabin as he resumed reading from the Thomas á Kempis book. Over the past two weeks he had been alternately reading it and angrily shoving it away.

This night he went back to it. He began to read an essay entitled, "Thoughts of Death," and it wasn't too long before it captured his attention. The words took on a prophetic theme: "Very soon your life here will end; consider, then, what may be in store for you elsewhere. Today we live; tomorrow we die and are quickly forgotten. . . . Therefore, in every deed and every thought, act as though you were to die this very day. If you had a good conscience you would not fear death very much. It is better to avoid sin than to fear death."

John thought about the words of his friend from the *Harwich,* James Mitchell, who had said that death was merely the extinguishing of life— no hell to fear, no judgment, no God.

Now Newton was not so certain. Something in the words of this fifteenth-century monk had the ring of truth. He could not escape their power:

> Tomorrow is an uncertain day; how do you know you will have a tomorrow? . . . Many die suddenly and unexpectedly, for in the unexpected hour the Son of Man will come. . . . Ah, foolish man, why do you plan to live long when you are not sure of living even a day? How many have been deceived and suddenly snatched away! How often have you heard of persons being killed by drownings, by fatal falls from high places, of persons dying at meals, at play, in fires, by the sword, in pestilence, or at the hands of robbers!

John's mind responded quickly and vividly to the words, and he recalled several incidents in which he had narrowly escaped death: being thrown from a horse and nearly impaled by hedgerow stakes as a boy; tripping with a musket and nearly blowing off his head; the drowning of his friends when he missed the longboat to visit the man-of-war;

missing a shore patrol with his mates who were all drowned; nearly dying at the hand of Peh'eye; and almost being killed by the sadistic Clow.

On all these occasions he had been miraculously saved from certain death. As John thought about his close calls with fatal mishaps, he sensed these events were more than mere coincidence.

God? John wondered. *How can it be that I believe in God in spite of my efforts to deny his existence?* He read another passage from the book:

> Gather for yourself the riches of immortality while you have time. Think of nothing but your salvation. In all things consider the end; how you shall stand before the strict Judge from Whom nothing is hidden and Who will pronounce judgment. . . . And you, miserable and wretched sinner, who fear even the countenance of an angry man, what answer will you make to the God Who knows all your sins? . . . For a man will be more grievously punished in the things in which he has sinned. . . . The wanton and lust-loving will be bathed in burning pitch and foul brimstone. . . . You must, therefore, take care and repent of your sins now so that on the day of judgment you may rest secure with the blessed. . . . He who loves God with all his heart does not fear death or punishment or judgment or hell, because perfect love assures access to God. . . . It is good, however, that even if love does not as yet restrain you from evil, at least the fear of hell does.

John's heart began to race for no apparent reason, but he was conscious of it. What were these feelings that overwhelmed him? Guilt? Fear? Shame?

He slammed the book shut and threw it across the cabin, then got up and paced the small room, trying to sort through his feelings and thoughts.

After an hour or so, he went to his bunk to try and sleep, but he couldn't. He tossed and turned fitfully. As he lay there, a solitary idea crept into his consciousness: *What if these things are true?*

Newton wrestled with the implications. If God does exist, then I am condemned. I have made my choices, and I will have to live and die by them. I can't turn back now.

Yes! You can turn back! He was startled by the thought. *What? How?* From the inner recesses of his memory came his mother's words, reading a Bible verse he had learned on her lap decades earlier: *"If we confess our sins, he is faithful and just to forgive us our sins, and to cleanse us from all unrighteousness."*

This reassuring memory of his mother calmed his spirit, and the tumult of thoughts subsided. Soon he fell asleep.

He was awakened several hours later by being violently thrown from his bunk onto the floor. The floor was cold and wet, and the shock of it jolted him awake. A huge wave had struck the ship broadside and washed into the cabin. Several inches of water covered the floor. The *Greyhound* was listing several degrees, and it took John a moment or two to regain his balance and footing.

He put on his wool jacket and oilskin coat and headed for the cabin door just as Captain Hiram burst inside. He took the precious sextant and compass and stored them in their wooden containers for protection, then grabbed the charts that had fallen into the water on the floor and patted them as dry as possible before locking them in a cabinet.

"It's a bad storm," he told Newton. "I'm afraid we're really in for it. Will you help me wake the rest of the crew? We'll need all hands to battle this one."

"Of course, Captain," John answered.

The storm was fiercer than anything John could recall. Winds were gale force and drove the rain sideways into his face with stinging intensity. He had difficulty walking along the deck rail—now pitched at an angle because of the listing of the ship.

He had to lean his head into his chest to even breathe. With some difficulty he reached the entryway to the crew quarters, clambered down the steps, and yelled out, "Ahoy! Everybody up! Captain wants all hands on deck."

The men jumped up quickly and put on their shoes and coats. John waited at the steps to the deck to make sure everyone was up.

As he started up the steps, Captain Hiram came to the entryway and yelled down to him, "Get a knife, Newton. We'll have to cut some of the rigging lines. The wind is shredding the sails!" With that order issued, the captain ran back to the quarterdeck to resume command.

John backed down the narrow steps and told the man behind him, "You heard the captain. Go get a knife."

"Get it yourself," the sailor snapped at John. "I've got my own knife. Captain wants you to earn your own way." He roughly pushed John aside and climbed up the stairs.

Newton quickly ran to the supply cupboard, grabbed a knife, and raced back over to the stairs and up to the deck. As he got there, the sailor who had pushed him aside was at the top and just stepping on deck. Suddenly an enormous wall of water struck him. Its force carried the sailor across the deck, swept him over the rail, and dropped him into the black, churning sea.

The huge wave also dropped gallons of icy water into the crew entryway. Its full weight fell on Newton and knocked him onto the floor of the crew quarters. Sputtering, he got up and hurried up to the deck.

On deck another sailor yelled, "Man overboard!" But the ship was moving too fast to go back for the sailor. Besides, the temperature of the water was just above freezing—he wouldn't survive more than a minute.

When John got up on deck and learned that the sailor just ahead of him was gone, he shivered, not so much from the cold as from the shock of knowing that *he* would have been the one washed overboard and killed if he hadn't gone back for the knife.

Once more his life had been spared. *Why?* he wondered. But there was no time to dwell on it now. The ship was in danger and so were the lives of the rest of them. The winds had blown out the running lights, and it was so dark the men had to feel their way along.

The occasional flashes of lightning provided light to see that the damage to the *Greyhound* was serious. Not only were her main sails shredded, some of the topsails were also completely blown away. The stern mast was splintered and tilted dangerously toward the port side.

Several crew members wrestled at winding thick ropes around that mast in what was probably a futile attempt to make a splint to keep it from breaking altogether.

One sailor was nearly killed as a heavy rigging pulley fell from the top of the mast and crashed onto the deck. The pulley grazed his hip, but another few inches to the left would have crushed his head.

The commotion seemed chaotic; yet each sailor knew exactly what to do. John entered into the frenzy of activity with experienced hands. Skills he had not used in years suddenly returned to him, and he made himself useful in trying to save the *Greyhound* from sinking.

Another flash of lightening lit up the horizon and revealed another huge wave approaching. The captain called, "Hard to starboard!" The pilot put his back into turning the wheel. Both he and Captain Hiram tried to turn the ship's rudder in time for the *Greyhound* to meet the surge head-on and keep it from capsizing the ship. The *Greyhound* groaned and turned ever so slightly as the men braced for the approaching wave. This time the wall of water caught them at a better angle. The wave broke over the bow and knocked down several of the seamen, but they had tied themselves to the ship and were not carried overboard.

"Captain," one of the sailors called out, "I've just been below. We're takin' on water really bad. If it keeps up, we're going to sink!"

"Woods and Kennedy—you go below and see if you can stop the leaks. Newton—you and Tyler man the pumps."

All four men responded in unison, "Aye, sir!" and headed belowdecks. The sailors grabbed oil lamps and tools and tried to find where the hull had splintered and was letting in water.

"Over there!" John called. He pointed to an area where water was spraying from several foot-long gaps in the hull. The men grabbed oakum and a barrel of wooden wedges to drive into the holes.

Meanwhile, John and the other sailor found the pumps and put their backs into the effort of getting the water in the hold into the hoses where it could be pumped outside the ship.

John worked furiously, but no matter how hard he pumped, the water level kept rising. When things had been stabilized on the decks, several sailors were sent below to help bail. It was a pathetic, impossible effort. They formed a human chain and passed buckets, pots, pans, and small barrels of water from one man to another in the chain, from deep belowdecks in the cargo hold—then up and out the portholes.

Spurting streams of icy water marked the leaks and made it easier for the men to find them and then try to caulk them. But these same leaks sprayed water onto the oil lamps, forcing the men to work in total darkness.

After nearly four hours of intense work, the winds let up a little. It was dawn—but there was no sign of the sun. In the greenish glow of morning, the men labored unrelentingly.

Since they were already shorthanded, the sailor that was lost at sea only aggravated their dilemma. John had taken his place, however. No more a mere passenger, Newton was as much a part of the crew as any man. He was hard at work by the pumps, resting only a minute or so before going back at it with all his might. The one good thing about his

slave labor in the fields was that he was in good physical shape and was able to keep up with the other sailors.

The water was still rising in the cargo hold, but at least the huge waves had quit breaking over the decks and filling the hold from above. Now, with the advantage of daylight, the sailors were beginning to find the leaks and make temporary repairs. However, they soon ran out of oakum and wood.

The captain came below to inspect the damage. "It's hopeless," cried one sailor.

Newton offered a suggestion. "Captain, why not send the men to scavenge bedding and clothes to pack into the holes. Then we can nail pieces of furniture to the walls of the hold. It might hold. If not, may God have mercy on us!"

The captain looked at Newton strangely. To hear a prayer come from the blasphemer's lips was as startling as a curse from a parson.

Bedding, clothing, and furniture were brought to the hold. The clothing and mattresses were stuffed into the holes, and then boards from tables were nailed over the stuffed holes. Legs of tables and chairs were used to pound the bedding into the gaping wounds of the *Greyhound* and also used to hold the material in the repaired hole.

Newton was grateful that the ship carried a light cargo of camwood and beeswax. If she were lower in the water, the two earlier swells that struck the ship would have sunk her for sure.

John tried not to dwell on the present misfortunes of the *Greyhound*. He thought of other things to distract him from their desperate situation, but present matters were becoming more and more hopeless.

He kept up with the laborious pumping. The rhythm of the pumps somehow put his mind into rhythms for words. In his mind he let the pumps lead him in songs and poems he had memorized as a child—mostly hymns and Bible verses, which should have seemed strange to him, but didn't.

A proverb he had learned as a boy was especially troubling because the words seemed so appropriate right now.

> Because I have called,
>> and ye refused;
> I have stretched out my hand,
>> and no man regarded;
> But ye have set nought all my counsel,
>> and would none of my reproof:
> I also will laugh at your calamity;
>> I will mock when your fear cometh;

The words were like a slap in John's face. He was in the most desperate situation of his life, and now God was laughing at his calamity. He kept pumping, his anger adding to his efforts. But the words still came to mock him:

> Then shall they call upon me,
>> but I will not answer;
> They shall seek me early,
>> but they shall not find me.

Newton could not shake the feeling that for many years God had been pleading with him to seek him and change his ways. Now his words were so plain that John could not ignore them, but it was too late. *I've already made up my mind to reject God,* he thought. *Now the Almighty is laughing at my calamity and mocking my fears.*

In addition to the sheer physical strain of the pumps, John's thoughts and emotions were also overwhelming him. After eight grueling hours of incessant pumping and fearful thoughts, Captain Hiram finally sent a sailor to relieve John about noon. Newton was nearly exhausted and

went to his bunk to rest. He had no mattress or bedding, so he flopped onto the hardboards and was soon in a deep sleep.

Newton slept only an hour before being awakened to return to the pumps. It was impossible to keep up with the leaking water. When he reported for duty, Captain Hiram stopped him. "Newton," he said, "you're in no condition to work the pumps. Why don't you relieve the helmsman at the wheel?"

John did as he was told and grabbed a rope on his way. He didn't want to be washed overboard by a wave or fall down exhausted and allow the ship to wander aimlessly with no one at the helm. He tied himself to the wooden frame of the helm, right next to the ship's wheel.

The storm continued all day, although with less intensity. Snow mixed with the rain, and soon ice formed in John's beard and hair, and his stocking cap was soon crusted with ice. He had tried to protect his hands by wrapping them with some rags, but they grew numb as he held the wheel, and he nearly collapsed several times.

Mountainous waves filled John's vision all the way to the horizon. He was almost afraid to look behind him where the wind-driven swells were up to thirty feet high. As these waves approached the ship from the stern (which was now in a proper direction to meet the swells), they lifted the *Greyhound* high onto the crest of the wave.

For a brief moment the ship was held suspended on the mountaintop of water. John looked over the forward deck and couldn't even see the sea below, so precipitous was the drop-off from the crest of the wave. Then, suddenly, the ship pitched forward and dropped to the bottom of the wave, some thirty feet below. John was able to anticipate the drop-off, but his stomach fell dizzily each time—even though he knew what was coming. It was both frightening and exhilarating, and this cycle repeated itself once every minute or so and continued for most of the day.

The captain and the crew were still frantically trying to keep water out of the ship. Though they bailed and pumped until the men were

unable to work any longer, the *Greyhound* still listed badly toward the port side.

John was terrified as the wind began to pick up in intensity once more. There was no doubt in his mind that they were truly doomed.

Suddenly the emotional strain caught up with John and he began to sob. Then he cried out, his voice swallowed by the winds, "Oh, God! Save us! Almighty God, save *me!*" The prayer surprised him. He had no right to call upon God—he had no faith to back up his words. It was a sad, pathetic cry from his tortured soul.

✝ ✝ ✝

Just as daylight was fading in the western sky, Captain Hiram came back to the helm. "It seems that the worst of the storm has passed," he told John.

By midnight the water had receded to less than dangerous levels below deck, and the men had regained control of the ship. The men rested fitfully at their stations until the next morning when they took inventory of their situation.

The chickens and few pigs that had been kept in coops on deck had drowned or were washed overboard in the storm. Flour and meal were reduced to a salty paste by the seawater that had soaked into all the barrels in the galley. The same was true of the hardtack and dried beef. A few pieces of salted codfish the crew had caught off the coast of Newfoundland and some moldy grain used to feed the pigs were the only salvageable foods that remained.

Fortunately, the water barrels appeared to be undamaged, so the crew members had plenty of water to drink. The captain ordered the cook to make soup with a little codfish in order to conserve what little food they had left. The captain had no idea of their position or how far they were from land. "It is important to save our resources for as long as possible," he told his men.

John Newton was perplexed. God had answered his prayer. He could think of no other explanation for why they were not all dead. The ship should have been swamped or smashed by the huge waves. Yet, here they were—still alive. And with that, John felt a sense of hope.

The idea that God had not given up on him (even though he had given up on God) kindled John's spiritual energy. After breaking every commandment and mocking God in every profane way, Newton felt ashamed and overwhelmed by guilt.

A deeply felt sense of sorrow made him cry at his apparent stupidity. His mind reeled with scenes of countless wrongs. He remembered his drinking, brawling, and whoring of the past decade and thought of how he had robbed young Job Lewis of his faith in Christ. Newton also remembered his callous misdeeds against African slaves, especially taking black women and forcing them to be his sexual slaves.

"My sins are too numerous to count," he prayed. John knew that the scales of divine judgment weighed heavily against him.

Then, from somewhere deep within his mind, he unexpectedly recalled some simple Bible verses from his youth:

> For the LORD your God is gracious and merciful, and will not turn away his face from you, if ye return unto him.
>
> Let the wicked forsake his way, and the unrighteous man his thoughts: and let him return unto the LORD, and he will have mercy upon him; and to our God, for he will abundantly pardon.
>
> For sin shall not have dominion over you: for ye are not under the law, but under grace.

"—under grace!" Newton repeated. "Wonderful, amazing grace—greater than my sins."

John was emotionally spent. He wept at last, his tears a mixture of genuine contrition, gratitude, and regret. He could not erase these wrongs from his memory, but he believed that he was truly forgiven. He had not deserved it, but God had forgiven him in an act of incredible mercy and amazing grace.

Chapter
Twenty-two

Experiencing Grace

The crew members tried to keep busy as the *Greyhound* struggled to keep afloat. The weather was still ugly and the skies always overcast. Captain Hiram had no idea where they were but estimated that they were getting closer to land—either Ireland or England—or, if they were too far north, maybe Scotland.

Actually, the winds had buffeted them into crosscurrents that had taken them back to the west, away from their destination. They had been going in circles for three days and nights.

John used the time to read the Bible and rebuild his faith. He was completely sure of his forgiveness and looked for ways to nourish his soul after so many years of spiritual starvation.

The captain was startled at the sudden and complete change in the former infidel. As quickly as Newton's faith surfaced, his swearing

stopped. This change also surprised Newton. Without even trying, he was able to talk without profanity.

The crew members were unimpressed, however. Perhaps they weren't as perceptive as Captain Hiram was. In any event, they still thought of Newton as something of a jinx, a Jonah. He was aware of their grumbling and furtive conversations.

After a week they were still adrift, now in becalmed waters. Without sails they were imprisoned on the immense sea, day after monotonous day.

At dawn on the sixth day after the storm, a lookout shouted that he saw land. The crew crowded the aft railing to see. They cheered when they saw what they believed to be the dark mountains of western Ireland. Land seemed to be just at the horizon—an easy day's journey—even with a crippled mast and shredded sails.

The captain told the cook to take the remaining fish and some of the pigs' grain meal that had remained dry and make it into a real meal. He also gave his men extra rations of the remaining rum to celebrate.

However, as the sun rose higher in the sky, the "mountains" of Ireland began to fade. The entire landmass was a cloud formation that had fooled them all. Angry and bitter, the men worried about food now that their last rations were eaten.

One crew member died during the week following the terrible storm. He had collapsed either from exposure, hunger, or sheer exhaustion. The captain led the service in which the man was buried at sea. As the crew watched his body drop into the ocean, each man wondered when it would be his turn to die.

A few days after the sailor's death, some of the men began to grumble. The rations were nearly gone. If they were unable to catch any wind, they could be trapped for up to a month.

One of the men said he wished they had not buried their shipmate at

sea but had kept his body. "It might have saved some lives," the man said quietly. The meaning of his words was not lost.

John overheard the man. There were, of course, tales of cannibalism in other extreme situations like this. But John had always thought they were just that—tales. Yet, he had no firsthand knowledge either way. It was *possible*. The conversation made him nervous. It was a small step from eating the corpse of a dead comrade and making another corpse of one still living. John had no illusions about who such a "volunteer" might be in a macabre situation like that. Disliked by all, he'd be their first choice.

The doldrums continued to keep the ship captive. Another week went by with scant food for the crew. The men tried their luck at fishing, but with meager results.

By the end of the second week, even the captain grew superstitious about Newton. John overheard Captain Hiram talking with his first officer.

"We've had nothing but bad luck ever since Newton boarded the *Greyhound,*" commented the first mate.

"Yes," the captain agreed. "I've lately been obsessed with the idea that the man is a Jonah. I believe that man Newton has provoked the anger of God. It's one thing to use a little profanity now and then, but he is utterly wicked and filled with such hateful blasphemy that I think God might be punishing this entire ship on account of him. I go back and forth about throwing him overboard in order to calm the waves and storms, so we might be saved."

Newton was about to step out of the shadows and let them know about the change in his life and reassure them when the first mate chuckled. "You're too late, Captain. We haven't had the huge waves and fierce storms in over a month. You should've tossed him overboard then. He can't calm the storm now when there isn't one! Besides, you told me yourself that he isn't swearing anymore."

The captain did not laugh at his joke. "Look," he said, "I am to the

place where I believe I must throw him overboard in order to save our ship. It may be the only way. God is a severe judge, and Newton has no doubt tempted him too long."

The captain seemed at a loss about what to do. Instead of acting on his impulse, he merely shook his head and walked away.

John wondered about their extreme situation. Nearly everyone was weak from hunger. They still had enough water to drink, but John knew the crew members were thinking—perhaps even talking and planning— to do something about the hunger aboard ship.

✝ ✝ ✝

John avoided the captain and crew for most of the following week. He was afraid to be placed in a situation where he might meet with an "accident" of some kind and end up in the cook's galley!

During the day he stayed on duty at the helm. The wheel required little activity, so he read during most of his waking hours—the Bible and *The Imitation of Christ,* along with a book of sermons he found in Captain Hiram's library.

The captain stayed in his cabin most of the time and only ventured out on deck on occasions that offered a rare hope of the sun poking through the clouds long enough for him to fix the ship's position. He was almost able to complete the sextant reading a few times, but the sun didn't stay out quite long enough to check his numbers. Captain Hiram was fairly certain of their approximate latitudinal position and felt somewhat confident that they would sight land by maintaining their present course. However, by not knowing their longitudinal position, he had no idea how far from land they really were.

Since everyone was so fatigued, they no longer bothered Newton. Combined with John's keeping to himself, the captain and crew had no real chance to observe the remarkable change in Newton's life since his encounter with God in the storm.

Even if they had noticed, however, they would likely have chalked up his new piety to some trick to get their minds off the thing that had to be done to insure the survival of the rest of the crew.

The *Greyhound* continued to limp eastward. The sailors had pulled the remnants of the sails from all of the masts and sewed together two fairly decent sails from the pieces. They placed these on the main mast and managed to wring some additional speed from the April breezes.

It was now exactly four weeks since the storm had crippled the ship, and the crew members were so weakened by now that they were nearly helpless. The tired lookout had climbed the rigging with great difficulty for the watch. After several hours of vainly looking through his telescope, he thought he saw something. He cleaned the lens on his shirt and looked again. It was land! Then he remembered the last time he had spotted the landmass that turned out to be a cloud formation and did not want to make the same mistake again.

The lookout waited and then looked again, wanting to be certain.

At the helm, John Newton had put aside the book he had been reading and was praying for the ship and crew. As he opened his eyes and looked to the east, his heart fluttered excitedly.

"Land! Ahoy!" the lookout called from above.

The men were restrained when they went to look. No one wanted it to be another mirage. The captain brought out a bigger telescope on a tripod that had greater magnification. He set it up near the helm and looked through the lens. After adjusting the lens for sharpness, he cried out, "It *is* land! I can see some houses and buildings!"

Then the men cheered. It was really true. They were saved.

"Thank God," Newton said with a smile.

Captain Hiram looked up from the telescope and smiled back at John. "Yes, Mr. Newton. Thank God indeed," he said.

The captain noted in his log entry for 8 April 1748 that land had been sighted and the *Greyhound* was making slow progress toward a harbor.

He had studied his charts to see if any of the visible land shapes matched those on his maps. The captain finally determined with reasonable certainty that they had spotted Tory Island just off the north coast of Ireland.

Although he didn't mention it in his log, Captain Hiram also noted that the *Greyhound* might have made landfall a few days earlier if they had maintained their original southern position. As it was, they had drifted nearly two hundred miles north. Even so, if they hadn't seen Tory Island, they would have sailed on to Scotland and arrived there a few days later unless beset by storms, hunger, or mutiny.

The exhausted crew and fragile ship spent the rest of that day and all night trying to steer the *Greyhound* around the mostly uninhabited north coast of Ireland to the northeast Dunree Head area, then safely into the harbor at Lough Swilly. The ship had just anchored and the crew was preparing to go ashore when another violent storm suddenly arose.

In the galley, the men were anticipating a last meager meal aboard the *Greyhound*. One of the sailors had filled a musket with birdshot and killed several seagulls that had landed on the ship. The cook had already cleaned the birds and had thrown them into the stewpot when the storm arose. He went to the storeroom to get some more water to make the soup. When he got there, he commented to his helper, "Well, at least we still have plenty of water. There's still a whole row of full barrels in the back there."

As he went to take the barrel nearest him, he braced himself for the weight of the container and lifted. He nearly lost his balance, however, because the barrel was empty and much lighter than he was expecting. "Hey, what's this?" he asked.

Turning the barrel, he saw that it had been smashed against the hull in the storeroom, and the water had leaked out. He reached for the next barrel. It was also empty. In fact, the entire remaining stock of water barrels was empty. The cook looked at his mate with astonishment and felt

a queasy knot in his stomach. They wouldn't have made it more than a few more days without water.

The captain watched the storm from his cabin window as the winds buffeted the *Greyhound* again. This time, however, the ship was protected by the calm waters of the bay. Captain Hiram knew that if they had not made anchorage when they did, the *Greyhound* never would have survived the battering from the storm. Or, as the captain mused, even if the *Greyhound* had been able to stay afloat after the storm, it's quite likely that the ship would have been blown further off course and missed *both* Ireland and Scotland, in which case all the crew members could have died of hunger or thirst in the northern Atlantic before eventually finding landfall weeks later in Norway.

✝ ✝ ✝

Later that day the terrible storm passed, and the men of the *Greyhound* went ashore. John took the little money he had brought with him from Africa and bought some new clothes, food, and lodging in Londonderry, not far from the ship's anchorage.

He conferred with Captain Hiram about sailing on to England after repairs were made on the *Greyhound,* and the captain told him it would take many weeks to repair all the damage. John thought about finding another way back home but felt an obligation to both the ship's owner, Mr. Manesty, for going to the trouble to bring him back to England and to the captain and crew. He decided to wait until the necessary repairs were completed and sail home on the *Greyhound.*

Meanwhile, Newton wrote letters in his rented room. The first was to his father. John poured out his heartfelt apologies for his rebellion, disobedience, and wickedness and asked for his father's forgiveness. He intended the next letter for Polly but was unable to finish it. For one thing, he didn't know if she was still unmarried or what had happened in her life since he last saw her more than four years ago. He also felt

great shame for the life he had led since he had last seen her. He wondered if it would ever be possible to see her again, let alone expect anything more of a relationship. He decided to wait awhile before writing to Polly.

To Newton's surprise, he received an answer to the letter he had sent his father. John wept as he read the letter from his father, rich with words expressing his great joy and affection. Since their last letters—when John was still marooned in Africa—John's father had heard a rumor that his son was aboard the *Greyhound*, which had been reported missing for almost a year. Captain Newton had presumed the worst and mourned the loss of his son at sea.

The letter also expressed Captain Newton's happiness at John's newfound faith. He told his son that he had almost given up hope that John would ever be swayed from his erring ways.

The letter closed with news about the captain's recent appointment as governor of Fort York, in Hudson's Bay, in the North American colonies. "Thomasin and the children will remain behind in our home near London for this duty," the captain wrote, adding, "I can take you along with me as my assistant. Please try and return in time to sail with me in May."

✝ ✝ ✝

The *Greyhound* was finally repaired and made ready to sail. Captain Hiram proudly stood by the helmsman on the beautiful May morning when the ship set sail. It took the ship, still laden with its cargo of camwood and beeswax, only a few days to reach Liverpool.

John packed his few things and made a final tour of the *Greyhound* before going ashore. He shook hands with each crew member and climbed over the rail into the longboat. Newton was rowed to the docks, and when he stepped back on land that he hadn't seen in more than four years, his eyes grew misty.

John immediately strode to the offices of Joseph Manesty to introduce himself. The owner of the shipping company hurried out of his
office when he was told that John had come to see him. John had never
met Mr. Manesty before and smiled when the older man introduced
himself. Manesty was a tall, distinguished-looking man with a strong,
imposing presence in the room.

"Mr. Newton! How good it is to meet you!" Manesty exclaimed, shaking John's hand enthusiastically. "Your father and I are old friends. I
received a letter from him just this morning—along with a letter he
wrote to you as well. In my letter he writes that his ship sails this very
day from the anchorage at the Nore, outside of London. I'm afraid you've
just missed him," Manesty said quietly.

John suddenly felt overwhelmed with sadness. He had wanted so
much to meet with his father before he left for his new appointment in
the colonies. Now it would be another three years before he could tell
him in person all that had happened to him.

Manesty ordered tea to be brought to his office, and he asked John
to join him. "Well," Manesty said after sipping from his teacup, "you
don't look anything like I imagined."

John grinned. "Sir, I must apologize for being so rude and disrespectful when you first offered me an opportunity in Jamaica. No doubt
things would have been quite different if I had taken that job."

Manesty waved his hand and shook his head. "That is all in the past.
What is important now is that you have learned from your adversity."

"Yes, sir. I have," John said contritely.

Manesty put his cup down and leaned forward in his big leather
chair. "While you were preparing to leave the *Greyhound* today, Captain
Hiram came ashore. He has already reported to me and told me of all
that has happened to him, to you, and the crew. He also tells me that he
was quite impressed with you after the storm struck the ship and you
were all in such danger."

John looked at Manesty quizzically. Captain Hiram—the one who so thoroughly disliked him, who wanted to throw him overboard, who couldn't stand to be in his presence? Could it be the same man?

"He told me that things were a bit rough at first, but he suspects you were angry at him for lying about an inheritance in order to get you to come back to England," Manesty smiled. "I'd be upset, too, I think. We apologize for the subterfuge, Mr. Newton, but your father wanted your rescue from Africa, and I'm afraid we had to bend the truth in order to accomplish it."

In the past John would have reacted in terrible anger and outrage upon being told now that he really wasn't coming into a great fortune. This time, though, he simply nodded and remained calm. (He had often thought about the inheritance during the long voyage but had convinced himself that it was too good to be true.)

Manesty continued, "Mr. Newton, based on the way that you handled yourself and took responsibility aboard the *Greyhound,* I have talked at great length with Captain Hiram, and we both believe you are ready to command your own ship. How would you like to be captain of one of my vessels?"

John was overwhelmed. He had been thinking about Polly. Too afraid to write to her, he had hoped to approach her about marrying him—if he wasn't already too late. Now, he had something to offer her. Still, he was cautious.

He thanked Manesty but modified his offer. "Sir, you and Captain Hiram are kind to say such good things about me. I appreciate your confidence, but I'm afraid that taking on such a responsibility based on a few weeks of reliability might be unwise. You already know my past. I've been *un*reliable. I let you down before. I don't want to disappoint you— or my father—again.

"Mr. Manesty, I have always given far less than my best. As I think about it, it might be best if I made another voyage first—serving under

another captain. I need to learn how to submit to authority," John explained.

Manesty could not believe the change in the man who sat in his office. His honesty and humility were refreshing.

John continued, "Sir, I think I can also benefit from learning more about the slave trade from the shipping company's point of view. You see, I have a great deal of experience from the 'land' side of things, but I only worked a few months aboard the slave ship. If you would, sir, kindly employ me to serve under another captain until I can prove myself worthy of command."

The shipowner sat for a long moment and stroked his mustache while he thought. Finally he spoke. "Newton, you continue to surprise me by your maturity and wisdom. It's a deal. I'll make you the first mate on the *Brownlow* when it sails in a few months."

"Thank you, Mr. Manesty," John replied, standing to shake the tall man's hand.

Chapter Twenty-three

Other Chances

Mr. Manesty had given John the letter from his father, and John read it eagerly:

Dear John,

We are still in a mood of great rejoicing at hearing that you are alive and safely returned to England. I write this as I am about to leave for the New World and my appointment as governor of Fort York. I regret that I was unable to see you before I left and that it will be another three years before we see each other again.

I should tell you that as I left to meet the ship, I traveled by way of Chatham and met with the Catlett family. They welcomed me warmly, and we discussed your former interest in a courtship with Miss Catlett. I assured them that you

had my blessing on this endeavor, and I prayed that they would likewise approve. Mr. Catlett then told me that he knew of no other suitors for his daughter's hand and assured me that he shall give his blessing to this match. I believe that your mother would be proud of your choice in a wife.

Your father,

J. Newton

John read the letter several times, taking in every word and relishing the good news. His father's warmth and affection amazed him—he even referred to his dead wife for the first time in sixteen years.

The match was approved! Yet, he had received no word from Polly. She had not written, and he had not heard from her for several years. Would *she* approve of the match?

John's mood changed suddenly as he thought about her. His memories were tarnished by his own carnality. He was nearly twenty-four and she was twenty. The difference in their ages was inconsequential, but the difference in their experiences was vast—a difference that weighed heavily on John's heart. How could he possibly tell this chaste and unspoiled young woman all that he had done—how depraved he had become and how utterly low he had sunk?

Then words he had learned as a child came into his mind:

He will not always chide:
    neither will he keep his anger for ever.
He hath not dealt with us after our sins;
    nor rewarded us according to our iniquities.
For as the heaven is high above the earth,
    so great is his mercy toward them that fear him.
As far as the east is from the west,
    so far hath he removed our transgressions from us.

John recalled another Bible verse promising that God had already taken his sins and had "cast them into the sea, to remember them no more."

He decided that if God could forgive him and even erase all of his sins from his memory, perhaps Polly might also be forgiving. Yet, he still couldn't write her directly, so he wrote to Polly's aunt and told her of his safe return and sincere desire to see Polly again, if she were still interested in seeing him.

Polly's aunt told Abigail about the contents of John's letter. Abigail then decided to write to John while he was still in Liverpool, on the opposite side of the country. He was invited to visit Chatham whenever he was free.

John looked at his dwindling finances but decided to pay for a stagecoach ticket and visit the family. Everyone welcomed him, including Polly, who had by now graduated from a women's seminary. (It was not a theological training school but rather a kind of finishing school that prepared girls for a life as wife and homemaker.) She was taller and no longer a child. She had blossomed into maturity in a way that took John's breath away as soon as he saw her.

Polly wore her best dress, which had a flowing skirt and long sleeves. Her hair was fixed in a tumble of curls and twin ivory combs. She smiled, extended her hand, and gave him a slight curtsy. Her greeting seemed to be platonic—as if he were her brother, and not the man she loved.

John wanted to take Polly in his arms and embrace her, but Polly was reserved and kept him at a distance. She smiled and conversed with him at dinner, but no more than Abigail and the rest of the family. They all asked questions about Africa and his adventures.

He stayed overnight but had to leave the next morning. Not willing to jeopardize his new appointment by overstaying his leave as he had done so many times before, he told them he had to go and asked Polly if they could go for a walk before he left.

The parents excused the couple, and John was bursting to talk with Polly and ask her to consider marrying him after he returned from his next voyage. She did nothing to encourage him, however. In fact, he was puzzled by her cold and aloof demeanor toward him.

As time slipped by, he tried to broach the subject but could only stammer general banalities. Frustrated, he took her back to the house, then asked her, "Polly, will you let me write to you?"

Polly answered cryptically, "If you like. I cannot forbid you."

John's emotions were in complete turmoil by the time he left the Catlett home for a brief visit to Thomasin and her children. After a genuinely happy welcome, he sat down to talk with Thomasin.

"I don't understand it," he told her. "When I left England four years ago, Polly seemed pleased when I asked to court her. Now she seems as if she has no interest at all."

"Well," Thomasin said, "what about her parents? Do they encourage you?"

"Yes. I sort of made things difficult before I left. I was forbidden to have any contact with Polly, but now they seem happy that I'm back and encourage me in every way. I don't understand," he said with a deep sigh.

"Well, John," Thomasin said with a smile, "you have a great deal to learn about women. She was probably just trying to show you how grown up she has become. The last time you saw her she was a silly, giggling girl. Now she's a woman and needs to be more reserved. It was probably nothing more than that."

"Really?" John asked.

"Why don't you write her a letter before you go? Tell her exactly how you feel."

That evening John wrote to Polly and bared his deepest feelings:

My dearest Polly,

How wonderful it was to see you and your good family after so many years away. Please give to your mother and father my sincere thanks for their hospitality and friendship.

There are so many things I wish we could have talked about during my visit. The time went by so quickly that I was unable to share the deepest thoughts of my heart and to ask you about the matters most important to me.

You did not forbid me to write to you, and so now I do, but I must complain that I have written so many letters and have received no replies from you. I beg for your charity! Please give me a morsel before I starve!

If you could show any encouragement to my letters with a crumb of even a few words, I would be so delighted. A letter from you would mean so much to me and not obligate you in any way. I pray you will give me time to show you the quality of my feelings for you before you reject me. However, if you reject my serious thoughts of marriage, please let your mother write to me and inform me of your unwillingness to pursue such a relationship.

I pray that you will forgive my boldness and will understand my deep feelings for you. I long for the day when I can show the world what I have often told you, that I have the most sacred regard for you, dear Polly.

I am your most faithful and ardent admirer and servant,
J. Newton.

John posted the letter and made arrangements to return to Liverpool. He had not said anything to the Catletts or Thomasin about his meager

finances but discovered that he did not have enough money for a coach
or wagon ride back to Liverpool. It took him more than a week to walk
across the country, occasionally hitching a ride on a peddler's cart or
farmer's wagon. For the entire two-hundred-mile trip he was alone, hungry, and without a place to sleep.

He immediately went to the Manesty shipping office upon his return
and began to get ready for the next voyage. Two days after his return to
Liverpool, he was surprised to receive a letter. When Manesty's assistant
presented him with it, he recognized its seal and took it with reverence.
It was from Polly.

> Dear John,
>
> Thank you for your kind letter. I have passed along
> your salutations to Mama and Papa. They also send their
> greetings.
>
> I shall take your admonition to heart and try to reply to
> your letters. I confess that I have not always done so in the
> past. Your letters are so wonderfully written, and I fear that
> my humble thoughts and weak efforts of expression will
> not match your eloquence. That is why I have been so fear-
> ful to write in the past. However, I shall make every effort
> to reply to your kind letters from now on.

John felt much better. It was apparent to him that Polly was not reject-
ing his marriage overtures. If she were, she would have had Abigail
write him a formal letter of rejection. His heart soared that the way was
cleared for him. He was ready to leave now, with the knowledge that he
still had a chance to win Polly's love.

✝ ✝ ✝

Six weeks later John was rereading Polly's letter as the *Brownlow* lay
at anchor in the waters off Sierra Leone, near the Plantain Islands where

he earlier served as Clow's slave. He put the letter safely back in a small wooden box inside his sea chest and went up onto the deck of the ship. It was just past sundown and starting to get dark. The ship was close enough to shore that John could hear the tree frogs calling in the evening air. Further inland, he heard the muffled sounds of African drums.

John's heartbeat quickened. His thoughts wandered to memories of his days in Africa—especially the times when he danced with the slaves and they gave themselves over to spirits. He was breathing faster as he thought of his life before his dramatic conversion in the storm aboard the *Greyhound*.

John had been sincere in his break with evil and efforts to emulate Christ. When he was in Ireland, he had gone often to church—not just Sunday worship but to vespers and midweek services as well. It seemed that he could not get enough of church, praying, and Bible study. However, while he attended church, he did not spend any time with a pastor who could have helped him grow in his faith and understanding.

By the time he set sail on the *Brownlow,* he was less passionate about those habits of piety. He had no Christian companion aboard the *Brownlow* with whom he could enjoy fellowship and mutual encouragement. As a result, John neglected prayer, Bible reading, and regular efforts at reform and redemption. By the time the *Brownlow* reached Africa, he had slipped back into old habits.

Miraculously, his speech had not regressed, however. The swearing and blasphemy did not return, for which he was grateful.

Tonight, however, John wasn't thinking about God. Female slaves had been brought aboard the *Brownlow,* and it was a good night to seek companionship. Other sailors had already selected sexual partners from among the captives, and John was feeling an urge to do the same. He struggled with his thoughts of lust for awhile, then abandoned his new-found scruples. John went below, unchained a young African woman, and brought her up on deck where he had sexual relations with her. In

the past such acts had never troubled him. This time, however, John had the distinct knowledge that he had raped her.

✛ ✛ ✛

Not long after that, a longboat came out to meet the *Brownlow.* John was stunned to see his old nemesis, Clow, sitting between the oarsmen.

The trader came aboard and introduced himself to Captain Rogers who shook Clow's hand, then called for John. "Mr. Clow, let me introduce my first mate, Mr. Newton," the captain said.

"Mr. Clow and I have already met," John said stiffly but politely. Clow looked over at Newton. The sound of John's voice brought instant recognition. Clow smiled and extended his hand. At first Clow's arm was stuck out in empty space before John finally took it and shook it somewhat tentatively.

"Well, Mr. Newton," Clow said, "you're looking quite well. The last time I saw you, you had a beard and long hair. I almost didn't recognize you. I didn't think I'd see you again. They told me you went back to England to claim a fortune."

"That's not quite correct," John muttered. "But I am quite well, thank you. And how is your 'wife,' Mr. Clow?"

Clow ignored John's particular unkind emphasis on the word wife. "She is also well. In fact, she would be pleased to see you, I'm certain. Tell me, Captain," Clow said, "would you and Mr. Newton do us the honor of having dinner with us this evening? It has been some time since we have had the pleasure of dining with civilized people."

"It would be our pleasure, sir," Captain Rogers replied before John had time to object.

John, of course, had never discussed Clow and Peh'eye with the captain. When they took the longboat to Plantain Island and walked the path to the Clow compound, John grew more and more uncomfortable—even afraid.

He saw the lime grove he had planted almost single-handedly, along with his old hut, the slave quarters, and the storeroom buildings. Several familiar faces among Clow's servants and slaves were stunned to see Newton back at the Clow compound. They stared at him as one back from the dead.

Peh'eye welcomed the guests from the *Brownlow* politely. Clow must have warned her that John was coming to dinner because she held her feelings in check and actually smiled at John when she gave him a seat of honor next to Clow.

John's fear of his old enemies dissipated after a few glasses of wine. Clow and Peh'eye were surprised at John's confidence. They both began to show him respect. After awhile, John himself even warmed to Clow's conversation and Peh'eye's presence. Despite her depravity, Newton was still struck by her beauty.

After a leisurely smoke and brandy after dinner, Clow stood up to address his guests. "I hope you will take advantage of our further hospitality," he said, "and be our guests for the night. It is too late to go back to your ship tonight, with the tide so high. Stay with us. Can you not go back in the morning after a good breakfast?"

"Why, thank you, Mr. Clow," the captain answered. "We appreciate your kindness, don't we, Mr. Newton?"

John wasn't as inclined to stay but didn't say so. "Yes, we'll be pleased to accept."

Clow smiled broadly. "Captain Rogers, I have already taken the liberty to send word to your men that you'd probably be staying the night, so that's all taken care of."

"Why, thank you, Mr. Clow," replied the captain.

"I have also taken the liberty to choose a companion for your bed, gentlemen," Clow said. The captain smiled. It was common practice among those in the slave trade to entertain guests by giving them a choice female from their inventory.

"Captain Rogers," Clow continued as he walked down the hall to a bedroom, "this will be your room. If you are in any way disappointed, simply let me know. I will not be offended if your taste is different from mine, but this female has proven charms."

The captain looked inside the room and saw a nude girl sitting on the floor near the bed. "She's lovely," he said. "She'll do just fine. Thank you, Mr. Clow."

"You're most welcome," Clow said. "And Mr. Newton, we'll give you your old room." John recognized the room where he had lain the time he got so desperately ill and watched from the window as Clow left him in the hands of Peh'eye.

John was anxious not to allow Clow to win this game of subtle intimidation. He smiled broadly and told his host, "How thoughtful of you to remember," he said.

"Oh," Clow added, "I almost forgot. You shall have a companion tonight as well. You may even remember her."

John opened the door to the bedroom and held his lamp higher. The soft glow of the lamp lit the room, and John saw the familiar form of his former mistress, Ruby, standing inside.

✝ ✝ ✝

Over the next few months John took the longboats of the *Brownlow* upriver on trading expeditions. He bought slaves and took them back to the ship. The weather, even in February, was unbearable. The temperature was always over one hundred degrees, and it rained nearly every day. Six men of the *Brownlow* died from fevers and reduced the ship's crew to twenty-four.

The captain of the *Brownlow* was only too glad to give First Mate Newton charge of the inland trading because he could now stay behind and be at less risk of contracting fevers and facing other dangers. He could also benefit from the hospitality of Clow and his mistress. Clow

had maintained his friendship with the officers of the *Brownlow,* and the captain stayed at Clow's compound. Whenever John returned from his trading trips, he also stayed there.

After one trading excursion, John dined with Peh'eye and Clow and suddenly became violently ill. It gave him a strong feeling of *déjà vu.*

Clow went to John's room the next morning and said, "Your fever has returned. Captain Rogers says that you were expected to leave on another trip to collect some slaves upriver. I told him I would go in your place and bring them back. He will go with me. You wait here. Peh'eye will take good care of you."

As John looked out the window, he saw Clow's boat pass from his sight. In addition to his fever and aching head, he felt a great uneasiness in his stomach. The memories of what had happened the last time were indelible as he recalled them with a growing fear.

After awhile, Peh'eye came into the room as he was drifting in and out of sleep, trying to shake the illness. He opened his eyes after sensing the presence of someone in the room.

She laughed loudly when he noticed her standing at the foot of his bed. "You *do* remember!" she exclaimed. "I see it in your eyes! You remember the last time, don't you?" Then she turned and left him to his suffering.

Newton tried to sleep off the fever but was unsuccessful. At first he vomited violently. After several days without food or water, his fever turned to delirious tremors, then chills, and back to burning fever. His entire body ached, and since he had nothing left in his stomach to vomit, he began to cough up blood.

John felt all strength leaving him and sensed that he was ready for death. Once more his life flashed before him—but this time he recalled more current memories. He recalled the storm, his calling out to God to save him, and the changes he had made in his life following his conversion—but he also saw that not all that much had changed. He was still almost as great a sinner as he had been before.

In his delirious state he imagined he was outside where the whipping post stood, looking at a cross that was erected in its place. On the cross was Jesus, and Newton was hammering spikes through his wrists and feet, nailing Christ to the cross.

Then John heard Jesus speak from the cross—*Why do you crucify me again? I died for you once. Now you are crucifying me again.* He then saw Christ's head fall limply on his breast as he gasped a final breath.

Forcing himself to return to reality, John awoke in the bedroom in Clow's compound. He was terribly weak and barely conscious. but forced himself out of bed and outside. He had to reassure himself that Christ was not on a cross in the yard.

Staggering, falling, and crawling, John somehow made his way to the beach where he had often gone to be alone when he was Clow's slave, the same place Barker had found him drawing algebra theorems in the sand. John collapsed and sat with his back against a huge rock. He cried out to God once more. His prayer was brief but sincere:

God, forgive me! I have been trying to crucify Jesus again. I have failed miserably in trying to reform my life. I cannot make any more promises. I have broken all the promises I made to you and failed to live up to the resolves I gave you. I have realized that I can't change myself. But you are a God of amazing grace. You can give me what I want more than anything else—peace of mind, forgiveness, and the ability to live a life of goodness.

Lord, I surrender. Take my life. I'm so tired, so sick. You saved me from drowning in the storm, but now I know that I should have died. I embody everything you find abhorrent.

Take my life, now, God. Let the tide take me. Bury me in the sea. Amen.

Following this heartfelt prayer, Newton was totally exhausted and lay against the rock with his head back, resting on the rock. Within moments he was asleep. Soon the incoming tide began to lap at his legs.

For more than an hour John lay still where he had dropped. Even when the tide brought the level of water to his waist, he still seemed to be unconscious. Before long, seawater was swirling around his chest and eventually lapped over his ears and around his mouth. Finally the water level stopped rising and began to drop again. John awoke when the beach was once again dry. When he opened his eyes, he had an unusual sense of peace, tranquility of soul, and an inner assurance that he was getting better and would get well again.

With great difficulty he made his way back to the Clow compound where Captain Rogers met him. The men had just returned from their upriver trading expedition and helped John back to bed. John slept peacefully that night and the next day was remarkably improved—so much, in fact, that within two days he was fully recovered and ready to go back to his ship.

John returned to the ship reassured in his faith that God had not forsaken him. Despite his backsliding and inability to keep his promises about reform, Newton discovered as he read more from the New Testament epistles that it was impossible for him to keep himself from sinning. Only God could do that. His part was to obey and to trust him.

A week after returning to the ship, John was planning to take a longboat party on a routine excursion to collect fresh water and firewood. His job as first mate was to supervise the work detail. As he was ready to climb over the rail onto the ladder to the longboat, Captain Rogers called out, "Newton! I want you. Please come back."

Another man was sent in John's place. He went over to the captain and asked, "Yes, sir, what can I do for you?"

"Uh . . . nothing. I'm sending Jim in your place, that's all," Captain Rogers answered.

"But you called me back. Why?" John asked.

"No reason. I want you to stay on the ship today," the captain muttered, not quite sure himself what it all meant.

"I don't understand, Captain," John said. "You must have had some reason to call me back."

"Forget it," the captain replied, shaking his head. "It's nothing."

The next morning an African canoe came toward the *Brownlow.* The native called to the sailor on watch and tried to communicate in Pidgin English.

Captain Rogers was summoned.

"This African says that our longboat sunk at the river entrance and that our crew is marooned on shore," the sailor explained to the captain.

"Was anyone hurt?" Captain Rogers asked.

"Yes, sir," the sailor replied somberly. "Jim was drowned. Went down with the boat."

The hair on Newton's neck rose at that word. Jim was the man who took his place the day before. Once again God spared his life. Captain Rogers looked over at John. In an instant they both knew the reason the captain had called John back. When they discussed it later, Captain Rogers simply said it was fate. John, however, knew better.

Several days later John wrote Polly about his various narrow escapes (but in rather general tones, sparing her the details) and finally got up the nerve to ask her to marry him. The letter was posted with a trading ship that would soon be on its way back to London.

Chapter
Twenty-four

Polly's Refusals

✠

When the *Brownlow* sailed from West Africa, her hold was filled with slaves. In past voyages John had only seen them in what was called "loose packed," where each slave had enough room to lie down and sleep on his or her back. This time, however, the ship had a total of 216 slaves crammed into the cargo hold. Such confinement forced the slaves to lie "spoon packed" on their sides with absolutely no room between them.

The air in the cargo hold was so stinking, hot, and thin that even candles would not burn. The conditions were absolutely unbearable.

These same conditions had been the cause of another narrow escape for John after the *Brownlow* was on her way to the West Indies. One night, after a slave had secretly stolen a marlinespike (an iron spike used as a giant "needle" to braid and repair ropes) and had somehow hidden it from the crew, an uprising took place. The muscular young black who

INFIDEL

had hidden the spike had it with him when the slaves were brought on deck for exercise and washing.

The slave immediately killed the helmsman with the marlinespike and attacked another sailor. Other slaves soon followed his lead, intent on killing their captors and taking over the ship. A violent free-for-all immediately occurred on deck. One of the sailors sounded the alarm bell, and other sailors came up on deck with muskets. Several shots were fired into the cluster of slaves.

John ordered the sailors to climb the rigging where the ankle-chained slaves could not follow. That way the sailors could take their time and pick off the rebels one at a time with their guns. Soon the skirmish was over, and four slaves lay dead, along with the helmsman. Two other sailors were injured, but their wounds were fairly superficial.

The rest of the renegade slaves were whipped publicly while the others watched as punishment for their rebellion. The rest of the journey to the West Indies was uneventful.

By the time the *Brownlow* arrived at the small island of Antigua, many of the slaves had died of disease or had suffocated in the close "spoon packed" cargo hold. This was an "acceptable" loss, however, since most slavers lost 20 percent of their cargo enroute.

First Mate Newton had the slaves brought on deck. He was the only one who knew enough of the African dialects to communicate with them; he told the slaves, "Your long voyage has ended. I know you are glad. Do not be afraid. I know that many of you have heard tales about the bad magic of whites—that we bring you here to be eaten. That is not true. Whites do not eat Africans. When you are put ashore you will be given food, clothes, and housing. Whites will take you and give you these things in exchange for your work. If you obey and work well, you will have a happy life."

The sailors hosed down all the slaves and shaved the men, then gave the slaves oil to rub on their skin. This made them glisten like polished

ebony, an appearance that was quite attractive to the bidders at the slave auction. However, many of the blacks resisted the oil, recalling the tales of being eaten by the white men. It seemed to them that they were only being basted for cooking!

As John was preparing the final paperwork for transferring the slaves, Manesty's agent in Antigua rowed out to the *Brownlow* to tell the captain and first mate about a change in plans. "The Antigua slave market is glutted with too many Africans," he said. "There is no market for slaves this month. You must go on. Take your cargo to Charleston, South Carolina, in the colonies. I'm told that the market there is good."

John was disappointed. Charleston was another eighteen hundred miles away. He had to tell the slaves that they were not getting off the ship after all. This proved to be a disaster, the final straw for many of the slaves. They had no idea why they were not let off the ship and no concept of how much longer their voyage would last. A number of the slaves went berserk, murdering other slaves and killing themselves. Every day the crew of the *Brownlow* had to throw more bodies of dead slaves overboard. By the time they landed at Charleston, the ship had lost 62 of its 218 slaves, but it was still within the "acceptable" range of loss.

First Mate Newton watched the slaves being sold in the market. Amazingly, many families had managed to stay together during the horrific trip and its conditions. Yet, now the white men were separating them. The African men generally were taken for work in factories and farms. The women were used as domestic help and for "lighter" work on the plantations—lighter only in comparison to the work of the male slaves. Children were sent to various places, usually with some thought to their anticipated potential as workers. In any event, it meant a terrible wrenching away of loved ones in different directions. Mothers screamed hysterically as their husbands or children were dragged off. This would be their last sight of each other. Once they were sold, they would never see one another again.

When the sale was over, the captain of the *Brownlow* netted a little more than £7,000 for the entire cargo of men, women, and children to take back to Joseph Manesty in Liverpool.

✝ ✝ ✝

The *Brownlow* stayed in Charleston for several months. Newton supervised the cleaning and airing out of the cargo hold and repairs of the ship, most of which was delegated to the crew and the bosun's mate in charge of the work. That freed John to go ashore and be alone with his thoughts.

He reasoned that since he had been so corrupt he could not trust himself for guidance in spiritual truth and lifestyle matters. He needed a mentor, someone who could be trusted to lead him down the right path.

John visited the church of an independent minister, Joseph Smith, and was impressed with his sermons. Yet, for some reason he never approached Reverend Smith for help. He did not know the reason for Smith's fiery sermons and practical Christian wisdom. It was not until much later that he learned it was Smith's association with an English preacher who was traveling in the colonies—George Whitefield—who became world renowned and a major influence in the life of John Newton.

As the *Brownlow* was being outfitted with its provisions for the return trip to England, John read the printed sermons of the frontier clergymen. They reminded him of Dr. Jennings, a dissenter who addressed the issues of sin and salvation straight on—whereas the traditional clergy seemed to be more focused on politics and other more worldly matters.

After almost four months in Charleston, the *Brownlow* had been repaired, loaded with cargo of tobacco and cotton, and made ready for the return voyage to England, with a planned arrival just before Christmas.

The trip along the North American coast and past the Newfoundland banks was uneventful. John recalled his trip of the previous year along the same route when the *Greyhound* was nearly lost with all hands in the terrible storm. He was grateful for good winds and an able ship.

The *Brownlow* sailed into Liverpool harbor a week before Christmas 1749. Manesty was delighted at the timely return with a good cargo as well as the gold and silver earned through the sale of the slave cargo.

When the captain and John were ready to leave the shipping office, Manesty asked John to stay. "I want to talk to you about your next voyage," he said.

When the two men were alone, he asked John, "Well, Newton, you've done quite well. Your experience is evident in the reports and accounting papers that were turned in. You are a born administrator as well as sailor. You'll make a fine sea captain. So, tell me. Are you ready to take command of your own ship next time?"

"Yes, sir. I believe I am ready," John replied.

"Good. I planned as much. I am giving you command of the *Duke of Argyle,*" Manesty told him. "She's an older ship but sound. Dignified. You'll like her."

The two men then discussed Newton's compensation as captain. This was the crucial information John wanted to pin down. He planned to use it when he asked Polly to marry him, to convince Polly and her father that he was finally ready to settle down.

John wrote a letter to Polly while he was still in Liverpool. He reckoned that it was already too late to get to Chatham in time for the holidays. He did not lay out all the particulars on his heart but let her know that he had "a matter of great importance to discuss with her."

Right after New Year's Day of 1750, John received a reply to his letter to Polly. It was brief and didn't really offer him any encouragement, but she did give permission for him to visit her and her family.

Newton began the two-hundred-mile trip to Chatham a few days later. Once again he was love-struck when he saw her. She represented purity and innocence—a stark contrast to his life of guile, corruption, and violence. He longed for those qualities to be present in his own life.

After a wonderful dinner and shared stories and laughter, John excused himself and asked Polly to go for a walk with him. He reached to hold her hand as he had done when she was younger, but Polly skillfully put her hands into the felt muff she carried.

It took a little time for John to cover the inconsequential matters, the small talk that helped him build up courage to speak his heart.

"I wanted to wait to tell you about my new ship and promotion to captain," he began, "but your father asked me first thing.

"With this promotion I will earn enough to be able to support a wife. For seven years, Polly—seven *long* years—I've been in love with you. I've always looked forward to marrying you, but that decision is yours." He cleared his throat and felt his heart racing. He stopped and looked into her face. "Will you do me the honor of marrying me, Polly?"

Polly stared down at the ground and did not reply for a long while. Then she replied softly, "I-I am sorry, John, but I cannot."

Newton was stunned. "But why?"

"I have deep feelings for you as well," she said, "but I have thought about this matter for a long time. I'm afraid I have to refuse."

The two of them walked back to her home in silence. John told George Catlett that he had to leave early. "My stepmother is ill, and I want to stop and see her family before I go back to Liverpool. I'd also like to see if there are any recent letters from my father."

Polly's father nodded, and from the expression on John's face, understood what must have taken place when the two took their walk. He shook hands with John. Abigail went over to John as he was buttoning his coat and embraced him. "Please stay in touch, John," she said. Then she whispered in his ear, "Don't give up. Keep trying."

All the way back to Liverpool, John was discouraged. Yet the words of Abigail gave him hope that Polly might change her mind.

John wrote Polly again from Liverpool, pleading his case and asking her to reconsider. He got no reply.

Several weeks later he received a letter from Abigail. She spent most of the correspondence bringing him up-to-date with local news. Only at the end of the letter did she come to the point. "When Polly and I were talking earlier this week, she said, 'You know, Mother, *if* John and I were to be married, I think that we should do well together.' Please take this, as I do, as encouragement that she is reconsidering your kind proposal."

John wrote to Polly again, asking for her to permit him to visit so that he could once again propose to her. She replied this time, telling him, "I give you my permission to come."

He thought about the brief, almost terse reply. If she did plan to turn him down again, she would not have bothered to invite him to make a two-hundred-mile journey to be told no.

Two weeks later John was back in Chatham. This time he had fortified himself with the same courage and bravado that he had as an officer of a ship. He would assert himself and plead his case once more.

Polly listened to his renewed proposal. When he paused, she spoke. "My mother asked me why I turned you down last time," she began in a quiet voice. "I told her that I was afraid.

"As I thought about the happy-go-lucky way you looked at life, I wondered if you would be serious about marriage," she told him.

"I assure you, Polly," he interrupted, "I take the idea of marriage with the utmost respect and solemnity."

"Then I thought about the times when you overstayed your leave and got into trouble," she said. "I remember my father telling me how irresponsible that was, and I was afraid that this might be a mark of your character and you might take leave of your marriage and family one day."

John was too embarrassed to reply as Polly continued to tell him her reasons for not wanting to marry him. "Then Father came to me after you left last time. He told me that he sees a dramatic change in your life. He thinks that something has happened to you to turn you around.

"If that is true," Polly said softly, "I am willing to reconsider."

"Polly," John whispered to her, "I regret a great deal of what has happened in my life. I cannot change the past. But your father is right. I *am* a changed man." Then he told her what had taken place in his life during the storm aboard the *Greyhound*. "I believe that God has given me another chance, and I don't want to throw it away. And if *you* will give me another chance, I promise you with all my life that I will not disappoint you."

They talked for several hours, at the end of which John finally asked her once more to marry him. Polly smiled, looked into his face, and lifted her hand in a symbolic gesture of agreement. He tenderly kissed her hand and squeezed it gently to affirm his feelings for her.

The next day John and Polly made plans to marry right away and set the date of February 1, 1750. They decided that Polly would continue living with her parents while John was at sea, but until he sailed, they would have several months of married life together.

Chapter Twenty-five

A Captain of Slave Ships

✝

The couple had to make many adjustments in their married life. As they worked through these matters, John also felt uneasy about his spiritual life. He wrote to his old pastor, Dr. Jennings, who remembered the seven-year-old boy he had put on a coach alone when his mother had died. Now John was almost twenty-five years old and asking serious questions about how to make up for lost years.

Dr. Jennings wrote back and sent John copies of sermons and books to help him in his quest. Newton's life was filled with enormous regret for those wasted years. Even in the years since his conversion at sea, Newton saw little progress or change in his spiritual character. He had a hunger that could not be satisfied by simply attending worship services. John felt that something was missing in his life and was eager to see that hunger satisfied.

May 18 was John's departure day. He kissed Polly and embraced the rest of the Catlett family as he said his good-byes. Then he traveled to Liverpool, where the *Duke of Argyle* had been outfitted, and prepared to sail.

When John got his first glimpse of the *Duke of Argyle,* his heart sank. The ship was small, old, and quite decrepit. To Newton, the *Duke of Argyle* didn't look shipshape enough to cross the channel, let alone sail to Africa, across the Middle Passage to the New World, and all the way back to England. In fact, the ship was in as much need of repairs as the *Greyhound* had been before it was caught in the storm.

John convinced Mr. Manesty that at least some repairs should be made before undertaking the voyage. Manesty agreed and put the ship in dry dock for another six weeks. He assigned John to care for some business for him back in London, so Newton arranged to spend more time with his bride while he awaited his ship. The *Duke of Argyle* was finally ready to sail, and on Saturday, August 11, 1750, the ship pulled away from England, on its way to Africa.

The crew of the *Duke of Argyle* matched its ship. The usual press-gang thugs, thieves, and rapists made up most of the sailors. Only three officers stood between the twenty-seven men and anarchy: the captain, John Newton; the first mate, John Bridson; and the second mate, Robert Arthur (who was also the ship's surgeon).

John had turned twenty-five just a few weeks earlier and was afraid that his youth might be misconstrued as a weakness. He had to prove his mettle as a leader of men and demonstrate his ability to maintain order and authority.

Ironically, he modeled his leadership as a captain on what he had learned from his father. The older Captain Newton used a number of eccentricities, thinking they made the crew respect him more. Unfortunately, the opposite was often the case.

John established a petty protocol that no one could eat, talk, laugh, or even ask the time without his permission or recognition. He even used the ceremony (generally used only on naval vessels) of piping the captain on and off the ship when he went ashore. Also, when Newton went ashore, he expected his men to wait up and not go to their hammocks until he returned. Rather than foster respect, these idiosyncrasies only made the crew members think that their captain was petty and rancorous.

Young Captain Newton also copied his father's habit of having a Sabbath worship service aboard ship. To the godless bunch of men serving aboard the *Duke of Argyle,* this practice only added to their irritation with him. Furthermore, John not only called the men to worship at eleven o'clock each Sunday morning, he also called them together again for midafternoon prayers and for a mandatory Bible lesson at four o'clock.

Most of the time the men either sat in disgusted resignation or with eyes glazed over in utter confusion. They had no idea what the captain was talking about, they didn't know the hymns, and they couldn't understand much from the Scripture passages.

Ironically, had Captain Newton used himself as an illustration of man's sinfulness and God's grace, the men would have understood. He had been like them for most of the years he served aboard ships until God did something in his life, which changed him. That simple story would have had more power to convince the crew about the reality of God and his power than all the religious services John offered. Instead, John's piety was only a means of further irritating his bad-tempered, anarchistic crew.

Some of the men were intimidating and defiant. Will Lees and three of his friends were the worst. Lees actually refused an order to stand watch when his time for duty came up. He threatened the life of the bosun who had given the order. The bosun backed down and put

someone else on duty, and Lees knew then that he had wrestled control of the men from the bosun.

Word got back to Captain Newton, who knew he had to regain control. He confined the bosun to quarters for not acting as the one in charge, and he put Lees on a work detail and warned him that any further insubordination would be met harshly.

The next day Lees went in the longboat as part of the work detail. He and two others were charged to row a trading party ashore and return. Instead, the three deserted and climbed aboard a French ship anchored nearby and got drunk with some of the crew. Then they got into a brawl with the French crew and left that ship. In their drunken stupor they couldn't row and ran the longboat into a rocky shoal and couldn't get it off.

Newton was angry and frustrated. Not only had they taken the only available longboat, but now he needed it to go ashore to buy slaves. If he did not hurry, the slaves would be sold to other ship captains whose longboats were not hung up on the rocks.

When Lees and his two friends, "the terrible Toms" (Tom True and Tom Creed) were freed from the rocks by the *Duke of Argyle* crew, it was too late to buy slaves. The three men were brought harshly to stand before the captain by the other officers. Captain Newton ordered the men to strip to the waist and had them bend over the ship's guns where they were tied. Then Newton himself gave them a severe caning. Lees was locked up for his insolence and as ringleader, and the two Toms were given a warning to reform.

John's reaction did not make things better. He had forgotten that not too long ago he was like Lees. He could drink, swear, and show disobedience and disrespect as well as any man serving aboard the *Duke of Argyle*. The captain's memory was short, however. John expected better of his men.

A few days later Lees was back at his old tricks of festering unrest. He found some sympathy from others who had begun to grumble.

"I say we kill those bastards and take over the ship," Will Lees told the men. He emphasized his words by swinging his dagger and driving it into a tabletop. Then he told them the rest of his plan. "I say we slit their throats and toss 'em overboard. We'll sail the ship to some port where they won't know the *Duke of Argyle*. We can sell the slaves and divide the money. Then we can sail to somewhere nobody will think of lookin' for us and either sell the ship or sink it."

"You're talkin' mutiny, Lees," Tom Creed reminded him. "We can all hang for that."

One of the other sailors spoke up. "Listen. Will's right. We're only halfway through our voyage. I, for one, don't want to think about another year with those sissy officers—and especially the captain—he fancies himself a parson, not a sailor! I wouldn't mind havin' a share of the money we'll get for the slaves either."

Tom True added his allegiance to the plot. "I agree. Besides, the odds are in our favor. There's twenty-seven of us and only three of them."

"Yeah, but maybe not all the crew will come over to our side," Creed said.

"How many crew can we least get by with?" Lees asked.

The mutineers argued about that for several minutes and came to no conclusive answer. They decided to feel out the men and see how many they could depend upon.

Meanwhile, John had already decided that he had had enough of the rebellion of Lees and his companions. He told his first mate that as soon as they met a British naval ship he planned to exchange the worst four troublemakers.

That opportunity came while they were still in African waters. The HMS *Surprise* lay at anchor at the mouth of the Rokel River. John acted quickly; he took Jamie Dorset, the two Toms, along with Will Lees (whom he handcuffed and put in ankle irons first) by longboat to the

Surprise. Her commanding officer, Captain Baird, was agreeable to an exchange.

"We know how to break a troublemaker," he said loudly enough for the four to hear. "Take them below and keep them in irons until I decide what to do with them," Captain Baird ordered.

He then found four replacements who were more than eager to transfer from the naval warship to a slaver. John smiled. He recalled his own such transfer some years earlier.

The next day Captain Newton addressed the crew and told them from his personal experience the kind of life and treatment they might expect if they were exchanged with another British naval ship. He left a clear impression that he was not going to tolerate any more insolence or disobedience. John also used the occasion to instruct the men about some new policies he was putting into effect.

"I have found it to be better to treat the slaves more humanely. For this voyage we will not 'spoon pack' the slaves. This causes them hardship, and many of them die before we reach the New World," he announced.

The men grumbled inside but said nothing.

"We will also change the way we treat the females," the captain added. "No one is to take a woman or a girl and bed her. Raping and other deviant acts will no longer be tolerated. I will enforce this rule absolutely."

The men groaned at this latter rule. No captain had ever curtailed the crew's sexual appetites before. Captain Newton had given the matter a great deal of thought, however. He wanted to stay faithful to his wife, so by forbidding the men to have sexual contact with the African women, he was also making it easier to avoid temptation himself.

John then listed several other new policies he was putting into effect and dismissed the men.

JOE
MUSSER

Later, Robert Arthur, his second mate and the ship's surgeon, asked him about the new policies. "Why are you showing these savages such Christian charity?" he asked.

"Am I?" Newton replied. "I hadn't really thought about it. I suppose I am."

"I've served on a slaver most of my adult life, and I've never thought about those things. We just pack them in and take them to the colonies. But I suppose that taking better care of them means fewer of them will die—and that means more money for the company."

Captain Newton nodded but said nothing.

Arthur then asked, "But why don't you want the men to have their way with the women? I can't see what harm it'll do."

John thought for a moment then replied, surprising himself with his answer. "Because it's the right thing to do," he said.

Later that day John took a longboat and visited his old nemesis, Clow, on his island. When he greeted the trader, John noticed that the lime trees he had planted years earlier were now ripe with fruit.

"Well, Mr. Clow," John said grinning, "I am here just as you prophesied. Do you remember? You told me that one day I might return with a ship of my own and buy these limes from you."

Clow seemed edgy. He knew well of his words, but he had spoken them with cynicism, intending to rub Newton's nose in the hopelessness of such a reality. Now John seemed to be enjoying the moment.

"How much do you want for the limes?" he asked Clow.

Clow shrugged. "How many do you want?"

"All of them," Newton replied. "I'll buy them all."

Now Clow was smiling. The two men bargained for awhile over the value of the limes and settled on a price. Clow made arrangements for the fruit to be picked and crated, and John said he would see to it that they were brought aboard the *Duke of Argyle*. It took a little over a week to get the job done. Meanwhile, John continued to buy slaves for his voyage.

✝ ✝ ✝

The *Duke of Argyle* finally set sail from African waters in early May 1751. The crew was glad to be leaving for the New World. John led a special Sabbath service on Sunday morning and offered prayers for the journey.

Several days into the voyage, Captain Newton saw a burly sailor beating a pregnant African slave. He went over to the sailor and pulled him off the woman. To set an example of the enforcement of his new humane policies, he ordered the offending sailor to be flogged.

The rest of the men were called on deck to witness the flogging, but its intended effect backfired on John. The men sided with the sailor and began to grumble about the crazy new policies.

Then the grumbling became more structured. The men, in clusters away from the officers or while at work, began to talk about the ideas that Will Lees had fostered before he was exchanged. As if to complement the talk of mutiny, the weather turned sour. It stormed and rained almost constantly and got so cold that it became impossible to bring the slaves up for periodic washings and to clean the hold.

After awhile the stench belowdecks became unbearable. The crew begged for the slaves to be brought up and washed and for their quarters to be hosed. They were not all that concerned about the slaves' welfare. They were only concerned that the smells emanating from below were troubling them, even abovedecks in the fresh air.

To make matters worse, some of the slaves were sick with diarrhea. If the rest of them caught it, the situation could become disastrous. John decided to bring the slaves up and clean the cargo hold while they were being hosed off. In addition, he changed their diet from beans to rice after several of the slaves died. That more bland diet worked—the slaves got better, but at a price. The rice was more expensive than beans. John would have to make an accounting when he returned to Liverpool to justify his actions.

Captain Newton felt depressed. He stood at the stern of the *Duke of Argyle* as several corpses were dropped into the sea. One was a sailor who had died that morning. A brief funeral service was held for him, but the slaves were buried at sea without ceremony. Newton watched as sharks approached the floating cadavers and attacked the human remains in a feeding frenzy.

One of the sailors came to the stern rail and emptied the garbage from the galley. Another man emptied a barrel filled with dead rats that had been killed during the night as feed for the sharks.

Rats always outnumbered the crew and slaves. At each port hundreds would find their way on board and multiply during the voyage. This trip, however, the number of rats on board was exceedingly high. Each night dozens were trapped or killed. In spite of the kills, the rats still scurried all over the ship. All of the food barrels and containers were breached and contaminated. Most of the time the crew members were not bothered while they slept—their hammocks were well off the floor. However, with so many rats aboard even the hammocks were not free of them. At night sailors awakened with rats gnawing on their feet, hands, or ears. Everyone was bitten—some of the sailors had vicious bites.

The slaves were even more vulnerable to rat bites. They had no hammocks, and the detestable rodents were everywhere. An infant was killed when rats swarmed all over it and attacked it much as the sharks feasted on the corpses in the ocean.

On May 26, still six weeks from the end of their voyage, Newton had to put down another slave uprising. Twenty male slaves had found a way to pick the locks on their shackles and were about to free the others when they were discovered. After regaining control of the cargo hold, the sailors brought the ringleader up on deck where he was flogged to set an example. That ended the trouble for the remainder of the journey.

On the first of July, the slaves were brought topside and cleaned. By July 3, the men had been shaved and oiled just as the *Duke of Argyle* approached St. John's harbor in Antigua.

The slaves were unloaded and taken away to be sold. Mr. Manesty's agent, as usual, was on hand to supervise the transaction. John reported to the agent that six of his crew had died during the Middle Passage voyage while only six of the 174 slaves died.

"You were lucky," the shipping agent told Captain Newton. You should have carried more slaves—'spoon packed' in order to protect yourself. If you had lost the usual 20 percent, I'm certain you would have drawn the wrath of Mr. Manesty and his shareholders by returning to Liverpool with a loss of revenue."

Newton argued. "I believe that if the slaves are given more humane treatment and better food, fewer are lost."

"Maybe," the agent countered, "but you can't take that chance. We did a calculation on whether it was better to work a slave hard and wear him out or go easy on him. The study shows that working slaves hard means they only live about nine years, but it's cheaper to replace them than to spend money on better care."

"I see," said John. However, the facts of the matter seemed rather cruel to him.

The crew members busied themselves cleaning and fumigating the ship so the *Duke of Argyle* could load cargo for its return voyage. After hosing down the cargo hold, they prepared to fumigate the area. A mixture of pitch, tobacco, and sulfur was burned inside a kettle. The smells of burning tar, sulfur, and tobacco overwhelmed the other stenches—the tobacco adding some fragrance to the burning smell that was otherwise almost as noxious as the original stench.

Captain Newton delegated the assignments and left the first mate in charge of the work crews while he went to see if any letters had arrived for him. He was looking forward to receiving letters from Polly that he

could read now and re-read during the voyage back to England. John also hoped to find a letter or two from his father. The senior Captain Newton's tour of duty as governor of Fort York in the Hudson Bay Territory was ending, and John looked forward to seeing his father again soon.

John was pleasantly surprised to find, in addition to several letters from Polly, a letter from Dr. Jennings, one from his father, and one from Thomasin. For some reason, he opened Thomasin's letter first, as if to savor the others.

It was brief, and John expected it to contain bad news. It did. Thomasin wrote that John's father had drowned in a lake—apparently disabled by a cramp and unable to swim to safety. It happened only a few days before he was scheduled to leave for England.

John sat on a stump under a huge banyon tree and wept softly. He and his father had never been close, but in these later years they had begun to develop a deep affection for one another. Now his father was dead. John cried not so much from grief as for the many regrets he suddenly felt. Greatest among these regrets was his wish that his father could have seen the changes in his life. The older Captain Newton, after all, had only witnessed his son's estrangement and his slide into rebellion and sinfulness.

However, for these past three years everything about John was changed. His character, behavior, habits—all were being brought closer to the model he had read about in the book *Imitation of Christ* by Thomas á Kempis. Many other regrets were piled on top of these thoughts, and he continued to weep.

John suddenly sensed his own mortality, and depression overwhelmed him again. He didn't even read the other letters but put them in his pocket and walked back to the ship.

Chapter
Twenty-six

Thoughts on the Slave Trade

✝

Five weeks after news of the death of John's father, the *Duke of Argyle* set sail for England. Captain Newton was still grieving for his father when another calamity struck. Robert Arthur, the ship's surgeon and John's best friend aboard the *Duke of Argyle*, became ill with a tropical fever while they were in the West Indies. John had suggested that Robert stay in Antigua to recuperate, but he was anxious to get back home to England.

John did not insist on his staying—after all, Robert was the ship's surgeon and should have known whether he was well enough to travel or not. Several days into the voyage, however, he got worse, and he died the next day.

Now Captain Newton also grieved the loss of his dear friend, companion, and confidant. John tried to keep busy to overcome his grief. He had his crew catch the winds to maximum force. The *Duke of Argyle* ran

fast with the autumn winds and seasonal storms pushing them furiously through the North Atlantic. It was the time for hurricanes, but the experienced crew pushed their ship relentlessly.

The *Duke of Argyle* sailed into Liverpool on October 3, 1751. The details of the cargo and manifest kept him busy for a month, so John didn't get to see Polly until Saturday, November 2. His wife had missed him greatly, as he had missed her. Their reunion was something like a honeymoon. Although she still lived with her parents in Chatham, they stole away for a time alone. Then John decided they should rent a house in Liverpool when he was home.

Polly had learned her lessons well at the women's seminary near Chatham before she was married. Yet, her lessons had more to do with becoming a good homemaker than equipping her for intellectual activity. Polly was pretty, dressed well and modestly, and was a stimulating partner and conversationalist. She read many of the books John had read earlier but found them to be a little too theoretical.

During his furlough, John continued to read Christian books and the Bible, and he prayed during his own daily quiet time.

One day Polly interrupted his meditations. "John," she asked, "may I join in your prayer time? Would you pray aloud?"

"Of course," he replied, feeling a little ashamed that he had never thought to include her before.

His list of prayer requests included Thomasin and his father's other children, thanksgiving to God for his safe return from the last voyage, and petitions for his next journey. He also prayed for God's care of his wife and wisdom to learn the discipline of serving Christ.

When he finished, he saw Polly still kneeling beside her chair. Without looking up, she asked, "Could you pray again for me—that the Almighty will favor me with a child?"

John appended that request to his previous prayers and was hopeful that the Lord would indeed favor Polly and him with a child. It wasn't as

if they had not *tried* to have a baby. True, he was at sea much of the time but when he was home they enjoyed lovemaking and looked forward to having a child. Now that they had their own rented house, they were also less inhibited in their lovemaking and enjoyed more times of playful pleasure and bliss.

One day John ran into an old acquaintance and physician, Dr. William Whitney, on the street outside his Liverpool office. After the usual small talk, John asked the doctor, "My wife and I are having some difficulty trying to conceive a child. Can you give us some advice? Is there something we can take to help?"

"Well, Newton," Dr. Whitney laughed, "you *do* know how to make babies, I trust?"

Seeing John's serious expression, the doctor didn't pursue his joke. He put his hand on John's shoulder and leaned in to speak more quietly. "Tell me, son, did you ever get a disease while sailing?" he asked.

"A disease? Of course—I've had all kinds— fevers, malaria—"

"No," Dr. Whitney interrupted. "I mean syphilis or gonorrhea," he said bluntly.

The doctor did not need to wait for John's answer. His face became flushed, red with embarrassment.

The doctor told him quietly, "I have found that when a man has . . . uh . . . been with other women, he usually catches these diseases. It's nearly universal with sailors. If you've had syphilis, especially, you may *never* be able to have children, John. I'm sorry."

John mumbled his thanks and excused himself. As he walked away, he felt terrible. One of the consequences of his earlier promiscuity was now taking its toll. John was reminded that while he had been *forgiven* of his sins, he couldn't eradicate the human consequences of his former actions. He felt sick and ashamed, mostly because her barrenness was something he could neither explain to Polly nor receive her forgiveness for.

John spent the next few months showering his wife with affection and constant attention, as if to make up for the fact that Polly would never conceive. He felt hypocritical to continue praying that Polly would have a child, but he reckoned that he should not extinguish her hopes.

✝ ✝ ✝

In April 1752, word was sent from Manesty's office that a ship was ready for John to sail on another voyage. He was told to report to the Liverpool dockyards in order to make ready for the journey. The ship was brand new, just recently arrived from the shipyards and appropriately named the *African*.

The *African,* being new, had some modern refinements. For one thing, it had a great deal more headroom belowdecks so the crew could walk without stooping.

While the carpenters were still on board, John ordered that a barricade of sorts be constructed in the slaves' quarters in the cargo hold. After two previous attempted mutinies by the slaves, he felt that an additional protective wall would add some security.

At last the *African* was ready to sail. On the evening before departure, Captain Newton spent his final hours with Polly. After dinner he read from the Scriptures and prayed. He could sense something was making his wife uneasy. "Can you help me, John?" she asked. "I want to have your faith. I don't see things as clearly as you do. I want God in my life—as he is in yours—so that while you are away I can talk to him as you have done here."

John smiled. He felt an enormous sense of love for Polly and gratitude to God for speaking to her spirit in this way. The two of them knelt, and John prayed for Polly. Then, in a soft voice not much above a whisper, Polly spoke to God—first with the usual formal approach to him, then with words from her heart.

"Almighty and all-knowing God, Lord of all the earth and heaven, I beseech thee to hearken unto my voice," Polly began. Then the words tumbled out from her heart, not just her head. "I ask for your forgiveness. I have been disagreeable with my husband and spiteful to my family. I have been selfish and impatient," Polly continued. "You have convicted me with all that I have read in the Scriptures. I am a great sinner, and I now confess my sinfulness to thee and ask for thy forgiveness."

John almost smiled. Her litany of sins was so tame weighed against his. Why, Polly was a saint compared to him. Yet, in *her* eyes she knew she had failings and found it impossible to measure up to God's standards as she understood them. John was amazed to see that she recognized her own shortcomings and still felt the need to be delivered from them.

Halfway through her prayer, Polly began to weep in real repentance. She asked God to forgive her and for Christ's Spirit to come and live in her as he had done for John.

At the conclusion of the prayer they were both weeping, not tears of regret and repentance now, but expressions of deep joy. At last the two partners were one. They felt a sense of love and unity that was deeper and greater than their marital affections for each other. It was mystical, amazing, and wonderful. That night their lovemaking had unusual passion and accord.

The soft breeze drifted in their bedroom window, and the fragrance of summer flowers was still fresh in the air. The two of them lay naked in each other's arms, talking softly and lovingly. John cupped her face in his hand and kissed her with great tenderness. Polly's hair fell over her shoulders, and she seemed wistful as her arms held John tightly, as if to keep him from leaving England. Their night of love would sustain him for months to follow as he recalled it many times in moments of loneliness or tension.

The next day, June 30, 1752, the *African* set sail for her namesake continent. Within six weeks the ship was making initial arrangements to take on slaves for its maiden voyage to the colonies. It took more than eight months to buy enough human cargo for the trip.

John's letters to Polly were frequent and filled with spiritual insights he had found in his reading. He didn't say much to her about the violence and cruelty of the slave trade. He only shared two major events with her, and these were glossed over so as to not worry her.

The first was a death threat by a deranged and jealous trader who made a false accusation against John and planned to lure him ashore where he could murder him. The night before this was to happen, John had a dream that he took as a warning. John decided not to be in the longboat that went ashore that day, so the murder plot never went forward. (It was only revealed later when the man who plotted against John was found out.)

The second event took place after the *African* was about to sail to Antigua with its cargo of slaves. John uncovered another plot. This time two slaves had stolen a chisel and were trying to break their chains when they were caught. A subsequent search of the slave quarters belowdecks turned up more chisels, some knives, and even some gunpowder.

The ringleaders were punished but continued to cause a great deal of noisy unrest and trouble. John pulled out these troublemakers and put them aboard another British ship. This move brought quiet aboard the *African,* and the remaining slaves almost seemed glad that the troublemakers had been taken away.

That night John thought about the slaves—the troublemakers as well as the obedient ones. Then a thought came to him to pray for the slaves. He wondered, *Why don't I pray for them?* It was an audacious idea. He had never prayed for an African before in his life. *Why not?* He realized that he had never before thought of them as human beings—only cargo.

With that, John began to pray regularly for the slaves below in the cargo hold. He also went to see them and began to take notice of them. He saw that they were individuals, human beings in desperate need of God's help and protection.

John's knowledge of African dialects helped him to talk with individual slaves. He was surprised, however, that one man, Owolabi, could speak fairly decent English. Owolabi told him that he was the son of a powerful chief. "I have much learning. I have learned the languages of eleven tribes and traveled to many lands," he said.

"One day a white man came to our people from a land you English call Scotland," Owolabi told John. "We called him 'Mr. White Man,' and he taught us how to read and write. He told us of the one true God and his Son, Jesus. All the people in our tribe became followers of Jesus. Mr. White Man taught us how to pray and ask the Spirit of Jesus to walk with us and fight evil spirits and voodoo magic.

"Then one day, Mr. White Man was killed. We knew him no more. After that, other white men came. They told us they were followers of Jesus also, but they lied to us. They really came to capture us and kill our old wise ones. They raped our women and took us to the slave ships.

"I cannot understand," Owolabi told John. "Why do these evil men call themselves followers of Jesus?"

John shuffled his feet uncomfortably and said nothing, but his conscience said, *I am one of those evil men who call themselves followers of Jesus, and I am killing these people.* It was a powerful accusation, and for the rest of the voyage Owolabi's unsettling question troubled Captain Newton.

As he reflected on his thoughts, John made several changes aboard the *African.* He ordered his crew to treat the slaves in a more humane manner and forbade them to abuse them in any way—especially the women. He felt somewhat better, but his conscience still bothered him—about the whole system of slavery to be sure—but specifically about his role in it.

The change in Newton's attitude was also reflected in the Sunday services. John shortened them and made them more understandable. Instead of the long readings from obscure Scripture texts and the *Book of Common Prayers,* John often gave a brief homily based on a relevant Bible passage. He explained, "My policies regarding the treatment of the slaves are not new. Jesus told us in Matthew's Gospel about the Golden Rule—'do unto others as you would have others do unto you' is our 'rule' for the treatment of the slaves."

The crew may not have agreed with his change in attitude toward the slaves, but at least they no longer fell asleep during worship services, and that was something.

✝ ✝ ✝

The *African* was plagued with summer storms, another uprising, and a near mutiny during the Middle Passage crossing. The strain was showing on Newton, and he began to spend more time than usual in his cabin reading. The ship finally arrived in the West Indies and was diverted to the island of St. Kitts instead of Antigua.

As usual, Mr. Manesty's agent, Francis Guilchard, was on hand to greet Newton and take charge of the cargo. Of the more than two hundred slaves brought aboard in Africa, twenty-eight died at sea. John busied himself and the crew with the task of cleaning and fumigating the ship and loading cargo to take back to Liverpool. Six weeks later the *African* was on its way back to England with her cargo holds filled with tobacco, cotton, and sugar.

Not long after their departure from St. Kitts, Captain Newton found himself missing the slave Owolabi. On the Middle Passage journey, John and the African had had many conversations. John was impressed with his intelligence and amazing faith. The African's faith was simple and uncomplicated in contrast to his, but John felt that Owolabi was in many ways closer to God. However, Owolabi was sold on the island, and

John felt enormous shame for his traitorous role in condemning this intelligent and pious slave to a slow death of forced servitude. After that, Newton began to question the whole idea of slavery—especially slave *trading*. He was troubled about these thoughts all the way back to England and prayed that he might find another occupation.

With favorable winds the *African* reached Liverpool by late August, just fourteen months after sailing on her maiden voyage. After unloading the cargo and seeing to the refitting of his ship, Captain Newton took a coach to Chatham to bring Polly back to Liverpool where they would have only two months of time together before he had to sail again.

John was glad to be with his wife, and she had missed him terribly. They spent much time together talking and catching up on what had happened in their lives during their separation. Newton also shared with Polly his misgivings about the slave trade and his desire to get out of the cruel, violent business.

"That would be wonderful," Polly told him. "I worry constantly for your safety on these trips."

"But I am concerned more and more that I am becoming callous toward those poor wretches that are taken into slavery. I learned that they typically live only nine or ten years and are literally worked to death. It seems too cruel for an accident of birth that makes them vulnerable to marauding mercenaries who kidnap them from their homes and tear them away from their families," John said with a deep sigh, then added, "We give better care to our livestock than to these poor souls."

"Then let us pray that God will give you another occupation," Polly said.

"Yes, that's what I have been praying for these past months." Yet, it never occurred to either John or Polly to pray for an end to the terrible slave trade itself. That evil was already far too pervasive in the world to change it.

Chapter Twenty-seven

Final Voyage

✠

John had talked with Mr. Manesty about the next voyage of the *African* and learned that it would sail in late October. As the days approached, John became more and more morose about the trip. There was only one bright note—Manesty wanted the *African* to be in St. Kitts in six months, the shortest trip John had ever made.

As the time grew nearer for departure, John was on the docks supervising the loading of cargo aboard the *African* when he heard a familiar voice call out his name.

"Newton! Hey John!" It was his friend and shipmate aboard the *Harwich,* Job Lewis. "Man, I still remember the day you connived your way off the Harwich and out of the Royal Navy."

"Job! Is that really you?" John called out excitedly. "What are you doing here?"

"I've finished my tour on the *Harwich* and have worked my way up on other ships."

"Any luck?"

"Yeah," Lewis replied. "I've finally been given command of my own ship. Can you imagine that, Newton?"

"Hey, Job. It's really good to see you again. How long has it been? How are you?" The two had run into each other several times over the past ten years, but it had been three years since their last meeting.

Job shrugged and grinned, "I'm the same old fellow. You taught me well, Newton. I can drink most of my shipmates under the table, and I've been busy corrupting the saintly ones who come under my—uh—'tutor-age.' Remember how we used to show the young recruits how to find the road to hell?" Lewis laughed and slapped his friend on the back, but Newton could only master a sheepish, ashamed grin.

"Well, that was the old Newton," John said. "I've changed. I'm married too. How about you?"

"Me? Nah—you know the old saying, 'Why buy a cow when you can take from the entire meadow?'" Lewis joked.

John felt increasingly uncomfortable in the presence of Job Lewis. True, his speech was corrupt, but the real reason John was so troubled was because Job's vile habits were of Newton's making. He was sick to think about it.

The two men exchanged news about all that had happened during the past ten years, and then Job said, "I'm scheduled to sail at the end of the week." The men then shook hands and Job walked away. As he watched his old friend walking the docks to his ship, John wished he could have a chance to undo all that he had done to corrupt Job's morals.

Two days later John ran into Job again. He seemed upset and had been drinking. "Have you heard?" he asked John.

"Heard what?"

"My ship. It's gone," Job muttered.

"What do you mean, 'gone'?" Newton asked.

"The whole bloody damn business went bankrupt. The lenders have foreclosed and taken the ships." Job went on to explain his situation, peppering it liberally with the most vile and blasphemous language. John cringed but was sympathetic to his friend's dilemma.

"Let me talk to Mr. Manesty. He runs the shipping company that I work for. I'll ask him to let you serve with me so he'll see how well you do. Then when we return from this voyage, he can give you command of your own ship," John suggested.

Job's eyes, glazed from too much rum, cleared for an instant in recognition of John's idea.

"Go get yourself a room and get cleaned up. See if you can sober up in case Mr. Manesty will want to see you," Newton told him.

When John told Manesty his idea, Manesty agreed to the plan.

The *African* sailed on October 21, 1753. John had created a special position for Job Lewis as an assistant to the captain, and it was Job's responsibility to learn as much of the slave trade seafaring business as possible in order to command a slave ship of his own on their return. John also hoped to use their months at sea to undo much of the damage he had done to the character and habits of his friend. He began by telling him of the miraculous events surrounding his conversion aboard the *Greyhound.*

"You were just calling out to God because you were afraid of death," Job countered. "I'd probably do the same. It was just luck, not God, that your ship was saved."

"But how do you explain the difference in my life?" John asked. "These past several years God has become even more real in my life. He has saved my life on many other occasions—just as miraculously as he did on the *Greyhound.* He changed my speech, my habits—everything.

And the Lord has given me a hunger for prayer and trying to live as Christ would have me live."

Job laughed and swore belligerently.

Newton would not give up on his friend. "I am praying that God will help me reverse that terrible thing I did ten years ago when I corrupted your faith and taught you to sin."

"Don't lose any sleep over me, Captain," Job sneered. "If it hadn't been you to open my eyes, I'd have never experienced all that life has to offer."

Over the next weeks Job Lewis confounded every effort of Captain Newton to undo his depraved condition. At Sunday worship he mocked Newton and God, and he undermined the captain's orders at every opportunity.

When they got to Africa, Lewis contemptuously disobeyed John's orders on how to treat the slaves. At first, whenever he wanted to have sex with one of the women, he at least did so when the party was ashore and out of the captain's sight. As time went on, however, Job grew bolder in his efforts to abuse and corrupt other crew members.

Once he convinced someone to break into the storeroom, steal a keg of ale, and pass out mugs of it to the crew, getting most of them drunk. Another time he made someone else steal a case of snuff. When the thefts were discovered, Captain Newton had the two men flogged with the vicious cat-o'-nine-tails. Job jeered from the sidelines as the men were beaten. From the looks on the faces of the crew, John figured out what had taken place but did nothing to punish his old friend.

Every time Newton tried to reform or convert Lewis, he was thwarted by the man's vile, depraved actions. It was hopeless, and John was growing more irritable toward the man.

When the *African* reached the Sherbro Islands off the coast of Sierra Leone, it was already December. Just off the starboard bow of his ship, Captain Newton noticed another slave ship. It seemed empty and lay

derelict at anchor in the harbor. When they went ashore, John inquired about the ship. He learned that it was a British ship called the *Racehorse* and that African slaves had murdered her captain and crew in an escape attempt. Local traders, who now offered it for sale, had recaptured the ship.

During the next few days Captain Newton negotiated to buy the *Racehorse*. Manesty had ordered the *African* to be in St. Kitts within six months—hardly enough time to get enough cargo to make the trip profitable. John could leave Job in command and have the *Racehorse* stay behind for awhile longer to take on more cargo of slaves and cam-wood. The added profitability from two ships' cargo would go a long way in paying for the *Racehorse,* which Newton had acquired at a bar-gain price.

The emotional bonus of this transaction was just as important—John would be rid of Job Lewis and wouldn't have to worry about unrest or mutiny resulting from the man's unrestrained, unregenerate nature.

John hired crew for the *Racehorse* from some of the land-based traders. He wrote out a letter of commission appointing Job Lewis as captain, but he hedged his bet by sending along his first mate, Mr. Taylor, to keep an eye on Lewis and run the ship.

The *Racehorse* sailed on January 18, 1754. It was to rendezvous with the *African* a fortnight later, after both ships made efforts to buy cargo. However, when the *African* reached Bonthe ten days later, the other ship was nowhere in sight. Newton waited. The next day a lookout sighted the *Racehorse* to the north. When the *Racehorse* came into view, John noticed that her colors were flying at half-mast.

After the ship anchored near the *African,* Mr. Taylor was the first man into the longboat. Captain Job Lewis was neither in the boat nor on deck. Newton watched as his first mate climbed aboard the *African* to report.

"What is it, Mr. Taylor?" Newton asked.

"I'm sorry, sir," the first mate said softly. "It's Captain Lewis. He's dead, sir."

The hair on the back of John's neck stood up. He bit his lip and asked for more details.

"Well, sorry to say, Captain Lewis got drunk right away when we left you, sir. And when slaves were brought on board, he treated them shamefully, Captain. He cut some of them up pretty bad. And one of the women—uh—well, she died, sir. He got terribly violent, and some of the crew got scared and threatened to go back to shore.

"Then, three days after we left you, the captain got a bad fever. He was ranting and raving like a madman. I've never heard such awful swearing—and mind you, I'm a sailor. It was like he had a devil inside him. The next day, he died—still screaming hate and vile things. We buried him at sea."

"Did he call out to God at the end?" John asked hopefully.

"Well, not really. He did say that he knew he was dying and going to hell," Taylor replied.

"But he didn't call on God?"

"No sir, he didn't. The whole crew watched him die. We were afraid that lightning might strike us from heaven the way he was screaming those awful things. But he never said anything about God. He just kept repeating over and over that he was dying and going to hell," Taylor said.

"He didn't believe in hell," John observed. *Thanks to me,* he thought. "I knew him well. He didn't believe in God, and he didn't believe in hell either," John said.

"Oh, he believed in hell," Taylor observed. "No doubt about it. He believed in God *and* hell."

John sighed. "He told me that we all call out at death because we're afraid. He said that God didn't exist, but I argued that when I was faced with death I was convinced that God *does* exist. I'm afraid that when he died he was only convinced of hell. He had no hope. It's sad."

"Yeah, but we're all the better off for his dying, sir. The man was wretched, worse than ever I saw before," Taylor said, shaking his head.

"Mr. Taylor, there was one who was every bit as 'wretched' as Captain Lewis. May God forgive me," John muttered.

That night John wept for the lost soul of his former friend. He also cried out of shame and regret for having been every bit as wicked as Job but somehow escaping God's judgment.

✝ ✝ ✝

The *Racehorse* sailed for St. Kitts shortly after Job's death, with Mr. Taylor as acting captain. The *African* sailed with the *Racehorse*. The slaves on board the two ships were fewer and less likely to cause trouble, so John spent much of his time reading and meditating about the strange ways of God.

Halfway across the Atlantic, John was stricken with a terrible fever, reminiscent of the one he had when he was a slave in Africa on the Clow plantation. For more than a week he was too sick to get out of bed and was delirious most of the time. He could not tell the difference between his nightmarish hallucinations and reality.

The ship's surgeon stayed by his side and tried to help but could offer no solutions for the strange illness. Occasionally John had a lucid moment or two, and when he could think, he felt he was dying, just as Job had.

"What do you think, Mr. Booth?" John asked the ship's surgeon.

The surgeon shook his head. "I've done all I can do, sir. I'll keep using this wet cloth to try and bring down your fever, but I can't think of anything else to help. Captain, it may be that you *are* dying."

John nodded. "But I won't go screaming at God and terrified about hell," he said in a hoarse whisper. "I'll go with praises on my lips for God's grace to me, for his protection and other blessings as well. I'm not afraid of dying, Mr. Booth. The Scriptures assure me that 'he is able also

to save them to the uttermost that come unto God by him.' Because Christ has died in my place, I am ready to face my judge."

That night his fever left him. It was as if he had validated that he was indeed ready to die and God no longer required him to prove it.

God then gave Captain Newton another blessing. The *African* and the *Racehorse* had an uneventful and trouble-free voyage to St. Kitts while John recuperated from the illness. Still weak, he stayed in his cabin and spent the time in constant prayer, offering up two major matters to God. He prayed that he would be given a greater understanding of his faith in Christ so that he might be used of God in undoing the harm he had brought to Job Lewis through his reckless and godless behavior and beliefs. His second prayer petition was for God to find another occupation for him so that he would not have to continue in the slave trade.

Despite his illness, John was able to maintain the schedule Manesty had given him. When the *African* and the *Racehorse* arrived in St. Kitts that April afternoon, the Manesty Shipping Company agent, Francis Guilchard, was on hand to meet the ships. He was astounded that not one slave had died during the Middle Passage crossing.

John rested a great deal during the time his ships were being cleaned and outfitted for the return trip to England. One night, at a party given by the Guilchards at their home in Basse Terre in St. Kitts, John was introduced to another sea captain. His name was Alexander Clunie, but unlike Captain Newton, he was not a slave ship captain. John envied that of the man.

As the two carried on a casual conversation, John could not help but notice the results of his own occupation all around him. Two African children were dressed in Western clothes and sat in a corner pulling on the ropes that operated a huge ceiling fan. Other slaves brought food and drinks on trays to offer the guests. The food was no doubt the result of the labor of field hands toiling in the hot sun, day in and day out. Outside, just beyond his view of the veranda, John watched still other

slaves attend to the horses and carriages. They went about their work without expression, their eyes empty and seemingly soulless.

John welcomed the distraction of meeting Clunie. It took his mind off the distressing guilt and remorse that was a growing part of his work.

"Tell me, Mr. Clunie, how long have you been a sea captain?" Newton asked.

"Please. Call me Alex," Clunie replied in his thick Scottish accent. The man was some years older than John and a bit taller and heavier. John immediately liked the man. He was friendly but not overbearing and seemed genuinely interested in the person he was talking with.

The two men talked about their respective experience as sea captains and gradually turned to other topics. John told him about his recent illness and how he had expected to die. "However, I believe that God may still have a use for me, so he spared my life again," John explained. Then he told him about his conversion at sea aboard the *Greyhound*.

Clunie's facial expressions encouraged John to tell more of his story. He gave an account of the death of his friend, Job Lewis, and his deep regrets for having caused his friend to take the road that had led him to hell. Clunie put his hand on John's shoulder as Newton's eyes welled with tears at the telling of the story.

"I can tell that you are man of God," Clunie said simply. "You are an answer to my prayers. I asked God to lead me to another Christian for fellowship. How about having dinner aboard my ship tomorrow evening so we can talk some more?"

"I'd be delighted," John replied with a broad smile.

Nightly dinner conversations between the two men continued for the next two months. As it turned out, Alex Clunie belonged to an independent church in Stepney—just a short distance from John's birthplace near London. The two men had even more in common. Clunie's minister was the Reverend Samuel Brewer, whom John knew to be a friend of his own clergyman, Dr. Jennings.

Alex was a mature believer and helped John with his progress in refining his faith. John had read the Bible and a number of books but lacked the interaction with others to shape and understand the ideas he read about. Clunie was an able advocate for spiritual truth and served as a sounding board to Newton's queries. In the two months of their conversations (most of them lasting until the middle of the night or until daybreak), John's insights began to take shape, and his understanding was confirmed.

Alex Clunie also helped John to become discerning about Christian matters. Until now, John had thought that anyone who said he was a Christian should be taken at his word. Clunie pointed out that the devil often uses "wolves in sheep's clothing" to confuse and create doubt. Alex said, "Not everyone who claims to be a minister of Christ is really what he says. You must listen to his words and observe his actions. If he denies the truth of the Holy Bible with either words or actions, then be careful. You may be listening to a false prophet."

It was Clunie who explained to Newton that he should be an "evangelical" in matters of faith—to believe all of the Bible implicitly, to believe in the deity of Christ completely, and to rely on the Holy Spirit for guidance. Alex also told John that he ought to be more open about sharing his faith, telling others about God. "If you can influence another person to seek God by your willingness to talk boldly about him, perhaps your remorse for having led your friend Job Lewis astray will lessen," he told John.

The conversations between these two sea captains cemented their friendship. John felt that he had benefited most from their times together. When it was time to sail back to England, the two men parted with a bond between them that was greater than two blood brothers.

✝ ✝ ✝

The *African* and the *Racehorse* sailed into Liverpool harbor in mid-August, making the round-trip journey in record time. Manesty commended Captain Newton for his exemplary accomplishments. Not only was the voyage the shortest ever, but John had lost no slaves during the crossing. Manesty was also quite pleased with his new ship, the *Racehorse,* which John had brought back with him.

"I appreciate your fine work, Captain Newton," he told John, "but I'm disappointed in the ship. I was hoping the *African* would have performed better than it did. I have another ship coming from the shipyards in a few weeks. I think you'll like her much better."

"I'm sure I will, Mr. Manesty," John said.

"I want you to be involved in the final touches to the shipbuilding. You should even pick a name for her, since you'll be sailing her. The ship should be ready to sail in five or six weeks," Manesty explained.

John hurried to Chatham for a reunion and brought Polly back to Liverpool to live in their rented house until he was to sail around the first of October. The couple was happy to be together once more and sought to make the most of their brief time in Liverpool.

As he supervised the final shipbuilding activities for the *Bee* (as he had named the new ship), John was unexpectedly depressed. It was hard for him to sleep at night. His dreams were filled with recollections of the terrible things he had faced during his times in Africa. During the day he was equally troubled as he thought about the cruelty and violence of the slave trade. He knew he should have no part of it but was unable to think of a way to extricate himself from it.

As the ship was finished and launched, this work should have distracted John from his dilemma, but it didn't. He was busy making final arrangements for their departure. John had signed on a brand-new

crew, the cargo had been loaded, and the ship was ready to sail. Yet, John didn't want to leave.

Joseph Manesty decided to celebrate the occasion with a party for John and Polly. Mrs. Manesty's servant girl brought in a tray of canapés and tea from India. The two women chatted about Polly's planned trip back to Chatham while the men naturally talked business.

Manesty was congratulating Newton on how smoothly everything had come together for the *Bee*'s crew and cargo. He was in midsentence when John suddenly stood up and stared wide-eyed at his host. No words came out of his mouth, and his face was drained of its color. Then, as a tree falling in the forest, his stiffened body dropped forward onto the Manesty's parlor floor with a force that rattled the teacups on the tray.

Polly screamed and ran to her husband as Manesty jumped up to also help John. Newton was unconscious but breathing in shallow breaths. Manesty loosened John's collar and unbuttoned his jacket. Then he called to a servant to fetch a doctor. A physician came quickly and examined the still unconscious sea captain. He held a small bottle of spirits under John's nose and it revived him after several passes. John was then placed on a couch in Manesty's home while the doctor ministered to his needs. By evening John was able to speak, but his speech was slurred and he had a terrible headache.

The physician diagnosed John as having had an apoplectic stroke or seizure. He told him to stay in bed for a week or more in order to gradually regain his strength.

Meanwhile, Manesty found another captain for the *Bee,* and the ship sailed.

In a few days the doctor returned to examine Newton again. He informed John that he could never again go back to being a sea captain. John was twenty-nine years old.

Concerned about making a living for Polly and himself, John asked Manesty if he could find him land-based work. His employer urged him

not to worry about that now. "You just concentrate on getting well. We'll take care of you when you're ready to go back to work."

Weeks passed as John rested and could finally talk without slurring his words. After a year of recuperation, John was feeling better.

Then, in late summer of 1755, John received news about the *Bee*. The ship was taken over in a bloody, violent slave uprising. The ship was recaptured and eventually brought back to Liverpool, but the captain of the *Bee* along with most of the ship's crew had been killed.

Chapter
Twenty-eight

No More Voyages

✠

John Newton thought often about his friendship with Alex Clunie in the West Indies and their times of spiritual fellowship and learning. In June 1755, John took Polly to London where she could see her family while he visited Clunie's church in Stepney.

Reverend Samuel Brewer greeted John as an old friend. Clunie had written his pastor about the sea captain he had met and their discussions together in St. Kitts. John appreciated his conversation with the minister and told him of his desire to be used in service for God.

Reverend Brewer told John about a young evangelical preacher, George Whitefield. Whitefield had been holding large meetings in England and America. He and another Church of England minister, John Wesley, had the religious community radically off balance by their preaching. Each had the audacity to proclaim to "Christian" people that

despite their cultural ties to the church, they were sinners who needed to be "born again."

The staid clergy establishment criticized Whitefield and Wesley as being too "emotional" about religion. However, the common people who heard the two preachers were transformed by their fiery messages. Religious revivals broke out all across England and in the American colonies—everywhere the two had been.

At the end of John's conversation with Reverend Brewer, the minister wrote a letter of introduction for John to meet Whitefield, who had just returned from America.

Newton traveled to London and looked up the address Reverend Brewer had given him. John was driven to a small flat in the city where he got out of the carriage and told the driver to wait. He walked up the brick walk, reached for the large brass knocker on the door, and announced his presence. After a minute or two, the door opened.

John thought the man at the door was probably Whitefield's secretary. He was about forty and appeared to be friendly.

"Excuse me," he told the man. "My name is John Newton. I have a letter of introduction from Reverend Brewer in Stepney. Would you kindly give it to Reverend Whitefield with my request for a meeting?"

"I'm Reverend Whitefield," the man said, "but I must apologize for not being able to see you just now. I have some important letters to finish right away—a ship is sailing today for Carolina, and I must send these letters with her. But let me give you a ticket for my services on Sunday. Perhaps I can see you after one of the services."

John took the ticket and thanked Whitefield. As the hackney cab took him back to his rented room, John stared at the ticket. He had never known anyone who needed an admission ticket to attend a worship service. It all seemed quite strange.

On Sunday John arrived early at the place advertised on the ticket and saw that a thousand people were already there. A huge wooden

"tabernacle" had been erected as a temporary facility to protect the listeners from the weather. Within a half hour the tabernacle was completely filled, with most of the audience standing.

Whitefield lived up to his reputation. His voice, like thunder, proclaimed the truths of God to the masses crowded inside the tabernacle as well as the hundreds who stood outside. Newton had never heard anything like it. The fiery oratory seemed to overwhelm the listeners. Whitefield presented his sermon in plain, direct, uncomplicated English. The concepts of heaven and hell were made clear, and the preacher asked his listeners to respond to what God was telling them.

John felt an unusual consonance about the place. At times the hair on his neck stood up—he was so excited by what the preacher was saying. But there was something else. It seemed to Newton that a supernatural quality had infused the entire tabernacle. *God is here in this place,* he thought.

The morning service lasted more than three hours, yet to John the time seemed to slip away in an instant. Whitefield's booming voice declared, "All of you here today are sinners! You can't get away from that fact. I didn't say that. God did. He said, *'All* have sinned and come short of the glory of God.' Yet, you can go to church all your life and miss this great truth. The Bible says we must be born again in order to go to heaven.

"I plead with you to act on what the Spirit of God is telling you today. Yield to that 'still small voice' within you that is convicting you of sin and drawing you toward Christ. Come forward and repent! Repent and be delivered from damnation and hell, I say!"

John was astounded to see several hundred people, many of them sobbing openly as they moved forward unashamedly. They wasted no time in pushing through the crowd toward the "penitent's bench" at the front of the tabernacle where they fell to their knees and cried out to God.

This part of the service was a bit noisy but still restrained. Then a spirit of calmness prevailed while the seekers wept and cried out to the Lord. John had never seen anything quite like it before, and he was entirely energized by the experience.

He never got a chance to speak with Whitefield, but many of the questions he had hoped to ask him were answered through the words of the sermon. John reviewed the events of the morning all Sunday afternoon. Then he remembered that an evening service was to be held at the tabernacle as well. He returned in the evening and was as excited about that service as the morning one.

When John returned to Chatham, he had much to tell Polly.

✚ ✚ ✚

Joseph Manesty knew that Captain John Newton could not return to sailing but was hard-pressed to know what to do with him. John had asked Manesty to help him find a land-based job, but Manesty had not been successful. He was persistent, however, and did try to help his former sea captain and protégé.

John continued to look for almost a year. Then, miraculously, Manesty was able to use his influence in getting John a "plum" appointment as a tide surveyor for the British Customs and Excise Bureau.

John gladly accepted the position. John and another man took turns searching inbound ships for contraband and figuring the British excise tax for the ships' cargo. Every other week Newton stayed in the tiny dockside office while his partner inspected ships. Then they alternated. The work was hard and often lasted well into the night, but it had an interesting benefit. Whenever the agents found smuggled contraband, it was confiscated then sold by the government. The agent was permitted to keep half the value for himself.

In less than a month after starting his new job, John was pleased to learn that George Whitefield was coming to hold meetings in Liverpool.

Newton again visited the services, this time held outdoors and not in a tabernacle, and was once again lifted up by the sermons of the impassioned preacher.

On one occasion John got an opportunity to see Whitefield and asked to meet with him privately. The two men finally met and soon became good friends. This extraordinary clergyman was an encouragement to John. He gave Newton some books and some of his printed sermons and pamphlets to read to further bolster John's faith.

One of the books, written by John Wesley, captured John's interest. In it Wesley condemned the usual practice of accepting bribes or other payments in business. Wesley declared that the practice was wrong.

John was bothered by this sermon. He had followed the traditional practice of accepting gratuities from shipowners or captains but had always tried to maintain an honest approach and not let the gratuity become a bribe. Still, he was now bothered by even the "appearance of evil."

Newton continued to study and read. He always tried to put into practice the things he read about. In 1756 he put his own thoughts on paper and paid a printer to publish a number of copies. The essay, *Thoughts on Religious Associations,* contained ideas for improving society. He mailed a copy to all the ministers within the greater Liverpool area.

That same year he also began to speak in public. Many had heard him tell the story about his conversion, and it had a tremendous impact upon them. Once he was even asked to testify at an outdoor meeting. Eventually, as he became more polished, his dramatic message was increasingly effective.

In 1758 several of Newton's friends suggested that he should become a minister, an idea John dismissed because he didn't believe he had the powerful gifts of oratory possessed by Whitefield and Wesley.

Still, he studied Greek, Hebrew, and Latin to improve his understanding of the Bible and theology. His self-study was comparable to a university education but probably would not have impressed the church

leaders who normally approved the credentials of their clergy. Newton, nevertheless, impressed Harry Crook, a friend of John Wesley, who was a member of the Church of England despite his associations with the Methodist Wesley.

Crook asked Newton, "Would you consider being a curate in our church?"

John was humbled by the man's confidence in him. "I'm honored, sir, that you would offer me such a position. Let me talk it over with Polly and get back to you with my answer," he said.

After some discussion, he and Polly agreed. He'd resign his job as tide surveyor and take a position as assistant to the vicar at a fraction of the government salary. They both felt it was God's will and made plans to accept the appointment.

However, Archbishop Hay Drummond did not approve his appointment. John was stunned. He suspected that the bishop thought that his views were too "evangelical" for the diocese. Sadly, he continued as tide surveyor and did occasional preaching. Two years later he received another call. This time John lacked the confidence in being given the appointment and was afraid to quit his job as tide surveyor. Instead, he asked for a three-month leave from his job in order to candidate for the pastorate of a small independent congregation in Warwick.

At the end of the three months, the congregation voted to call Newton as their permanent pastor. John was not certain of his calling to that church, and after praying about it, sent the congregation a letter declining the position.

Several years later, in 1764, through the influence of a friend, the Earl of Dartmouth, Newton won an appointment to be curate at a small chapel in Olney. The town was a tiny industrial center, and its chief claim to fame was its lace-making industry.

As his appointment was being considered, John still faced the prospect of having his credentials challenged by Archbishop

Drummond. However, Lord Dartmouth intervened and pressed the case. Not wanting to be on the wrong political side, the archbishop did as Lord Dartmouth suggested and approved Newton's appointment to Olney.

✝ ✝ ✝

The Reverend John Newton took seriously his role as clergyman to the people of Olney. He preached twice every Sunday as well as for various midweek services. Through the generosity of Lord Dartmouth, who lent one of his run-down mansions, Newton introduced a rectory-sponsored children's ministry as sort of a Sunday school.

His ministry continued for many years. In addition to his preaching (which wasn't at all polished), John discovered that he had a talent for writing. His letters had always been a treasure for Polly when they arrived from far-flung seaports. He had also written several pamphlets and circulated handbills that were used to influence people.

His friend, Alex Clunie, whom he had met in St. Kitts and who had helped him learn more about Christian doctrine, had also retired from the sea. Clunie, like Newton, had taken a post as tide surveyor with the Custom and Excise Bureau. Clunie encouraged John to write.

"Wesley and Whitefield have a gift of oratory and have converted many thousands," he told John one day. "But you have another gift, that of an author. People who might never go to a Whitefield meeting may read your books. And if they respond, they'll be just as converted to Christ as if they'd gone to hear Wesley or Whitefield."

The challenge intrigued John, and he began working on his auto-biography in 1763, using letters he had written to Clunie and another friend, Thomas Haweis. Newton reasoned that since so many people were affected when he told his story in person, perhaps a written account would be as effective.

It was. His autobiography, with the cumbersome title of *An Authentic Narrative of Some Remarkable and Interesting Particulars in the Life of **** (Anonymous), was published a year later. Although he wrote the book anonymously, nearly everyone knew that it was Reverend Newton's story.

The book reached into all strata of society and class and became an instant "best-seller," not only in John's community of Olney but all across Britain. In towns all over England, illiterate people would each contribute one or two pence to buy the book, hire a literate reader, and listen transfixed to the narrative. The autobiography gave Newton an opportunity to share some of the horrors of slavery with a basically uninformed public. The success of the book inspired Newton to write other material that proved just as effective. He was even motivated to write poetry.

In 1767 John met and became friends with the poet William Cowper. In addition to a mutual love for Christ, each man had a penchant for poetry. They agreed to collaborate on writing hymns. For many years the two men enjoyed their partnership, but in 1774 Cowper became mentally ill and left Olney. Three years later Newton published *Olney Hymns,* a collection of 348 hymns (most of which had been written by John).

A small boy in Newton's Olney congregation took particular interest in his sermons and dramatic stories. His name was William Wilberforce, and he attended Sunday worship services with his aunt and uncle. Young Will had been placed in his uncle's home after the boy's father died suddenly. Will was a homely lad whose tiny frame seemed too small for his age. He was about eight when John was introduced to him, and now was ten, but still looked much younger. When he was born he was sickly and nearly blind; he wasn't expected to live, and his early years were filled with continuous illnesses. However, Will's family was wealthy and could afford the best doctors, who somehow kept the boy alive. He

was studious and serious, and John noticed that little Will was captivated by his life stories and the Bible stories he preached.

Young Wilberforce came every Sunday and listened attentively to Reverend Newton's sermons; he even became a disciple of sorts.

John made it a point to get to know the boy and encourage him. He knew what it was to lose a parent at such an early age and the devastating effect that such an experience could have in a boy's life. Young Will responded to the attention and love that his pastor gave him. For several years they had frequent serious talks, and Will made a serious commitment to the church and the Christian faith. That commitment turned out to be troublesome for the boy's mother. She noticed that when he came to visit her in the city, he, now fifteen, seemed "too religious" to her.

Will's mother decided to bring him back to live with her, not at all happy with the "fanatical" Christian influences that the boy's uncle and those around him had on Will.

John noticed immediately that Will was no longer attending church services and asked his uncle about it. After hearing the uncle's account, John shook his head sadly. "It is difficult enough to try and influence a young man when you have him sitting under your preaching. I fear for his faith when he gets under the influence of his peers and those in his mother's household," he said.

Two years later, when he was seventeen, Will Wilberforce wrote a letter to his former pastor. He reported that he was attending St. John's College in Cambridge. He also wrote: "I was introduced on the very first night of my arrival to as licentious a set of men as can well be conceived. They drank hard, and their conversation was even worse than their lives."

John was somewhat reassured that maybe he had misjudged the depth of young Wilberforce's Christian character. At least he could hope for the best. However, he later learned from the reports of the boy's uncle and others that it did not take long for Will to fall into the same

habits he had earlier criticized. He began to drink as hard as any of them and all but abandoned the values and character he had learned from hearing Reverend Newton in Olney.

The pastor shook his head in dismay, recalling his own youthful indiscretions and transgressions. He decided to make Will's lifestyle changes a matter of personal prayer.

Chapter
Twenty-nine

Ultimate Test of Faith

In 1774 John Wesley published a pamphlet condemning the slave trade, and it encouraged Newton to speak out more frankly about his own experiences and his determined opposition to the cruel economic practice.

Newton was fifty-four years old, and his writing had made him famous. The small chapel at Olney was filled every Sunday with parishioners and travelers who came to hear stories about his life experiences. His friends counseled him that his fame and notoriety as an author could expand his pulpit beyond any reputation he might have as a country preacher. They urged him to seek an appointment to a larger church as a means of reaching more people—meaning, of course, his readers.

John and Polly discussed the idea and both felt they could stay in quiet Olney forever. John wanted to write; he attempted several serious

themes, thinking that his autobiography and other writings, taken mainly from his letters to others, were not scholarly or theological enough in content, but it was his letter writing that brought the greatest ministry and reader response. Readers could relate to his earthy stories and identify with his human failures.

John's friends interceded when an opening in a larger church presented itself. John was secretly relieved when someone else was appointed as vicar of that congregation.

Another friend, Lord Dartmouth, approached Newton with an offer to become the president of a college in Savannah, Georgia, in the newly formed United States. That offer did not seem suited for the gifts that John felt God had given him, and he soon forgot about making a move from Olney.

Then, in 1779, John Newton was approached to become the vicar of St. Mary Woolnoth Church, a tiny but influential and prestigious chapel in London. His friend, John Thornton, offered him the position and said that he would personally see to John's compensation.

The minister told Thornton that he enjoyed the tranquil life of Olney and its peaceful woods and river and wasn't sure about the bustling, polluted living in the big city. However, after discussing the matter with Polly, John finally agreed. He began his ministry at St. Mary Woolnoth in early January 1780. Polly joined him in London in March.

In London now, John became more aware of the politics and other topics of society. Due to his preaching and writing, others (like John Wesley) were now also attacking the slave trade in order to outlaw it. Newton's voice in opposition to the slave trade soon made his ideas a *cause celibré*.

For fifteen years this ex-slaver had spoken out about the evil of slavery, and now people were finally beginning to pay attention. One of these was a young member of Parliament, William Wilberforce.

John had not seen Wilberforce since the young man left Olney to return to his mother's home and later go to college.

In 1785 John received a letter from the twenty-seven-year-old member of Parliament. Wilberforce asked for a private and *secret* meeting with Reverend Newton. John made arrangements to meet with him at his parsonage.

The meeting began without fanfare or preliminary talk. "Reverend Newton," Wilberforce began, "I need to talk to you."

John found it hard to believe that this was the same Will Wilberforce who used to look up at him from the third row pew and in their talks asked questions in a high, squeaky, girlish voice. Now his voice was deep, and his words had the sound of authority and strength. John gestured for Wilberforce to continue.

"I came under the conviction of faith when I listened to you at Olney, but then I left and a bit later went off to college. I was afraid to surrender to Christ for fear of what others might say," he explained.

Newton was fully aware of how evangelicals were despised and how hard it was to shake off old traditions. "And now?" John asked his young guest.

"Now I have come to a crisis of soul. I am afraid I've turned my back on Christ, and that bothers me, but I also fear losing face and prestige. If my constituents were to hear that I embraced the Methodist religion, my already-brief career would be over," Wilberforce said quietly. "But maybe that would not be so bad. You have always inspired me, Reverend Newton. When I used to go to Olney and hear your sermons, I felt like jumping up and asking you to help me be a preacher like you.

"That enthusiasm cooled when I went away to the university and then got into politics. Still, as I read the Bible and Christian books, I am convinced that I must act on what I have read. I've come to see you before I go out of my mind about this. I feel pulled in every direction.

"I know I must yield myself to Christ," Will continued, "but if I do, I feel I should give up my post as a member of Parliament and become a clergyman like you. I am torn between following my head or my heart. What do you think, Reverend Newton?"

John didn't answer him at first. Instead, he encouraged Will to "consider first things first." John pulled the conversation back to the initial subject. He then listened patiently as Wilberforce told him how he had been convicted of his shallow life and loose moral values while on a holiday in the south of France.

"I was with a friend who let me read one of his books. It was written by Phillip Doddridge, and it presented a serious and sincere case for Christianity that is more than mere lip service. I felt then and feel now that God was holding a strong light over my life and showing me just how pitiful and awful I have been," Will said quietly. "I feel terrible about the way I have abandoned all that you taught me as a boy, but I don't know how to act on those feelings of regret and guilt."

This was the opening Newton was waiting for. The preacher told Will what he expected John would tell him—that he must surrender to Christ.

Then, with quiet logic based on his own experience of faith, Newton took his Bible and explained salvation to his young visitor. When they both had prayed and Wilberforce wept—tears of relief and repentance— John added a new thought for him to consider. "If God can use an ex-slave trader for his work, imagine what he can do through a gifted member of Parliament," he said.

Will looked up at his mentor, a bit surprised. "That's an odd thing for a minister to say," he said. "I'd expect you'd want to see me become a Christian clergyman."

John shook his head and smiled. "Well, you certainly have the voice and intellect to be a great preacher," he told his young visitor, "but there is nothing that says you have to be a clergyman to follow Christ. I know

of nothing in the Bible that says you cannot be a Christian statesman. True—it may be that these qualities are not always found in our political leaders, but it happens."

That meeting was the first of many encounters between the two men. Over the next few years they met regularly to discuss their faith and the need for a Christian worldview and values to guide political decisions. Their conversations sharpened the faith of both of them and created a bond that helped Wilberforce form an agenda of political independence. Because of John's firsthand experience, he was able to see more clearly the evils of slavery. He constantly spoke on the need to end that terrible institution while Wilberforce led the long fight in Parliament for the same cause.

✦ ✦ ✦

In 1788, when John was sixty-three, Wilberforce came to see his friend with the news that he had finally found a sympathetic audience. "But I'm afraid it will cost you something to help me," Wilberforce told John.

"What do you mean?" Newton asked. "I've already told you that I'd help you in any way I can. When we last discussed this, I told you that I would go before Parliament and give firsthand testimony about the slave trade and my part in it whenever you can make it happen."

Wilberforce smiled and said, "That may happen before you know it. I finally have an opportunity to bring our case before Parliament through committee hearings. For the first time, I think we can gain some sympathy for our cause. As you know, I was hoping you would come forward and testify as to your experience in the slave trade."

"I'll be happy to, but what can I add to what I have already written about the evils of slavery?" John asked his friend.

"I need you to truly enlighten the members of Parliament even more. It will mean that you will have to tell them what you have told me about

your role in it. It will have to be the unvarnished truth. You will be baring yourself before them, and ultimately the entire nation. Do you think you can do that?"

John sat for a long moment in contemplation. His frame was draped casually in the wooden captain's chair in his study while the younger man paced the floor. "Well," John said quietly at last, "it is only because of God's grace that I am still alive. If he had not allowed a stroke to keep me from going back to sea, I would have been killed when the ship I was assigned was lost at sea. Even if I had survived the rigors of the sea, I am certain the slave trade would have killed me by now. What could be worse?"

"Some things I haven't told you may give you pause," Wilberforce replied. "Many people have much to lose if the slave trade is abolished. They have strong voices and even stronger alliances.

"You know that I have sent an Abolition Bill before Parliament every year, and every year it is defeated. However, the margin of defeat decreases every time. I plan to keep bringing it before Parliament until it finally becomes law, but those who oppose me do so with great antagonism," the young man said quietly. "On several occasions they have even had thugs attack me. Once I was beaten unconscious and nearly died. While no one was caught, everyone seems to know who these attackers are."

"Then why don't you prefer charges?" Newton asked. "Otherwise they'll keep after you until serious harm is done."

"I know. But I don't know any of the men who attacked me, and even if I did know who sent them, I have no proof. I have received a number of death threats over the past month. These people are serious about stopping those who interfere with their slave trading. As you know, John, slavery has become entrenched in just about every facet of society and commerce.

"The men who wish me harm believe that I am just a rabble rouser who simply wants to bring down the frame and fabric of our nation,"

Wilberforce said ruefully. "It's ironic. I want more than anything to help my country. That's why I've taken on these hopeless causes—you know, my work with child labor abuses, the exploitation of the poor, and now, slavery. For every cause I take up, there are those who find social, economic, and even patriotic reasons for shutting me up and maintaining the status quo."

"If you're receiving death threats and have been attacked physically, they are breaking the law. This must stop," John said, raising his voice and displaying unusual emotion. "Will, are you suggesting that if I go before Parliament to testify that these thugs will come after me too?"

"No, John," Wilberforce replied. "I don't think so. They won't come after you with clubs but with something worse."

"What do you mean?"

"They won't hurt *you*, they'll hurt your wife," Wilberforce said quietly.

John looked puzzled. "I don't understand. Are you saying they will threaten or harm Polly if I go before Parliament to testify against slavery?"

"In a way, yes." Wilberforce strode across the room and sat in the chair opposite his friend. He leaned forward and spoke barely above a whisper. "John, you were brutally honest and forthright when you wrote your autobiography and your personal views of the slave trade. Many were surprised that you shared your life and experiences with such candor."

Newton nodded but did not reply. His friend continued. "But as open and candid as you were, I am certain you left out a lot of details."

Leaning closer, Wilberforce said quietly, "John, someone came to me earlier today to warn me about bringing you in to testify. This person was associated with Mr. Manesty, your benefactor for so many years. He apparently heard from Manesty before he died concerning some things about you that you did not put in your book."

"What kind of things?" John asked.

"He said to ask you about your African wife, and about your half-African offspring—something about female slaves pregnant by you. And there is more—"

John waved his hand and interrupted, "Yes, I know. I lived as a son of Satan. My life was every bit as shameful as anyone can charge. If anything, I was far worse than these people could possibly know. And except for the grace of God, I'd have done even more evil. If they want to bring all that up, fine. I'll simply turn it over to the Lord again. He's forgiven me—although it's taken many, many years for me to forgive myself. That, my dear Will, took monumental effort!

"Let them make their charges. It will only help prove our case as to the evil of slavery and what it does to people," John said sharply, pounding his fist on his desk for emphasis.

"John," said Wilberforce in a low voice, looking toward the door to the other room where Polly was sitting while they talked. "It's not *you* I'm worried about."

Newton immediately checked himself. It was true. Polly didn't know much about his former life—it was far too foul. John was not afraid of the threats of exposure of his past deeds, but he was not willing to put Polly through the pain and humiliation that public exposure of these deeds would bring.

He told Wilberforce. "I can't put Polly through that kind of experience. She has been emotionally fragile ever since my stroke, and more recently, she's been quite ill. If these awful things about my past come out in public testimony, it could devastate her. I can't do that to her."

"I understand," observed Wilberforce, "but it may already be too late."

John felt the hair on the back of his neck stand up. "What—?" he asked quickly.

"Lord Nelson has been quite outspoken in his criticism of anyone opposed to the slave trade. You and John Wesley have written about it.

Some call Wesley a heretic and discredit him. They'll do the same to you, whether you testify or not. If you testify, they'll call you a hypocrite and accuse you of covering up the kind of person you really were. I've even heard that they plan to bring witnesses from your past to testify against you.

"These are people who have no qualms about telling the world the kind of things you did in the past. They'll make a big public show of assassinating your character. Whatever turn this takes, they'll make political gain from it. I'm afraid I've put you between a rock and a hard place," Wilberforce said, grimfaced.

Then he stood up. "I must go now. Think this over, John, and let me know what you decide. If you choose not to testify, I'll be sorely disappointed, but I will understand."

Newton nodded but said nothing. He shook his friend's hand and helped him with his topcoat. Then Wilberforce left. John heard his carriage pull away from the curb outside as he sat back down in his study.

John stared blankly at the bookcase across the room and thought about his dilemma. Before Wilberforce's visit, his path was plain. He was even eager to go before Parliament and plead his case against slavery. Wilberforce wanted him to do it because of his fame and renown. Although his autobiography was now more than twenty years old, it was still being read by a vast number of readers. His tract on abolishing the slave trade also made him something of a famous figure in society. All that could change now. In order to discredit John's testimony, the opponents of abolition would assassinate his character.

John thought about the events of the evening. He was no longer sure he could testify.

John thought of Polly. He truly wanted to spare her from knowing all there was to know about John Newton, the slave ship captain and

self-described infidel. For nearly forty years he had protected her from the most sordid aspects of his life. Now, in her later years, fragile and ill, he wondered what might happen if she were exposed to the vile and repugnant facts. True, God had forgiven him. But Polly—naive Polly—knew nothing about these things, and it would surely punish and cripple their relationship if he had to tell her at this late time in their marriage all that he had done to betray her.

John put his face in his hands and began to weep. All the sorrow and regret surrounding his past as well as his feelings for Polly suddenly engulfed him, and his body shook with deep wrenching sobs.

✝ ✝ ✝

The next morning John awoke early and returned to his study to pray and read his Bible. He had not slept much the night before, and his thoughts were jumbled and confused. He was no closer to knowing what to do.

John was still sitting at his desk in the study when a visitor came calling later that morning. Polly ushered the Reverend Thomas Scott into the room. Reverend Scott was a clergyman from the Olney area.

Not many fellow clergymen had accepted John when he assumed the Olney church post, probably because he had come into his role through such a remarkably untraditional path. More than a few turned up their noses at his unconventional education, especially how he had taught himself Greek and Hebrew, although none could fault his mastery of them. Still, they kept their distance. For the most part Newton had been shut out of the established ecclesiastical circle, but it never seemed to bother him.

Reverend Scott, however, had not kept John at arm's length. He and John had become acquainted when John served the Olney congregation. In fact, although they were quite different in style and temperament, they even became friends.

Often the two met and discussed theology or other church business and enjoyed each other's company. Their friendship was not that close, but they were comfortable with their differences and similarities.

Polly brought a tray of tea and biscuits as the two men exchanged small talk. Finally, John asked, "What brings you all the way to London? Surely not to have tea with an old friend."

"No, John," Reverend Scott answered. "I have heard things about you that I thought you ought to know."

"Really?" John replied with a smile.

"Yes. I know you have been invited to address Parliament on the issue of slavery."

John looked at his guest and said nothing for a moment, then answered, "Well, not exactly. I have been asked to speak to a select committee of Parliament, that's all. Wilberforce thinks it may carry some weight for them to hear from someone who has had firsthand experience in the slave trade."

"Then, you've agreed?"

"Not yet. There seem to be some complications he wanted to warn me about before I make a decision. Is that why you're here?"

The minister nodded. "John, I believe some people are out to totally discredit you and your reputation if you go forward with this plan to testify against slavery."

"Well, I've heard that already. But my reputation has never been spotless. You know my background."

"I do," Reverend Scott said. "I know that the life you've lived for the past forty years ought to carry more weight than the reputation you earned as a reckless youth. But you know as well as I do that people can be very fickle and petty. I'm here today, John, to convince you not to testify. You have nothing to win and everything to lose."

John put his cup and saucer on the desk and sat back in his chair. "Go on," he said simply.

"If you go forward with this, a group of ministers plans to petition the bishop to have you defrocked and excommunicated," Reverend Scott said.

John sat back in his chair. He had not expected ecclesiastical leaders to go so far to distance themselves from him. "But I'm not the only voice against slavery," he said.

"True. John Wesley and others are also speaking out, but they are radicals already outside the traditions of the Church of England. You, however, have been given great credibility even though you are one of those 'evangelicals.' I don't understand your success. You're self-taught, and you didn't attend university. Why, no one even knows whether you're a Calvinist or Arminian in your theology."

"Most of the people I talk to don't care about such distinctions. They just want to hear about Christ," John replied.

Reverend Scott dismissed the answer. "That's not what I mean. Look, John, these people mean business. They are organized. They have influence and power. The word is out—if you go to Parliament, they'll have you booted out of your church."

He added, "Some highly placed church leaders even question your faith as genuine."

"What!? How can that be? Those who know me know that this old 'servant of slaves' is now Christ's servant. There is no mistake about that."

"Nevertheless," Scott interrupted, "you can't go ahead with this. You don't know what you're getting into. Here is their argument. You claim you were converted, but conversion implies repentance and change. You say you were converted but did not give up your slave ship. You only left the slave trade because you had a stroke."

"But—" Newton protested.

"And when you were appointed to be a minister, did you not follow many of the false doctrines of the evangelical sect?"

"What false doctrines? My beliefs are as sound as—"

Scott ignored John's responses and hammered him with other accusations. "The bishop who oversees the work at Olney, along with the church authorities over your work here at St. Mary Woolnoth, are prepared to bring charges against you."

"Then so be it," John said sharply with some resignation. "God is my final authority. I have not betrayed him. If he chooses, I will stay or I will be let go. Whatever he decides."

"That's crazy, John. What will you do? You can't start over at your age."

"I can write and publish—"

"No, you cannot. They will see to it that your views will be labeled heretical and forbid their congregations to get your books," Scott said with a deep sigh. "Look, John. This is real. They mean business. Some would even kill you if they could. Destroying your reputation and career is the next best thing."

"I won't betray my conscience," John said.

"No one is asking you to," Scott replied. "Just allow your conscience to admit that the other side of the debate contains just as much truth as your side does. The institution of slavery has been around for more than a century. In other cultures it's as old as the Bible itself. True, the slave trade could be more humane, but it serves a useful purpose for mankind. The standard of living of the entire civilized world has benefited from slavery. Just think of what the price of sugar, lumber, or cotton would be without slaves to keep the costs of production at a reasonable minimum."

"But how do the *slaves* benefit?" John asked sarcastically.

"Well, they are fed, clothed, and given a place to live. In Africa their lives were miserable. We have saved them from that," Scott answered.

John laughed derisively. "You have just described what a man might do for his dog—feed it and keep it in a shed out of the bad weather. But

even a dog enjoys companionship with his master. Slaves are treated worse than dogs," John said bitterly, adding, "I know what we have done to these poor people. We take them from their homelands, abuse them terribly, make slaves of them, and kill them with hard work and lack of care. Don't tell me their lives are better than they were in Africa because I have been there. I was part of it!"

"John," Scott responded, "we're talking about primitives—savages. As such, according to church doctrine, they do not have souls. They are subhuman, John. You're making it sound as though they have the same rights as ordinary human beings."

Newton's eyes flashed in anger and he opened his mouth, but Scott ignored him and continued to argue his case. "John, they are going to crucify you! They'll ask you why you condemn them for their treatment of the slaves when *you* are the hypocrite. You are the one who sent hundreds of female slaves to the New World with your offspring inside them!"

John turned as if stabbed, then motioned for Scott to keep his voice down. "Where did you hear that?" Newton asked.

"One of the Parliament members has found someone who was a former sailor on one of your ships. He is going to testify to what he has described as your sexual habits—he calls it 'bestiality'—and what he defines as inhumane acts against slaves aboard your ships," Scott said quietly.

John said nothing for several minutes. Scott let him mull over their conversation. Then he added, in a voice suggesting how a member of the parliamentary committee might ask a question, "Reverend Newton, is it true that you had a black wife and a number of black mistresses?"

"Quiet, man!" John said sharply, gesturing to the door to the parlor where Polly was. "Where are you getting these stories?"

Reverend Scott sat down again. "They have dug deeply into your past, John. They mean to keep you from testifying. I met with them.

They asked me to talk sense to you. If you don't listen, they mean to ruin you for good. They've found over a dozen men who will be brought in to tell how you destroyed the faith of young sailors and led them into debauchery and harlotry. They'll ask you why you lived with heathen and practiced witchcraft. They want to know why you—"

"Enough!" John cried. "Enough."

Scott leaned toward Newton and placed an arm on his shoulder. The older man was devastated at this turn of events. Scott talked quietly, reassuringly, to his friend. "Look, John, they may be using the wrong tactics, but they truly want to do the right thing. In their eyes, you have betrayed your church, your God, your country's commerce, *and your wife.*"

Scott emphasized this latter phrase, sensing vulnerability in Newton's nature. John picked up on that emphasis. He said, "These men are going to destroy Polly, not me. I have not lied about these things, but I've never volunteered them either. I wanted to shield my wife from knowing all the foul and profane things I did before Christ changed me. If she hears these things as public gossip or reads about them in the newspaper, in her fragile health it'll kill her."

"Then if you won't change your mind for your own well-being, do it for Mrs. Newton," Scott urged. "Besides," he added, "speaking before a committee of Parliament will have no effect anyway. You can't undo centuries of policy and practice with a speech. Why would you jeopardize your wife's well-being with something that will change nothing? We both know that slavery is too much a part of the British Empire to be affected by a sermon."

Newton said nothing. He was thinking the same thought. *It's true,* he thought, *I'm crazy to think I can make a difference. The cause is hopeless. I am better off by not testifying.*

Scott persevered. As if sensing John's melting resolve, he said, "Think of Mrs. Newton. Why would you subject her to such terrible

punishment for something that will have no effect and no lasting consequences?"

✝ ✝ ✝

John Newton agonized over the choice before him during the next several days. He hardly slept at all and was continually troubled by having to relive the experiences of his ungodly life. As much as his tormenters knew about him, Newton knew more. It was as if Satan came to him by night to remind him of his past, question his conversion, and doubt his salvation. In Newton's mind, God had countless good reasons to have abandoned him during those years—but he never did. John hung onto that fact—that if God demonstrated love and faithfulness to John and Polly then, John had no reason to doubt him now.

John turned to his large, worn Bible for consolation. His favorite readings during times like this were the Psalms. His hand carefully turned the pages, and he found all kinds of encouraging passages. Then he silently read Psalm 25, and it seemed as if it were written for him and for this occasion. It became his prayer:

> O my God, I trust in thee: let me not be ashamed, let not my enemies triumph over me. . . .
>
> Remember not the sins of my youth, nor my transgressions: according to thy mercy remember thou me for thy goodness' sake, O LORD. . . .
>
> Look upon mine affliction and my pain; and forgive all my sins. Consider mine enemies; for they are many; and they hate me with cruel hatred.
>
> O keep my soul, and deliver me: let me not be ashamed; for I put my trust in thee. Let integrity and uprightness preserve me; for I wait on thee.

As he grappled with the issues involved in his proposed testimony to the parliamentary committee, he also reviewed the stakes. He had already exposed many of his experiences in his autobiography, which he had written some twenty years earlier. Of course, his words were not as explicit as they could have been, nor did he tell everything about his life. Even so, the book had had a profound effect on thousands of readers.

However, now he was faced with a real test of his faith. He had risked little by writing about his experiences—he'd published it anonymously to begin with. People soon found out it was written by the country parson, but it made no difference—in fact, it may have been even more intriguing because it was written by a clergyman.

Now, however, things were different. He would not be the author— he'd have no control over the words and descriptions that would be delivered. These men had threatened to humiliate and ruin him in the most public of forums, and John knew they had the influence and power to do so. If he went ahead with Wilberforce's plan, he risked losing his church, his reputation, and—more important to John—his wife's emotional and physical health. Everything he valued most was at risk of being lost.

John was tempted to tell Wilberforce that he couldn't testify. He reasoned that the committee members, for the most part, had already made up their minds. His testimony would be a futile effort, and nothing he said could help the cause of abolition anyway. And he really had no idea what terrible things might happen if he did testify.

William Wilberforce found Newton in his study when he came to visit. He was on his knees in prayer. Polly greeted Will and ushered him to the door of her husband's study. Newton had not heard Wilberforce knock, and the young man entered tentatively.

"I'm sorry to intrude, John," he said quietly, seeing his friend at prayer. "Shall I come back later?"

John looked up at his friend. Wilberforce was startled to see how awful his friend looked. He blinked but did not otherwise react to the sight of Newton. The aging clergyman showed the signs of lost sleep, spiritual agony, and struggle. John's eyes were swollen and red. His face was ashen and unshaven.

"Shall I come back later?" Wilberforce repeated.

"No," John said, rising to his feet and extending his hand in greeting. "I am glad you are here."

"Have you made your decision?"

Newton nodded. "Polly and I talked most of the night. I felt that all of this is still likely to come out even if I don't testify. There's too much momentum already. So I decided to tell Polly what was going on. Then I began telling her what might come out if I testify. I thought it might be easier if she heard it from me." Then he shrugged. "I don't know. Maybe it was still the wrong thing to do."

"How did Mrs. Newton respond?"

"I don't know. At first she said she didn't want to hear about it—that all those things happened so long ago. But then I explained to her that others might bring it up and set it out for all to see. I told her that they'd likely tell horrible things about my past that no one else knows about—including her. That worried her more than my telling what I did. She's a proud woman, and naturally she's upset thinking about what those people might say," John told him.

Wilberforce tried to be encouraging. "She's a fine and noble woman, John," he said. "God will give her the strength to deal with this."

"But she shouldn't have to," John snapped. "I'm the one who should suffer. It's ironic, isn't it? No other person I know has lived such a wretched life as I have. Yet I have had such a sense of God's love and forgiveness that my spiritual, emotional, and physical well-being have never been in doubt. But Polly is innocent of my perversions and infidelities. Even though she says that none of this will make any difference, I know

it will. Women are more emotional creatures than men. It's going to have a terrible effect on her, and I despair of it."

"Maybe not," Wilberforce said. "She is, as I said, a fine and noble woman. She'll find the strength to cope."

"I pray that you are right."

"What have you decided then?" Wilberforce asked his friend.

"I told Polly that I must do what is right even if it has no effect. The threats by the opponents to abolition make it clear to me that they mean me harm whether I testify or not. So my answer is yes. I will testify," Newton said with a deep sigh. "May God have mercy on us all," he added.

Chapter Thirty

Amazing Grace

In the halls of St. James's Palace, the Reverend John Newton waited to be called to testify. His friend William Wilberforce was encouraging when they met earlier in the day. He had just seen Parliament pass a new law that he had introduced requiring all chimney sweepers to be at least eight years old. Younger children were used because they could navigate the tight spaces inside the old chimneys. The trouble was, chimney sweeping was a very dangerous job. Now, at least, some initial efforts at child labor reform were finally taking place.

Wilberforce had hoped for similar success in his opposition to slavery. The year before, Wilberforce and his friends, Thomas Clarkson and Granville Sharp, had formed the Society for the Abolition of the Slave Trade. Clarkson was asked to collect information to support their cause and took to the task with serious commitment. He arranged for interviews with some twenty thousand sailors to talk with them about

their role in the trade. He also collected a wide array of equipment used in the control and torture of Africans captured for delivery to the New World or England, which included such frightening, strange implements as handcuffs, leg irons, thumbscrews, branding irons, and iron face masks. These would be presented to the members of Parliament to consider along with other testimony concerning the slave trade.

As John sat on a bench outside the stately room where he was to give his testimony, he was struck by the irony of it all. Here he was, a former slave ship captain, infidel, libertine, and corrupter, sitting in a hall surrounded by the massive portraits of kings, queens, and prime ministers. He shook his head in disbelief.

In his imagination, standing next to a portrait of Queen Anne beside her royal carriage was little John Newton, the seven-year-old boy, watching his mother get into a carriage and leave him forever.

Blinking, he looked away. Then he noticed the portrait of William Pitt, the youngest prime minister in the history of the empire. As he looked he imagined a teenaged John Newton climbing out of the longboat taking him to the *Pegasus* from the H.M.S. *Harwich*.

As he gazed at a portrait of King George II, it seemed to him that he saw a young John Newton in rags, as if just in from the slave fields of Mr. Clow, standing nearby.

Underneath the portrait of Oliver Cromwell, John imagined that he saw the crumpled form of the terror-stricken John Newton on the deck of the *Greyhound* when hurricane-force winds nearly sank the ship and caused him to cry out to God.

A voice interrupted his reverie. The page standing nearby snapped to attention and announced the arrival of Prime Minister Pitt, who was striding toward John. "Reverend Newton, I am pleased that you could be with us today. Mr. Wilberforce is just now finishing his remarks, and the committee is ready to see you now," the prime minister told him.

Newton stood, smoothed his black frock coat, straightened his pow-
dered wig, and walked into the room. He felt uncomfortable in this garb,
such a contrast to the clothes he wore in his recent daydreams in the
corridor.

As Prime Minister Pitt escorted John to his seat, John looked around
and saw the attentive faces of some of the most influential people in
England. Some of them turned their attention from Wilberforce to
watch him enter the room and walk quietly to his seat.

Wilberforce was not distracted. He spoke fervently to the assembled
leaders. "I believe that God Almighty has set before me two great objectives, the suppression of the slave trade and the reformation of society
and its morals," he said.

"In regard to slavery, gentlemen, where is your outrage? You have
seen some of the instruments of torture and death. You have heard testimony about the hardships of bringing Africans from their native land
to the New World and to England. Imagine, slaves are picked up in West
Africa and shipped thousands of miles away, never to see their homeland
again," he told them.

Continuing, Wilberforce said, "They are taken in chains, in ships
with no sanitation, and under conditions that are unbearable. When they
get to their destinations, they are oiled and fattened up to disguise the
ravages of months of starvation, whippings, and seasickness. Then they
are paraded naked before buyers so that they can be appraised and
given a market value."

As John watched the members of the committee, they showed scant
interest in what their fellow member of Parliament was saying.
Wilberforce ignored their indifference and finished his speech. He told
them, "From ships that sailed from just one British seaport, over three
hundred thousand slaves were sold as part of this shameful trade. I have
a report to enter into the record of the testimony of this hearing. It is a
report about a captain of a British slave ship who threw 132 living slaves

overboard during a storm in order to lighten the ship. When this captain
returned to England, he had the nerve to file an insurance claim on the
'lost cargo' that was tossed overboard! There was no public outrage, but
I declare to you today that never—never I say—will we desist until we
extinguish every trace of this bloody traffic, of which our posterity, looking back to the history of these enlightened times, will scarce believe
that it has been suffered to exist so long a disgrace and dishonor to this
country!"

A shuffling of papers and a few mumbled remarks were heard at the
conclusion of Wilberforce's speech, and it seemed to John as if most of
the words fell on deaf ears.

John then listened as the prime minister introduced him to the
assembly.

"Reverend John Newton is the learned rector of St. Mary Woolnoth
and formerly curate of Olney Chapel. He is a man of great piety and yet
possesses an equal measure of humility. Reverend Newton is an author
of world renown whose writings have been published widely. His name
is famous in his homeland, and he is also well-known in America and
Europe as an author and public speaker. Reverend Newton comes to us
as an authority on the subject we have under consideration before us
today," Pitt said to the parliamentary committee. He made some
impromptu remarks of his own appreciation for Newton, and when his
flowery written introduction was finished, he turned the podium over to
John.

For a moment Newton thought about telling this august body to forget what Mr. Pitt had just told them about piety, good works, and great
learning. When he slowly rose to speak, his voice was strong but tempered with years of humility and authority. He said to them, "The
Honorable Mr. Prime Minister gives me credit I do not deserve. I am
simply the worst of the worst sinners. Except for the grace of God, I
would long be dead—or if alive, I would still be defiling his world.

"I know that some of you think you know as much about the life I lived forty years ago as I do, and you may wonder whether I have really changed since then. In fact, there are some who tried to keep me from coming here today in order to protect me from what might be said about me in public. But gentlemen, no one here can condemn me any more greatly than I do myself." John told the men assembled before him that he was, like the apostle Paul, "chief of sinners" and "deserving of every punishment that God—or you gentlemen—might consider for me.

"The fact that I can even stand before you today is a miracle in itself," he told them. "It's a miracle of forgiveness. By the grace of Almighty God, he delivered me. That's an experience I can talk to you about with great authority and understanding. Let me tell you about it." He then proceeded to tell them how he was drawn into the slave trade, then set out all the reasons—social, economic, and religious—why slavery should be abolished.

"Slavery is an evil abomination in the sight of God. Yet apart from that, if you judge it solely on its economic merit, it will not hold up. Slavery makes a handful of men rich but does nothing for the other classes. Furthermore, it destroys countless lives from the lowest classes of all—classes unable to protect themselves from its evil. For every slave who dies, one Englishman dies. Every year more than fifteen thousand *English* lives—mostly sailors—are lost through storms at sea, uprisings, drownings, armed conflict with the natives, fevers, and other rampant tropical diseases," John said.

"Also, no fewer than fifteen thousand slaves die each year at the hand of white slave traders. And that does not take into consideration the thousands more that die of 'natural causes' once they are bought by slaveholders—who believe it's more economical to work their slaves to death because buying new ones is cheaper than providing the ones they have with good care, decent food, clothing, and shelter.

"We go into their villages and steal men, women, and children from their families. We force march them to the sea where they are taken aboard filthy, crowded ships—packed so tightly that many of them are smothered on the way.

"The women are taken and defiled by the white traders and sailors. Sometimes even the children are abused in the worst ways. I know, because I was once one of these devils. I am ashamed to tell you that there may be dozens, even scores, of mulatto children of slaves born with the blood of John Newton in their veins."

Newton paused. Many of his listeners were shifting uncomfortably in their seats. Some were moved at his explicit description of the evil system and his role in it. Others were distressed because he was telling the assembly all the terrible things they had intended to say to ruin him.

Newton continued, telling them of the abhorrent marauding raids, the intense torture and abuse, and the terrors of the slave ship. "The slaves lie in rows, one above the other on plank benches on every side of the ship's cargo hold. They are packed like books on a shelf. There's scarcely room to walk without stepping on them. They're shackled in irons, both hands and feet, and can't turn over to get comfortable."

John described in graphic detail how up to a quarter of the slaves died on the way and how their corpses were fed to the sharks. "Every morning the sailors went below to carry out the corpses of the ones who died in the night."

Newton told them how it was a policy to kill the slaves who *did* survive the voyage by hard labor—that the typical male slave working in the fields or factory lived only nine years after his arrival. "I doubt sincerely that any of you gentlemen farmers would treat a plow horse with such callousness and cruel indifference," he told them.

His own eyes filled with tears, and his voice broke as he recalled seeing little children snatched from their nursing mothers, of the terrible

sores that result from wearing the leg irons and chains, of torture, abuse, and worse.

"Gentlemen, what England has established through the system of slavery is nothing but genocide. It has the effect of totally destroying an entire race within only a few generations. What will we say to the Almighty on Judgment Day for our part in this horror?" he asked in a voice reduced to a whisper. Then, regaining the strength and authority in his voice with which he began, he told them, "There are those who told me not to speak out on this matter—that my words will offend a great many people. But I am not afraid of offending every man in the world by declaring the truth. The truth is, no man here has seen the slave trade through eyes like mine. If you had, you would never argue in favor of a form of commerce that is so evil, so cruel, so oppressive, and so destructive, as the African slave trade.

"Gentlemen, I am not afraid of humiliating myself before you today by sharing my shame and offering this public confession of my own sins. I do not know how many thousands have died—it may be *hundreds of thousands*—over the years. And may God forgive me for my part in it.

"I cannot be silent. I know in my *changed* heart what is right. It is as if God has carved the words on my very soul. That is why I plead with you today, in God's name, *stop it!* You cannot let this evil continue! You have to stop it because it is the right thing to do. You must abolish slavery throughout the empire, before slavery destroys Great Britain." With those words he sat down while the shaken body seated before him gave his presentation careful deliberation.

✝ ✝ ✝

That night, at home in his parsonage, John was unable to sleep. As often happened, whenever he shared the grim stories of his past, he had nightmares. These vivid scenes were imposed onto his thoughts, and he would lie awake for hours, trying to go back to sleep.

Many times he would rise and go to his study and read from the Bible or a devotional book. When calmness at last gave him peace of mind, he would once again retire.

Tonight, however, he simply paced the floor for awhile. He carried a small candlestick with him into his study as he perused the shelves of his bookcases. His eyes fell on a copy of *Olney Hymns,* published nine years earlier. Strangely, sometimes his own writing had the ability to calm and restore his soul.

He put down the candle and lit an oil lamp for more light. Then he sat down at his writing desk and opened the book. The pages were already worn, and he was familiar with the location of every hymn from frequent use.

John opened to one he had written for a weekly church service, a hymn that was extremely autobiographical. Even as its author, he felt that the words were inspired.

Ironically, the melody was said to be an African folk melody introduced by slaves. John closed his eyes and was transported back to Africa. This time, instead of the nightmarish scenes that disturbed him, he recalled the beauty of the land and its peace-loving people. He began to hum and "sing" the words in his head:

Amazing grace! How sweet the sound
That saved a wretch like me!
I once was lost, but now am found,
Was blind but now I see.

It was absolutely true. No one (except maybe Job Lewis) had been more dissolute and immoral as John Newton, and because of the undeserved grace of God, this miserable creature was saved and his friend languished in hell. Amazing. Amazing grace.

He read the other verses—verses written by the "chief of sinners" to contrast his corrupt life with the work God had done:

'Twas grace that taught my heart to fear,
 And grace my fear relieved;
How precious did that grace appear,
 The hour I first believed!

Through many dangers, toils, and snares,
 I have already come;
'Tis grace has brought me safe thus far,
 And grace will lead me home.

Epilogue

Continued Grace

John and Polly never had children of their own, but when Polly's brother and sister-in-law died, leaving a five-year-old daughter an orphan, the couple took her in. They adopted little Elizabeth (Betsy), who lived with them even after her marriage.

When John had his stroke at the age of twenty-nine in 1754, his beloved Polly never really recovered, although he did. She suffered from depression brought on by the strain of that event. Then, in October 1788, she was diagnosed with breast cancer. From then on Polly went downhill. By October 1790 she was in great pain and had to take drugs that clouded her mind.

John patiently sat by her bedside and read to her, prayed for her, held her hand, and wiped her brow. He helped her sit up a little in a chaise, but when the cancer ate away at her spine, she was paralyzed and could not move. She only had feeling in her hands and head. John stroked her hair and squeezed her hand to let her know of his continuing love for her.

John's guilt over betraying Polly in his profligate years laid heavily on his soul. He also worried that what he shared with her before giving his testimony before the parliamentary committee might have somehow contributed to her present situation. His thoughts were dark and depressing. He blamed himself for her impending death.

The struggle lasted almost three months. In December 1790, Polly died. She was sixty-two, and the couple had been married forty years.

John Newton continued his preaching and writing until old age, blindness, and infirmity kept him out of the pulpit. His authorship of *Thoughts on the African Slave Trade,* published in 1787, provided the abolitionist cause in Britain its mightiest weapon. William Wilberforce, himself, distributed thousands of copies.

On May 1, 1807, just before Newton died, the British Parliament passed a law making it illegal to ship slaves from any British territory. Only a few weeks after his death, on March 2, 1808, another law was passed that went hand and glove with the first. This law made it illegal to land slaves on any British territory.

Reverend John Newton played an important and significant role in these efforts as well as the eventual abolition of slavery, which finally came in 1833.

Newton's mind never failed, and he became a counselor to hundreds in the same way he had mentored Wilberforce. Even in the years after Polly's death, he continued his influence and ministry. He lived to see the fruits of his testimony favoring the abolition of the slave trade. After eighteen years of presenting the bill before Parliament, William Wilberforce finally achieved success. Parliament voted to completely abolish the slave trade on March 25, 1806. Wilberforce came to give John the news and personally thank him for his role in that accomplishment. While Newton humbly dismissed his part in the matter, Wilberforce reminded him of his testimony that helped to change the course of the thinking of the British Empire.

"In a way, you provided our nation an opportunity for redemption. I think you thought that your action was your own test of faith—that when you stepped into that arena, you were the one being tested. Maybe that was true. But the effect of your words changed hearts and minds on that day, and more were changed by your example," Wilberforce told him.

The bill had passed in Parliament by 267 votes, making it a definitive triumph for Newton and his protégé, Wilberforce.*

John Newton at last felt vindication. He had never felt that anything he had done had in any way offset the evil of his younger days. While his friends and Polly tried to let him know that he was wrong—that he had accomplished much good and had a profound effect on hundreds if not thousands of lives because of his preaching and writing—Newton himself was never quite sure of his own contribution, yet he lived long enough to see one good thing result from his life.

Following the March passage of the abolition bill, John grew progressively weaker. Betsy (the niece they had adopted) had devoted herself to care for John and now hardly left his side.

His strength gave out just before Christmas that year. He died at age eighty-two on December 21, 1807.

Before John died, he insisted on writing his own epitaph. His friend Henry Martyn came to visit, and the two conversed for awhile. Martyn told him that the people of London thought quite highly of the Reverend John Newton, and there was talk about having a monument erected in his memory. Newton would have none of it.

"In my way of thinking, there are just two categories in our experience—human happiness and human misery. For much of my life I traded happiness for misery. Now, if I can take away even the smallest amount of misery and trade it for happiness, it will be worthwhile," he

---

*Wilberforce lived to see total emancipation of slaves in the British Empire a quarter of a century later. In 1833, when he was 74, the law was passed, and Wilberforce died two days later.

said in a voice tempered by old age. In his own mind Newton had come to terms with the idea that at last his life had been of use.

Still, he could not rid his thoughts and his conscience of the one fact that could not be erased—he was once a corrupt and vile man who trafficked in human misery.

"Here is what I want on my headstone," he said. "There is to be no monument, only a simple marble slab with these words."

He handed Martyn a sheet of paper. The handwriting had lost some of its artful script, but it was still easy enough to read:

John Newton

Clerk

Once an Infidel and Libertine,

A Servant of Slaves in Africa,

Was

By the Rich Mercy of Our Lord

and Saviour, Jesus Christ,

Preserved, Restored, Pardoned,

And Appointed To

Preach the Faith

He Had Long Labored to Destroy.

He Ministered Near 16 Years As

Curate And Vicar Of Olney In Bucks

And 28 Years As Rector Of

These United Parishes.

On February First 1750 He Married Mary*

Daughter Of The Late George Catlett,

Of Chatham Kent,

Whom He Resigned To The Lord

Who Gave Her, On December 25, 1790

---

*John's wife's given name was Mary, but John called her by the affectionate nickname Polly.

John's close friend, William Jay, came to visit him just before his death. The old parson could hardly speak, so Jay bent down over the bed to hear him. In a voice that was more breath than sound, the Reverend John Newton spoke his final words. "My memory is nearly gone, but I remember two things—I am a great sinner . . . and Christ is a great Savior."

The effort taxed him, however, and he fell asleep—not to waken until he left earth for heaven two days later.